Praise for *Awakening Love*

"In *Awakening Love*, Fr. Greg Cleveland gives us permission to fall in love with Jesus. The blending of the Song of Songs with the Spiritual Exercises reinforces the notion that a deep and loving friendship requires us to 'be with' our beloved (Christ). We are drawn by God into a human and spiritual union whereby having a disciplined and faithful life of prayer, we are now able to discern God's will and respond with confidence and affection."

— Christina Lynch, Psy.D.,
President, Catholic Psychotherapy Association

"Drawing on his extensive background as a retreat master, Fr. Cleveland applies the schema of the Spiritual Exercises of Saint Ignatius to the Old Testament book, the Song of Songs. The result is an inspirational set of reflections well suited for use as a retreat. The application of the Ignatian method to the book of biblical love poetry draws the reader into the mystery of the transforming power of God's love for each person. Having used this book of conferences and prayers for my retreat, it has opened for me a more profound understanding of how deeply God loves me and how I am called to respond in love, gratitude, and action. The spiritual renewal facilitated by the use of Cleveland's book is very much in line with the interior renewal preached by our Jesuit Pope, Francis."

—Most Rev. John M. LeVoir, author of *Covenant of Love* and
Bishop of New Ulm, Minnesota

"*Awakening Love* is the result of years of serious prayer, reflection, and experience in directing the Spiritual Exercises of Saint Ignatius. The author is true to the unity and meaning of the biblical text while, at the same time, engaging the wealth of the Church's tradition of patristic exegesis, principles of ascetical theology, contemplative insights of the great mystics, and the integrity of the Spiritual Exercises. This book achieves a profound 'awakening of love' for Jesus Christ through the process of a thirty-day retreat."

—Sr. Mary Timothea Elliott, RSM, SSD,
Theological Consultant to the Bishop and *Censor Liborum*,
Diocese of Knoxville, Tennessee

AWAKENING LOVE

AWAKENING LOVE

An Ignatian Retreat with the
SONG *of* SONGS

By Gregory Cleveland, OMV

Foreword by Kathryn J. Hermes, FSP

Pauline
BOOKS & MEDIA

Library of Congress Cataloging-in-Publication Data

Names: Cleveland, Gregory, author.
Title: Awakening love : an Ignatian retreat with the Song of songs / Gregory Cleveland, OMV.
Description: Boston, MA : Pauline Books & Media, [2017]
Identifiers: LCCN 2017020445| ISBN 9780819808578 (pbk.) | ISBN 0819808571 (pbk.)
Subjects: LCSH: Ignatius, of Loyola, Saint, 1491-1556. Exercitia spiritualia. | Spiritual
exercises. | Bible. Song of songs--Devotional literature. | Spiritual retreats--Catholic Church.
Classification: LCC BX2179.L8 C54 2017 | DDC 248.3--dc23
LC record available at https://lccn.loc.gov/2017020445

Scripture quotations are from *Revised Standard Version of the Bible—Second Catholic Edition* (Saint Ignatius Edition), copyright © 2006, National Council of the Churches of Christ in the United States of America. Used by permission. All rights reserved.

Excerpts from the English translation of the *Catechism of the Catholic Church* for use in the United States of America, copyright © 1994, United States Catholic Conference, Inc. — Libreria Editrice Vaticana. Used with permission.

Excerpts from papal and magisterium texts, copyright © Libreria Editrice Vaticana. All rights reserved. Used with permission.

Excerpts from *The Spiritual Exercises of Saint Ignatius of Loyola* by Louis J. Puhl, S.J. (Newman Press 1951). Reprinted with permission of Loyola Press. To order copies of this book call 1-800-621-1008 or go to www.loyolapress.com.

Excerpts from *Illustrated Sunday Homilies* by Mark Link © 1992, RCL Benziger. Used with permission.

Every effort has been made to trace copyright holders and to obtain their permission for the use of copyrighted material. The publisher apologizes if there are any errors or omissions in the above list. If any permissions have been inadvertently overlooked, the publisher will be pleased to make the necessary and reasonable arrangements at the first opportunity.

Cover design by Rosana Usselmann

Cover photo istockphoto.com/© SrdjanPav

Published by Pauline Books & Media, 50 Saint Paul's Avenue, Boston, MA 02130-3491
Printed in the U.S.A.

www.pauline.org

Pauline Books & Media is the publishing house of the Daughters of St. Paul, an international congregation of women religious serving the Church with the communications media.

2 3 4 5 6 7 8 9   22 21 20 19 18

Contents

Foreword

In my early twenties I discovered the Spiritual Exercises of Saint Ignatius. I was especially drawn in those young adult years to Ignatius' Principle and Foundation: the truth that we come from God our Creator and that our goal is to return to him through the gift of salvation. But even after thirty years of plodding my way through my own spiritual development, using the tools Ignatius provides in his Spiritual Exercises, I have to admit that I have always felt something vital was missing.

Recently at a conference where I was a presenter, a priest approached me and asked with a sincerity that was extremely moving to me, "People have told me that I am too intellectual. I need to learn how to pray from my heart. Can you help me?" I stammered a few suggestions, but I knew that they fell short of what he really needed. My difficulty in responding reminded me of the chasm that can exist between being a person of faith and experiencing the power of God's love radiating through your life. Though people, for example, find guidance and comfort in my own *Surviving Depression: A Catholic Approach*, I have found that after reading it some still can experience a sense of separation from God.

So when I was asked to write the foreword for Father Greg Cleveland's *Awakening Love: An Ignatian Retreat and the Song of Songs* I didn't just read the book, but submitted myself completely to an experience of awakening love under the author's guidance, and I realized that Father Cleveland has put together precisely what we in today's spiritual environment most need. *Awakening Love* presents the Spiritual Exercises as a school of prayer through which we prepare ourselves to receive the divine gift of prayer: the kiss of God. This "lover's kiss," Father Cleveland explains, is a movement of the spirit felt at a very deep level of our being, close to the center, that bridges any distance and removes any sense of separation. And isn't this what we all long to know: that we and God are intimately united through God's overflowing and never-ending tenderness?

Awakening Love integrates the dynamics of Saint Ignatius' Spiritual Exercises with the intensity and tenderness of the lovers' intimacy recounted in the Song of Songs. *Awakening Love* speaks to the deepest core of our being through the spiritual experience of God's thirst for us and his nearness, leading us to dedication and commitment to God's dream for us in the world.

Awakening Love makes both the Song of Songs and Ignatian spirituality accessible and understandable to people who are searching for God. Beginners will discover the riches of both the retreat experience of the Spiritual Exercises and the mystical content of the Song of Songs. In these past decades, the Spiritual Exercises have become a welcome and familiar landscape when we make retreat. However, some advanced pray-ers can grow weary of making the same Spiritual Exercises and are looking for new approaches and adaptations of the traditional text. *Awakening Love* will bring fresh insight using the Song of Songs, opening new horizons for the retreat experience.

For those of us who are intent upon growing in the spiritual life, the process takes time. We may feel unsatisfied or empty or insufficient because we feel we are continually collecting pieces of information—as though our spiritual life is a puzzle and we are being given only a few of the pieces. We hear something in a homily here, read something else in a book, treasure a nugget of inspiration shared with us by a friend, and try to understand our spiritual development in this fragmentary light. Even after a lifetime of puzzle pieces, we often don't understand how things "hang together." I have always felt that somehow the process of the Spiritual Exercises helped me understand how the few pieces of the puzzle that I had come to understand were a small part of the whole picture. This is one of the gifts that the Spiritual Exercises can give you: a framework for understanding your spiritual experience, one that is robust enough to grow with you as you progress through the years.

Time is a precious commodity in today's world. That's why books such as *Awakening Love* are such a treasure. They can cut the time needed for the reader to find this personal path of growth in the spiritual life in half, and maybe in half again, when the reader surrenders to the process of the "retreat." Father Cleveland has specialized in preaching and directing the Exercises and concentrated on the study of both the Spiritual Exercises and Christian spirituality in general for the past twenty-five years. As a good retreat master, Father Cleveland has succeeded in writing a book that doesn't tell us one way to follow in order to discover God's love, his way, but mentors the reader gradually into surrendering to the way the Lord wants to show us how he loves us personally. Father Cleveland doesn't give a list of tasks but rather evokes in the reader's heart a "longing for the beauty and immensity of God." A good director will help us apply the wisdom of the word and of the spiritual tradition wisely to our own personal situation, by hearing what God says directly to us so that we can find God in everything. That is what this book does so well.

Here one finds a structure that guides the reader to an openness of heart that enables her or him to listen more and more deeply to the Lord of their heart. And we can listen to that Lord everywhere.

With *Awakening Love*, Father Cleveland brings a splendid integration of Scripture, prayer, the spiritual tradition, the writings of the saints, the legacy of recent popes, and a wholesome understanding of the dynamics of conversion and sanctification to the field of retreat work and spirituality. A great book is like a tree that offers shade to anyone who needs it. *Awakening Love* is such a tree. I am confident that many people will find their longing for the Lord met by the Lord's even greater thirst for them—and their soul will be stretched to infinite horizons.

KATHRYN J. HERMES, FSP

Author of *Cherished by the Lord: 100 Meditations* and *Surviving Depression: A Catholic Approach*

Introduction

The Spiritual Exercises of Saint Ignatius have had a tremendous impact in the history of the Church, while the Song of Songs is the most sublime book of Scripture describing mystical union with God in prayer. Both of these works can awaken in the reader a passionate desire to love and serve the Lord. Both books describe a deeply personal encounter with the living God, and both encapsulate the entire Christian spiritual journey. In my prayer I have long pondered the profound connections between these two masterpieces. As a retreat director, I have often proposed to retreatants texts of the Song of Songs that pertain to the themes of the Spiritual Exercises, and these texts—in tandem with the Exercises—have yielded rich results in their prayer experience. In *Awakening Love*, I explore the deep correlation between the two books and provide the reader with abundant food for prayer and reflection.

The Spiritual Exercises of Saint Ignatius are a systematic way to God that is tailored to the individual. The Exercises have a dynamic methodology, an interior logic and flow. As we pray through the great themes of God's revelation in and through the sacred Scriptures, we will see a structured system and a dynamic personalism. In the midst of the systematic pattern of prayer, God reveals himself personally and uniquely to the individual. Dialogue with a spiritual director fosters this personal approach within the framework of the retreat.

The twin goals of the Exercises are union with God in prayer and the discernment of God's will for our lives. Toward the first goal, the retreat experience begins with the *Principle and Foundation*, a meditation that sets out the conditions for achieving spiritual freedom. At the heart of this freedom is a desire for God and a strong awareness of his personal love, so we focus our prayer on this desire and awareness. The Exercises then progress through "weeks" or phases, during which we contemplate specific themes. In the first week, we meditate on sin and the reality of evil in the world and within ourselves, arriving at repentance and awareness of God's tremendous mercy. In the second week, we contemplate Christ and the mysteries of his life to gain a more intimate knowledge of him so that we may follow him more closely. We consider the call of Christ more intensely and apply principles of discerning God's will in our vocations, and so move toward the second goal. In the third week, we journey in greater union with Christ in his passion and death and are confirmed in our call to follow him more closely in suffering. In the fourth week, we rejoice with the risen Christ and are confirmed in the joy of following him.

We emerge from the Spiritual Exercises better attuned to God's presence and will in all the circumstances of our lives. More conformed to Christ and his call, we can better choose according to his values. The Exercises are therefore geared to the apostolic life of an active person making choices to follow Christ in the Church and in the world.

Building upon the Gospel's message of service to God and neighbor, the Spiritual Exercises have been described as a service-oriented spirituality. Saint Ignatius seeks to orient us to the service of Christ and others out of gratitude for what God has done for us. We make a self-offering in service to God who has offered himself for us. This beautiful note of self-offering is sounded throughout the retreat, based on a relationship of love and friendship between creature and Creator. In the Exercises, however, Saint Ignatius mentions love only a few times, which some criticize as a deficiency given love's importance in the Gospels. Saint Ignatius emphasizes that "love ought to manifest itself in deeds rather than in words" (SpEx 230). Still, words are vital to love if love is to convey itself in actions.

In contrast with the service mentality of the Spiritual Exercises, bridal spirituality is a very different approach to prayer. Best exemplified by Carmelite saints such as Teresa of Ávila, John of the Cross, and Thérèse of Lisieux, bridal spirituality explicitly emphasizes verbal expressions of love, while orienting love toward service. One of the bridal mystics' favorite sources for this fervent articulation of love is the Song of Songs, a book of love poetry that speaks deeply of God's ardent love for us and our loving response. On the surface, the Song of Songs appears merely to be a passionate dialogue between two lovers, a bride and a bridegroom,* that intensifies their union and appreciation of one another. A deeper reading of the Song of Songs, however, reveals the bride's transformation as she grows in awareness of the bridegroom. This transformation parallels our growth in holiness as we experience the Spiritual Exercises. *Awakening Love* will show how the bride's spiritual development parallels the schema of the Spiritual Exercises.

Many are drawn by the beauty of the Song of Songs but may quickly become confused by its content. Because the bridal language can seem foreign to how people experience spiritual reality, they may question the Song's relevance and wonder how it applies to ordinary Christian life. Through the themes and prayer exercises that follow, I will strive to make the Song of Songs relevant and accessible. For those looking for new approaches and adaptations of the traditional text of the Spiritual Exercises, these subjects will also bring fresh insight and open new horizons for the retreatant.

At first glance the Song of Songs is a book of love poetry describing lovers' bliss on their wedding day. The import of this expression and "sacrament" of nuptial love that unites a man and a woman should not be understated or lightly skipped over on the way to deeper spiritual meanings. Underscoring the importance of this scriptural nuptial language, John Paul II calls his reflections on the Song of Songs the "crowning" of his teachings on the theology of the body. He notes how the words, movements, and gestures of the spouses correspond to the interior movement of their hearts.[1] We can realize the profound expression of love through their declarations and body language.

The rich literal meaning of the Song of Songs includes references to the Temple and Israel's love and worship of the Lord. It also reveals the Lord as the Bridegroom of Israel, his bride. Other Hebrew Scriptures, such as the Psalms, Isaiah, and Hosea, corroborate this meaning. For example, in Hosea 2:19 the Lord declares to Israel: "And I will take you for my wife forever; I will take you for my wife in righteousness and in justice, in steadfast love, and in mercy." These passages clearly reveal the Lord as the divine Bridegroom who

---

* In the quotes from the Song of Songs that follow, the bride is indicated as B; the bridegroom as G; and the daughters of Jerusalem as D—Editor.

1. See John Paul II, *Man and Woman He Created Them* (Boston: Pauline Books & Media, 2006), 549ff.

espouses Israel as his bride. The Song of Songs describes the nature of their love relationship.

The Song of Songs is not limited to this literal understanding of the nature of love but expands to an inexhaustible treasure of wisdom based on a spiritual interpretation. As the Church has always held, the Holy Spirit is the primary author behind the word, ever ready to lead to deeper levels of divine truth those who seek to understand his word in the Spirit of the Church.[2]

The Scriptures have a literal meaning we can grasp through study. But in prayer we are led to deeper spiritual meanings by the same Spirit who is the divine author of Scripture. Metaphor and analogy often describe our experience of union with God according to this spiritual understanding of God's word. The Fathers and Mothers of the Church describe the Song of Songs as an expression of the love of God for Israel, of Christ for his Church, and of Christ for the individual Christian—especially, then, for the Blessed Virgin Mary, as she is the perfect disciple and representative of the Church in her holiness and purity.

Given the logic the Church provides for reading and pondering scriptural texts, throughout this book we will primarily consider the spiritual understanding of the Song of Songs by using insights from the great mystics in the Church's tradition. Sometimes we will also examine the historical circumstances surrounding the text in order to clarify the author's intention and literal meaning. Finally, we will consider the text's relation to the Spiritual Exercises.

When reading the Song of Songs, women might easily place themselves in the role of the bride alongside the divine Bridegroom, while men may find that more difficult. But for all of us, Christ is the Bridegroom of our souls. Some virtues that might seem more feminine are common to all of us, male and female. Men and women both must cultivate them in order to be receptive to God's grace. All Christians, for example, are called to imitate Mary in her receptivity and responsiveness to God. While men excel at giving themselves in a way that is receiving of the other, women excel at receiving the other in a way that is giving to the other. In relating to God, we are all called

---

2. Hans Urs von Balthasar has explored this topic in *The Word Made Flesh*, vol. 1 of *Explorations in Theology* (San Francisco: Saint Ignatius Press, 1989), 21.

to first excel at receiving in a giving way, as shown in the instance of Martha and Mary. Mary chose "the better part" (see Lk 10:42); she received Jesus in hospitality by sitting at his feet and listening deeply to his words. As the Lord gave himself to Mary, she simply received him, and in doing so, she also gave him love.

God desires to give himself totally to each one of us. By receiving God, we are giving ourselves back to him. God is pleased to give himself to us and delighted when we receive his gift of self in prayer.

In prayer, we remain primarily in this receptive mode before God. The bridegroom in the Song of Songs delights in his bride's reception of him, just as God delights when we receive him through prayer, a receptivity that begins primarily in being before doing. We receive our created being as a gift from God before we communicate ourselves to others and act on their behalf. As the only-begotten Son, Christ himself receives his divine being and mission from the Father from eternity. At the moment of the incarnation he received his human nature from his mother through the power of the Holy Spirit. As man, he was then able to give of himself as the incarnate Son of God. Christ calls his disciples to be with him as companions before he sends them out on mission. In the Spiritual Exercises, we are similarly called to be with Christ in contemplation, to receive his divine life and let it flow into our apostolic activity. Saint Ignatius admitted that his way of being led in God's grace was more passive and receptive than active and controlling.[3]

---

3. See Jose Ignacio Tellechea Idigoras, *Saint Ignatius of Loyola: The Pilgrim Saint*, trans. Cornelius Michael Buckley, S.J. (Chicago: Loyola University Press, 1994), 584.

How to Use This Book

This book may be used: *As a way to pray through the Song of Songs.* The Song of Songs is a very attractive yet mysterious book, hard to understand on a spiritual level. *Awakening Love* provides a key to understanding the profound yet elusive meaning of this mystical Scripture text and helps to apply it in one's life.

As a way of making the Spiritual Exercises: It is nearly impossible to make the Spiritual Exercises by reading them in their raw form and making the retreat without some explanation and guidance. *Awakening Love* "fleshes out" the Exercises and offers a spiritual compass to guide you through them. I also recommend that you reflect on your experience of God in prayer with a spiritual director, who can help you make more sense out of what is happening to you.

As a companion to making the Spiritual Exercises: If you are formally undertaking the Exercises with a spiritual director, *Awakening Love* will help you understand their dynamics and content, fostering greater receptivity to God's grace. The final seven chapters also make for an excellent transition into daily living at the end of the retreat. The Appendix shows how each chapter of this book corresponds to the relevant theme of the Exercises.

As spiritual reading: In his Spiritual Exercises Saint Ignatius provides a complete spirituality of the Christian life and gives wise advice about practicing our faith. *Awakening Love* unfolds the great truths of Ignatian spirituality and offers solid spiritual nourishment.

The end of each chapter offers questions for personal reflection and group discussion, prayer exercises based on the reading, and suggested graces to ask for in prayer. Ordinarily I recommend taking one week to digest each chapter and engage in the accompanying prayer material, but the time frame is not fixed. Seven prayer exercises are given, one for each day of the week. You may wish to linger more deeply with certain Scripture passages and themes, without completing all seven exercises in a given week.

Although the full Spiritual Exercises are sometimes referred to as the thirty days' retreat in a closed setting, I provide thirty-two chapters and themes. There is no magic to a fixed period of thirty days in a closed retreat setting, or thirty weeks adapted to a daily life setting. In both cases, one can complete the Exercises in a longer or shorter time. Saint Ignatius allows for adaptation of the Spiritual Exercises (see SpEx 18–20):

- *In time*, such as over a weekend, or eight days, or a full thirty days, etc.
- *In space*, either in a closed retreat house setting or in daily life in one's home (over a number of weeks), or even in a parish setting.
- *In content*, according to our desires, needs, and readiness. One may focus on any particular theme, such as desire, mercy, call to mission, suffering, resurrection, finding God in all things, etc.

You can read and pray with the Exercises at your own pace, privately or with the guidance of a director.

CHAPTER I

The Kiss of Life

[B] —Let him kiss me with the kisses of his mouth! . . .
Draw me after you, let us make haste.
    The king has brought me into his chambers.
[D] We will exult and rejoice in you;
    we will extol your love more than wine;
    rightly do they love you. (Song 1:2, 4)

It is more suitable and much better that the Creator and Lord in person communicate Himself to the devout soul in quest of the divine will, that He inflame it with His love and praise, and dispose it for the way in which it could better serve God in the future. (SpEx 15)

Saint Ignatius invites anyone making the Spiritual Exercises to come to the retreat with great desires. The drama of love in the Song of Songs begins with the bride's desire for the kiss of her beloved in a quest for union. Through kisses, lovers attempt to give themselves entirely to one another, even to exchange breath, which symbolizes life. If it were possible, they would give the breath of life to each other and become one in a fusion of lives.[4] Human beings have a drive toward union, yet fall short of this complete one-ness of heart. The quest for union between human beings is a good analogy of our desire for communion with God—our ultimate goal. God created pas-sionate human love to mirror his own passionate desire for us. The image of marital union in the Song of Songs is the best image for the depths of union we experience with God.

God is a Holy Trinity of complete self-giving of persons to one another in perfect knowledge and love. In his desire to share his love with other beings, God chooses to create the universe and fill it with the very gift of himself. The Lord not only creates natural life, he also breathes the super-natural life of the Spirit into us by the grace of our baptism, uniting himself completely to us. The kiss that the bride mentions symbolizes the divine life God imparts to us, which leads us to desire to grow in it. Just as a lover's desire for greater bonding with the beloved is insatiable, so our desire for God is unquenchable, because God has first desired us with an infinite thirst.

Prayer is simply getting in touch with God's thirst for us and our longing for him. The founder of the Oblates of the Virgin Mary, Venerable Bruno Lanteri, writes that prayer basically begins with desire: "In order to facilitate prayer, it is necessary to know that force, study is not required, but only a word, a sigh, a desire ever so light, a desire in its birth, a desire that we haven't developed fully in the heart; this same disposition of the heart to pray has already passed into the heart of God."[5] Our desire for God has already passed through the heart of God as his desire for us, just as the bride's desire for her bridegroom flows from her response to his love.

Because God first desires us and initiates his relationship with us, prayer is God's initiative, just as the lover takes the initiative in kissing his bride. The Spiritual Exercises are a school of prayer through which we prepare ourselves to receive the divine gift of prayer, the kiss of God. Saint Ignatius offers many forms of prayer exercises as ways to dispose ourselves to receive God's grace. As we ponder these exercises, a combination of prayer and Scriptures, we use

---

4. See Patrick Regan, *Advent to Pentecost: Comparing the Seasons in the Ordinary and Extraordinary Forms of the Roman Rite* (Collegeville: Liturgical Press, 2012), 187–189.

5. David N. Beauregard, OMV, ed., *The Spiritual Writings of Venerable Pio Bruno Lanteri* (Boston: Oblates of the Virgin Mary, 2001), 114.

the powers of our soul—the memory, intellect, will, and imagination. God works through our faculties to reveal himself to us in prayer. We might be tempted to believe prayer flows from our own efforts, but we only respond to God's drawing us—like the bride focusing her entire attention on her bridegroom as the object of her affection.

The kiss between lovers suggests their immediate union. The Song of Songs begins with the bride dreaming of her lover in the third person. In the Hebrew, she expresses her wish as such: "Oh, that he would kiss me with the kisses of his mouth." Here her lover seems distant. But in the line that immediately follows, she addresses him personally, "Your love is better than wine." What happened to change her perspective? It was her longing for him. In crying out for the bridegroom she was inviting him to draw close to her. Now she finds him present. In fact, he was never distant at all but was always close.

God is so close that he touches us. Even the notion of adoring the Lord is rooted in the Latin words *ad* and *ora*, or "to the mouth," in the sense of kissing God. Just as the lover's kiss bridges any distance the bride had previously perceived, so adoration of God in prayer allows God to deal directly with us, removing any sense of separation from him. God is closer to us than our inmost selves. No wonder Saint Ignatius states that "it is much more suitable . . . that the Creator and Lord Himself should impart Himself to His devout soul, embracing her to His love and praise, and disposing her for the way in which she can better hereafter serve Him."[6] The word "embracing" suggests immediate contact of God with the individual soul and has conjugal connotations that resonate with the bridal spirituality of the Song of Songs. The person whom God embraces will be more inflamed with love and desire to serve than if another human being had urged the person to do so. On a related note, Saint Ignatius exhorts the director of the Spiritual Exercises to "permit the Creator to deal directly with the creature, and the creature directly with his Creator and Lord" (SpEx 15). The director does not inspire the retreatant but simply narrates faithfully the events of salvation history, enabling the retreatant to encounter God directly.

---

6. SpEx 15, based on studies of the original Spanish autograph edition of the Spiritual Exercises redacted in 1969. This revised translation is almost universally held by scholars. Footnote 72 in *Ecclesial Mysticism in the Spiritual Exercises*, Michael Buckley, S.J., *Theological Studies*, September 1995, vol. 56, no. 3.

Saint Ignatius knew that God dealt with him directly, teaching him just like a schoolmaster teaches a child.[7] He had many distinct experiences even as a beginner in the spiritual life while he was staying in a cave near Manresa, Spain. While praying and atoning for his many sins, he had overwhelming experiences of God's forgiveness and mercy. These led him to an intimate knowledge of the Incarnate Christ, moving him to love and follow Jesus more closely. Saint Ignatius encountered the suffering Christ and sorrowed with him. The risen Lord filled him with joy and consolation, leaving him with a profound awareness of God present in and through all things. He could see with the eyes of Christ and feel with his heart. These experiences in Manresa formed the core of what Saint Ignatius would eventually call his Spiritual Exercises. Just as God dealt directly with Saint Ignatius, in the Spiritual Exercises the Lord deals directly with each person who seeks deeper prayer and spiritual growth.

Saint Ignatius' prayer experiences did not remain only at the head level but resulted in his deep devotion and conviction to follow the Lord more closely. Although we distinguish between thinking about God and knowing him personally, these two things are not opposed but complementary. Our thinking about God should lead us to love him more deeply, just as when we love another person we seek to know that person better. But our knowing cannot remain at the level of mere intellectual speculation. Saint Ignatius explains early in the Spiritual Exercises that "it is not much knowledge that fills and satisfies the soul, but the intimate understanding and relish of the truth" (SpEx 2). It is easy to fill our heads with book knowledge and remain solely on the level of the intellect, but much more challenging to move to the level of the heart. Real prayer begins when God's grace touches our hearts, just as the bride in the Song of Songs has been deeply moved by the bridegroom to crave his kiss and embrace.

We have often heard about the Lord from others, and that has led us to believe in him. But now we seek his personal and unique revelation to our individual hearts, just as the bride desires to experience her lover directly in receiving his kiss. Origen, one of the earliest and greatest commentators on

---

7. See *The Autobiography of Saint Ignatius Loyola*, trans. Joseph O'Callaghan, ed. John Olin (New York: Fordham, 1993), pars. 27–31.

the Song, exclaims, "To you I turn, Father of my Spouse . . . send him to me, that he may speak to me no longer through his servants and prophets, but that he himself come, that I may hear him speaking and teaching, and he may kiss me with the kisses of his mouth."[8] We want to hear the Lord directly at the source of our being, where the Spirit of God kisses our human spirit.

Sometimes we might be living more in the context of someone else's understanding of divine revelation and less our own. We certainly need the witness and teaching of others, but God's grace is established uniquely in each one of us. Joseph Ratzinger once explained that there are as many ways to God as there are people; even within the same faith, each person's way is an entirely personal one.[9] While certain patterns are common to all of us in the journey to God, spirituality is not "one size fits all." Each person's relationship with God is marked by distinctive features, as John Paul II comments: "We all know this moment in which it is no longer sufficient to speak about Jesus by repeating what others have said. You must say what you think, and not quote an opinion."[10]

Going Deeper

As important as it is to know and love God, much of this relationship escapes our awareness and remains at the level of our spiritual unconscious. The Carmelite Ruth Burrows explains that the most vital aspects of our being occur at a level beneath our awareness. Thus genuine contemplation in its substance evades our immediate awareness.[11] The Gospels themselves show us how little Jesus' disciples understood his nature and mission. As Christ walked the earth and performed signs and miracles, his followers

8. See Origen, *The Song of Songs, Commentary and Homilies*, Part One, Book One, trans. Edmond de Pressensé, manuscript dated 1862.

9. See Joseph Cardinal Ratzinger, *Salt of the Earth: The Church at the End of the Millennium, An Interview with Peter Seewald* (San Francisco: Saint Ignatius Press, 1987), 32.

10. John Paul II, Homily during the Mass for Brazilian youth in Belo Horizonte, July 1, 1980 (Vatican web site, https://w2.vatican.va/content/john-paul-ii/en/homilies/1980.index. 4. html, last accessed October 27, 2013).

11. See Ruth Burrows, O.C.D., *Essence of Prayer* (Mahwah: Hidden Spring/Paulist, 2006), 32–33.

began to believe in him, but that faith fell woefully short of the truth about who he was. The disciples constantly failed to comprehend Jesus and often reduced his supernatural teaching to a merely natural level. For example, Peter thought Jesus' washing his feet was merely a matter of hospitality and hygiene, when it was meant to be a cleansing from sin and a share in Jesus' very life and ministry of service (see Jn 13:6–8). Nicodemus thought that being "born again" meant going back into his mother's womb, and he didn't understand it as being born of water and the Spirit (see Jn 3:1–15). Like the disciples, we are limited in our ability to receive much of the fullness of God's revelation.

Movements of grace occur when the Lord reveals himself in our hearts and minds, allowing us to receive more of his fullness; Saint Ignatius describes this as "spiritual consolation."[12] Saint Ignatius speaks of the touch or "kiss" of God that the bride experiences in these deep encounters, these profound interior movements: "I call it consolation when some interior movement in the soul is caused, through which the soul comes to be inflamed with love of its Creator and Lord; and when it can in consequence love no created thing on the face of the earth in itself, but in the Creator of them all. . . . I call consolation every increase of hope, faith, and charity, and all interior joy which calls and attracts to heavenly things and to the salvation of one's soul, quieting it and giving it peace in its Creator and Lord" (SpEx 316).

Spiritual consolation is a spike in the ordinary experience of our life of grace. It is a movement of spirit felt at a very deep level of our being, close to the center, where God kisses and embraces us. In moments of consolation, we perceive that we are in a blessed union with God. We have an awareness of being "in tune" with God and his plan. When tuning a radio, we hear static as we move the dial. When we land on our favorite station, the static gives way to the beautiful music we were looking for; now we are clearly connected. In consolation, we experience the beautiful music of being united with God and doing his will. We also feel at peace and most at home with ourselves in God. It is important that we pay attention to these gifts. The Lord often speaks to us in consolation for various reasons: to make us aware of how much he loves

---

12. For an in-depth teaching on spiritual consolation, refer to Timothy Gallagher's books: *Discernment of Spirits* (New York: Crossroads, 2005) and *Spiritual Consolation* (New York: Crossroads, 2007).

us, to give personal meaning to our relationship with him, to make us aware of his call, and to lead us to follow him more closely.

When we receive spiritual consolation, we may often notice it for a moment and then, sadly, quickly forget. Saint Ignatius suggests that we should drink deeply of God's consolations, savoring their comfort and "storing them up" for difficult times. In the Song of Songs, the King (God) has drawn the bride (us) into his chamber or "wine cellar" (v. 4). He desires that they both drink deeply of the intoxicating love they have for each other. Saint Teresa of Ávila remarks: "It doesn't seem the King wants to keep anything from her. He wants her to drink in conformity with her desire and become wholly inebriated, drinking of all the wines in God's storehouse. Let the soul rejoice in these joys. Let it admire God's grandeurs. Let it not fear to lose its life from drinking so much beyond what its natural weakness can endure."[13] God's consolations are meant to be savored deeply and permeate our whole being. We ought to drink in his kiss, to yield to his love in our heart, allowing the experience to have its powerful and lasting effects on our being.

This does not, however, lead us to exalt ourselves. Saint Ignatius reminds us that we should humble ourselves (see SpEx 324) in moments of spiritual consolation, realizing they are God's gift and not our own doing. At the annunciation, Mary accepts God's proposal and adds, "Here am I, the servant of the Lord" (Lk 1:38). In her Magnificat, Mary rejoices and exults in the Lord's gift, drinking fully of the moment of consolation and expressing her love and praise to God: "My soul magnifies the Lord, and my spirit rejoices in God, my Savior, for he has looked with favor on the lowliness of his servant" (Lk 1:46–48). She is convinced of her own humility and dependence on God for all she is and does. Mary, like the bride, has experienced the kiss of God in the most profound way—in his being conceived in her heart and taking flesh in her womb. As she ponders in her heart that God who is mighty has done great things for her, she becomes more alive in his presence. Like the bride, she is led to rejoicing, to deep communion with her Beloved. The goal of the Spiritual Exercises is to lead us into this same direct union with the Lord.

---

13. Saint Teresa of Ávila, Meditations on the Song of Songs, *The Collected Works of St. Teresa of Ávila*, Volume Two, trans. Kieran Kavanaugh, O.C.D., and Otilio Rodriguez, O.C.D. (Washington, D.C.: ICS, 1980), 251–252.

Questions for Reflection and Discussion

1. Do you perceive God as distant or close? Are you aware of the Lord's touch or "kiss" to you that bridges any perceived distance? What is it like?

2. When have you experienced greater awareness of the Lord's presence? How might this help you to discover those things that might still be unconscious in your relationship with God?

3. Saint Ignatius described God as a divine schoolmaster who taught him directly. He also learned from other trusted guides in the spiritual life. What have you learned from others about you relationship with God? What have you learned directly from God? What is unique about your religious experience?

4. Have you ever experienced the divine "kiss" of spiritual consolation? How would you describe it? How did it affect your spirit, soul, and body? What meaning did it have regarding your relationship with God and the direction of your life?

5. How have you expressed your heart or articulated your thoughts and feelings to the Lord? How did it impact your relationship with God?

Prayer Exercises

1. Read Venerable Bruno Lanteri's words about desire and prayer (p. 10). Pray with Song of Songs 1:1, and ask for the grace to desire God more fully.

2. Pray with Exodus 3:1–6, and ask the grace that God will reveal himself to you personally.

3. Ponder the comments of John Paul II about knowing God personally (p. 13). Pray with Matthew 16:13–20, and ask for the grace to know and express who Jesus is to you.

4. Consider the apostles' lack of understanding of who Jesus was. Pray with Luke 7:11–17 or Matthew 8:14–15, and ask for the grace that what is unconscious in your relationship with the Lord may come to light.

5. Pray with Song of Songs 1:2–4, and ask for the grace to express yourself to the Lord in prayer.

6. Ponder Saint Ignatius' description of spiritual consolation (p. 14). Pray with Luke 1:39–51, and ask for the grace to rejoice in the gifts God has given to you.

7. Repeat any of the above meditations and return to the experiences of greater insight or deeper feeling.

CHAPTER 2

Desire Is Prayer

[B] Let him kiss me with the kisses of his mouth! . . .
Draw me after you, let us make haste.
   The king has brought me into his chambers.
[D] We will exult and rejoice in you;
   we will extol your love more than wine;
   rightly do they love you. (Song 1:2, 4)

I will ask God our Lord for what I want and desire. (SpEx 48)

S aint Ignatius exhorts anyone beginning the Spiritual Exercises to pray with great desires, namely for the infinite and lovely things of God that lead to our salvation and sanctification. We can emulate the bride in the Song of Songs, whose passionate desire is expressed in the longing for her bridegroom to kiss her "with the kisses of his mouth." Jesus knows our great yearnings and aspirations. He began his ministry with a question for his first followers, "What are you looking for?" (Jn 1:38) Other translations are: "What do you seek?" or "What do you desire?" All point to the primacy Jesus gives to desire. We should allow Jesus to ask us this question and, in response, ponder what we seek. At the beginning of the spiritual journey it is crucial to orient our longings, because they indicate the end we are striving for. A ship pointed a few degrees off course at its origin will not reach its destination. Likewise, our perseverance and success in reaching our goal depend on the clarity and intensity of our desires, which keep us on course. The French novelist Antoine de Saint-Exupery once explained that if you want to build a ship, it's best not to herd people together to collect wood or to perform other tasks; rather you teach them to long for the immensity of the sea.[14] In the same way, as we begin to pray, we need to focus not on tasks but on our longing for the beauty and immensity of God.

Since Jesus presumably knew the hearts of his first followers, why did he ask them what they desired? Though *he* knew the answer to his question, perhaps they didn't. The disciples had been following John the Baptist, a prophet of the Most High, which certainly indicated their desire for God. John piqued their curiosity by pointing to Jesus, and they began to follow him, leading to his query. They simply responded, "Rabbi . . . where are you staying?" (Jn 1:38). Since Jewish rabbis often lived with their disciples, this response may have indicated their desire to follow Jesus in a radical way as his disciples, eating and drinking with him and sharing his life while he taught them. The question may also have meant they were simply interested in Jesus. In either case, Jesus invited them to "come and see," and their lives would never be the same.

As we begin the Exercises, Jesus asks us the same question he asked the disciples, and we can begin to wonder about our own desires. We know we have many, more numerous than the hairs on our heads, as Saint Augustine put it. Some of these desires might frighten us, as they did C. S. Lewis, who looked within himself and discovered the covetousness and hunger for power that had been driving him.[15] Like Lewis, we have probably experienced desires pulling us in multiple directions, threatening to derail our fundamental purpose in life. Even if we have only one or two errant desires, their intensity could menace our happiness. The addict painfully experiences the tyranny of one desire that dominates all of life and how its consequences can

---

14. See *Citadelle*; the origins of the quote are not certain: http://quoteinvestigator.com/2015/08/25/sea/.

15. See C. S. Lewis, *Surprised by Joy: The Shape of My Early Life* (New York: Harcourt Brace Jovanovich, 1966), 226.

ruin relationships, work, and health. As substitutes for God, disordered desires become idols in our lives that demand our homage and turn us away from our fundamental desire for God.

Even the good things we desire and pursue may mask our deeper, more fundamental desire, preventing us from seeking it and leaving us dissatisfied. The literary enthusiast enamored of Shakespeare still asks if the playwright's graceful lines can yield more meaning. The sports fan cheers his team to win the big game, yet finds the victory hollow. The musical devotee attends the great opera but leaves with an insatiable appetite for more beauty. We should also not suppose that our desire for God will be satisfied in this life. The more we have of God, the more we will desire him. Still, we will only have him when we behold him face to face. In her *Dialogues*, Saint Catherine of Siena echoes this truth as she addresses God, exclaiming that each time she seeks him, she finds him all the more, and each time she finds him, the more she seeks him. In her seeking she can never be satisfied, for what she discovers of him leaves her even more eager to discover, know, and experience.[16] When the Lord fills our souls, we crave his presence all the more.

Humans are given to extremes, even in the spiritual life. One extreme is to follow our desires indiscriminately. Many people do just this, looking for God to bless their fundamentally disordered attachments. Such persons take the reins of control of their lives and make decisions without consulting God in prayer. When they do invoke the Lord, it is only to ask God to give them what they want without pondering if their desires are God's will for them. Desires, instead, have to be discerned in God's presence. We need to ask God to provide what is best for us and to instill his desires in us, for only he knows what will satisfy us.

Discernment

Saint Ignatius was a man of many desires. Before his religious awakening and return to faith in God, he lived a very worldly life in the court of the Duke of Nájera. Driven by the passion for courtly life with its honors and privileges, Saint Ignatius wanted to distinguish himself on the battlefield, to

---

16. See Saint Catherine of Siena, *Dialogues*, taken from *The Liturgy of the Hours*, vol. II, Office of Readings (New York: Catholic Book Publishing Corp., 1976), 1794.

bask in the glory of a Spanish victory. The opportunity arose when a French force of 10,000 men invaded his Basque territory of northern Spain. Though Saint Ignatius was leading a battalion of only a few hundred, he insisted on defending the fortress at Pamplona against the much larger force. As the fight ensued, a cannonball exploded, shattering his leg, and he was carried off to his home at Loyola for surgery and convalescence. During his recovery, Saint Ignatius asked for his favorite books full of tales of chivalry and errant knights. None were available, only books on the lives of Christ and the saints, so he read those. He began to desire to follow these saintly examples. But at other times Saint Ignatius went back to daydreaming about chivalry and the heroic deeds he would perform in the service of a great and noble lady, seeking to win her hand. As he dwelled on these fantasies, he found himself inflamed with desire, just as he had been when reading about the lives of Christ and the saints. In particular, Saint Ignatius experienced the desire to imitate Saint Francis and Saint Dominic in their lives of prayer, penance, and charity. Which desire and lifestyle would he therefore follow—to serve a noble lady or to serve God?

When Saint Ignatius noted his internal reactions that resulted from pondering each desire, he noticed a key difference. After fantasizing about the noble lady and chivalric deeds, he felt dry and discontented. But after thinking about imitating the saints, he felt inflamed with a lasting love and desire. This observation marked the beginning of his understanding that though he had many desires, only some were deep and satisfying. Once he discovered them, he did in fact follow his truest and most profound desires to love and serve God.

Saint Ignatius illustrates a point known in the field of psychology: all people have certain vital desires. The American psychologist Abraham Maslow devised a six-level hierarchy of motives that, according to his theory, determine human behavior. Maslow ranks human needs as follows: (1) physiological: food, shelter, exercise, etc.; (2) security and safety; (3) love and feelings of belonging; (4) competence, prestige, and esteem; (5) self-fulfillment; and (6) curiosity and the need to understand. God certainly works through these good and healthy desires, which ordinarily should be pursued on a natural and even supernatural level. Mark Laaser, in his book, *The Seven Desires of Every Heart*, encourages readers to consider their soul's greatest longing. He explains that the longings of our souls illustrate the desire to be heard and understood; to be affirmed; to be blessed; to be safe; to be touched; to be chosen; and to be included.[17] As we seek the Lord in prayer, we realize he wants us to desire these fundamentally good things and wants these desires to be fulfilled. By getting more in touch with these fundamental desires, we will hopefully come to realize that they are leading us to their ultimate fulfillment in God.

Sometimes for various reasons we fail to recognize that we have deep and authentic desires. Perhaps we don't trust our desires enough to face them. If we were stuck in superficial or sinful desires in the past, we may have learned to uproot all desires and desire nothing at all. A kind of Christian stoicism can lead to this elimination of desire. The Stoics taught that we can attain happiness through an internal calm that comes through repressing all feelings. So they would desire very little until no person or thing was important anymore. This attitude is far removed from Christian anthropology, since as human beings in love with Christ we desire the good as Christ desired it. At the Last Supper Jesus declared, "I have earnestly desired to eat this Passover with you before I suffer" (Lk 23:15), showing that he clearly desired the good of his disciples. Christ's great desire, his food, as he described it, was to do the Father's will. In expressing his well-formed desires, Jesus is our model to imitate.

Even as we follow the Lord's example, we may be unable to voice our desires. Maybe we have been taught to satisfy others' desires first, so we don't pay attention to our own. Many people laudably sacrifice themselves for the sake of others, like the mother who always gives to her children. Some people may have been told what to want,[18] such as the young person who is expected to follow in his father or mother's footsteps in a career or relationship. Other people, sadly, have been raised to see their own desires as selfish. They seek to meet others' needs and don't know how to accept their own. Yet Jesus still asks us, "What do you desire?"

Attitudes that inhibit us from considering our desires could be frustration, fear, or comfort with mediocrity. Some people are so used to feeling unfulfilled that they may wonder, "What's the use of even hoping for something different, something more?" Many people reach midlife only to find

17. See Mark Laaser, *The Seven Desires of Every Heart* (Grand Rapids: Zondervan, 2008).

18. See Janet K. Ruffing, R.S.M., *Spiritual Direction: Beyond the Beginnings* (New York/Mahwah, N.J.: Paulist Press, 2000).

their dreams unrealized, and they lack the strength to seek yet another dream. Others may observe the popular religious caveat: "Be careful what you ask God for, you might get it!" That saying implies a fear of the changes that ful-filling a desire would demand in one's life. I could be mired in a relationship that is not really life giving to me, but fear the pain of leaving it. I might be stuck in a career that doesn't allow me to use my talents or doesn't fulfill my dreams, but feel paralyzed over not knowing the next move. I might also feel perfectly comfortable in this mediocrity, this inertia that stifles my willing-ness to face my true desires and make the changes they might demand. As an example, I pursued an education and career in business because my father and older brothers had done so and I had never considered other career options. I had a certain interest in and penchant for marketing, and I had never pondered anything else. Discovering the call to follow Christ in priest-hood and religious life awakened a great passion in me. By God's grace, I left my business career behind in order to follow his invitation, breaking away from a choice that sprang from my having followed the status quo.

Other Obstacles

Another great obstacle to discovering our desires is thinking that we don't even have any that are worthwhile. John Eldridge, a Christian psycholo-gist, describes his counseling process with Ted and Diane, a couple whose marriage was on the rocks because they failed to look at their real issues. They were making good progress until Diane asked Ted about his deepest desires: what did Ted secretly wish Diane would do for him? Certainly any man would love to hear his wife ask him such an intriguing question. The sky was the limit. But did Ted ask for greater intimacy or respect? No, he asked for clean socks! For Ted, life would be better and their marriage would be richer if Diane would keep his drawer filled with clean socks. Eldridge mused that he wanted to throw Ted out the window—not because Ted was bad, shallow, or inconsiderate, but because he didn't even know what he wanted. His desires for love and adventure were an inaccessible mystery to him.[19]

Perhaps, like Ted, we're afraid that if we dig deep, beyond our desire for clean socks, we'll come up short—that nothing truly valuable will emerge.

---

19. See John Eldridge, *The Journey of Desire* (Nashville: Thomas Nelson, 2000), 165.

We may have to pray for the courage to ask that God instill deep desires within us. Saint Paul affirms the truth that God, in his good will toward us, produces in us any measure of desire or achievement (see Phil 2:13). Just as we can ask God to instill desires in us, we can also ask him for the ability to discover even our unconscious desires. When we do, we will likely discover that, first of all, we desire greater intimacy with God. William Barry, a master of the Spiritual Exercises, reminds us that God desired us into being and continues to sustain us, arousing in us a desire for an enigmatic divine totality that we do not know and cannot name.[20] At the heart level, God's desire for us is the foundation for the development of our relationship with God. Our corresponding desire for "I know not what" spurs us on to search for God's peace and leaves our hearts restless until they rest in God. Our desire for "I know not what" is the first step toward fulfillment in God.

Any desire we have for God is born of his intense desire for us. In commenting on the Gospel passage about the Samaritan woman at the well, Saint Augustine taught that we thirst for God because he has first thirsted for us. Jesus' dying words on the cross, "I thirst," express his thirst for each one of us. The Lord's desire for us engenders our desire for him. God creates holy desires within our hearts. It is important for us to pay attention to our desires, to listen deeply for them, so that we can discern whether or not they are from God. We should notice how God is already in some way fulfilling our deepest desires and be grateful for his generosity.

While all good desires come from God, he may not fulfill them in the way or time frame that we expect. Saint Thérèse of Lisieux desired to be many things, some of which she attained in this life and others only in eternity. One of the things Thérèse wanted to be was a ministerial priest; being a woman, however, she knew God was not calling her to that vocation. So she chose to pray for priests and support them by her letters. Yet today she is the patroness of priests, undoubtedly a great blessing and unexpected fulfillment of her desire. Thérèse also desired to be a martyr, often choosing to dress up and play the part of her heroine, the martyr Saint Joan of Arc. Though Thérèse didn't suffer martyrdom in the traditional sense, she suffered tremendously and heroically with the tuberculosis that eventually

---

20. See William Barry, *Letting the Creator Deal with the Creature* (Mahwah: Paulist Press, 1994), 24.

took her life. A final major desire of hers—to be a missionary in foreign lands—was impossible because she was a cloistered nun. Yet she interceded for missionaries throughout her life and is now the patron saint of missionaries. Each of Saint Thérèse's desires was important, having been placed in her heart by God. None was realized in the way she might have supposed. Still, God, who does not inspire impossible desires, ultimately did fulfill them for Saint Thérèse.

When our desire for God remains only partially fulfilled, our longing for him stretches our soul, giving it the capacity to better accept what God desires to give us. In his greatness, God desires to give us more of himself, so he must increase our capacity to receive him. Even with Mary, always "full of grace," God worked throughout her lifetime to increase her capacity to receive him and his grace. But why does God need to stretch us? It's because we often put limits on God's desires as well as our own. An anecdote will help to illustrate this. Two men—one an experienced fisher and one a novice—went fishing. Every time the experienced fisherman caught a big fish, he put it in his cooler to keep it fresh. Whenever the inexperienced fisherman caught a big fish, he threw it back. The experienced fisherman observed this dynamic all day without comment until finally, tired of seeing this waste of good fish, he exclaimed, "Why do you keep throwing back all the big fish you catch?" The novice replied, "I only have a small frying pan."

Is the "frying pan" of our desires big enough to hold what God wants us to have of himself? The likely answer is no. Our desire for God, therefore, needs to increase.

Ultimately, desire for God will bind us to God in prayer. As we become more aware of the Lord's thirst for us, we will thirst for him all the more, and our amazement and gratitude will increase along with our thirst. It might surprise us that the Lord would find us pleasing and attractive, that he would seek us. We respond to this truth with gratitude for his having chosen us despite our unworthiness. The bride's initial expression of desire is for the kiss of her bridegroom, which is realized. She is now led to deeper levels of fulfillment of desire. She exclaims, "The king has brought me into his rooms," places of greater intimacy and union. Explaining this dynamic, Saint Augustine states that the essence of prayer is a desire for God that comes from faith in his presence: "For it is your heart's desire that is your prayer; and if your desire continues uninterrupted, your prayer continues also. . . . If you would never cease to pray, never cease to long after it. The continuance of your longing is the continuance of your prayer."[21] Our expressed longing for God becomes our prayer to him and disposes us to contemplation. The Lord instills our very desire for him into our hearts. In prayer we grow more aware of our fundamental desire for him and, like the bride, seek ever deeper levels of satisfaction.

Questions for Reflection and Discussion

1. What is your personal history of considering and following your desires? How have you been taught to do this? What obstacles keep you from understanding and acting upon your desires?

2. Consider Maslow and Laaser's list of human needs (p. 22). How are your desires already being satisfied? What more do you desire in life? What more do you desire in your relationship with God?

3. How do you experience and live out your desire for God? Saint Augustine describes desire as prayer and foundational to our connection with God. How might you better keep desire for God at the forefront of your awareness?

Prayer Exercises

1. Pray with the Song of Songs 1:2–4, and ask the Lord to reveal his desire for you and your deepest longing for him.

2. Consider the story of John Eldridge and the married man who was unaware of his deeper desires. Pray with John 1:35–39, and ask for the grace to notice and formulate your desires.

3. Consider Saint Ignatius' conversion story and his discovery of his passion to follow the Lord. Pray with Isaiah 55:1–6, and ask for the grace to follow your deeper desires and to delight in the Lord.

4. Pray with John 4:3–29, and ask for the grace to know and break any addictions that sap your desire for God.

5. Pray with Mark 10:46–52, and ask for the grace to follow your deepest desires in the face of discouragement.

---

21. Saint Augustine, *On the Psalms*, 37, 13–14 (CCL 38, 391–392).

6. Consider Saint Thérèse's seemingly unfulfilled desires. Pray with Psalm 63:1–8, and ask for the grace to express any frustrations you have and to persevere in seeking what you truly want.

7. Make a repetition on any of the above contemplations, moving to places of greater insight or deeper feeling.

CHAPTER 3

Love's Right Order

[B] For your love is better than wine,
    your anointing oils are fragrant,
your name is perfume poured out;
    therefore the maidens love you. . . .
[D] We will exult and rejoice in you;
    we will extol your love more than wine;
rightly do they love you. (Song 1:2–3, 4)

Man is created to praise, reverence, and serve God our Lord, and by this
means to save his soul. . . . Our one desire and choice should be what is more
conducive to the end for which we are created. (SpEx 23)

Tuesday is my day off—or better, day out because there's no day off from
being a priest. Weather permitting, I usually head to the golf course to
play the greatest game in the world. I am never disappointed. Even if my
game is poor, I can enjoy the beauty of nature, the camaraderie of friends, and
the endless challenge of hitting difficult shots. Golf is a great diversion from
the ordinary routine that absorbs a person's total attention. Maybe that's why

Miguel was golfing that autumn morning, completing our foursome. As we golfed, we began to get to know one another. On the third hole he told me he was a busy and successful construction manager. But on the seventh hole he dropped a bomb: his wife had left him that morning, taking their one-year-old son.

Naturally I was stunned at the revelation and wondered why he was golfing. I thought that perhaps he was trying to take his mind off his problem, off his pain. As he continued to pour out his heart to me, Miguel explained that to take advantage of the housing boom, he'd been working long hours. In response, his wife had been sending signals that he was never home for them and that she was starving for attention and affection. He ignored the signs and continued his pursuit of the almighty dollar.

"Did you do anything to harm her?" I asked.

"If getting her all kinds of nice things is harming her, Father, then I guess I did," he replied, his response betraying his lack of perspective on what was of value in his life.

We continued to talk about marriage, the importance of practicing his Christian faith, and what he might do to win her back, ending our round on a hopeful note. That day, golf wasn't much of a diversion from my pastoral work. But it gave me an excellent opportunity to reflect on how easily people lose sight of the most fundamental values in their lives.

The Principle and Foundation

Saint Ignatius begins his Spiritual Exercises with a deliberation on the purpose of life simply entitled *Principle and Foundation*:

> Man is created to praise, reverence, and serve God our Lord, and by this means to save his soul. The other things on the face of the earth are created for man to help him in attaining the end for which he is created. Hence, man is to make use of them in as far as they help him in the attainment of his end, and he must rid himself of them in as far as they prove a hindrance to him. Therefore, we must make ourselves indifferent to all created things, as far as we are allowed free choice and are not under any prohibition. Consequently, as far as we are concerned, we should not prefer health to sickness, riches to poverty, honor to dishonor, a long life to a short life. The same holds for all other things. Our one desire and choice should be what is more conducive to the end for which we are created. (SpEx 23)

This opening statement may first appear to be an obvious truth, as are most first principles. For example, the Declaration of Independence speaks of the right to life, liberty, and the pursuit of happiness. As with the Principle and Foundation, those ideas seem obvious because they are largely self-evident truths. Therefore, we need to be careful not to lose sight of them, for if we did, crucial things would crumble. In the case of the Declaration, the whole structure of rights, freedoms, and responsibilities in our nation would fall apart. In his Principle and Foundation, Saint Ignatius asserts the truth that we come from God, our Creator, and that our goal is to return to him through his gift of salvation. The truth that we are meant to be with the Lord for all eternity is as simple as it is profound—something we must never lose sight of.

Myriad forces militate against this truth in our lives. In the previous chapter we meditated on desire. We realize the fundamental truth that our primary desire for God must be the pre-eminent goal we strive for. Everything else is secondary. Similarly, in the first line the bride of the Song of Songs seems to suggest that "he" is the one she is interested in. He, as a metaphor for God, is the one, *the only one*. His primacy is so self-evident that she assumes she need not state his identity. Shifting to addressing her lover more directly, she exclaims: "Your love is better than wine" (1:3). All else pales in comparison to her lover.

In saying that her lover is better than wine, the bride is also suggesting he is the true wine that brings delight. In the Scriptures wine is the primary symbol of the joy that accompanies God's presence. In Psalm 104 we hear of "wine to cheer men's hearts." The prophet Isaiah regales us with God's promise to prepare a banquet of fine wines when he restores his chosen people Israel (see Is 25:6). Wine will flow in abundance when the Messiah comes (see Am 9:13, Joel 3:18). Jesus manifests himself as the true Bridegroom who will provide wine for the wedding feast, as he does in Cana (see Jn 2). At the Last Supper, Jesus gives his blood as wine to drink, and he pours it out for us on the cross for our salvation. We "taste and see that the LORD is good" (Ps 34:8) and prefer him above all other goods. The blood of Christ, his love of the covenant poured into our hearts, is the foundation of our very existence, something we have to be sure of before we can grow in the spiritual life. God says, "I have loved you with an everlasting love; therefore, I have continued my faithfulness to you" (Jer 31:3). We need to take this message from our heads to our hearts and let it seep into our bones, into the center of our beings.

After comparing her bridegroom to wine, the bride uses a metaphor to further describe him: "delicate is the fragrance of your perfume." Scent is an evocative, recurring image in the Song of Songs, symbolizing the desirability and enticement of the bridegroom. Just as the bridegroom's desirability enters the bride's heart, so the perfumed oil seeps into and permeates her very being, leaving a lasting impression of the bridegroom's abiding presence. Saint Paul speaks of the "aroma of Christ" (2 Cor 2:15), which refers to the beauty and attractiveness of Christ's person and his virtues. Building upon Saint Paul's idea, Origen points out that none of the scents the bride had encountered to this moment possessed the sweetness of this new perfume: Christ. The queen of Sheba gave rare, exotic perfumes to Solomon, which surpassed whatever scents the bride might have desired. But they all faded away when compared to the perfume of Christ.[22] Again we realize, as Saint Ignatius tells us in the Principle and Foundation, that nothing compares with the goodness and attractiveness of Christ. We learn to see all goodness and beauty as caught up in him.

Moving from the bridegroom's association with perfume, the bride now uses the image of oil. In particular, she associates his name with oil, as "an oil poured out." Besides its myriad natural uses, oil connotes a religious significance in the anointing of priests, prophets, and kings. The word Messiah means "anointed one," bringing us back to the image of the Messiah as the one who has been blessed with oil. We cannot read this line without reference to Christ as the Messiah, of whom it is written in the psalms, "Therefore God, your God, has anointed you with the oil of gladness beyond your companions" (Ps 45:7). Like perfume, oil suffuses the skin and the very being of the one anointed. This makes it not only an apt association with the anointed Messiah but also an appropriate image of the Holy Spirit coming from Christ. William of St. Thierry, the Belgian theologian and mystic, reflects:

> And soon, in the odor of sweetness and the power of health, the oil of this same name of yours is poured out from you and poured into me, softening all my rigidity, smoothing all roughness, and healing my infirmities. . . . For

---

22. See Origen, *The Song of Songs: Commentary and Homilies*, Part One, The Commentary, Book One, 82–83.

the sound of your name—"Lord," "Jesus," or "Christ"—straightaway gives to my hearing joy and gladness, because as soon as your name sounds in the ears, the mystery of your name also shines forth in the heart and your love in the affection.[23]

The name of Jesus is his presence in our hearts as our sole treasure.

The outpouring of perfume and oil is Christ's gift of himself to us. In return we offer ourselves to him. This self-giving is dramatically symbolized by Mary of Bethany's anointing of Jesus with expensive nard and ointment, which fills the whole room with its fragrance (see Jn 12:3–4). She anoints the feet of Jesus and wipes his feet with her hair in a lavish outpouring of love and total dedication to Jesus. The cost of the nard is equivalent to 300 days' wages, as Judas protests. Jesus defends Mary's excessive gift, connecting it with his own death and burial as a symbol of his total outpouring of life unto death. Since Christ is our all, we want to imitate Mary in our total self-giving and dedication to Christ, above all other persons, places, or things. Receiving his beauty in love, in love we want to return to him all that we are and have. The Principle and Foundation exhorts us to "praise, reverence, and serve the Lord" with the totality of our being in response to God's complete gift of himself to us.

Jesus tells us to "love the Lord your God with all your heart, and with all your soul, and with all your mind" and to "love your neighbor as yourself" (Mt 22:37–39). The Principle and Foundation echoes Jesus' words, exhorting us to love God in and above all things, and to love nothing apart from him. Jesus presents a hierarchy of love, saying that our love of God is meant to surpass all other loves. The bride's maidens exclaim, "We will extol your love more than wine" and "rightly do they love you" (v. 4). A certain righteousness is involved in putting love of God above all creatures. Jesus' first commandment is "to love the Lord," and his second commandment is "to love neighbor as self." If we love God first and above all things, we are likely to experience other loves in their proper proportion. Our lives will be ordered. Those who put love of creatures first are likely to experience disorder in their lives and fail even in love of neighbor, self, and things. Jesus tells us to "strive first for the kingdom of God and his righteousness, and all these things will

---

23. William of St. Thierry, *Exposition on the Song of Songs*, trans. by Mother Columba Hart, O.S.B. (Shannon, Ireland: Irish University Press, 1970), 31.

be given to you as well" (Mt 6:33). If we have put the love of God and his kingdom first, the "other things" will also be ours, in due proportion. The American poet and Carmelite nun Jessica Powers puts it eloquently: "Here where we walk the fire-strafed road and thirst for the great face of love, the blinding vision, our wills grow steadfast in the heart's decision to keep the first commandment always first."[24] By seeking the face of Christ in prayer as the center in our lives, we will be strengthened in loving God first, in and above all things, and our love will be ordered.

When we seek first the kingdom of God and his righteousness, Jesus tells us, we receive the other things we need. God is the highest goal—our heart's desire—to be sought in himself, who brings along with himself all other benefits. In African rural villages, a child is often asked to gather into shelter a mother hen and her clutch of chicks. The child usually begins with the chicks. But as they run away, the child falls many times before catching even one. Worse, the mother hen comes after the child with her beak and claws in order to defend her chicks. After so many falls with little results, the child often gives up. Then the child's mother comes to the rescue. First she gets a large basket, lures the mother hen into it, and covers her. The mother hen then clucks for her chicks, which gather around and rush into the basket. Just as the mother hen brings all the chicks along with her, if we put God at the center of our lives, all other blessings will follow.

All Things Lead to God

Saint Ignatius continues with his next insight in his Principle and Foundation: "The other things on the face of the earth are created for man to help him in attaining the end for which he is created. Hence, man is to make use of them in as far as they help him in the attainment of his end, and he must rid himself of them in as far as they prove a hindrance to him." God created everything good, and we are to regard all creatures as good, keeping in mind that they are meant to lead us to God. We should use things according to the purpose for which God created them and, more importantly, allow them to lead us to God. Every person, place, and thing should be seen

---

24. Jessica Powers, *The Selected Poetry of Jessica Powers*, ed. Siegfried and Morneau (Washington, D.C.: ICS Publications, 1999), 43.

in Christ and enjoyed in the context of God's plan of salvation. Anything that cannot be used in this way is to be relinquished, because it would lead us away from our fundamental goal of life in Christ Jesus. This principle could be applied to money, among other things. It is good to earn money to be able to purchase the things we need to live well. We are called to use money to help others, especially the poor, and to give some of it away. Jesus even says to use money to win friends (see Lk 16:9). Money is a good servant but a poor master. It should be used in order to lead us to God and godly values. Yet how many people grow attached to money, either excessively saving or spending it. Money becomes the goal of peoples' lives and work, and capital is valued even more than human beings. People become preoccupied with financial security and grow distraught when it is threatened. Even if our currency says "In God We Trust," the money itself feels more trustworthy. Jesus warns us, "You cannot serve God and wealth" (Lk 16:13). Only God can be our master and goal in life; money must serve our ultimate purpose.

Beyond the use of goods, this dictum of using creation insofar as it leads us to God has a more profound meaning: any situation can be an occasion of God's grace if we have the eyes to see and the ears to hear. Even trials and sufferings are meant to lead us to God, assuming that we perceive and use them properly. This truth is illustrated by the life of Archbishop Nguyen van Thuan, who spent thirteen years in Communist prisons in Vietnam, including nine years in solitary confinement. In his book, *The Road of Hope*, he reveals the secrets of his survival. During those days and months, his mind was plagued with many confused feelings, sadness, fear, and tension. Being separated from his flock nearly broke his heart. In this dark night of anguish, he slowly woke up and faced the reality that he was in prison. Van Thuan realized he had precisely the opportunity to serve God in his concrete situation in prison. He wondered how he could contact his people as their pastor in their time of greatest need. The Catholic bookstores had been confiscated, the schools closed, the religious dispersed to forced labor in the villages. One night a light came to the archbishop: "Francis, it is very simple. Do as Saint Paul did when he was in prison. Write letters to the different communities." Van Thuan obtained old calendars from a seven-year-old altar boy named Quang. Every day in October and November 1975, he wrote messages to his people from prison. Each morning Quang smuggled the messages out and brought them home so that his brothers and sisters could recopy them.[25] Van Thuan's words became a great source of consolation and hope, a means through which he strengthened his flock. Behind his dire situation the archbishop discerned the divine will. As the Principle and Foundation teaches us, we can use occasions of suffering to lead us to God.

This ability to use or relinquish things insofar as they lead us to God requires an attitude of indifference to all creation. Saint Ignatius continues in the Principle and Foundation to explain this attitude of indifference: "We should not prefer health to sickness, riches to poverty, honor to dishonor, a long life to a short life" (SpEx 23). When we speak of indifference, we are not talking about apathy, carelessness, or lack of desire toward God's creation. We have already established the importance of desires and deep concern for what matters to us and to God, and apathy would go against that. But we are still called to be detached even from the good desires God places in our hearts. Detachment may even presuppose that we have strong attachments to certain persons, places, things, and events. All these must still be surrendered in an act of trust to God, who places these desires in our hearts.

At first we may think it is easy to achieve the indifference recommended by Saint Ignatius in his Principle and Foundation. Nothing could be further from the truth. Saint Ignatius requires us to complete this exercise in order that we might realize just how difficult it is to abandon ourselves into God's hands, surrendering our strongest desires. The difficulty of surrender is illustrated by the clever way that African hunters trap monkeys. They cut a coconut in two and hollow out the insides. In one half of the shell they cut a hole just big enough for a monkey's hand to slide through. They insert a ripe, juicy orange and fasten the two halves of the coconut back together. Then they fasten the coconut to a tree with a rope, hide in the jungle, and wait. When an unsuspecting monkey comes along, it smells the delicious orange in the coconut. The monkey slips its hand through the hole and grabs the orange, but can't get it through the hole. Meanwhile, the hunters approach with their nets to capture the monkey. The monkey sees them approaching and could easily let go of the orange and flee, but it desperately desires the orange and frantically tries to take the it along. This hunting system works because the monkey doesn't realize it cannot have both the orange and its

---

25. See Francis Xavier Nguyen Van Thuan, *Testimony of Hope: The Spiritual Exercises of Pope John Paul II* (Boston: Pauline Books & Media, 2000), 52–57.

freedom. We are a lot like the monkey. We know what we want and grasp at it. Even when we know it endangers us, we continue to hold onto it, sometimes more intensely and anxiously. Though Jesus wants to free us from our excessive attachments, we do not want to let go. We need to pray for the grace of detachment.

In the Principle and Foundation, Saint Ignatius wants us to realize how difficult it is to relinquish our attachments and arrive at indifference and freedom in loving and serving God. He wants us to abandon ourselves into God's hands and rely on God's grace in order to achieve detachment. In the process we discover it is only through love of a greater good that we can relinquish a lesser good. When we direct our desires to God as our ultimate goal, we are freed from the grip of lesser desires at the natural level. We gain sufficient freedom to choose according to Christ and his value system out of love.

The bride prefers the bridegroom, symbolizing Christ, to all things, and has achieved the indifference needed to follow him in freedom. She is convinced that her lover is the only one who matters and so she is free to follow him as he calls. She cries out, "Draw me in your footsteps," indicating that she is ready and willing to come after him and awaits his initiative; she waits for him to move her. Notice that her request reflects the abandonment to God counseled by Saint Ignatius. Often, unlike the bride, we move ahead of God; we move toward him instead of waiting for him to move toward us. The bride shows great wisdom in waiting for him to act in drawing her. Saint Augustine affirms, "No one comes unless drawn, so will you not be drawn? Pray to be drawn."[26] We need this spirit of detachment and surrender in all things, especially in our prayer. Ignatian meditation[27] disposes us to be open to God as the primary initiator. While this method helps to dispose us to God's grace, the method itself does not bring about prayer. We might act, but prayer is always God's initiative. Saint Paul teaches that "we do not know how to pray as we ought," but that we need not worry because "that very Spirit intercedes with sighs too deep for words" (Rom 8:26). Jesus emphasizes this need to be led and also says, "No one can come to me unless drawn by the Father who sent me" (Jn 6:44). Following Saint Ignatius' dictum, even a prayer

---

26. Quoted in Pio Bruno Lanteri, *Spiritual Writings*, 110.

27. For a full treatment of Ignatian prayer, read Timothy Gallagher, *Ignatian Meditation and Contemplation* (New York: Crossroads, 2008).

method should be used only insofar as it leads us to God. We should cry out, "Draw me in your footsteps," just as the bride does, aware of her inner poverty and longing for union with her beloved.

Once the bridegroom has drawn the bride close to himself and she is aware of his call, she hastens to his side and says, "Let us run." Similarly, Saint Ignatius wants us to run in the Lord's ways—to come to him more effectively in our prayer and through our choices. The final sentence in the Principle and Foundation emphasizes this desire as it calls us to remain free to choose whatever is "more" for the glory of God. We often discover this "more" in what God is already doing in our lives, sometimes despite our preferences. At other times, however, we are called to amend our lives so as to answer God's call to seek his greater glory. We need to recognize his plan and attune our hearts to it. The Jesuit priest Walter Ciszek exemplifies this conformity to God's plan. Captured by the Russian army during World War II and convicted of being a "Vatican spy," he spent twenty-three agonizing years in Soviet prisons and Siberian labor camps. Father Ciszek struggled with the frustration of being unable to establish any Catholic connections or support. Then one day it dawned on him. He received "the grace not to judge our efforts by human standards, or by what we ourselves wanted or expected to happen, but rather, according to God's design. It was the grace to understand that our dilemma, our temptation, was of our own making and existed in our own minds; it did not and could not coincide with the real world ordained by God and governed ultimately by His will."[28] Ciszek learned to look at his daily life with the eyes of God and discover God's purpose in bringing him into contact with every person and situation. In accepting God's will in the present moment and responding in faith and love, Ciszek chose what was for God's greater glory, just as Saint Ignatius suggests and the bride exemplifies. By living the Principle and Foundation, we too can run in his ways.

Questions for Reflection and Discussion

1. How do you understand what it means to love God above all things? How does this translate into daily practice?

---

28. Walter J. Ciszek, S.J., with Fr. Daniel Flaherty, S.J., *He Leadeth Me* (San Francisco: Saint Ignatius Press, 1995), 37.

2. What things do you tend to put ahead of God? What obstacles prevent you from living according to the Principle and Foundation of Saint Ignatius?

3. Saint Paul wrote, "We know that all things work together for good for those who love God, who are called according to his purpose" (Rom 8:28). How have you sensed God's grace even in the seemingly negative things that have happened to you?

4. How do you experience Ignatian "indifference"? What things are you attached to? Do you feel sufficiently "detached" or free to choose according to Christ and his kingdom?

5. How do you find that fixing your heart on greater things helps to free yourself from the lesser things to which you are attached?

Prayer Exercises

1. Pray with Song of Songs 1:2–4, and ask for the grace to realize the goodness of God. Ask to be able to desire God alone and above all things.

2. Pray with Matthew 6:25–34, and consider the African story of the mother hen and her chicks. Ask for the grace to trust that in having Christ, you have all you need, and that all else necessary will be provided for you.

3. Meditate on Saint Ignatius' Principle and Foundation. Pray with Wisdom 9:1–6, and ask for the grace of wisdom to choose according to the values of Christ and his kingdom. How would you formulate your own personal Principle and Foundation?

4. Consider the story of Archbishop Van Thuan and pray with Romans 8:26–39. Ask for the grace to realize God's plan and care for you in all circumstances.

5. Pray with Philippians 3:7–16, and ask for the grace to count all as loss in comparison with the surpassing worth of knowing Christ Jesus.

6. Pray with Philippians 4:4–13, and ask for the grace to be content in any circumstance to which the Lord calls you.

7. Make a repetition on any of the above meditations, paying attention to moments of greater movement of feeling or thoughtful insight.

CHAPTER 4

Dark and Beautiful

[B] I am black and beautiful,
    O daughters of Jerusalem,
like the tents of Kedar,
    like the curtains of Solomon.
Do not gaze at me because I am dark,
    because the sun has gazed on me. . . .
[G] I compare you, my love,
    to a mare among Pharaoh's chariots.
Your cheeks are comely with ornaments,
    your neck with strings of jewels.
We will make you ornaments of gold,
    studded with silver. (Song 1:5–6; 9–11)

Here it will be to ask for a growing and intense sorrow and tears for my sins.
(SpEx 55).

I will conclude with a colloquy, extolling the mercy of God our Lord, pouring out my thoughts to Him, and giving thanks to Him that up to this very moment He has granted me life. I will resolve with His grace to amend for the future. (SpEx 61)

The bride begins this stanza of the Song of Songs with strongly contrasting, almost contradictory, images of darkness and light. She compares her look to that of the tents of Kedar in northern Arabia, known for their hideous appearance. She echoes the psalmist's lament: "Woe is me . . . that I must live among the tents of Kedar" (Ps 120:5). The Book of Lamentations has a similar reference to disfigurement in describing the princes of Israel who, once purer than snow, are now ill regarded: "Now their visage is blacker than soot; they are not recognized in the streets. Their skin has shriveled on their bones; it has become as dry as wood" (Lam 4:8). In the Psalms, Lamentations, and the Song of Songs, bewailing is a metaphor for the disfiguring effects of sin on both one's external appearance and inner being.

Despite the bride's sinful past, she can feel affirmed in her beauty, for she has repented of her sin. In comparing herself to the white curtains hanging in Solomon's temple in Jerusalem, she shows that despite her regrettable past sin, God has restored her to a new life of grace with him. Saint Ambrose sings here of the bride's pain and triumph as he describes the Church wearing a bright baptismal garment, having bathed in God's grace. Despite the frailty of her human condition and her sinfulness, she is nevertheless beautiful because of God's presence through her baptism.[29] The bride's testimony emphasizes the truth that although sin can injure us, it cannot destroy the image of God in us. We may be deeply wounded, but not wholly depraved. Instead, through repentance God restores us to his grace and beauty. We must cooperate with this restoration, but it is fundamentally his work. The grace that touches our hearts and calls us to repentance is unmerited. It proceeds solely from God's love and mercy. Like the bride, we may accept this inspiration of God and turn to him. Or we may reject God's gift and remain in sin.

We can easily deny our sin and the resulting guilt. Like our first parents, we may deflect our basic responsibility and say with Adam, "The woman made me do it," or with Eve, "The serpent made me do it." Here we hide the obscure side of our being, and by denying our guilt, we overemphasize our

---

29. See Saint Ambrose, *The Mysteries*, in *St. Ambrose: Theological and Dogmatic Works: The Fathers of the Church, A New Translation*, vol. 44, trans. Roy J. DeFerrari (Washington, D.C.: Consortium/Catholic University of America Press, Inc., 1963), 17–18.

own goodness. Even so, the shadow side exists, and we are much better off acknowledging it and the faults that make it up. Saint James advises, "Confess your sins to one another" (Jas 5:16). Still, in myriad ways we disavow our guilt, cover it up, and even project it onto others.

Despite the difficulty, the bride does not try to hide her sinful past. Now that she is redeemed, she is quite open about it before her lover and the other women. She admits, "My own vineyard I have not kept," evoking Israel in her history of infidelity to the Lord. Israel is the unfaithful bride who worshiped false idols and became like a prostitute. The Lord had to bring her back, cleanse her, and espouse her to himself anew in his great fidelity and steadfast love (see Hos 2:19).

Our focus on the bride's sin and repentance in the Song of Songs brings us to the Spiritual Exercises, where Saint Ignatius leads the retreatant to look at sin in both its objective and subjective forms (SpEx 91). We begin by pondering the history of sin in the cosmos and for the human race.

First the angels sinned, and then "through the devil's envy death entered the world" (Wis 2:24), death followed sin. We then consider the fall of Adam and Eve, which shows us that all sin is an act of disobedience. Their sin resulted in their loss of grace and friendship with God and unleashed the effects of sin upon generations to follow. After we spend time contemplating sin on a grand scale, we ponder sin on an individual scale. We look at the consequences for any person who falls into mortal sin and does not repent, these being hell and isolation from God and others.

As we pray with the broad sweep of sin in the cosmos, the world, and throughout human history, we may be deeply impressed—perhaps overwhelmed and disturbed—at the vast extent of sin and its impact on humanity (cf. Rom 1–3). We shouldn't stop at collective humanity, however; we must also realize that the fault lines of sin in the world extend into our own hearts. Sin in the world affects you and me personally as a corrupting influence. In this dire and seemingly hopeless situation, we might feel sadness, confusion, and pain. We might feel powerless to change much about our morally polluted world. These feelings only point us all the more emphatically toward our need for a Savior. As the Apostle Paul points out, "Where sin increased, grace abounded all the more" (Rom 5:20). As terrible as sin is, God has nevertheless taken pity on our world in sending the Redeemer.

Our Personal History of Sin

After observing sin in its objective form, we move on to consider it subjectively in our personal history of sin. The story of David and Nathan (2 Sam 12:1–13) can instruct us here.

David has designs on Bathsheba, the wife of Uriah. To eliminate his rival, David places Uriah on the front lines of battle, where he is killed. Knowing what David has done, the prophet Nathan tells David a parable and asks him to judge the case of two men, one rich and one poor. While the rich man had many flocks and herds, the poor man had only one little ewe lamb. He raised the lamb, which would eat his morsels, drink from his cup, and lie in his bosom. The lamb was like a daughter to the poor man. When the rich man received a guest, instead of taking one of his own herd to serve the guest, the rich man took the poor man's lamb and had it killed.

When David hears this story, he grows angry and tells Nathan that the rich man deserves to die for his evil deed. Nathan then shocks David by saying, "You are the man!" Despite having been filled with God's blessings, David took cruel advantage of the poorer man, killing him and taking Uriah's love, Bathsheba, as his own. David is stung to the heart by Nathan's accusation and confesses to him, "I have sinned against the Lord."

Through the parable Nathan intentionally moves from the objective to the subjective. He thus enables David to see his sin, acknowledge it, and repent. David then pens the *Miserere* (Psalm 51), expressing his heartfelt contrition and firm purpose of amendment of life.

After we, like David, have come to see the reality of our sinfulness, the Spiritual Exercises lead us to look back over our lives, period by period, in order to realize our great number and kinds of sins against the Commandments and to ponder their gravity. As a prelude to this meditation, Saint Ignatius calls us to consider ourselves as imprisoned and separated from all that is good, much like the prodigal son in his self-imposed exile. This exercise brings home the reality that sin leads us into exile from our true homeland in God. In the Song of Songs, the bride has been similarly exiled from Jerusalem, enslaved by the conquering nations. Her situation is like ours: just as her conquerors enslave her, so the world, the flesh, and the devil enslave us through our addiction to sin. We need to be liberated by God's grace. The Lord promises to break the snare of sin that entangles us. Thus we hope to experience what the psalmist declares: "We have escaped like a bird from the snare of the fowlers; the snare is broken, and we have escaped" (Ps 124:7)!

Before grace can free us, however, we must feel the full weight of our sins. Thus, Saint Ignatius asks us to request the grace of "shame and confusion" in response to our having sinned; the knowledge that we deserve condemnation for our sins (SpEx 48). In this exercise, we contrast our sinful selves with God's attributes and perfections (SpEx 59) in order to increase our awareness of our wretchedness. While some forms of shame are toxic, we can also experience a certain natural and healthy shame. Saint Paul confesses his shame and confusion over his own weakness, calling himself "carnal" and "sold under sin." He laments, "I do not understand my own actions. For I do not do what I want, but I do the very thing I hate" (Rom 7:14–15). Saint Augustine also keenly felt the distress of being unable to make his will follow his reason in doing the good. Similarly, the bride possesses a healthy sense of shame about her past life of sin, and like Saints Paul and Augustine, she admits it in all humility. In her shame, she asks that no one look at her skin, sunburned from her exile. She humbly admits, "My own vineyard I have not kept," fully acknowledging that she has been a sinner.

At this point in the Exercises, we may consider not only the history of our many sins, but also the pattern of sin that dominates our lives. The seven capital or "deadly" sins describe not only objectively sinful acts but the underlying attitudes of heart that are evil. Often we have one predominant fault that we struggle with the most, a sinful pattern that flows from one particular sin, such as pride, envy, or avarice. As we become more aware of these patterns, we ask the Lord to cast his light into the dark areas of our hearts and free us by his grace. We can also act against these sinful tendencies by making the particular examination of conscience (SpEx 24–31), daily working on our predominant fault in a specific way. The bride faces her own primary sin of sloth. Her remark, "My own vineyard I have not kept," indicates her lack of attentiveness and responsiveness to her bridegroom. The bride's fault is neglect of her inner life and practice of prayer. Saint Ignatius was no stranger to patterns of sin. His predominant fault was vainglory, shown by his life of self-interest and self-glorification before his conversion. To combat his sinful tendency, he not only regularly examined himself regarding his vice, but he also sought to acquaint himself with and practice the opposing virtues. His program worked, for he became known for doing all "for the greater glory of God," *Ad Maiorem Dei Gloriam*.[30]

Sin and Redemption

Saint Ignatius' last meditation on sin (SpEx 65–71) shows us where sin can lead—even to hell itself. There nothing but sheer misery is found. Sin alienates us from ourselves, from others, and from God. In order to drive home the evil effects of sin, Saint Ignatius asks us to consider the vast nature of hell—its length, height, breadth, and depth. Because hell can seem like an abstract concept, perhaps some images from the darker side of human life, of hell on earth, will be useful.

When I was newly ordained, one of my first assignments was to a maximum security prison surrounded by concrete walls twenty feet wide and barbed wire laced all along the top. The building itself had been condemned on three separate occasions and was terrifying to behold and enter. One day I was called to minister to a longtime inmate who was dying of a terrible disease. I quickly realized that all he truly needed was a listening ear. He explained his very unhappy childhood: how his parents had taught him to drink as a young teenager, how drinking had led to drugs, how drugs had led to stealing and all kinds of crimes. He expressed great sorrow at his choices and at how his life had turned out. I asked him if I could do anything for him, expecting the usual request of writing the parole board in his favor. To my surprise, he broke down, saying, "Father, save me from my sins. I lived my life in hell, and I'll die in hell here in this prison. I don't want to go there forever." Moved with the deepest pity for this man, I continued to listen to him and to encourage him. By the end of our conversation, he told me that he wanted to go to heaven. I am confident that when he died, Jesus said to him, as he said to the repentant thief, "This day you will be with me in paradise." There is such a thing as a hell on earth, and it is a foretaste of the eternal reality—just as heavenly experiences on earth can speak to us of the blessed hereafter.

---

30. A general examination of conscience (SpEx 32–43) can be profitable in helping us to see our own predominant faults by looking at patterns of sin throughout our lifetimes. This topic is treated more fully in chapter 15.

Even as we face the misery of our own sins and ask for "shame and confusion," Saint Ignatius draws our eyes to the Lord on the cross, so full of mercy. We can exclaim in wonder that we have been saved from condemnation.

The movie *Once Upon a Time in America* has a very poignant and moving scene involving David, an ex-con who returns home after ten years in prison. David had spent those ten years thinking about Debbie, the sister of his childhood friend, and wondering if she has married. On his return from prison, David, flat broke, feels like a social outcast, a total disgrace, a misfit with nothing to offer Debbie. David and Debbie happen to meet one night in her brother's restaurant. Now that she is grown up, Debbie is the most gorgeous woman that David has ever seen. Debbie's brother signals the orchestra to play their favorite song as David and Debbie meet. They start dancing and David, nervous because he feels so inferior, finally asks Debbie the burning question: did she ever think about him while he was in prison? Looking at him tenderly, Debbie tells David that she *always* thought of him while he was away.

As shameful as David felt before Debbie's radiance, he was even more overwhelmed by her constant thought of him. The scene reminds us of the father of the prodigal son, who, even after his son abandoned him, never stopped thinking of his son, looking for him even upon his return. As terrible as the son's sin was, treating his father as though he were dead in order to gain his inheritance, the father's steadfast love and tender mercy were amazing. As we ponder our own redemption from sin, we should focus on God's steadfast love for us and the great joy in heaven over one repentant sinner.

We ought to have the same perspective as the bride, who is clearly more focused on her own redemption, even in the face of her previous life of sin. Saint Gregory of Nyssa remarks about God's ability to transform our ugliness into lasting beauty as he did for the bride:

> Do not be surprised due to my sin and my works, I was loved (by my Bridegroom) because he made me beautiful through his love by exchanging his beauty for my deformity. . . . This is why the bride does not allow the souls she instructs to despair of becoming beautiful when they look at their past life; rather, they ought to look at her and learn from her example that the present can become a veil covering the past.[31]

---

31. Saint Gregory of Nyssa, *In Canticum Canticorum*, Homily 2, 789–792, in *The Cantata of Love*, Blaise Arminjon, S.J., trans. Nelly Marans (San Francisco: Saint Ignatius, 1988), 96.

We should never despair of the reality of sin in our lives, but only cast ourselves upon the loving mercy of the Bridegroom who continues to love and redeem us in his mercy. As Saint Gregory points out, the Lord not only redeems us but also exchanges his beauty for our ugliness, enabling the bride to experience and proclaim her own beauty.

Akin to the renewed bride is the woman who falls at the feet of Jesus and washes his feet with her hair. This scene wonderfully illustrates the power of God's mercy and of true repentance (see Lk 7:36–50). Whereas she previously felt shame, now in Jesus' presence the woman cannot even find the disgrace she once felt. In spite of the hateful gaze of the judgmental Pharisee who seeks to humiliate her into inaction, she causes a spectacle: weeping, falling to Jesus' feet, anointing his feet with her perfume and her tears. She does not hide the fact that she had previously been a harlot, but does not let her admission of guilt keep her from focusing solely on her redeemer. Formerly a sign of her harlotry, her hair let down is now a sign of love. Jesus affirms these gestures of hospitable love and gratitude and even contrasts them with Simon's lack of them. The woman's tears bathe Jesus' feet, which Simon had failed to wash. The oil she provides makes up for Simon's lack of anointing. Her kiss replaces Simon's nonexistent kiss of welcome. Jesus affirms her true repentance in contrast to Simon's self-righteousness. He acknowledges that the woman loves much because she has been forgiven much. The more the woman considers her sin, the more she is filled with gratitude toward Jesus for his mercy. Her sin has become the very occasion of his mercy and of her salvation. No wonder we can sing in the Easter *Exultet* that Adam's sin was not only required but even delightful because it gained for us so magnificent a Redeemer to totally abolish that sin.[32] Because of Christ's great mercy, our sin has become our happy fault, the occasion of our greater closeness and union with God. We should not become discouraged by our failings, for God can bring tremendous good out of them. As we recognize how far we are from perfection, we can grow in the virtue of humility and have greater compassion toward others in their sinfulness.

In the same way, knowing the good that can come from her fallen nature, the bride in the Song of Songs discovers that the very instruments of her slavery have become adornments of her beauty. With his first words, her

---

32. See *Roman Missal*, "The Exsultet" at the Easter Vigil.

lover compares her to a mare harnessed to Pharaoh's chariot, a comparison that might seem peculiar to us. In ancient Near East tradition, however, the bride is often compared to a noble mare, known for its style, grace, and charm, a mount of royalty. Egyptian horses represented that great nation's pride and strength. Still, God's mare, Israel, whom the bride represents, is more outstanding in grace and power than the Egyptian horse and even Egypt itself. Though enslaved by Egypt—bound in neckbands and chains —in the service of Pharaoh, Israel remained beautiful.[33] Those instruments of oppression have now, by God's grace, become ornaments of beauty that attract her Bridegroom, as God once spoke to Israel: "I adorned you with ornaments: I put bracelets on your arms, a chain on your neck. . . . You grew exceedingly beautiful, fit to be a queen" (Ezek 16:11, 13). Through Israel's repentance and her trials of suffering and exile, she has been perfected in endurance and adorned with virtue.

So too for us. In Christ the very things that symbolized our slavery to sin become, through his mercy and love, occasions of grace that adorn our persons. The place of my weakness and failing becomes the place where the Lord manifests his power, achieving great things in my life. Look at Saint Paul; once the greatest persecutor of Christians, he became the greatest promoter of the Christian faith in missionary lands. Saint Paul could boast of his weakness because God had become his strength.

An example from medieval British history also illustrates this point. At that time harsh sentences were the norm; for example, as a penalty for stealing, people's hands were often cut off or their body was branded. When a certain man was caught robbing sheep, the authorities branded on his forehead the letters S.T. for sheep thief. The man changed his ways and spent the rest of his life repenting of that disgraceful incident. As an elderly man, the letters S.T. were still noticeable on his forehead. But when children asked their parents what the letters meant, their parents replied, "He is a *saint*,"[34] highlighting the powerful work God had done in this man's soul.

At the moment we become aware that God has saved us from our sins, Saint Ignatius instructs us to look at Jesus on the cross and ask, "What have

---

33. See Arminjon, *The Cantata of Love*, 108.

34. See Mark Link, *Illustrated Sunday Homilies*, Series II, Advent 2B (Allen, TX: Tabor, 1990), 4.

I done for Christ? What am I doing for Christ? What ought I to do for Christ?" (SpEx 53). Forgiveness of sin releases new energy, new vitality, and new gratitude, which lead us to desire to serve God more ardently, to become a saint. In the Scriptures we find individuals similarly touched by God's mercy, who, like the bride, discover a newfound energy in the service of Christ. Even though Peter had denied Christ three times, Jesus mercifully gave him the opportunity to redeem himself in his threefold confession of love for Christ. Peter realized the gift of mercy he was given, which transformed him. It gave him the willingness to fulfill his role as leader of the Church. Jesus also forgave the sins of Zacchaeus, a notorious tax collector. When Jesus announces his intention of dining with him that evening, Zacchaeus shows his willingness to go far beyond what the Law requires regarding restitution for fraud. We have seen how Saint Paul's conversion led him to promote the Gospel with even more zeal than he had shown before as a persecutor of Christians. Like the woman at the feet of Jesus, those who have been forgiven much now want to love much. The bride is similarly aware that, despite her sinfulness, she is now espoused and made beautiful by her Bridegroom. Adorned with ornaments of virtue, she is ready to run with zeal in the ways of her Beloved.

Questions for Reflection and Discussion

1. How have you experienced repentance as being primarily an act of God's grace and initiative? How can you surrender to his grace more fully?

2. How do you experience the paradox of being deeply wounded by sin but at the same time made beautiful by the grace of God?

3. How are you affected by the presence of evil and sin in the cosmos and the world? What are the organized structures of sin that you face in the world? What troubles you most about our sinful world? How do you see God's redemption breaking into this world?

4. What capital sin are you most inclined toward? How do you experience God's grace in the midst of that weakness? How do you act against that tendency in prayer and life?

5. What does God's mercy mean to you? How have you experienced it? What is the sense of freedom you have felt in being liberated from sin?

6. In gratitude for the gift of salvation, how have you been motivated to serve Christ more fervently?

Prayer Exercises

1. Pray with Genesis 7:3–24 or Romans 5:12–21, and ask for the grace of shame and confusion about original sin and about its effects and pervasiveness in the world and in you.

2. Pray with Romans 7:14–25 or Luke 18:9–14, and ask for the grace of shame and confusion about your own sin.

3. Consider the story of the prisoner (p. 46). Pray with Matthew 25:31–46 or Luke 17:19–31, and ask for the grace to see that hell is the consequences of mortal sin. Ask for gratitude that you have been spared such punishment.

4. Reflect on the scene from *Once Upon a Time in America* (p. 47). Pray with Psalm 51, Luke 7:36–50, or Luke 15:1–32, and ask for the grace of gratitude to God for having shown you so much mercy.

5. Ponder Saint Gregory of Nyssa's quote (p. 47). Pray with Song of Songs 1:5–7, and ask for the grace of knowing the love of the Lord, your Bridegroom, for you as a sinner who has been redeemed.

6. Recall the story of the man branded with the letters S.T. (p. 49). Pray with Song of Songs 1:8–11, and consider how God has helped you to grow precisely in the places where you have been sinful. Reflect on Saint Ignatius' question, "What will I do for Christ?" What new energy do you experience in your desire to serve the Lord?

7. Make a repetition on any of the above meditations, paying more attention to moments of insight or greater spiritual feeling.

Chapter 5

Stronger in the Broken Places

[B] My mother's sons were angry with me;
    they made me keeper of the vineyards,
    but my own vineyard I have not kept! (Song 1:6)

[I will ask for] a deep knowledge of my sins . . . ; an understanding of the disorder of my actions that . . . I may amend my life and put it in order. (SpEx 63)

The great British violinist Peter Cropper was once invited to Finland to play at a special concert during the celebrated Music Festival in Kuhmo. Because of his exceptional musical prowess, the Royal Academy of Music in London offered Cropper their priceless 258-year-old Stradivarius for the occasion. Taking its name from the Italian violin maker, Antonio Stradivari, who brought the art of violin-making to perfection, this instrument is made of eighty pieces of specially selected pine, boxwood, and ebony. Then, by a unique process, the Stradivarius is covered with thirty types of soft-textured varnish. A Stradivarius produces wonderfully resonant notes, which intensify the farther they travel.

As Peter Cropper hurried on stage, filled with anticipation, the unthinkable happened. He tripped on a loose extension cord and landed on the Stradivarius, breaking it into several pieces. With amazing self-composure, Cropper played for the audience using a borrowed violin. Afterward, in a state of shock, he flew back to England. The members of the Royal Academy tried to comfort Peter, but he was devastated. Back in London, a master craftsman named Charles Beare offered to repair the Stradivarius. After two months of seemingly endless work, Beare had reassembled the Stradivarius, bringing it back to life. Elated, he showed the repaired violin to Cropper who stared at it, astonished, as the craftsman pointed out the areas of repair. The repair marks were so well hidden that even those expert eyes could not see them. As wildly successful as the viewing was, the crucial test was yet to come. How would the Stradivarius sound?

Cropper's heart pounded as he gingerly raised the Stradivarius to his chin. Saying a quick prayer, he began to play. As each soaring note reverberated through the shop, the mesmerized group of music experts became more and more entranced. How was it possible that the violin's tone seemed even more perfect than before? In the months that followed, Cropper took the violin on an international tour where, night after night, he drew beautiful notes from the once-ruined Stradivarius, and night after night he received standing ovations. His success was due to the hands of a master craftsman who brought his masterful touch to bear.[35]

God made each of us precious, like the Stradivarius violin, able to bring forth beauty for his sake. Yet we are born into a broken world where we experience tragedy and suffering. In our first experiences of the world, our families, we may experience dysfunction or even betrayal. A father becomes a workaholic and ignores his family, while a mother become domineering and smothers her children. Loved ones die in accidents or from illnesses. Misfortunes can leave us in a state of shock, like Peter Cropper with his broken violin. All of this can lead us to feel apprehensive, vulnerable, out of control, or even existentially threatened. We may develop false and constraining beliefs—I am insecure, I am incapable, I am bad—because we often blame ourselves for tragedies that are not our fault.

---

35. See Link, *Illustrated Sunday Homilies*, Series I, Ordinary Time 6B, 59.

Healing Our Wounds

Traumatic events may shatter our self-image, harm our relationships, and even undermine our trust in God. Naturally in questioning why our Lord would allow evil to happen, we might grow distant, unable to trust him. We might feel we don't deserve God's love or we can't live up to his expectations. We might feel as Jeremiah prophesied the Israelites would: "For thus says the LORD: Your hurt is incurable, your wound is grievous. There is no one to uphold your cause, no medicine for your wound, no healing for you.... Why do you cry out over your hurt? Your pain is incurable" (Jer 30:12–13, 15). Yet, despite these laments, God ultimately restores Israel and renews his covenant with his people, uttering this healing promise: "You shall be my people, and I will be your God" (Jer 30:22). As God was with the Israelites, God is with us in tragedy, abuse, and distress. He never abandons us, for we are his people and he is our God.

Forced into hard labor as keeper of the vineyards, the bride in the Song of Songs carries deep wounds; she exclaims, "My mother's sons were angry with me" (1:6). She still bears the painful marks left by blows from her relatives. In her cruel exile from her family, the bride represents Israel in exile. Her words hearken back to the psalmist's lament, "I have become a stranger to my kindred, an alien to my mother's children" (Ps 69:8). Some background is helpful: Abraham, Israel's ancestor, came from Chaldea, meaning that Chaldean blood flows in Israel's veins, that Israel and Chaldea are brothers, or, more precisely, cousins (see Gen 11:28, 31; 15:7; 22:20–23; Deut 26:5). Sadly, though, the Chaldeans are the enemies who despoil Jerusalem, causing Israel's exile.[36] In their anger, they have imposed hard labor and servitude upon her, making her work in their vineyards. Israel has experienced the pain and agony of being exiled from her homeland, symbolic of the true self. She is deeply wounded and needs healing just as the bride does.

Our sins often originate in experiences that left us emotionally wounded, yet we may be unaware of the connection between our past wounds and our present sins. In the Spiritual Exercises, Saint Ignatius wants us to "consider

---

36. See footnote in *The Jerusalem Bible*, gen. ed. Alexander Jones (Garden City: Doubleday, 1966), 993.

the causes, origins, and roots of our faults."[37] He emphasizes this probably because he himself was a great sinner before his conversion. In a family that was long on piety but low on morals, Saint Ignatius grew up to be a womanizer, a gambling addict, and a violent man. These sins very likely emerged from a core wound in Saint Ignatius' life, the terrible tragedy of his mother's death shortly after she gave birth to him. Deprived of his mother, he was raised by an aunt who gave him very little attention. Saint Ignatius developed what psychologists today call a deprivation neurosis.[38] His sinful actions later in life betrayed a desperate need for attention and affection. At the time, Saint Ignatius was hardly aware of what he had been missing in motherly love and care. Once the Lord's love enlightened him, however, he faced his wounds and sinfulness and entrusted his life to God.

It takes courage to face our wounds and so become aware of our own need for healing. Often we pretend everything is fine, preferring the comfort of the status quo over the discomfort of delving into a painful past. Some even use religion to mask their pain and wounds instead of healing them. For instance, an abused wife might spiritualize the problem by thinking that God wants her to suffer. Someone else may take on the role of helping others without recognizing one's own need for help, because it's more comfortable that way. As a helper, one can remain in control and feel good about oneself, while ignoring one's pain. Henri Nouwen reminds us that we are "wounded healers" who need to heal our own wounds before we can help to heal others. Otherwise we might transmit to others what we don't transform, becoming "wounded wounders." Nouwen explains that we have to do the hard work of naming our experiences and opening ourselves up to the Lord's healing touch. When we go to the doctor and are asked how we are, we point out what hurts us. When we imagine Jesus, our divine Physician, asking us the same question, we can admit our pain. Our wounded emotions lead us to the sore spot that needs God's healing.

As the bride in the Song of Songs considers her own hurts, she names the cause of her wounds: her brothers' anger and their having forced her to

---

37. *On Giving the Exercises: The Early Manuscript Directories and the Official Directory of 1599,* trans. Martin Palmer (St. Louis: The Institute of Jesuit Sources, 1996), 309. Cf. SpEx 63, "a deep knowledge of my sins."

38. See William Meissner, *The Psychology of a Saint* (New Haven, Yale University Press, 1992), 362–363.

slave in their vineyard. Anger pointed at us can injure us terribly. While anger can be beneficial when it shows us something wrong to be addressed, it can also be very destructive. Parents and authority figures use anger to control people and situations, often with violent or dramatic outbursts to keep people in fear. Sometimes anger is expressed in ways that harm and berate others.

Besides anger, three other emotions point to our wounds and to our need for healing: fear, shame, and grief. Though fear can be a healthy emotion, it often becomes distorted and exaggerated when we are faced with an evil to be overcome or a good to be enjoyed. Fear can constrain our freedom, even to the point of paralyzing us. Jesus tells the disciples, "Do not fear. Only believe" (Lk 8:50). Here he intends to begin to lead us to the place where he can calm our fears.

Shame can also be toxic for someone who's been deeply wounded. If guilt tells us we *made* a mistake, shame tells us that we *are* a mistake. We might have received the messages of shame from parents, friends, and loved ones, in response to our physical or personality traits or our behaviors. Sometimes feelings of shame come from within, rooted in our failure at tasks or inability to relate well to others. We need to renounce this toxic thinking and realize the affirmation of God's unconditional love, precisely in those places of hurt and shame.

The emotion of grief often goes unrecognized. Our culture teaches us we should be happy all the time and that something is dreadfully wrong if we're not. But sadness and mourning often make up a greater part of life than happiness. Moved by the deepest emotions, Jesus wept at the death of his friend Lazarus, showing us the importance of grief. A parent's divorce or absence could cause a great sense of loss. The loss of loved ones, friends, co-workers, or others due to death or changes in life situations might also affect us deeply.

Matthew Linn, a Jesuit priest involved in healing ministry, describes a traumatic loss in his childhood. When he was seven years old and his brother Dennis was five, their younger brother John caught bronchitis and died suddenly in an ambulance. Matthew was angry at the ambulance driver, the doctors, and even God. Eventually, whether consciously or unconsciously, he blamed himself for his brother's death, thinking he must have done something wrong for God to take John. Matthew's guilt caused him to dislike himself, make mistakes in school, and feel inferior to his classmates. In high school he compensated for that by achieving honors.

Eventually, Matthew joined the Society of Jesus and, as a novice, made the thirty-day Spiritual Exercises of Saint Ignatius. During the retreat, he made an examination of conscience for his whole life. He wrote a twelve-page list of things he didn't like about himself and gave it to his novice master. Instead of focusing on the list, the novice master asked Matthew what he was most sorry for in his life. Breaking into tears, Matthew immediately replied that he felt responsible for the death of his younger brother. The novice master put his arm around Matthew and told him God loved him and that he did too. Matthew felt the hardened shell around his wound fall away, as he now found himself loved in the place he felt most unlovable.

Reflecting on his life and ministry, Matthew has discovered how that tragic event led to tremendous blessings in his life. When John died, Matthew drew close to his brother Dennis in what would become a lifelong companionship. And after losing John, his family adopted Mary Ellen, who became Matthew's sister.

Matthew considers the sacrament of Penance to be one of the highlights of his ministry; through it he helps others be relieved, just as he was, of their crushing burden of guilt. He helps people to experience forgiveness and to forgive others and themselves. Having dealt with the loss of his brother, he feels fulfilled working with parents who have lost a child. He listens with compassion and understanding as he journeys with them through grief. Finally, Matthew has excelled at the ministry of healing, offering retreats that have helped countless people who have suffered deep wounds to encounter Christ. He has witnessed amazing transformations of broken people who are now bearers of Christ's most precious gifts.[39] Matthew is a living example of Christ's power to bring great blessings out of the wounds we suffer.

Approaching Jesus

After becoming aware of my pain and need for healing, I must approach Jesus. He is waiting to heal me, but he respects my freedom and requires something from me: my assent. He asks, "Do you want to be healed?" Jesus doesn't presume upon our freedom; he wants to enlist our willing

---

39. See Matthew Linn, Dennis Linn, and Sheila Fabricant, *Prayer Course for Healing Life's Hurts* (Ramsey, N.J.: Paulist Press, 1983), 23–24.

cooperation in the process. Many barriers to this willing cooperation exist in people. Some have built their lives around their wounds and so are comfortable with the pain; it is all they've ever known. Others might be reluctant to do the hard work of forgiving others that is a necessary part of the healing process.

Jesus cannot heal us without our collaboration. A man who once made the Spiritual Exercises was aware that a certain darkness ruling his life was rooted in a painful wound. At first he did not want to ask for healing, and admitted his reluctance to the Lord. The man later reconsidered, but when he asked Jesus to heal him, he heard the Lord tell him that he couldn't heal him. Understandably upset by this reply, the man persevered in prayer until he heard Jesus qualify his previous response by saying that he could heal the man if they worked together.[40] The man realized he couldn't expect Jesus to wave a magic wand and heal him; he had to cooperate with Jesus in the healing process. Similarly, we ought to examine our own hearts to find out if we're ready to ask God for healing. If we find ourselves ready, we should be willing to cooperate in the process through self-examination and opening our hearts to God. In the Spiritual Exercises, Saint Ignatius wants us to come to a deeper knowledge of our sins (SpEx 63) by considering the causes, origins, and roots of our faults. We are to take an active role in our salvation, by accepting the grace that God is offering.

A significant part of the healing process in the Spiritual Exercises will be to tell your story to another person, to Jesus first of all. As you pray and enter into conversation with God, your undisclosed feelings will begin to surface. You can become more honest with God about these feelings, perhaps more honest than you've ever been. As you express your feelings to the Lord, you will hopefully sense God deeply and compassionately listening. He is profoundly concerned about you and wants to show his love for you now, exactly as you are. In Scripture Jesus' healing actions are always accompanied by a personal encounter. Before he heals the man at the pool at Bethsaida, Jesus allows him to explain his debilitating, long-term illness and how he could never get to the pool in time for healing. Another time Jesus notices that a woman suffering for twelve years from an internal hemorrhage tries to gain healing by merely touching the tassel of his cloak. Jesus does not allow her to

---

40. See William Barry, *Allowing the Creator to Deal with the Creature*, 29–30.

escape without an encounter. Realizing that she's touched him, he wheels around and addresses her. Jesus doesn't heal impersonally but wants us to tell him our names and who we really are—to speak to him about our past, our brokenness, our feelings of rejection, our family dysfunction, our difficulty forming relationships. Truly, he is compassionate and merciful to us. After we've told our story to Jesus, we can relay it to a spiritual director or trusted friend, and this telling, too, will facilitate healing. Saint Ignatius emphasizes the role of the director in giving the Spiritual Exercises (SpEx 1–20). The director is one who looks upon the other and listens with loving compassion as part of the healing process. This spiritual friend or guide creates a safe haven where one can share the most secret and intimate parts of one's soul.

Healing of Memories

We can tell our stories only by using our memory. Unsurprisingly, Saint Ignatius emphasizes using memory during the first week of the Exercises (SpEx 50, 56) to help us ponder our histories of sin and gain deeper insight into their root causes. Our memories are filled with painful episodes and hurts that need the healing touch of God's grace. One method of prayer in particular can lead to the healing of memories.[41] With this method we utilize our powers of memory to travel back to the hurtful event. While this method is difficult and potentially painful, and is sure to dredge up agonizing feelings, the freedom to be gained should encourage us.

We first use our memories to imagine the scene in all its details—the time of day, the persons involved, the situation. Next we can begin to grapple with the emotional content of the memory: the shame, anger, or fear that might drench this painful episode. Immersing ourselves in those emotions brings us back to the time and place where the traumatic incident occurred. Of course, we need not enter into this memory alone; we can and should invite Jesus to accompany us. After inviting Jesus into that painful place, watch what he does and says when he enters the scene. Only by walking back through the memory—with Jesus at our side—can we, in many cases, find healing from the wound connected to the memory. As we walk with Jesus or simply sit with

---

41. See Tad Dunne, *Spiritual Exercises for Today* (New York: HarperCollins, 1991), 128–137.

him in this painful space, we have the unique opportunity to ask him any burning questions we might have regarding our painful memory, such as: why wasn't he there to help us when we were suffering? Why did he allow the painful or traumatic situation? Why weren't things different? Jesus will answer us, and here we can listen carefully to his answer, attempting to take in what he might be saying. As we listen, we should be attuned to how Jesus is using our imaginations to speak to us in thoughts, words, or images. God works through our imaginations to speak to our hearts and touch us deeply.

Once when I did this exercise, I relived the pain of being harassed by fellow students in a new school just after my family had moved. I felt the presence of Jesus, compassionate and understanding, strengthening me until I felt ready to confront one of my taunters. And confront him I did: "Why are you doing this? Do you want to hurt me?" In an instant, I understood that he hadn't had such malicious intent. I could see that being oversensitive to criticism at the time, I had emotionally overreacted to the taunters. In Jesus' presence, these insights helped me to recognize my new willingness and ability to forgive my persecutors. Even greater healing came when I could finally see the silver lining: how these experiences taught me something about myself and ultimately had made me a better person, better able to endure persecution, less likely to want to hurt others through my words and actions, and more apt to love and affirm other people. Through my deepest wounds, God gave me the grace to love others with greater sensitivity, just as he can and will for anyone who has the courage to ask. The grace to love is a sign that healing has taken place.

Forgiveness

As we seek Jesus in the healing of painful memories, a need to forgive someone will often arise. We have built-up resentments and grudges toward others, some of them longstanding. Ideally, we would be able to face the people who have hurt us and hear them acknowledge the hurt they caused. Then we would offer our forgiveness, achieving reconciliation. We think of the father embracing the prodigal son in forgiveness and experiencing their new closeness as they stand face to face. Often we may not be able to meet the offender in person. Perhaps he or she now lives far away. Perhaps the person would not acknowledge the harm he or she has done and would only rub salt in our wound. Perhaps the pain is still too great, making us reluctant to meet this person and relive the pain. In such cases, we still need to let go of resentment and work toward forgiveness. As long as we hold on to resentment, it will bind us and harden our hearts even more. Resentment then turns into a formidable obstacle to love of God and neighbor. Jesus exhorts us, "Love your enemies and pray for those who persecute you" (Mt 5:44), but we can do neither if we are bound by hardness of heart. Jesus emphasizes that we won't receive forgiveness from our Father if we don't forgive those who have hurt us. If we fail to forgive, we will not only be trapped in resentment but we will also find ourselves utterly alienated from our Heavenly Father.

Still, sometimes the resentment and anger we feel from past hurts are so great that forgiveness seems impossible. In her book *The Hiding Place*, Corrie ten Boom describes her experience in Amsterdam during World War II, when she and her family hid and sheltered Jews from the Nazis. After an informant reported them to the authorities, family members, including Corrie and her sister, Betsie, were deported to the notorious Ravensbruck concentration camp. Betsie died in the camp, but Corrie survived. After the war, she went on a lecture tour throughout Europe, speaking about forgiveness and reconciliation. After one talk, a man approached Corrie and thanked her. To Corrie's horror, this man was one of the SS who had stood guard at the shower room door in the processing center at Ravensbruck. Glowing and bowing, he approached her as the church emptied out. He started telling her how grateful he was for her message that Christ has washed away our sins. The man thrust out his hand to shake Corrie's. She froze, unable to react, as the horror of the camp and the death of her sister leapt into her memory. Understandably filled with resentment and revulsion, Corrie tried to tell herself that Jesus had died for this man. Still, she could not forgive him. Flooded with emotion, she was unable to meet his outstretched hand. Praying silently, Corrie told Jesus that she could not forgive the man and begged Jesus to give her his own forgiveness. Immediately she felt something like a current flow through her shoulder, down her arm, and toward the guard. She took his hand in true forgiveness. At the same time, Corrie felt an overwhelming love for this man springing from her heart.[42] Then a powerful realization came upon Corrie: she needed Jesus' power in order to forgive and heal.

---

42. See Corrie ten Boom and John and Elizabeth Sherill, *The Hiding Place* (Washington Depot: Chosen, 1971), 214–215.

Like Corrie ten Boom, we ultimately depend on God for our own healing and the healing of others. "By his wounds you have been healed," Peter reminds us (1 Pet 2:24). Jesus' wounds—the stripes of the Roman scourging and the five wounds of the cross—though perhaps gruesome to behold, are the means through which we are healed. Saint Ignatius instructs us to look at Jesus upon the cross, to contemplate his wounds, and also to wonder at how he has stooped to become man and to pass from eternal life to mortality so that he might die for our sins (SpEx 53). As we contemplate, Saint Ignatius exhorts us to "a cry of wonder accompanied by surging emotion . . . extolling the mercy of God our Lord, pouring out my thoughts to Him, and giving thanks to Him that up to this very moment He has granted me life" (SpEx 60–61). Pondering Jesus' wounds, amazement fills us over the wondrous love he has for us that moved him to undergo such torment.

When Jesus rose again, he manifested those wounds, made glorious in his body, for us to see and touch, trophies of his sacrifice and vindication. A healing light and power shine forth from those wounds. We can bring our wounds to Christ, unite them to his sufferings, and experience in our bodies and hearts his resurrection and new life. Like the Stradivarius violin, though broken and repaired, we can produce even more beautiful music than if we had never been broken. Like the bride of the Song of Songs, we are disfigured by suffering at the hands of others and by our own sinful choices that emerge from wounded places. We too are made beautiful in the healing process by grace, more beautiful than we could have been if we had remained unscathed. Uniting our wounds to Christ, we are transformed by his healing love that enables us to radiate his light and life.

Questions for Reflection and Discussion

1. What are some tragedies you have experienced? What wounds do you still carry? How has your faith helped you in the face of tragedy?

2. Which emotions are most prevalent for you—anger, fear, shame, or grief? What has been your experience dealing with these emotions? What happens when you take these to the Lord for healing?

3. Whom do you need to forgive? What has been your experience of forgiving others?

4. Has suffering made you a better person or a bitter person? How?

Prayer Exercises

1. Consider the story of Peter Cropper and the Stradivarius (p. 53). Pray with Mark 5:22–43, and ask for the courage to face your wounds, hopeful that Jesus will heal you.

2. Use the exercise for healing of memories (p. 60). Continue to pray with Mark 5:22–43, and consider that Jesus wants to know you personally and hear your story.

3. Pray with Matthew 14:22–33, and ask for the grace to face your deepest fears and be given the courage to respond to the Lord and his call.

4. Pray with John 2:12–16, and ask for the grace to understand your anger and surrender it to the Lord, to be given his meekness of heart.

5. Pray with Luke 15:11–32, and ask for the grace to know the Lord's deep acceptance of you and for the ability to say "yes" to your own existence.

6. Pray with John 11:17, 32–35, and ask for the grace to understand your losses and to grieve them, then to move forward with hope.

7. Reflect on the story of Corrie ten Boom (p. 62) and her journey of forgiveness. Pray with Matthew 18:21–35 and consider whom you need to forgive in your life. Ask the Lord for the grace to be able to forgive.

CHAPTER 6

Strength in Our Weakness

[B] Tell me, you whom my soul loves,
    where you pasture your flock,
    where you make it lie down at noon;
for why should I be like one who is veiled
    beside the flocks of your companions?
[G] If you do not know,
    O fairest among women,
follow the tracks of the flock,
    and pasture your kids
    beside the shepherds' tents. (Song 1:7–8)

I will resolve with His grace to amend for the future. (SpEx 61)

It is characteristic of the evil spirit to harass with anxiety, to afflict with sadness, to raise obstacles backed by fallacious reasonings that disturb the soul. Thus he seeks to prevent the soul from advancing. It is characteristic of the good spirit, however, to give courage and strength, consolations, tears, inspirations, and peace. This He does by making all easy, by removing all obstacles so that the soul goes forward in doing good. (SpEx 315)

Having admitted both the sins that disfigured her appearance and her own failure to maintain her vineyard, the bride experiences a change of heart. Now she desperately desires to walk alongside her beloved in grace and virtue. But she still struggles with feelings of weakness and helplessness, not knowing how or where to pasture her flock. In answer to her fear, either the bridegroom or the chorus of women (the text is unclear) counsels the bride to follow her beloved as her shepherd, walking in the tracks left by his flock. This path is that of the Bridegroom and Shepherd of Israel, who foreshadows Jesus as the Way, the Truth, and the Life. Jesus desires to find the bride and set her feet on the right path, for he is the Good Shepherd who seeks the lost sheep in order to save it. Formerly, the bride traveled a faulty path, one leading to exile, but now she is being called to conversion, to walk on the right path.

The bridegroom is calling the bride to journey by a reverse path to the promised land of beatitude. As Israel was being led into exile, Jeremiah prophesied, "Set up road markers for yourself, make yourself signposts; consider well the highway, the road by which you went. Return, O virgin Israel, return to these your cities" (31:21). Like Israel, the bride will now return to her bridegroom by the very path on which she was led astray. In order to return, we as the bride must follow the teachings of our Shepherd, Jesus, and the way of virtue marked out by the holy shepherds of the Church. The bride's conversion begins in prayer, a sure way into the teachings of Jesus and into his way of virtue. Here, she will discover that this journey toward conversion of heart depends on the Shepherd's guidance.

The first week of the Spiritual Exercises deals with our conversion of heart. Saint Ignatius gives us an opportunity to experience true repentance as sinners who need God's mercy. In the process, we learn to depend on the Lord so that we might come to him and follow his ways just as the bride did.

The word "conversion" comes from the Greek word *metanoia*, which means to turn completely in mind and heart. In conversion from sin, we turn our hearts and minds radically away from sin and toward God who frees and fulfills us. As conversion leads us to greater dependence on God, we become more childlike—one of the major criteria Jesus sets for coming to him. When Jesus found the apostles arguing about who was greatest in the kingdom, he held up a child in their midst and said, "Truly I tell you, unless you *change* and become like children, you will never enter the kingdom of heaven" (Mt 18:3, emphasis added). In order to fully appreciate Jesus' point, we need to realize just how shocking a statement this was in his day. In that culture, one's status was based heavily on honor. As you might expect, people were eager to keep their honor pristine, while thinking nothing of exposing the scandal in others' households. Families, then, would employ their children for the purpose of spying on their enemies and discovering their dirty secrets. Children were therefore often viewed with suspicion or even despised. No wonder the disciples tried to keep the children from Jesus, who again amazed them by saying, "Let the little children come to me."

Jesus did not look at children with suspicion but with true admiration for their unique qualities: innocence, a sense of wonder and awe, honesty and frank speech, an ability to ask for what they need, and a trust that their needs would be met. Jesus wants us to become like little children in asking for whatever we need and trusting our Father to grant it. Our pride rebels against this childlike attitude, for we want to be in control and to assert our own will, even in our faith journey. When we feel ourselves wavering, we think greater willpower will strengthen our pursuit, ultimately creating a stronger faith. Increasing our willpower, however, often backfires, because it can inflate our pride. Rather than depending more on God, we depend more on ourselves. We associate willpower with being a strong and responsible adult, but willpower will get us nowhere in terms of becoming more childlike, a necessary aspect of faith. Only dependence on God and confidence in his care will get us there. The bride shows us the way to this right path. She realizes her own childlike weakness, her inability to find her way. Instead of relying on herself, she calls out to her bridegroom. She asks him where he shepherds his flock, relying on and clinging to him so that he can lead her in his ways.

The motif of the youngest child as the triumphant one is prevalent in the Bible. In stories that have to do with two siblings, the younger sibling almost always emerges as the protagonist. Such stories include Cain and Abel, Ishmael and Isaac, Esau and Jacob, Leah and Rachel, Joseph and his brothers, and David and his brother.

Psychologists have attempted to explain this pattern but without much success. Some approach it, however, from a different angle. They recognize that the human personality is driven by two energies, that of the older sibling and that of the younger—the senior and the child. The senior is wiser and more prudent, yet more calculating and cautious. The child, on the other hand, is more venturesome, more willing to take chances and so more prone to making mistakes. While the senior is security driven, the child is more prepared to let go. The senior is more geared toward competition, power, and success, whereas the child is more attuned to cooperation and celebration. The senior is more responsible; the child is more lighthearted. It often happens that parents transfer their senior energies to their older children and their child energies to their younger children.

In order to be fully human and alive, these two energies must find a balance in our personality. Our tendency is to give more weight to the senior, without allowing the child within us to emerge. [43] No wonder Jesus took a child into his arms and told his disciples, "Truly I tell you, unless you change and become like children, you will never enter the kingdom of heaven" (Mt 18:3). In order to follow Jesus in his ways, we must trust more in the Father's providence. We will then be more willing to let go and take chances, more given to celebrate and cooperate with others.[44]

Saint Paul had to become like a child in his conversion and then learn to travel a new path. We usually think of his conversion as turning from his vengeful, violent life. As a zealous Jew, Saint Paul persecuted Christians. On the road to Damascus, intending to round up Christians there, he was thrown to the ground. He encountered Jesus and afterward had a complete change of heart. He became a great champion of the Christian faith and its most ardent promoter. But Saint Paul had an even greater conversion in becoming like a child before the Father. As a prominent Jew who studied under the great rabbi Gamaliel, Saint Paul had a great deal of prestige. Explaining his impeccable credentials, he said, "If anyone else has reason to be confident in the flesh, I have more: circumcised on the eighth day, a member of the people of Israel, of the tribe of Benjamin, a Hebrew born of Hebrews; as to the law, a Pharisee; as to zeal, a persecutor of the church; as to righteousness under the law, blameless" (Phil 3:4–6). Despite his qualifications, Saint Paul was self-righteous, self-justifying, and self-reliant. Through his experience on the way to Damascus he was changed, broken of his self-centered thinking and self-reliant behavior. He later explained that whatever gain he had in credentials

---

43. See Father Munachi E. Ezeogu, C.S.S.P., *Sunday Homilies for Year B*, 25th Sunday in Ordinary Time, https://justmehomely.wordpress.com/2012/09/21/twenty-fifth-sunday-in-ordinary-time-year-b-4/.

44. In the early days of his conversion, Saint Ignatius thought that because he was slow and dull of mind, God treated him as a schoolteacher does a child.

and self-righteousness, he considered as loss in light of the surpassing worth of knowing Jesus Christ as his Lord (see Phil 3:7–9).

Saint Paul had a complete change of heart. Like the bride, he surrendered to the Lord and was led in a completely new direction. He truly became like a child, submitting himself to Ananias and taking instruction in the Christian faith. After spending years in the desert immersing himself in Christian truth and practice, he emerged ready to become a great apostle. He took risks in bringing the faith to foreign lands and leading new Gentile Christians into the Church of God. Through it all, Saint Paul depended totally on Christ. He became as a little child before God, ready to let God work in him. Knowing that he could do nothing by himself, Saint Paul learned simply to receive from his heavenly Father.

Saint Paul learned to be content with his weakness and his total dependence on God. In one of his most famous passages, he refers to a thorn in his flesh. When he begged the Lord to remove it, he was told: "My grace is sufficient for you, for power is made perfect in weakness." Saint Paul adds, "I will boast all the more gladly of my weaknesses, so that the power of Christ may dwell in me" (2 Cor 12:9). Whatever the thorn was—whether a physical ailment, a moral struggle, or a spiritual wound, such as a stigmata—it kept Saint Paul aware of his weakness and his dependence on God. In short, it kept him from becoming proud.

Weakness can do the same for us, causing us to turn humbly to God. In the midst of suffering we can seek his strength to realize that his grace is enough for us. It is good to be aware of our weakness so that we might better discover God's grace. Henri Nouwen remarks that Christ, the source of our peace, is found in our weakest places, where we feel most broken and most helpless. In brokenness we usually find that our successful methods for control are utterly useless. So what can we do? We can stop relying on our old self-sufficient ways. Nouwen suggests that we refrain from doing and thinking very much and instead latch on to our Lord in surrender, relying on him to help us. Like Saint Paul, Nouwen concludes that in our weakest place, at our weakest moment, we find Christ and his other-worldly peace.[45]

45. See Henri J. M. Nouwen, *Adam's Story: The Peace That Is Not of This World*, © The Henri Nouwen Legacy Trust. First published in *Weavings*, March-April 1988.

Years ago when I was rector of the Oblates' seminary in Boston, I was faced with my own weakness. As leader of the twenty-five seminarians, I absolutely felt I was in over my head. In this state I entered my yearly retreat, this time with a wise nun as my director. I was concerned with my own image, how the men perceived me, and who I was for them. After our first session together, this perceptive sister told me that I was too focused outside of myself and that I needed to seek Christ within. Later that morning, as I walked in the neighborhood by the retreat house, I came upon a landscaper working with music blaring out of his van. As I tried to hurry past to avoid being disturbed in my quiet wandering, I picked up the tune of a great old song, "Just the Way You Are." As much as I liked the song, I tried to ignore it. But those words had taken hold, striking me like lightning. I realized that God loves me—not some imaginary version of myself—just the way I am. Instead of trying to change who I am, I should let God love me and transform me. I was trying to live up to some false image of myself, which helped me feel justified yet insecure. The Lord enabled me to surrender to his grace in that moment and for the rest of the retreat. God loves me deeply, especially in my weakness. Just as the bride is content to be who she is—disfigured due to sin though beautiful in God's grace—I saw that I could rest in the reality of who I am: scarred but lovely. I didn't have to try to be someone I wasn't.

We often create obstacles to God's work in us because we can't accept ourselves as weak, even though God accepts us that way. We believe that we should measure up to an impossible ideal much different from our reality. When we see others' gifts, we quickly compare ours to theirs and find ours lacking. We desire gifts we don't have, and we wish we didn't have our faults and defects. This "compare and despair" attitude prevents us from accepting God's unconditional love. If we don't think much of ourselves, it's likely we will believe God doesn't think much of us either. But God loves us exactly as we are, and he wants us to love and accept the gift that we are. This means not only accepting our defects and misery, but also loving them as God loves them in us. Saint Francis de Sales advocates acceptance and love of our own misery by calling this love authentic humility. He says that acceptance of our misery should even be a source of delight for us. Because it is true humility, it can only lead us to understand God's utter majesty, since true humility shows that God is glorious in perfection and we are not. Besides, through honestly seeing our faults and defects, we are more inclined to hold up our neighbor as better than us (see Phil 2:3). Saint Francis goes so far as to say that if given the choice between having and not having defects, we should choose to have them, for nothing fosters perfect humility like imperfections.[46]

This doesn't mean being complacent about our weaknesses; rather we must be open to a change of heart. God's work will change our hearts, but we must cooperate by discovering what will motivate us to change. Knowing that God loves me in my weakness is the best motivation for becoming a better servant of God who relies on his grace. The bride accepts that she is scarred and has not kept her own vineyard; she is lost and doesn't know the way—yet she wants to run in the Lord's ways, convinced that she is loved. This is precisely the attitude Saint Ignatius wants to foster in us through the Spiritual Exercises: the discovery that we are loved sinners. The more I look at my sin and weakness, the more I can and should be convinced of the Lord's grace, mercy, and unconditional acceptance of me.

We all have faults and defects, but if we allow God to love us in our misery, he can make us into something beautiful for himself, just as he did the "dark but beautiful" bride. Saint Paul reminds us that "in everything God works for good with those who love him, who are called according to his purpose" (Rom 8:28). The Lord can take our sinful past and our present flaws and use them to fashion great goodness and beauty in our lives and in the lives of others.

During the Renaissance in Florence, the great artist Donatello was offered a tremendously large block of marble for his next sculpture. The marble, however, had an obvious flaw, so Donatello rejected it. Michelangelo was offered the same block of marble. He saw the same defect, but he also saw the marble's potential, and he accepted it. From that flawed block of marble that Donatello rejected, Michelangelo sculpted one of his greatest masterpieces: David. This story is a metaphor for the process through which God, seeing our potential, accepts us in our defective state. Indeed, God brings forth stunning beauty from those very defects, flaws, and wounds. The more we get to know ourselves with our strengths and defects, the more we need to accept ourselves just as we are, just as God accepts us. Only then will we be able to give ourselves to others and to God in love. Through our deep awareness of

---

46. See Saint Francis de Sales, *Introduction to the Devout Life*, http://www.ccel.org/ccel/desales/devout_life.vi.viii.html, Pt. 3, Ch. 6.

sin and grace in the first week of the Exercises, Saint Ignatius brings us to self-knowledge, self-acceptance, and self-gift. As we become aware that our being is a gift from God, we become much more willing to offer ourselves as a gift to God and others in service.

Discouragement and Desolation

In considering our sin, wounds, and brokenness, and those of others, we might be tempted to discouragement. Often the enemy spirit will attack us at our weakest point to make us feel worthless and abandoned by God, without hope of making progress in our relationship with him. We recall that Saint Paul, besides his thorn in the flesh, had "a messenger of Satan to torment" him (2 Cor 12:7). Saint Paul himself reminds us that we are involved in a spiritual battle: "For our struggle is not against enemies of blood and flesh, but against the rulers, against the authorities, against the cosmic powers of this present darkness, against the spiritual forces of evil in the heavenly places" (Eph 6:12). We need to arm ourselves for spiritual battle so that we might resist the devil and cause him to flee (see Jas 4:7).

This state of discouragement common to the spiritual life is called "spiritual desolation." Saint Ignatius gives us his first set of Rules for Discernment of Spirits (SpEx 313–327) especially for dealing with spiritual desolation. He describes how the enemy of our human nature attempts to severely discourage us from our goal of drawing closer to our Lord, especially as we consider our weakness and sinfulness. The enemy's attack can lead to what Saint Ignatius explains as "darkness of soul, turmoil of spirit, inclination to what is low and earthly, restlessness rising from many disturbances and temptations which lead to want of faith, want of hope, want of love. The soul is wholly slothful, tepid, sad, and separated, as it were, from its Creator and Lord" (SpEx 317).

When we are in a state of desolation, the enemy does not play fair. He will attack us where we are most vulnerable—our weak places—in order to discourage us from seeking God and serving him. The enemy will suggest thoughts to us that lead to lack of faith, hope, and love, seeking to further drive a wedge between us and God. Spiritual desolation is not to be confused with being in a bad mood or feeling depressed, but is a painful spiritual experience that can negatively impact our relationship with God.

When in a state of spiritual desolation, the all-important first step is to recognize and to name it. We are often unaware that this negative force is moving us, and simply recognizing it greatly reduces its hold upon us. Instead of being driven by the enemy spirit, we are now in the driver's seat, so to speak. Once we have named our state as desolation, we should realize that this experience is an aberration in our ordinary life of grace—our life of faith, hope, and love. God only allows it in order that we might profit through a testing of our fidelity when he withdraws consolation. He knows that we grow in virtue through spiritual battle with a challenging sparring partner. Saint Ignatius understands the enemy of human nature to be the traditional sources of temptation—the world, the flesh, and the devil, often working together. Just as God allowed Job to struggle through an affliction by Satan in order to draw Job into greater dependence on himself, so God allows us to be afflicted. And just as God restored Job's blessings, so he will soon restore us to a state of spiritual consolation.

In the Spiritual Exercises, Saint Ignatius suggests a few helpful methods for resisting spiritual desolation and the counsel of the enemy spirit. First, we should examine ourselves to see if we have sinned in some way that contributed to the downward spiral. We should also make acts of faith in God's presence, despite feelings to the contrary. Because desolation is a temporary state, we should resist the temptation to think we will always feel sad or separated from God. Instead, we should cling to hope that God's consolation will soon return. Once we have the right attitude about our desolation, we should make a few resolutions. First, we should not make any significant decisions while in desolation, since it is the enemy who is leading us with his counsel, which can never be good. We are to hold, rather, to the resolutions about prayer and Christian living that we made prior to finding ourselves in desolation. Second, we can elect to engage in some penance in order to realize our greater dependence on God and to obtain the grace of consolation.

The experience of working through and resisting spiritual desolation is valuable because we learn that we cannot of ourselves produce or earn spiritual consolation. We are given a greater sense of our own poverty of spirit and humility. If we find ourselves in spiritual desolation, we shouldn't hide it but manifest it to a spiritual friend or guide. Otherwise we will feel more alone and isolated in this painful experience. The spiritual director can help us to accurately name this negative movement of spirit and give us advice on how to resist it. Through all our efforts to resist spiritual desolation, God summons us to courage and spiritual battle, and we grow in virtue and faithfulness to him.[47]

We can find encouragement in the bride's example. Despite her darkness and her past life of sin and waywardness, she does not fall prey to spiritual desolation or self-loathing. In her childlike dependence and confidence, she stays aware of the bridegroom's unconditional love and her beauty in his eyes. She arrives at authentic self-acceptance and is prepared to give herself as a gift to her Bridegroom. We must do the same.

Questions for Reflection and Discussion

1. In what areas of your life do you need to experience conversion of heart as total dependence on God?

2. In what areas do you tend not to accept yourself? Are there any qualities you wish you had but cannot attain? Do you waste time and energy lamenting what you are not? How do you plan to deal with this?

3. How does your image of the ideal Christian help or hinder you from being more at peace as a Christian? Where do you need to adjust your conception of the ideal and improve on your real person?

4. Do you tend to measure yourself by your strengths? Are you aware of your weak areas? How have you discovered the power of Christ at work in your weaknesses in order to strengthen yourself and others?

5. What patterns of thinking make you spiritually desolate or discouraged? What are the sources of this discouragement? How can you better resist and reject it?

6. What temptations come to you when you are discouraged? Consider how you will try to overcome these temptations in the future.

7. How is the Lord affirming and encouraging you in your life and vocation right now with consolations of the Spirit? Can you name any real consolations in the recent past or in the present as you pray with Scripture passages?

---

47. For more information on dealing with spiritual desolation, consult Timothy Gallagher, *Discernment of Spirits* (New York: Crossroad, 2005).

Prayer Exercises

1. Pray with Song of Songs 1:7–8, and reflect on the bride's feeling of being lost. Ask for the grace to know and follow Christ the Good Shepherd as the Way, the Truth, and the Life.

2. Consider the qualities of the childlike (p. 67). Pray with Mark 10:13–16, and ask for the grace to become childlike in faith, hope, and love.

3. Ponder the story of how Michelangelo saw the potential in the marble (p. 71). Pray with Second Corinthians 12:7–9, and ask for the grace to realize that God loves you as you are in your weakness, just as he makes you strong in his grace.

4. Pray with Hebrews 5:1–10, and ask for the grace to realize how Christ shared in our human weakness and has compassion on us.

5. Pray with Psalm 139:1–18, 23–24, and ask for the grace of authentic self-acceptance and self-love in Christ.

6. Read Saint Ignatius' description of spiritual desolation (p. 72). Pray with Luke 24:13–35, and ask for the grace to understand spiritual desolation and to resist and overcome it in faith, hope, and love.

7. Make a repetition on any of the above exercises, focusing on those places of greater consolation or desolation.

Chapter 7

Love's Compassionate Gaze

[B] While the king was on his couch,
  my nard gave forth its fragrance.
My beloved is to me a bag of myrrh
  that lies between my breasts.
My beloved is to me a cluster of henna blossoms
  in the vineyards of En-gedi.
[G] Ah, you are beautiful, my love;
  ah, you are beautiful;
  your eyes are doves. (Song 1:12–15)

I will stand for the space of an *Our Father,* a step or two before the place where I am to meditate or contemplate, and with my mind raised on high, consider that God our Lord beholds me. (SpEx 75)

The bridegroom and bride now behold one another in a gaze of mutual admiration, each captivated by the other's beauty. The bridegroom is the first to exclaim, "Behold, you are beautiful, my love." This mutual beholding of lover and beloved is an apt description of contemplative prayer, which is a gaze upon Jesus. In the second week of the Spiritual Exercises, we learn the art of contemplation, beholding Christ, the Bridegroom, in the mysteries of his incarnation and public life. In contemplating Christ, Saint Ignatius has us seek an intimate awareness of the Lord's inner heart in order that we may love him more and follow him more closely (see SpEx 104). As we behold Christ in his inner beauty and outward virtue, we are drawn to greater love and imitation of him.

The contemplative moment in the Song of Songs begins with God the Bridegroom looking at us, his bride, and calling us beautiful. In the same way, Saint Ignatius begins his teaching on the method of contemplative prayer by having us be aware that God is looking at us. Attentive to his presence, we pray an Our Father to prepare ourselves for contemplation. As we consider ourselves in the Lord's gaze, we put aside any preconceptions we have of ourselves and imagine how God beholds us.

We begin contemplation by being aware of God's presence and knowing that he is already looking at us as we behold him. Likewise, when the bridegroom in the Song of Songs proclaims the bride's beauty, she becomes aware that he is already looking at her. God is always beholding us with love and sees our goodness and beauty. He sees not only our exterior person, but our interior being at its deepest center. The psalmist declares, "O Lord, you have searched me and known me . . . you discern my thoughts." His experience of God's interior gaze is one of marvel, "Such knowledge is too wonderful for me" (Ps 139:1, 2, 6). As we experience the Lord's gaze, we become aware that we are deeply known and loved, that God beholds us as his beautiful creation.

In the Gospels, Jesus gazes on those whom he loves. John frequently refers to himself as "the one whom Jesus loved." Here John intends not only to describe how he is keenly aware of Jesus' gaze of love; he also enables the reader to take his place and experience being the self-same "one whom Jesus loves." As Jesus gazes upon those he loves, he is caught up in awe and love for God's handiwork. He first recognizes their dignity and potential, and only then does he speak and act on their behalf.

Jesus spent the whole night in prayer before he chose his twelve apostles, contemplating each one of them in love in the Father's presence. Matthew tells us how on that day, as he walked by the Sea of Galilee, he saw Peter and Andrew casting a net into the sea. After truly seeing these men, Jesus spoke to them, saying, "Follow me, and I will make you fish for people" (Mt 4:19).

Jesus' gaze and words elicited a response from Peter and Andrew, who left their nets and followed him. As Saint Ignatius suggests, they came to more intimate knowledge of Jesus in order to love him and follow him more closely (see SpEx 104).

In the Song of Songs, the bridegroom (whom the bride now calls "king") contemplates his bride, speaks, and elicits a response. When the king sees and calls his bride beautiful, his words actually make her beautiful. It is important that we consider beauty as God sees it in us and not as the world sees beauty, which is often only at the superficial, physical level. We can first consider beauty as it exists and is manifested in God. Supremely beautiful in his unity, truth, and goodness, God is the source of all created beauty. God's beauty is especially manifest in Jesus Christ, who is God become man, visible and intelligible to us. Jesus is the beauty of God reflected perfectly in his humanity.

Through her creation and participation in the mystery of God as Bridegroom, the bride shares in his same beauty. We too share in the Lord's beauty by his work of creating, redeeming, and sanctifying us. We are made beautiful in his image, redeemed in Christ and given a share in his divine life. Gregory of Nyssa imagines the Lord saying: "You came to me . . . therefore you became beautiful, changed as it were into my own image through some kind of mirror. . . . You became beautiful as soon as you approached my light, drawing to yourself, through this very approach, a share in my beauty."[48] Our beauty, then, results from God having loved us first, giving us life and making us radiant with his beauty. Since the sight of beauty gives pleasure, God delights in the beauty he has brought about in us. More than being merely physical, beauty especially includes knowledge and appreciation. On perceiving beauty, one sees beyond appearances to the interior essence of a person or thing, and this interior beauty delights the mind. Having created, redeemed, and sanctified us, God truly knows our goodness through and through, and he finds us beautiful.

In her beauty, the bride in the Song of Songs becomes the sole interest of her bridegroom. Consumed with her beauty, he gives her his undivided attention. God looks at us with the same focused desire, as though we were

---

48. Gregory of Nyssa, *Homilies on the Song of Songs*, trans. Richard A. Norris, eds. Brian E. Daley, S.J. and John T. Fitzgerald (Atlanta: Society of Biblical Literature, 2012), Homily 4, 93.

the only person who matters. When the Lord gazed at the first man and woman he created, he found that they were very good, just as he finds us to be good.

While God loves one and all universally, God also loves each of us in particular according to our unique personality, needs, and temperament. How can God love us in this way? If a mother of several children is asked which one she loves the best, she will likely answer, "each of them," because each child is unique and lovable in her sight. This is even truer with God.

Our Lady of Guadalupe's appearance to Juan Diego gives us a clue into this particular yet universal gaze. When scientists studied the image our Lady had miraculously emblazoned on Juan Diego's tilma, they discovered Juan on the lens of our Lady's eye, displayed upside down as images appear in the lens of a human eye. Her eye was filled with the person upon whom she looked with such great love. So too God looks at us with a particular love that is specific to our unique souls.

Jesus beheld each of us personally as he lived his mysteries on this earth. The work of Natalia Tsarkova demonstrates this truth. She is a Russian painter who lives in Rome and has been commissioned as an artist for the Vatican. In one of her more remarkable compositions, a huge, magnificent canvas of the Last Supper, she illustrates the crucial truth that God always pays attention to each one of us. In the midst of the dramatic scene, Jesus' face is turned away from the swirling activity and is looking right at the viewer of the painting. Jesus' attention toward us challenges us, inviting our response. Nothing is more important to Jesus than you personally—your salvation, your well-being, your love for him in return for his love for you.

Jesus looked with love upon everyone he encountered. No one knew this better than Saint Peter. He experienced this loving look in his call to follow Jesus at the seashore in Galilee. Jesus looked at Peter with love again when he called him by a new name and gave him the role of leading the Church. Peter felt that gaze once more when he betrayed Jesus, who looked at him mercifully as he went to his trial and passion.

Saint John Paul II describes the effect of the loving gaze of Jesus upon us, especially in our most dire moments:

> Man needs this loving look. He needs to know that he is loved, loved eternally and chosen from eternity. At the same time this eternal love of divine election accompanies man during life as Christ's look of love. And perhaps most powerfully at the moment of trial, humiliation, persecution, defeat,

when our humanity is as it were blotted out in the eyes of other people, insulted and trampled upon. At that moment the awareness that the Father has always loved us in his Son, that Christ always loves each of us, becomes a solid support for our whole human existence. When everything would make us doubt ourselves and the meaning of our life, then this look of Christ, the awareness of the love that in him has shown itself more powerful than any evil and destruction, this awareness enables us to survive.[49]

John Paul's words give us insight into Peter's experience at his lowest moment of self-loathing and despair. When his beloved Lord was arrested and falsely tried, Peter denied even knowing him. Yet at this very moment, Peter felt Jesus' merciful love. Peter wept bitterly for his sins and never lost sight of Jesus' love for him. At the shore of the Sea of Galilee after the Resurrection, Peter would again experience that loving gaze of Jesus. This time Jesus offered Peter an opportunity to atone for his threefold denial by allowing him to affirm his love for Jesus three times. Peter would never forget the Lord's look of love, which enabled him to respond to Jesus' call to love him more and follow him more closely.

Jesus' Look of Love

The experience of a prayerful man named Richard can illustrate this loving look of the Lord in Ignatian contemplative prayer. As he began to pray one day, Richard took the place of Zacchaeus in the tree at Jericho (see Lk 19:1–10), waiting for Jesus to pass by.

Jesus did stop and look at Richard, who realized that Jesus was giving him all his attention, that Richard was his only concern. Jesus gazed upon him with his entire consideration, affection, and yearning to be with him. Richard responded with a loving look toward Jesus. The experience made Richard feel tranquil and cheerful, relieving his stress and self-questioning. He realized that Jesus desired to be with Zacchaeus, despite his wretchedness. The presence of Jesus who loved and affirmed Zacchaeus was enough to profoundly change him. Richard experienced Jesus being with him like that. He heard Jesus call him down from the tree and ask to visit him at home.

---

49. John Paul II, *Letter to the Youth of the World (Dilectic Amici)* (Boston: Pauline Books & Media, 1985), no. 7.

Finally they remained together in Richard's house without saying much, simply enjoying each other's company.[50]

Richard was first of all aware that Christ had noticed him, that he mattered to the Lord. Jesus stopped what he was doing in order to focus upon Richard, even calling him down to tell him he must dine with him that very evening. Jesus' sole focus became Richard. In contemplation, Richard had the sense that he was the only one who mattered in the Lord's eyes. This is precisely the experience of the bride in the Song of Songs, now aware that she has become the sole object of her bridegroom's attention.

As Jesus looks at us with love, he is filled with compassion. Sharing our human weaknesses and strengths, he knows us through and through, just as he knew his disciples. Jesus understands us, having taken upon himself our weak human flesh. He desires that we know his love and care. Jesus knew the potential and strength of his apostles as well as their weakness, and he had compassion on them. In his compassion Jesus identified with them, as he does with us. Derived from the Latin words *cum* and *passio*, compassion means "to suffer with." When Jesus encountered the widow of Nain (see Lk 7:11–17) at the funeral procession for her son, he was moved with the deepest compassion, at the innermost core of his being. Jesus felt the deep sorrow of a grieving mother's heart and performed a dramatic miracle to restore her son to life.

Jesus knows our hearts and wants to share in our lives. His compassion doesn't mean just giving us something, nor does it end by merely identifying with us, simply feeling our pain. His compassion leads him to address our situation, by either improving it or giving us the strength to bear it. His compassion leads him to speak and to act out of love for us. Jesus doesn't leave us in our ugliness and misery; he makes us beautiful by his loving gaze and words.

This compassionate gaze of Jesus is shown in the life of Kim, an autistic child who requires constant care and attention provided by her mother Jill. Jill's husband, Paul, writes:

> When I was studying how Jesus looked at people, I watched how Jill looked at Kim. Kim is bright and cheerful, but struggles getting around physically and has trouble communicating because she cannot speak. She has few

---

50. See Timothy Gallagher, *Meditation and Contemplation* (New York: Crossroad, 2008), 38–39.

friends. The local public school she attends has several floors with steep steps and difficult railings. Jill memorized Kim's schedule and prayed for her during the hard parts of the day. When Kim was navigating the steps, Jill was praying for her safety. When Kim was alone in the lunchroom eating, Jill was thinking about her. With her heart full of Kim, she quietly concentrated on her and prayed for her all day. She was "looking" at and looking out for Kim even when she wasn't with her. When Jill looked, she slowed down and concentrated. She moved outside of her world and into Kim's. When I think of how Jesus loved people, the word "cherish" comes to mind. When we cherish someone, we combine looking and compassion—we notice and care for that person.[51]

We can imagine that Jesus has a heart full of love for each one of us. He cherishes us as he beholds us with compassion. Jesus is constantly beholding us in our moments of prayer, when we are focused on him, and during our activities, when we are more likely to forget his presence. We could imitate him in looking at our neighbor with the same gaze of compassionate love, as Jill did for Kim.

The bridegroom's look of love engenders the bride's capacity to gaze with love. After calling her beautiful, he goes on to say, "your eyes are doves" (v. 15). The bridegroom is enraptured by the bride's dove-like eyes—lively, charming, and pure. The dove was the symbol of love and peace for Israel. In the New Testament, the dove symbolizes the Holy Spirit, as when the Holy Spirit descended upon Jesus in the form of a dove. In comparing the bride's eyes to doves, the bridegroom is suggesting their likeness to the Holy Spirit. By the grace of the Holy Spirit, the bride now has the capacity to see with spiritual eyes. Origen comments that with these new, spiritual eyes, the bride can see and understand in a spiritual way. Gazing more deeply into the beauty of her Spouse, with her eyes like doves, she can perceive the beauty of the Word of God. For no one can understand the wonderful splendor of the Word without dove's eyes, that is, a truly spiritual understanding.[52]

The bride is given the supernatural gifts of faith, hope, and love, and her vision is greatly expanded beyond the world's horizon, drawing her eyes beyond the natural. The graced look of the Lord bestows the beauty of

51. Paul Miller, *Love Walked Among Us: Learning to Love Like Jesus* (Colorado Springs: Navpress, 2001), 34.
52. See Origen, *The Song of Songs*, Part One, Book Three, 171–173.

supernatural vision to her eyes in the person of the Holy Spirit. In order to contemplate Christ and truly see his interior beauty, we need the gift of the Holy Spirit who opens our spiritual vision to divine realities.

Like the bride, we are given spiritual vision and enabled to behold others with the same compassion that Jesus has for us. Think of it in this way: God enables us to see others, to love others, with *his* very vision. The thought should thrill our hearts. The words of the lovely hymn "Be Thou My Vision" might inspire in us a desire to see—informed by the Holy Spirit—with the eyes of Christ.

As we begin to contemplate Jesus in the mysteries of his life, death, and resurrection with spiritual, "dove" eyes, we realize that he is contemplating us and has been doing so since time's beginning. He became man for us in order to share our very existence, an existence that was present to him in his incarnation. From all eternity, we have existed in the mind of God, even in our potential for being. God thought of us even before he created us. Jesus the Lord, in the unity of his divinity and humanity, retains this omniscience in his incarnation. In his divinity, and in some way in his humanity, he was able to see us throughout his life on earth, and certainly he now does so in his place in heaven. The Indian Jesuit Herve Coathalem asserts the reality that as Jesus lived the mysteries of his life, he was aware of our existence in his inner gaze—just as he gazes upon us now in his risen existence. As Christ lived the events of his earthly life, he interceded with the Father on our behalf, as he continues to do now. This is the basis of our ability to be present to the Lord in contemplative prayer.[53]

We can say we are truly present to our Lord as he lives his mysteries for us. As we begin to contemplate Christ in his mysteries, we know that he is already contemplating us. Our awareness of the Lord's loving look transforms us. As we are filled with wonder and awe at who God is, our amazement grows when we realize that this tremendous Lord is gazing at us with high regard, calling us beautiful. Our amazement moves us to awe, to extolling the marvels of his love. We can respond with the bride, "Behold, you are beautiful, my beloved."

---

53. See Herve Coathalem, *Ignatian Insights: A Guide to the Complete Spiritual Exercises* (Taichung, Taiwan: Kuangchi Press, 1961), 144.

Questions for Reflection and Discussion

1. Can you imagine God looking at you in prayer? What is your image of God? How does he look upon you?

2. Can you hear the Lord call you beautiful? How do you feel about this? Do you experience any resistance to this message?

3. When have you sensed Jesus or Mary having compassion for you? What did it mean to you to be totally understood? When do you experience the most compassion for others?

4. How do you experience seeing spiritually, according to the Lord's vision and the gift of faith? Can you contemplate reality more in this way?

5. As you pray with the mysteries of the life of Christ, do you ever perceive Christ beholding you in a more profound way than you behold him?

6. How has the Spirit enabled you to behold others in a more contemplative way, to see their dignity and treat them with love?

Prayer Exercises

1. Pray with Song of Songs 1:12–14, and ask for the grace to know the embrace of God and to hold his presence close within your heart.

2. Pray with Song of Songs 1:15, and ask for the grace to appreciate the beauty of Christ and to see with his vision and the spiritual eyes of faith.

3. Consider how God looks on you and calls you beautiful. Pray with Psalm 139, asking for the grace to be aware of God looking at you with love.

4. Pray with Luke 18:18–23, and ask for the grace to experience the loving gaze of Jesus.

5. Pray with Song of Songs 1:15. Ask for the grace to hear the Lord calling you "beautiful" and "my love."

6. Reflect on the story of Paul Miller's wife and child (p. 82). Pray with Mark 10:46–52, and ask for an awareness of Jesus' compassion for you.

7. Make a repetition on any of the above contemplations, paying attention to the places of greater spiritual consolation or desolation.

CHAPTER 8

Transforming Beauty

[B] Ah, you are beautiful, my beloved,
    truly lovely. Our couch is green;
    the beams of our house are cedar,
    our rafters are pine.
I am a rose of Sharon,
    a lily of the valleys.
[G] As a lily among brambles,
    so is my love among maidens.
[B] As an apple tree among the trees of the wood,
    so is my beloved among young men.
With great delight I sat in his shadow,
    and his fruit was sweet to my taste.
He brought me to the banqueting house,
    and his intention toward me was love.
Sustain me with raisins,
    refresh me with apples;
    for I am faint with love.
O that his left hand were under my head,
    and that his right hand embraced me!
I adjure you, O daughters of Jerusalem,
    by the gazelles or the wild does:
do not stir up or awaken love
    until it is ready! (Song 1:16—2:7)

This is to ask for what I desire. Here it will be to ask for an intimate knowledge of our Lord, who has become man for me, that I may love Him more and follow Him more closely. (SpEx 104)

As God has already fixed his gaze on us, we also fix our gaze on him as we begin to pray. The bride replies to the loving look of her bridegroom, admiring his beauty in turn, "Behold, you are beautiful, my beloved, truly lovely." In the Spiritual Exercises, Saint Ignatius suggests that we begin contemplative prayer with a desire to behold the beauty of Jesus: "Ask for an intimate knowledge of our Lord, who has become man for me, that I may love Him more and follow Him more closely" (SpEx 104). As the bride beholds the bridegroom, we behold the beauty of Jesus in the mysteries of his life, death, and resurrection. In doing this we will come to know and love him and be drawn to follow him more closely. The French bishop and theologian Jacques Bossuet explains that this attracting beauty of Christ begins as an admiration that mixes pleasure and pain, an ache to draw nearer. The admiration grows into an eventual total occupation with the beauty of Jesus Christ.[54] As we admire the Lord in contemplative prayer, we are wounded with love by his beauty and drawn to greater union with him.

Saint Ignatius' Exercises suggest that Jesus' beauty is most easily contemplated in the mysteries of his life. We can do this by using two different approaches. In the first approach, the retreatant might simply rest in the Lord with a profound awareness of his presence. This approach is akin to the bride's simply "being" in the company of her lover, exclaiming that "with great delight I sat in his shadow." Her words remind us of the "shadow" of the Lord, which accompanied Israel through the desert as a cloud by day. This "shekinah," or overshadowing presence of the Lord, is the same divine presence that overshadowed Jesus in his transfiguration on Mount Tabor, in which the

---

54. See Jacques-Bégnine Bossuet, "Lettres des Piété," *Lettres* (Paris: Plon, 1927), 250. In Arminjon, *The Cantata of Love*, 133.

Father's voice was heard saying "this is my Son, my Chosen; listen to him!" (Lk 9:35). Similarly, at the Annunciation the angel announced that the Holy Spirit would overshadow Mary in order to bring about the incarnation of the Savior, Jesus Christ, in her virginal womb. Just as the bride is content to linger in the shadow of the bridegroom's presence as a model of simplified contemplative prayer, so can we.

In Saint Ignatius' second approach to contemplation, we use the imagination to focus on the mysteries of the Lord. This act is akin to the lovers' use of many images to describe one another's beauty in the Song of Songs. Saint Ignatius allows a great deal of latitude in using the imagination, allowing us to envision persons, places, and events in our own way. In the prelude to this form of prayer, he describes a way of composing oneself by visualizing the place, instructing the listener to see "in imagination the way from Nazareth to Bethlehem." Saint Ignatius goes on to suggest that the listener "consider its length, its breadth; whether level, or through valleys and over hills. Observe also the place or cave where Christ is born; whether big or little; whether high or low; and how it is arranged" (SpEx 112). While respecting the essential objective content of the mysteries of the life of Christ, Saint Ignatius allows ample room for our imagination to fill in the details. He leaves it up to us to picture the dimensions and features of the landscape, allowing the Lord to work through our imagination in order to reveal himself to us.

All of our seeking and knowing of truth in some way involves using our imagination. Imagination is a necessary tool for knowing Christ. Imaginative experiences in prayer must be discerned wisely. How do we know if God is truly working through our imagination or if the images are merely our own fantasy, which might be tinged with falsehood? The world, the flesh, and the devil can influence our thoughts and imagination. Worldly values can creep into imaginations. Think of how we are bombarded every day with countless glamorous advertisements that give us a false sense of happiness. As fallen creatures given to fleshly desires, we can easily use our imaginations build up our own egos and a false sense of self. The evil one can also suggest imaginative fantasies that distract us from our true spiritual purpose.

On his sickbed Saint Ignatius came to realize the folly and lack of realism in his fantasy about winning the hand of a lady high above his station in life. The fantasy ultimately led to spiritual desolation and he therefore dismissed it, attributing it to the devil. However, he alternatively experienced his imagination rooted in spiritual reality as he envisaged imitating Saint Francis and

Saint Dominic in their lives of prayer, penance, and charity. God worked in Saint Ignatius' imagination to bring about lasting consolation, and so he actually did imitate these saints, embarking on his own life of prayer, penance, and charity.

Another good test of the authenticity of what we imagine is to compare it with the teachings of Christ and his Church. Ideas and images that diverge from the revelation of God and the deposit of faith are not from God and should be dismissed. It is, therefore, a good idea to maintain vigilance in our use of the imagination so we can discern which images are authentic, ideally by describing them to a trusted spiritual guide or friend. Still, Saint Ignatius wants us to experience great freedom in using our imagination with the upright intention of seeking the face of Christ, trusting that the Holy Spirit will in fact guide us to all truth.

Though some have more active imaginations than others, no one can claim to have no imagination, to be too literal a thinker without a figurative dimension. Perhaps too much emphasis, though, has been placed on the use of the visual imagination, while neglecting other imaginative modes, such as the auditory. We use the auditory imagination to hear sounds in our minds and hearts. With his highly developed auditory imagination, Mozart could actually imagine music in his mind, and so he composed full symphonies without using even one musical instrument. Saint Paul, too, gives the auditory imagination its due in its essential role in our coming to believe, writing that "faith comes from what is heard" (Rom 10:17). Naturally, then, Saint Ignatius invites us to go beyond simply seeing the persons in a Scripture scene in order to "consider, observe, and contemplate what the persons are saying" (SpEx 115).

Through use of the auditory memory, prayer can be a powerful experience of hearing God's word in the Scripture, hearing those words that speak profoundly to our hearts. Though the word may have a common meaning for every reader, often it will take on a specific understanding unique to the individual. For the bride in the Song of Songs, the words dear to her heart are those her lover speaks: "Ah, you are beautiful, my love"—leading her to a similar outpouring of admiration for her lover: "Ah, you are beautiful, my beloved." The person who prays is very free to discover which words one will take to heart, which words are meant just for oneself.

Beyond seeing and hearing the persons in Scripture, Saint Ignatius also wants us to notice "what they are doing" (SpEx 116), in other words, to use our kinesthetic imaginations. (Kinesthesis is the ability to feel the movements of the limbs and body.) This has to do with noticing actions and remembering and describing them to others. For example, as a child I would watch athletes and want to imitate them. It is not surprising, then, that one of my strongest prayer experiences involved Jesus calling me to action, to walk on the water toward him as Peter did when Jesus called him. As I pictured this scene in my imagination, I found confidence and courage to overcome my fears of what was pulling me away from Jesus, symbolized by the wind and the waves. Profound feelings washed over me as I experienced Jesus filling me with courage.

When using our imaginations in prayer, we might approach the Scripture scene either as a bystander or as a participant. When acting as a bystander, we watch the scene unfold, seeing and hearing the persons and their actions, noticing what attracts or repels us. Jesus may be drawing us to himself by what attracts us. By contrast, what repels us may reveal our resistances that could be obstacles in following Jesus. When we act as participants, our approach is more direct as we are now acting as characters in the biblical scene. For instance, instead of a participant watching the boy with the loaves and fishes being brought to Jesus, I could assume the role of the boy. In this role, I might imagine the disciples asking for food and wonder where the food will come from. Realizing I have food, I may feel reluctant to share it but follow the desire to be generous. I might be introduced to Jesus and feel awe in his presence, taking in his affirming look. Embarrassed that I have so little to give, I could experience the reassurance that comes when he accepts whatever I have to offer. I might grow in trust that he can do much more with the little I have and multiply it to feed others. Through this approach to contemplation, the story of the loaves and fishes jumps off the page and becomes the story of my life and my call. Here I am confirmed in my desire to give to Jesus and trust that he will transform my small gift into something marvelous.

What happens to us as we engage in this type of contemplative prayer? Nothing short of real transformation into the likeness of our beloved, the Lord Jesus. Saint Paul speaks of how we are being transfigured from one glory to another in God through prayer (see 2 Cor 3:18). Examples abound of holy persons being so transformed that even their faces seemed to glow. Moses' face became radiant when he prayed before the Lord in the meeting tent. Similarly, Conrad of Marburg, Saint Elizabeth of Hungary's spiritual director, wrote that eyewitnesses saw her coming forth from prayer with her face shining and light beaming from her eyes like the sun's rays.[55]

Of course, no list would be complete without the holy radiance of Saint Teresa of Calcutta. When the journalist Malcolm Muggeridge was working on a documentary on Mother Teresa, he decided one day to film the sisters as they picked up the dying in the streets and took them to their shelter. The sisters would wash and care for these people so they could die within the sight of a loving face, as Mother Teresa put it. Mother and the sisters agreed to participate in the documentary, but insisted that they pray before being filmed. The room that morning was dimly lit to the dismay of the film crew, who had not brought portable lighting. Most of the cameramen thought that they should not even attempt the shoot, but one of the crew suggested they film the scene anyway since it might be useful. To their astonishment, the footage turned out to be brightly lit, and the inside of the building glowed with a mysterious warm light. Ironically, some of the footage taken outside appeared markedly dimmer in comparison. The camera crew agreed that there was no technical explanation for the outcome. Muggeridge, a former atheist, wrote in his book that love—overflowing love—glowed in Mother Teresa's home for the dying. That love registered on the faces of Mother and her sisters, so it was no surprise that it also registered on photographic film.[56] By the grace of contemplative prayer, Saint Teresa was transformed into Christ and radiated his light just as we can.

As we practice contemplative prayer, praying for interior knowledge of the Lord, we are transformed. The more we come to know Jesus, the more we will love him. The more we come to love him, the more we will desire to get to know him. In this way, we will grow in friendship with Jesus and become like him, taking on his desires, his perspective, his attitude, his way of acting and responding to others. When we fall in love with the Lord, the effects transform our very being. Even our behavior begins to change. The former Superior General of the Jesuits, Pedro Arrupe, spoke spontaneously to a group of religious sisters about falling in love with the Lord: "Nothing is

---

55. See *The Liturgy of the Hours*, vol. 4, Memorial of Saint Elizabeth of Hungary, *Office of Readings*, November 17, Second Reading.

56. See Malcom Muggeridge, *Something Beautiful for God* (Garden City: Image/Doubleday, 1977), 30–31.

more practical than finding God, than falling in love in a quite absolute, final way. It will decide what will get you out of bed in the morning, what you will do with your evenings, how you spend your weekends, what you read, who you know, what breaks your heart, and what amazes you with joy and gratitude. Fall in love, stay in love, and it will decide everything.[57] Contemplating the Lord leads us to a deepening love relationship with him that will change our lives.

Imaginative contemplation brings about greater union with Christ. As Christians, by Baptism we are already united to Christ in his life, death, and resurrection. As members of his Body we live out the mysteries of Christ, the Head of the body. As we experience his love in contemplative prayer, we receive his life and power to love one another as he has loved us. Jesus penetrates us deeply with his mysteries and "enables us to *live in him* all that he himself lived."[58] Jesus lives his mysteries in us and exhorts us to "abide in me as I abide in you" (Jn 15:4). Saint John Eudes explains that Jesus' life and experiences are performed in us and that we can conform our hearts to his as we realize his mysteries in our lives.[59] Through contemplation we can better participate in the mysteries of the life of Christ and appropriate them into our lives. Using our imagination, we truly encounter Christ and receive the inspiration to live his way of life. Saint Paul even says, "It is Christ who lives in me ... the life I now live in the flesh I live by faith in the Son of God" (Gal 2:20). He participates in Christ's very being and experiences his power flowing through him.

This union in prayer results in complete identification of the lover with his beloved. We can see this dynamic in the Song of Songs where union results in oneness. Specifically, the bridegroom communicates his beauty to the beloved, in a way transmitting it to her and making it hers. By her very existence, her beauty becomes a participation in his beauty. Saint John of the

---

57. Pedro Arrupe, S.J., see Fall in Love, Jesuit Online Resources, Xavier University, http://www.xavier.edu/jesuitresource/online-resources/love-quotes.cfm, last accessed April 3, 2017.

58. CCC 521.

59. See Saint John Eudes, *On the Kingdom of Jesus*, in *The Liturgy of the Hours, Office of Readings*, vol. IV, Second Reading, Week 33, Friday (New York: Catholic Book Publishing Corp., 1976), 1794 (pars. 3, 4, Opera Omnia 1, 310–312).

Cross had this very experience in his contemplative prayer. He underwent transformation in Christ's beauty, such that he resembled the Lord. He could behold himself in Christ's beauty and come to possess that beauty, as does the bride with her bridegroom.[60] In the Spiritual Exercises, Saint Ignatius comments how a lover desires to share what one has with the beloved (SpEx 231). United to Christ our Beloved in contemplation, he shares gifts of wisdom, love, and glory with us, such that we become more like him in his beauty.

Using the Senses

When engaging in contemplative prayer with the imagination, the retreatant will do well to practice what Saint Ignatius says "will consist in applying the five senses" (SpEx 121). He is referring to a longstanding tradition in the Church of praying with the interior senses of the imagination and applying each sense to the mysteries we contemplate. Just as our physical senses operate and experience the realities of our physical world, so too our interior spiritual senses of the imagination are trained through interaction with the realities of the spiritual life. When Saint John speaks of "what was from the beginning, what we have heard, what we have seen with our eyes, what we have looked at and touched with our hands, concerning the word of life" (1 Jn 1:1), he describes precisely what we do in contemplative prayer using the senses of the imagination.

Origen describes how those who advance in the spiritual life develop these spiritual senses of the imagination. Sight discovers divine realities; hearing perceives the meaning of the Scriptures interiorly to the soul; touch enables one to examine the flesh of the Word; smell and taste express the delicacies of knowledge. The soul becomes more like God as it delights in the word of God in all its senses.[61] By a kind of osmosis we are taken into the life of God and participate in his being and virtue.

Thus Saint Ignatius invites us to pass the five senses of the imagination over the mysteries we contemplate. He encourages us to see Jesus (and other

---

60. See Saint John of the Cross, "Spiritual Canticle," Stanza 36, trans. Kieran Kavanaugh, O.C.D. and Otilio Rodriguez, O.C.D., *The Collected Works of John of the Cross* (Washington, D.C.: ICS Publications, 1991), 611–612.

61. See Origen, *The Song of Songs*, 78–79.

characters) with the sight of the imagination, just as Jesus allowed himself to be seen in his incarnation. Since the New Testament does not describe the physical appearance of Jesus, we can only imagine it. We are asked to hear the words spoken by Jesus and the other characters, using the auditory imagination. Interestingly, we are also instructed to "smell the infinite fragrance" (SpEx 124) of the divinity, directly corresponding to what Saint Paul describes as the aroma of Christ (see 2 Cor 2:15). The bride speaks of her lover's anointing oils as fragrant and pleasing (Song 1:3). Next, we are to "taste the infinite sweetness of the divinity" (SpEx 124). Here we are reminded of the psalmist's exhortation to "taste and see that the Lord is good" (Ps 34:8). The bride here speaks of the bridegroom's fruit as sweet to her taste (Song 2:3). Saint Ignatius then brings us to "apply the sense of touch" (SpEx 125). We should not fear to imagine touching Jesus, for he himself touched those he encountered and allowed them to touch him. We may have an awareness of being spiritually held or touched by the Lord, as here the bridegroom embraces his lover with his right hand, holding her head with his left hand (Song 2:6).

Contemplative prayer develops the interior senses of the imagination. Saint Bonaventure explains how the inner senses are restored to see the highest beauty, to hear the highest harmony, to smell the highest fragrance, to taste the highest sweetness so that the soul is prepared to spiritually advance in prayer.[62] The bride apprehends her lover more fully through her sense knowledge. She is caught up in delight at the sight of her beloved, at his beauty. As he speaks to her, she hears his affirming words. With his fragrant anointing oils, he is a "sachet of myrrh" lying at her heart. She tastes his delightful love at the banquet as he holds her in the embrace of his right hand. In these ways and others, the bride's senses are totally overwhelmed in the presence of the bridegroom.

The bride now rests in her lover's embrace in a sleep of love. This moment of rest and sleep is a metaphor for the experience of resting and soaking in God's grace in contemplative prayer, as Saint Ignatius reminds us to do (SpEx 323). We are to soak up and store the memory of grace from these divine consolations so that they may sustain us in the future. We should drink

---

62. See Saint Bonaventure, *The Journey of the Mind into God*, ch. 4.

deeply of consolation, savoring God's presence and gifts while they are being given to us, just as the saints did. When Saint Francis, for example, experienced the Holy Spirit's consolation, he would taste it to the full and savor it for as long as it lasted. He would stop what he was doing and slake his thirst with God's grace, always ready to welcome God in his visitations.[63] Because Francis appropriated and deepened the graces received, his life of contemplation bore fruit in a life of faith, hope, and charity. So too can it be with us.

One way to store up and deepen the grace received through contemplation is to perform what Saint Ignatius calls a "repetition" of the contemplation. By repetition he doesn't mean a complete review of the subject matter. Because our initial contact may have been superficial, Saint Ignatius intends us to return to the contemplation—those places where the individual perceived a greater movement of the spirit, either toward consolation or toward desolation. Repetition could be likened to shifting a camera from a panoramic, wide-angle view to a narrow, zoom-lens focus on specific details that concern me. Ultimately, through repetition, our prayer will become more focused and simple, and God's personal revelation will uniquely impact our lives and behavior. If the movement is toward spiritual desolation, we should remain attentive, for we might find some misunderstanding God desires to shed light upon or some wound God desires to heal. If, instead, the more profound movement is toward spiritual consolation, we should return to deepen and savor that experience of joy and peace. By revisiting the experience, we can hold and assimilate the grace received. God's favor becomes deeply personal to us and opens up new ways of being in friendship with the Lord. Saint Ignatius wants us to dwell in this moment and draw from the experience all it has to offer, like a bee that draws nectar from a flower before moving on. By making a repetition, God's grace will have a greater impact on our lives as we move forward from prayer.

Contemplation does not end merely in the union of the lover and beloved but continues to be fruitful. The marriage between bridegroom and bride is meant to be abundantly prolific. The bride exclaims that "our couch is green; the beams of our house are cedar, our rafters are pine" (Song 1:16–17), the verdant couch suggesting growth and new life resulting from their

---

63. See Saint Bonaventure, *The Major Life of St. Francis*, I. 10. 2–4, in Marion A. Habig (ed.), *St. Francis of Assisi: Writings and Early Biographies* (Franciscan Press: Quincy University, 1991).

union. Here, the cedar beams suggest those that support the Temple, reminding us of the strong support of Christ. Also, since in the Ancient Near East cypress was a symbol of death, the bride's reference can remind us of Christ who died to save us, in this way providing the ultimate support. As the bride's marriage bed brings fruitfulness, so too does Christ's death and dying—and ours in union with him, as Jesus tells us, "Very truly, I tell you, unless a grain of wheat falls into the earth and dies, it remains just a single grain; but if it dies, it bears much fruit" (Jn 12:24). Adherence to Christ in contemplative prayer entails dying to self in order to live for him as we strive to remain faithful to the Lord's inspirations. Our dying and faithfulness in following him will bear fruit in our lives and in the lives of others, as Jesus promised, so we need not fear.

The flowering that leads to fruitfulness is already coming forth in the bride. She relates herself to the coming fruitfulness of spring, with new growth and flowers springing up all over Israel, saying, "I am a rose of Sharon, a lily of the valleys. As a lily among brambles, so is my love among maidens" (2:1–2). The bride compares herself in all humility to the most common lily of the valley, the red anemone that blankets the valleys in beauty, its abundance symbolizing fruitfulness. Even more, the bridegroom calls the bride a lily among thorns, contrasting her beauty (the lily) with her suffering (the thorns). Because it will bring forth great fruit, her suffering only serves to highlight her attractiveness. The bride calls her lover "an apple tree among the trees of the wood." Christ, like the apple tree, is copiously productive and the source of all fruitfulness. His dying on the tree produced the fruit of our salvation, giving life to the members of his Body. The bride asks, "Refresh me with apples" (2:5). This fruit, so sweet to the bride's mouth, refreshes her body as she is "nourished in his banquet hall."[64]

Prayer is authentic if it bears good fruit. Jesus reminds us that "a good tree cannot bear bad fruit." Through prayer, we are restored, renewed, and

---

64. She also desires the fruitfulness of her bridegroom in asking him to "strengthen me with raisin cakes" (2:5). Raisins were seen as an antidote to impotence and she is desiring more ardor and fertility. Though the bride is "sick with love," she asks to be strengthened in bearing fruit for her lover. Jesus promised his disciples, "He who abides in me, and I in him, he it is that bears much fruit (John 15:5); See George Maloney, S.J., *Singers of the New Song* (Notre Dame, IN: Ave Maria Press, 1985), 46–47.

called to live the Gospel and proclaim Christ to others. In that vein, at the end of the first week's prayer on God's mercy, Saint Ignatius calls us to ask, "What have I done for Christ? What am I doing for Christ? What ought I to do for Christ?" (SpEx 53).

In the second week, the goal of contemplative prayer is a more intimate knowledge of Christ that leads us to follow him more closely (SpEx 104). Specifically, contemplative prayer during the first two weeks of the Spiritual Exercises should bear fruit in some kind of resolution about how I want to live more like Christ, in loving union with him. At times this resolution is expressed with strong feelings of faith, hope, and love, while at other times it is expressed with a concrete desire to act in a Christ-like way. Jesus cautions us, "Not everyone who says to me, 'Lord, Lord,' will enter the kingdom of heaven, but only the one who does the will of my Father in heaven" (Mt 7:20–21). The sign of sanctity, then, is not just the consolation one receives in prayer but the response in love to such gifts of God's grace.

The bride in the Song of Songs depends on her bridegroom in her desires for fertility and in being fruitful. The Bridegroom—Christ—brings about and affirms our fruitfulness. Both emotionally and physically, Christ supports the bride as she follows him and bears great fruit. He holds her with his left arm under her head as his right arm embraces her. She can succeed only by his power. Saint Ambrose explains that the great hands of Christ caress and cherish the bride, embracing her whole soul. His hands encircle and strengthen her as she is united with the Word of God in spiritual marriage. Eternal Wisdom places his hand under her head and embraces and supports her entire body of labors and virtuous deeds.[65] Through contemplative prayer, borne by the power of Christ, we are able to follow him more closely and bear fruit in doing his works.

---

65. See Saint Ambrose on Ps. 118; cited by Fr. Juan Gonzalez Arintero, O.P., *The Song of Songs: A Mystical Exposition*, trans. James Valender and Jose L. Morales (Cincinnati: Monastery of the Holy Name, 1974), 237.

Questions for Reflection and Discussion

1. What is your experience of using imagination in prayer? Do you have a vivid or weak imagination?

2. Which mode of imagination is dominant in your prayer: visual, auditory, or kinesthetic?

3. How has prayer transformed the interior senses of your imagination? How does prayer affect the way you interact with your environment? In what ways do you experience harmony or a clash with the culture in which you live?

4. What is your favorite mystery in the life of Jesus or image of Jesus in your prayer? How has it changed you?

5. How have you noticed your prayer bearing fruit in your life? How have you learned to measure the authenticity of your prayer in its effects in your life?

6. How can you do better at storing up moments of consolation for your future life in the Spirit?

Prayer Exercises

1. Pray with Luke 1:26–38, following Saint Ignatius' method of using the imagination. Ask for the grace of a more intimate knowledge of God made man for you in order that you may love him more and follow him more closely. Notice the persons in this Scripture scene and what they are saying and doing. What impresses you?

2. Pray with Luke 2:1–20 with the above method. As Saint Ignatius recommends, be a participant in the scene by making yourself a child helper to the Holy Family.

3. Make a repetition on the above contemplations, going back to the places of greater movement of spirit. Consider making a resolution about storing up the grace received and putting it into action in a concrete way.

4. Review Saint Ignatius' method of prayer using the spiritual senses (pp. 94–95). Make another repetition on the above contemplations,

this time passing each of the interior senses of the imagination over the mystery in order to savor it more fully.

5. Pray with Song of Songs 1:16–2:1 and consider the beauty of the Lord as he has revealed himself to you.

6. Read the summary of Ambrose's comments (p. 98) regarding the hands of Christ supporting us. Pray with Song of Songs 2:3–6, and ask for the grace of greater fruitfulness in the Lord's service.

7. Make a repetition on any of the above prayer exercises, paying attention to greater movements of spiritual consolation or desolation.

Chapter 9

Love Draws Close

[B] The voice of my beloved!
    Look, he comes,
leaping upon the mountains,
    bounding over the hills.
My beloved is like a gazelle
    or a young stag.
Look, there he stands
    behind our wall,
gazing in at the windows,
    looking through the lattice. (Song 2:8–9)

The Three Divine Persons . . . decree in Their eternity that the Second Person should become man to save the human race. So when the fullness of time had come, They send the Angel Gabriel to our Lady. (SpEx 102)

The Danish philosopher Søren Kierkegaard once told a parable about a great and noble king whose heart was melted by his love of a humble maiden from the poorest village in his kingdom. He wanted to marry her but hesitated because his people would have looked on it unfavorably. Kings simply did not marry peasants. Still, the king knew that he could marry this lovely maiden if he chose. Given his great power, no one would dare oppose him. But he worried that if they were married, both he and the young woman would be uncomfortably aware of the gap in their status. She would admire his grandeur as a king though she couldn't really love him as an equal, and he would love and admire her beauty but never see her as his true match. The king even considered renouncing his wealth and kingship so he could offer her his love as a man on her social level. This too, he thought, could go awry. She might think him foolish for leaving his wealth, power, and position, and might not be interested in him as a man of her own meager status.

Despite the risk, the king made the drastic resolution to renounce his wealth and position. One night, after all in the castle were asleep, he laid aside his golden crown and removed his rings of state. He shed his royal robes of silk and linen and dressed himself in the common clothes of the poorest of the kingdom. Leaving through the servant's entrance, the king left his crown, his castle, and his kingdom behind. As the next day's sun rose in the east, the maiden emerged from her humble cottage to find herself face to face with a stranger, a common man with kindly eyes who asked to speak with her and, in time, to court her for her hand in marriage.

How did the maiden respond? We don't know. Kierkegaard never tells us her decision or how the story ends.[66] He wanted to show us that the tale continues in our lives; we are like the humble maiden, while Jesus Christ is like the king. Having complete power and dominion, Jesus could rule over us but instead chooses to approach us like a humble beggar, as someone on our own level, to win our love as one human being to another. Saint Paul restates the ancient Christian hymn, "Let the same mind be in you that was in Christ Jesus, who, though he was in the form of God, did not regard equality with God as something to be exploited, but emptied himself, taking the form of a slave, being born in human likeness. And being found in human form, he humbled himself and became obedient to the point of death—even death on a cross" (Phil 2:5–8). Jesus emptied himself, as it were, of his divinity—a treasure infinitely greater than Kierkegaard's king possessed—in order to

---

66. See Søren Kierkegaard, *Philosophical Fragments/Johannes Climacus*, ed. and trans. Howard V. Hong and Edna H. Hong (Princeton, N.J.: Princeton University Press, 1985), 28–36.

assume our humanity. Of course, Jesus is still divine, but in the incarnation of the Word made man, he now becomes like us, meeting us on our own level.

In the Song of Songs, the bridegroom, like Kierkegaard's king, descends from his high place to make a proposal to his bride. She tells us with excitement of his coming from a great distance, "leaping upon the mountains, bounding over the hills" with great speed and agility. In this way the bride speaks of the seemingly vast distance from heaven to earth that the Lord surmounts in his coming from divine origins. These details remind us of the transcendence of God, who made and established all things, ruling them from his place in heaven. Mountains remind us of God's majesty and surpassing greatness, as God is always greater than what we can think or know of him. Isaiah reminds us that God's thoughts and ways are far beyond ours (see Is 55:8–9). Yet God's immanence stands side by side with his transcendence. In the incarnation, God has drawn exceedingly close to us human beings—closer to us than we are to ourselves. He knows our inmost thoughts and surveys all our deeds. The bridegroom, in a gesture illustrating how he probes the bride's thoughts and surveys her actions, "stands behind our wall, gazing in at the windows, looking through the lattice" (2:9). Jesus similarly approaches us in the incarnation, assuming our nature, peering into our inmost being, knowing us intimately.

In the Spiritual Exercises, Saint Ignatius tasks us with pondering the incarnation, God drawing close to us. Praying about the mystery of the Annunciation, we can see the Holy Trinity as they look upon the earth. They desire to save human beings through the willingness of God the Son to become man. We can then imagine the angel Gabriel appearing to Mary. In this foundational mystery, we ponder the tremendous grace of God the Son who loves us so much that he assumed and elevated our human nature. By God's action, our human nature is "divinized," that is, graced with a divine quality. Because he shares our nature in the incarnation, God knows experientially what it means to be human, and we, through pondering Jesus, understand what it means to be godlike. This sentiment is expressed in the Offertory of the Mass. As the priest pours water into the chalice of wine, he prays that we may share in the divinity of Christ, who through his humility lowered himself to share in our nature. The Lord desires us to share in his nature as he shares in ours.

This sharing of natures is wonderfully illustrated in Mark Twain's classic book, *The Prince and the Pauper*. The story is about an English prince who lives in a royal palace shielded from the world of ordinary folks. One day a pauper looks in the gate at the palace and is arrested. The prince intervenes and, after spending time talking to the pauper, comes to find him utterly fascinating. Desiring the pauper's friendship, the prince invites him into the palace. The two get along wonderfully and notice, as they look in the mirror, how much they look alike. Except for the way they dress, no one can tell them apart. Then they both get the same idea: to pull a prank and swap identities. The pauper cleans himself of the street's grime and exchanges clothes with the prince. After telling each other how to act in their new roles, each sets out to live the other's life for a time. The pauper lives the life of royal luxury and privilege, while the prince rubs elbows with the poor and downtrodden in the streets. When the prince and the pauper tire of their game and return to their former places, each finds that he now profoundly understands the other's life. The pauper knows what it is to live with great dignity and nobility. The prince knows what it is to be poor and mistreated, and grows up to become the most compassionate king that England has ever known.

This parable reminds us of the wondrous exchange of the incarnation. Christ exchanges the royal garments of his divinity for the ragged clothes of our humanity, thus coming to understand by experience what it is to be poor and mistreated. Similarly, we exchange the ragged clothes of our humanity for the royal garment of the Lord's divinity, now able to understand in some way what it means to live on the majestic level of God's grace. Grace transforms our lowly humanity. We literally "put on the Lord Jesus Christ" (Rom 13:14), not merely in an external way, like changing clothes, but interiorly in a way that changes our hearts.

At the incarnation, Mary enabled Christ to come near by her consenting to become the Mother of God. The incarnation was not a once-and-for-all event but continues in our own lives. The incarnation happens in our lives in very much the same way that it happened for our Lady. In the beginning of the Second Week, Saint Ignatius has us ponder the mysteries of the conception, birth, and infancy of Christ, with Mary at the center of these mysteries. As we ponder Mary and her role in bringing about the incarnation, we realize that in a very real way, by grace and the Spirit, we imitate her in conceiving and bearing Christ in our lives.

Mary is the paradigm of how to receive Christ. At the angel's invitation she consents with her *Fiat* and surrenders to God's request as the humble maidservant of the Lord. Likewise, the Lord offers his grace to us and gives us the choice to respond to his loving invitation. Mary conceived Christ in a way we never will, bearing the biological flesh of Jesus in her womb. However, Saint Augustine tells us that Mary conceived Christ in her heart before she did in her womb. We are similar to Mary in the sense of bearing Christ in our hearts. Through Baptism and its gifts of faith, hope, and love that God pours into our hearts, all Christians share in a conception of Christ in their hearts. Like Mary, we all spiritually conceive and bear Christ to the world. Jesus said that whoever hears the word of God and keeps it is his mother (see Mt 12:46–50). This motherhood is true of any Christian who brings forth Christ according to the Spirit when one accepts the word of God. By being receptive to divine grace in our souls, we conceive Christ in imitation of Mary.

In this ongoing incarnation in our lives, Mary shows us the way to accept the word of God. During her lifetime, she always pondered the word and was receptive to it. Echoing Hannah (see 1 Sam 2:1–10), in her Magnificat Mary expresses absolute joy in conceiving and bearing Christ. Later, Mary ponders in her heart all the events of the birth of her Son (see Lk 2:19). As Jesus grows, Mary continuously contemplates him. In one notable case, she fails to understand what Jesus has said at finding him in the Temple, but still she continues to ponder his words in her heart. This pondering means to "turn over" again and again in wonderment. That's a good description of contemplation for us as Christians, as we ponder God's word in the Scriptures and in the events of our lives. Like Mary we think over how "God who is mighty has done great things for us." We ponder and allow God's life and grace to permeate us more deeply, radiating through us. After noting how Christ's mother bore him in her womb, Saint Augustine remarks that we should bear him in our hearts, which should grow big with the faith of Christ. Mary delivered the Savior and we ought to give birth to praise. We should not be sterile but fertile with God.[67] Pondering the mysteries of Christ with Mary, we become filled with the very life of God.

---

67. See Saint Augustine, *Sermons*, 189, 3, in *The Works of Saint Augustine: A Translation for the 21st Century*, Part III, Volume 6, trans. Edmund Hill, O.P., ed. John E. Rotelle, O.S.A. (New Rochelle: New City Press, 1993), 35.

Bringing Christ to Others

Filled with God himself, we carry him to the world. Mary shows us the fruit of her conceiving Christ and bringing him forth for others. In the mystery of the Visitation, she journeys to Ein Karem to see her cousin Elizabeth who is six months pregnant. Saint Luke sees in this episode the mystery of Mary as the Ark of the Covenant. As Mary is the bearer of Christ's presence, so we are meant to be. Already, at the Annunciation, Luke shows us that Mary was overshadowed by the Holy Spirit just as the Ark of the Covenant was overshadowed by the cloud of God's presence (see Ex 40:34–35). As David danced before the Ark upon its return to Jerusalem, at the Visitation John the Baptist leaps in his mother's womb at the presence of Mary, the Ark that carries Jesus. And as David cried out, "How can the ark of the Lord come into my care?" (2 Sam 6:9), so Elizabeth exclaims, "And why has this happened to me, that the mother of my Lord comes to me?" (Lk 1:43). Now we hear in this passage from the Song of Songs, "The voice of my beloved! Behold, he comes, leaping upon the mountains, bounding over the hills,"[68] suggesting Mary's journey across the hills from Nazareth to Ein Karem as the Ark of the Incarnate Word who is the Bridegroom. The Bridegroom, carried in Mary, has come from the heavens to earth in order to dwell with his bride in her inmost self, to peer at her inmost being in love.

In the Spiritual Exercises, the reality of the incarnation has implications for our life of contemplation. Saint Ignatius wants us to give proper attention to both the divinity and humanity of Christ in our prayer. When we acknowledge his wisdom, power, and might, his ability to work miracles, and his divine authority over our lives as king of the universe, we attend to his divinity. We experience the power of his divinity to change our lives. But only to prayerfully consider his divine nature would fail to acknowledge Jesus' full human nature. His real humanity has implications for our life of prayer as we grow to understand that he shares our way of existence. So we should pay attention to Jesus' humanity. We can notice that Jesus was tired and thirsty at the well in Samaria, that he desired the companionship of his apostles and friends, that he was moved by the deepest emotions when his friend Lazarus

---

68. This passage is read during Advent for the Mass of December 21.

died. Because Jesus shares our nature, he knows what it is to be human and can be truly compassionate with us. Vatican Council II explains that "the Son of God . . . worked with human hands, he thought with a human mind, acted by human choice, and loved with a human heart."[69] We might give intellectual assent to the doctrine of Jesus' humanity, but we will only truly understand Christ and his relationship to us in prayer through an encounter with his true humanity.

Saint Ignatius emphasizes the point that in the incarnation the Son of God became man *for me* (see SpEx 104). God desired me into being from all eternity and now wants to share my life in his act of becoming man. Jesus is the Son of the Father from the beginning and has come in order to bring us into filial relationship as children by adoption. Saint John expounds on this crucial meaning of the incarnation in the Prologue to his Gospel: "But to all who received him, who believed in his name, he gave power to become children of God" (Jn 1:12). We become children of our heavenly Father not by biological generation, but spiritually by divine adoption through grace.

As children of God, we discover how deeply our heavenly Father desires us. Perhaps this is best illustrated by looking at the experience of those who are lost or forsaken in this world. Greg Boyle, a Jesuit priest and founder of the largest gang intervention program in the United States, Homeboy Industries, tells a story that shows by analogy the deep significance of divine adoption.[70] Father Greg first met a young boy named Cesar during the California earthquake of 1987, when a tent city emerged in Los Angeles after the housing projects were reduced to rubble. Wondering if the world was coming to an end, the young Cesar looked to Father Greg for reassurance. But the earthquake was the least of Cesar's troubles. Later, as a teenager and young adult, he spent more time in prison than out. When he was released from prison, he arrived home to find that his girlfriend, in a fit of rage, had burned all his clothing. So Father Greg took Cesar to a department store and bought him 200 dollars' worth of clothes. As they arrived home, Cesar confided his fears that his old gang would expect him to come back and he would

---

69. *Gaudium et Spes*, no. 22, par. 2. http://www.vatican.va/archive/hist_councils/ii_vatican_council/documents/vat-ii_const_19651207_gaudium-et-spes_en.html.

70. See Gregory Boyle, *Tattoos on the Heart* (New York: Free Press, 2011), 28–32.

end up in prison. Knowing that God was at the center of Cesar's big heart, Father Greg reassured him that all would be well. Late that night, the phone rang. It was Cesar, anxious to ask Father Greg a question. Cesar had always seen the priest as his father, and he asked Father Greg if he had been as a son to him. Father Greg said yes, by all means he had been like a dear son. Sobbing and relieved, Cesar replied that he would be Father Greg's son, hopeful that nothing would ever separate them. Reflecting on the episode, the priest suggests that Cesar did not simply discover that he had a father, but that he was a son worth having. In the midst of his miserable life, Cesar knew himself beloved by Father Greg.

It is difficult for many of us to imagine the experience of being orphaned, forsaken by parents, or feeling lost and abandoned. Some people who have parents experience the pain of rejection. Some carry the feelings of being unwanted by a mother or parents even from the womb. The Lord promises that even if father or mother forsake us, he will not forsake us (see Is 49:15). He has chosen us from all eternity to be his children, his prized possession. Such an experience as Cesar's of the love of adoption is the ultimate meaning of God's having become man, as Saint Ignatius says, *for me*. We realize that in the Father's eyes, we are sons and daughters worth having. God chose in advance to adopt us into his own family by bringing us to himself through Jesus Christ. It gave him great pleasure to do so, and we feel ourselves to be precious in his sight (see Eph 1:5). We are no longer strangers and aliens, but fellow citizens with the saints who belong to God's household (see Eph 2:19). Once, like orphans, we were people without any identity, but now we are God's people. Now we are a chosen race, a royal priesthood, a holy nation, a people for God's own possession (see 1 Pet 2:9–10). The Lord not only seeks to be with us, but to make us his sons and daughters.

The bridegroom intently seeks his bride in his longing to make her his own and to carry her away with him as his treasured possession. The bride wonders with amazement that the bridegroom has traversed mountains and hills at great speed in his exuberant yearning to be with her. In humility, he has stooped from his kingship to propose to her. He has drawn close and is intently gazing upon her, seeing into her interior with love. In Christ, God has traversed the vast distance from the mountains of heaven to the valleys of earth in his desire to become one with us, to enter into our very being in his ongoing incarnation. The Lord has emptied himself of his divinity in order to share in our humanity and to cherish us as his own.

Questions for Reflection and Discussion

1. How do you experience the divinity of Christ in prayer? Consider his wisdom, power, and might, his ability to work miracles, and his divine Person and authority over our lives as King of the universe.

2. How do you experience the humanity of Christ in prayer? Consider his assuming our human nature, his meekness and humility of heart, his sharing our weakness and limitations, and his achieving the fullness of human potential.

3. Saint Paul wrote: "It is no longer I who live, but it is Christ who lives in me" (Gal 2:20). How do you experience Christ living in you?

4. How do you imitate Mary in her essential role of motherhood toward Christ in conceiving him and bearing him to the world? How can you be more attentive to the needs of the humanity of Christ?

Prayer Exercises

1. Pray with Song of Songs 2 and consider Christ the Bridegroom drawing close to you in the incarnation. Ask for a greater awareness and appreciation of the Word of God become man for you.

2. Reflect on the story of the prince and the pauper (pp. 103–104). Pray with John 1:1–18, and ask for a greater awareness of sharing in the divinity of Christ.

3. Ponder Kierkegaard's parable of the king and the peasant woman (pp. 101–102). Pray with John 2:1–12, and ask for the grace to accept the Lord's invitation to spiritual union.

4. Pray with John 6:41–59, and ask for a greater awareness of Christ sharing in your humanity.

5. Consider Mary's role as mother to Christ as a paradigm for all Christians (p. 105). Pray with Mark 3:31–35, and ask for the grace to conceive and bear Christ to the world as Mary did.

6. Pray with Galatians 2:20, and ask for the grace to understand Christ's life within you by his indwelling grace.

7. Make a repetition on any of the above contemplations, paying attention to the places of greater consolation or desolation.

CHAPTER 10

Beloved Friend

[B] The voice of my beloved!
    Look, he comes,
leaping upon the mountains,
    bounding over the hills.
My beloved is like a gazelle
    or a young stag.
Look, there he stands
    behind our wall,
gazing in at the windows,
    looking through the lattice. (Song 2:8–9)

The colloquy is made by speaking exactly as one friend speaks to another.
(SpEx 54)

A desire for "an intimate knowledge of our Lord, who has become man for
me" (SpEx 104) will lead to friendship with Jesus. In this chapter, we
will see how contemplating the person of Christ brings about this
friendship.

The Hebrew word the bride uses for her beloved also means "friend."
Friendship is a very profound form of love. It is the best foundation for

marriage, and many spouses know one another as best friends. The bridegroom's intimate sharing of life with his bride indicates that their love is rooted in friendship. The word intimacy sounds like "into-me-see"; it suggests the transparency of the bride in allowing the bridegroom to see into her inmost soul. Indeed, he is "gazing in" at her through the windows, "looking through the lattice." God is the one who sees the heart, the deep interior of the person, and doesn't judge by mere external appearances (see 1 Sam 16:7). Jesus also sees into and knows what is in our hearts (see Jn 2:24) and desires our friendship.

Jesus drew many people into friendship with him, such as Martha, Mary, and Lazarus. When Jesus wept at the death of his friend Lazarus, it led the bystanders to comment, "See how he loved him!" (Jn 11:36). Jesus called apostles to himself, not just to train them to be ministers, but because he desired their companionship. Jesus told them, "I do not call you servants any longer, because the servant does not know what the master is doing; but I have called you friends, because I have made known to you everything that I have heard from my Father" (Jn 15:15).

As our friend, Jesus reveals to us what is in his heart, and we are privileged to share in it. Jesus led his band as a servant, washing their feet and giving them a participation in his very life (see Jn 13:8). Christ the Bridegroom, though divine, has humbled himself to become a man in order to meet his bride on equal terms. The bride is elevated to become the companion and equal of her lover, God. As such, she is lifted beyond mere servitude in the process of developing friendship. The mystic Saint John of the Cross describes the Lord's desire to make the soul equal to himself in friendship:

> If anything pleases him, it is the exaltation of the soul. Since there is no way by which he can exalt her more than making her equal to himself, he is pleased only with her love. For the property of love is to make the lover equal to the object loved. Since the soul in this state possesses perfect love, she is called the bride of the Son of God, which signifies equality with him.... As a result they are truly gods by participation, equals, and companions of God.[71]

---

71. "Spiritual Canticle," 28.1, in *The Collected Works of St. John of the Cross*, trans. Kieran Kavanaugh and Otilio Rodriquez (Washington, D.C.: Institute of Carmelite Studies, 1973), 584.

God desires to share his divine nature with us, as he shares in our human nature, so we can become like him by grace. Saint Ignatius comments how a lover desires to share all one is and has with one's beloved, including the thoughts of one's heart (see SpEx 231). Jesus does not want us to remain mere obedient slaves who take orders from a master. As a friend, he wants to reveal himself to us and he wants us to reveal ourselves to him. Jesus already thoroughly knows us, but when we reveal ourselves to him we come to greater self-discovery in Christ. This mutual self-revelation happens especially in the prayer of the Spiritual Exercises and is foundational to our relationship with God.

Mutual self-revelation in friendship is a gradual process, just as God slowly prepared Israel over the centuries to receive the fullness of revelation in Jesus Christ. Once God became man in Jesus Christ, he continued to display patience in growing accustomed to our humanity. As a child he grew in grace and wisdom before God and men, and for thirty years, before beginning his public ministry, Jesus slowly gained experiential knowledge of all things human. He was raised as a faithful Jew under the Law of Moses and became familiar with religious ritual and practice. Jesus gradually came to know his apostles more profoundly when he called them to himself and they accompanied him throughout his public ministry. We can imagine how deeply Christ knew his apostles through living with them day in and day out, sharing everything, including his vision of the kingdom. This must have led to deep conversations of the heart. Throughout this process, Jesus showed patience and determination in befriending the apostles. At the Last Supper, he could say to them, "I have called you friends" (Jn 15:15), revealing how greatly he loved them.

God's slow and patient cultivation of friendship with us is illustrated by Antoine de Saint-Exupéry's book *The Little Prince*, the story of a small boy, the Prince who came to Earth from another planet. On Earth, he felt very lonely and longed for a friend, until one day he met a fox who was equally desperate for friendship. He asked the fox to play with him, but the fox replied that he would first need to be tamed, that they needed to create ties. If the boy tamed the fox they would be unique to one another. The boy would be the only boy in the world for the fox, and the fox would be the only fox in the world for the boy. The fox's life would no longer be monotonous, but like sunshine. The sound of the boy's footsteps would be like music calling the fox out of his burrow. The boy then asked the fox what he must do to tame him. The fox told him that he must be very patient, that he must first sit down a small distance away in the grass. The fox would watch him from the corner of his eye and the boy would say nothing because language can be a source of confusion. But each day the boy would move closer to the fox. The little prince approved and they soon became best friends.[72]

This story speaks volumes about the very gradual process of two persons becoming friends. The Prince had to learn patience in coming to know the fox; spending time together was the only way to become friends. The Prince's experience parallels the way God befriends us: very gently and steadily. In becoming man, Jesus had a great deal to learn about being human in an experiential way. One could say Jesus tamed his apostles in friendship, and he continues to befriend us in the same gentle and gradual way. He draws closer and closer to us over time as we become more comfortable with his approaches and his desire for intimacy. It is a process Saint Ignatius wants to foster in his Spiritual Exercises. As we ponder the mysteries of the life of Christ, we desire to understand his vision and to share his lifestyle. We journey with Jesus as his companions, coming to share deep conversation with him as he gradually reveals his heart to us

The Path to Friendship

Just as the fox is sensitive to the boy's taming in *The Little Prince*, the bride is very attentive and responsive to the many approaches of the bridegroom. Saint Bernard notes how observant the bride is to the bridegroom's overtures. Notice the dedication and cleverness of the bride, Bernard says, with what a careful eye she looks for the bridegroom's arrival and examines the details about him. He appears, he comes more quickly, he moves close, he is here, he surveys, he talks, and not one of these subtle elements gets away from the steadiness or the readiness of the vigilant bride. . . . And when he at long last halted and hid himself behind the lattice, she still perceived his nearness and was intensely mindful that he was looking through the windows and

---

72. See Antoine de Sainte-Exupery, *The Little Prince*, trans. Katherine Woods (New York: Harcourt, Brace, & World, Inc., 1971), 80–84.

cross sections. Then as a reward for her extraordinary dedication and sacred enthusiasm, she listens to his words.[73]

The bridegroom is keenly interested in the bride and her inner life, peering at her through the lattice work, looking into her soul as it were. The bride has become sensitive to his loving gaze and approach. We too can learn to be more sensitive in prayer to the Lord's loving gaze and advance toward us, more aware of his presence and action in our lives and in our developing friendship and conversation.

Since the Lord approaches us on a human level to cultivate our friendship, we can expect our friendship with him to evolve in a very human way. Let us examine the patterns of how human friendship develops in order to better understand the process. As two people get to know each other, they begin to communicate on a superficial level, speaking about things like the weather, their favorite sports teams or hobbies, or basic facts about their families or jobs. These things are safe to talk about as they are not hugely revealing; they require no vulnerability. Similarly, some of us might feel safer remaining on the surface when in prayer without getting to matters of the heart. As we begin to move deeper into conversation, both with other people and with God, we are enabled to reveal ourselves especially when the listener is encouraging and not judgmental. The lay evangelist Matthew Kelly describes some of these deeper levels of communication that can make or break a relationship.[74] A person now ventures into sharing opinions with the other person. They may agree, which is easy, or disagree, which tests their relationship. When people disagree, the best approach is to try to understand and respect the other person's opinion, without trying to impose one's own. Disagreement can certainly introduce tension into the relationship, but also lead to growth in mutual esteem and understanding. Jesus, desiring to hear their opinions, frequently asks his disciples, "What do you think?" (Mt 21:28). In our developing friendship with Jesus, we could

---

73. See Saint Bernard of Clairvaux, *On the Song of Songs*, vol. III, sermon 57, trans. Kilian Walsh, O.C.S.O., and Irene M. Edmonds (Kalamazoo, MI: Cistercian Publications, 1979), 95–96.

74. See Matthew Kelly, *Seven Levels of Intimacy* (New York: Beacon Publishing, 2005), 151–172.

imagine him probing our ideas about life, understanding how we arrived at them through our education and experience, and respecting us, even while challenging us to see his point of view.

We must wade into even deeper waters of mutual self-revelation if friendship with Jesus is to develop. Kelly speaks of the importance of communicating hopes and dreams for one's life.[75] This may include one's goals in life and what one hopes to accomplish in the way of work, relationships, and future endeavors. Some of these dreams may reveal the depths of the person's identity, helping the other to understand what motivates the person.

In the Spiritual Exercises, Saint Ignatius has us contemplate Jesus' sending forth the seventy-two disciples. After they return from their mission, he tells them, "I came to bring fire to the earth, and how I wish it were already kindled!" (Lk 12:49). Through their apostolic mission, the disciples come to desire this same kindling of the fire of the Spirit. When the Holy Spirit comes upon them at Pentecost, they participate in the Lord's saving work and fulfill their hearts' desire.

Revealing one's motivations and goals also gives a friend the ability to help one achieve them. When we reveal our hopes, dreams, and legitimate needs to God, we may notice that, desiring the same for us, he wants to fulfill them. In some cases, he might think we've aimed too low and want to give us something infinitely better. We may also discover Jesus' desire for our self-gift to him, for our love poured into our efforts to help him bring about his kingdom. This dynamic is evident in the Song of Songs, as the bridegroom calls the bride to arise and come away with him in his desire for her companionship and her sharing in his mission.

Saint Ignatius encourages us to speak with Jesus during prayer "as one friend speaks to another" (SpEx 54). Friendship reaches deeper levels as two persons communicate their feelings to one another.[76] Feelings reveal not only our passion, but also our brokenness as human beings. It takes a trusted friend, one who will offer a compassionate listening ear, to help us be vulnerable concerning our emotions. Jesus certainly wants to be that listening friend as we express to him our true feelings, even the ones we think are inappropriate or negative. It is important for us to experience his deep listening and his

---

75. Ibid., 173–185.
76. Ibid., 186–202.

response of deep compassion. Saint Augustine experienced such compassion in prayer that he sensed the Lord placing his ear upon Augustine's heart, listening profoundly to his pain. This is something of a reversal of John resting his head on Jesus' chest at the Last Supper; it shows the reciprocal compassion that can exist in our relationship with the Lord. Just as Jesus has heartfelt empathy with us, we should have genuine empathy with Jesus in his feelings, which are so truly human.

Any friendship will have to face each person's failures and defects. Each person will have to learn to acknowledge and take responsibility for his own sins and mistakes, which are sometimes glaring. A friend will offer understanding and compassion, and, if necessary, forgiveness for offenses or omissions. In the first week of the Exercises we saw that as we approach our friend Jesus, he knows our sins and reveals them to us. As with any true friend, Jesus wants us to acknowledge what we've done wrong so he can offer understanding, compassion, and forgiveness. Before we've told him about our sins, he loves us nevertheless. As we express our sins to Jesus, we understand his limitless compassion. Our friendship with Jesus becomes closer as we discover we are loved even with our faults and defects.

The bride is also aware that she is loved by her bridegroom peering through the lattice work, which symbolizes his gaze at her interior soul with all-knowing eyes and compassionate heart. In this way he leads her to the knowledge that she is intensely loved. As we open our hearts to the Lord in prayer, we experience this genuine love that penetrates the inner depths of our hearts. We need to experience this love of God if we are ever to love as Christ loves.

The Lord loves us immensely, but his love is difficult for us to accept. We have not always received unconditional love from human beings and might not fully trust others to love us. As a result, we might resist Jesus' overtures toward greater intimacy with us, fearing rejection if we reveal ourselves. The temptation is to put up walls in our hearts in order to be safe rather than rejected, abandoned, or discovered to be deficient and damaged. But Jesus knows us completely and he loves us even though we are sinners, even to the point of dying for us on the cross (see Rom 5:7).

We can trust that even though we are sinners, the Lord passionately loves us and will never abandon us. Though others have mistreated the bride in the past, she understands that she is thoroughly known and completely loved as the bridegroom approaches and peers into her inner being. She is transparent and vulnerable in opening her heart to his love and is prepared to love him completely in return.

We still must face further obstacles to the deep, mutual self-revelation that brings about greater intimacy in interpersonal friendship. Karen Fischer and Thomas Hart, in their book *Promises to Keep*, explain four such obstacles that could apply to our relationship with Jesus.[77]

First, when I open my heart I make myself vulnerable, and what I say can be misunderstood, used against me, or dismissed as ridiculous, bad, or boring. Once the truth is revealed, I cannot take it back. But Jesus will never use my words against me or dismiss anything I say, for he is understanding and compassionate.

Second, I fear being shattered if I lose what I love. I may feel more secure not loving anyone or anything too much because losing that love may feel like total ruin. Anyone who as a child lost a parent through death or divorce knows this desolation. Persons who form a close bond of love and are rejected later in life feel the devastation. If that happens we might vow consciously or unconsciously to never let ourselves get that close again. But Jesus promises, "I am with you always" (Mt 28:20). He will never abandon us. The Lord tells us that even if a mother could forget her child, he could never forget or abandon us (see Is 49:15).

Third, if I have never experienced intimacy, I simply may not know how to get close to another. Some people desire closeness with others, but don't know how to proceed. Others are so deeply hurt by parental rejection that they move through life with a sort of distant numbness without aspiring to intimacy. Jesus is already close to us, closer than we are to our very selves, and he wants us to live genuinely in him as he already lives in us (see Jn 15:4). Though we might not know how to seek intimacy with the Lord, the Spirit intercedes for us with inestimable groaning (see Rom 8:26).

Fourth, I may fear that if I get too close in a relationship, I will be taken over by another, losing myself. I will no longer know my own identity or have a life of my own. If I express love to another, he or she will possess me, place demands upon me, and take away my freedom. But Jesus respects our

---

77. See Karen R. Fischer and Thomas N. Hart, *Promises to Keep: Developing the Skills of Marriage* (Mahwah: Paulist Press, 1991), 14–16.

freedom and will never force our will. He will only draw close if we allow him. He will always allow us to maintain and develop our unique personality, character, and interests—to be our authentic selves. Jesus will even invite us beyond ourselves to transcend ourselves in freedom.

We might also shy away from deeper intimacy and friendship with the Lord because we are afraid of what he might demand of us. In the Spiritual Exercises, Saint Ignatius helps us to overcome our fearfulness by having us contemplate many of our Lord's mysteries involving Saint Peter. When Peter and the apostles made the miraculous catch of fish, Jesus drew close to Peter who said to him, "Go away from me, Lord," (Lk 5:8); Peter feared what Jesus might ask of him. Jesus told Peter, "Do not be afraid; from now on you will be catching people" (Lk 5:10), helping Peter to overcome his misgivings and to follow Jesus. When Jesus gave Peter his new name and called him to be the rock, Jesus explained it would entail following him in his suffering and death. Peter tried to dissuade Jesus. At the end of John's Gospel, Jesus offers Peter the opportunity to make a three-fold declaration of love in reparation for his three-fold denial. Again we see Peter's fear of what Jesus wants. The first two times Jesus asks Peter if he loves him, Jesus uses the Greek word *agape*, which means sacrificial love—the same love Jesus showed to Peter in dying for him on the cross. Peter replies, "Yes, Lord; you know that I love you" (Jn 21:15), using the word *philia*, which means the love of friendship, admiration, and loyalty to another. Peter knew he was not up to the degree of love and self-sacrifice Jesus was asking. The third time, Jesus meets Peter on his own level, and he asks Peter if he loves him as a friend, using the word *philia*. Peter again says yes. Jesus accepts the type of love Peter can currently offer as a friend, knowing that this *philia* will blossom into *agape* when Peter will later offer his life in service of Jesus.

We have now seen how contemplating the mysteries of the life of Christ in the Spiritual Exercises foster friendship with Jesus; we discover not only who we are, but also who we are capable of becoming. The Lord calls us as his disciples first to friendship and only then to mission. Similarly, the bride-groom first calls his beloved bride "friend" and only then invites her to "come away" in mission. He sees into her inmost being and her potential for love, awakening her desire to offer herself to go forth with him. The Lord sees deeply into our hearts and invites us into his friendship, enabling us to go forth to extend his love more easily to all humanity.

Questions for Reflection and Discussion

1. How do you relate to Jesus as a servant and as a friend?

2. How has the Lord been gradual and patient with you in developing your friendship?

3. At what depths of yourself, from the superficial to the more profound levels, are you comfortable communicating with the Lord?

4. Read the paragraph about vulnerability and acceptance (p. 115), in relation to Jesus' great love for us (see Rom 5:7). Do you experience any resistance to opening your heart to the Lord and being known more deeply?

5. What do your human friendships teach you about friendship with Jesus? What does your friendship with Jesus teach you about human friendships?

6. What do you enjoy most about friendship with Jesus? What is most challenging about it?

7. What persons in your life have taught you by their example and friendship? What can you learn from that experience?

Prayer Exercises

1. Ponder the paragraph about vulnerability and acceptance in relation to Jesus' great love for us (see Rom 5:7). Pray with the Song of Songs 2:8–9, and imagine Jesus peering into your soul as a friend. Ask for the grace to open and reveal yourself more transparently to him.

2. Ponder the story of *The Little Prince* (pp. 113–114). Pray with Luke 4:16–30, and ask for the grace to know the patience and gradual nature of Jesus' revelation to you.

3. Pray with John 14:1–14, and ask for the grace to better know Jesus as a friend so that you may love him more.

4. Review the levels of human intimacy and self-disclosure (p. 115). Pray with John 15:12–17, and ask for the grace to deepen your friendship with Jesus.

5. Pray with John 11:1–16, and ask for the grace to understand Jesus' desire for friendship.

6. Pray with Sirach 6:5–17, and ask for the grace to be a faithful friend to Jesus and to experience his friendship as a life-saving remedy.

7. Make a repetition on any points of the above Scripture passages where you felt a greater movement of spirit.

CHAPTER 11

Arise and Come

[B] My beloved speaks and says to me:
[G] "Arise, my love, my fair one,
    and come away;
for now the winter is past,
    the rain is over and gone.
The flowers appear on the earth;
    the time of singing has come,
and the voice of the turtledove
    is heard in our land.
The fig tree puts forth its figs,
    and the vines are in blossom;
    they give forth fragrance.
Arise, my love, my fair one,
    and come away." (Song 2:10–13)

I will ask for the grace I desire. Here it will be to ask of our Lord the grace not to be deaf to His call, but prompt and diligent to accomplish His most holy will. (SpEx 91)

It is my will to conquer the whole world and all my enemies, and thus to enter into the glory of my Father. Therefore, whoever wishes to join me in this enterprise must be willing to labor with me, that by following me in suffering, he may follow me in glory. (SpEx 95)

123

The bridegroom now issues his invitation to the bride to arise and come away. With this compelling and challenging invitation, he summons her to greater life and fruitfulness.

An example of such a fruitful life is found in Saint Elizabeth Ann Bayley Seton. She was born in New York City in 1774, just before the Declaration of Independence was signed. Her mother died when she was only three years old, and her father remarried. Elizabeth grew to be a resilient and resourceful woman. Part of New York high society, at the age of twenty Elizabeth married William Seton, also a blue blood. In time the couple had five children. As a young wife and mother, Elizabeth felt a deep spiritual restlessness, which developed into deep sadness when William developed tuberculosis. He moved his family to Italy, hoping that the climate would help his condition, but his illness proved incurable and eventually fatal. After William's death, the family moved back to the United States with the assistance of a benevolent Italian Catholic family. The generosity of that Italian family led the young widow to explore the Catholic Church, and two years later she was received into the Catholic Church. Elizabeth's relatives and friends were stunned and practically disowned her.

In order to provide for her five children, Elizabeth was forced to take a job teaching. When the children grew old enough to be on their own, Elizabeth became a religious sister dedicated to educating the young, establishing the American branch of the Sisters of Charity. Working tirelessly with her fellow sisters, she forged the great Catholic school system in America. Elizabeth once told a friend that she would like to step back from the world's havoc and lead a simple life of prayer, but that God had other plans for her and that God's will must come first.

Elizabeth Ann Seton endured the winter of trials and sufferings as a young mother, and when her children were raised, felt called by her beloved Lord to come and bear greater fruit. Her natural desire to retire and live a simple life may have indicated some resistance to the Lord's invitation, but she overcame it by her commitment and diligence. Similarly, the bride in the Song of Songs has endured a difficult season of trials, as her bridegroom exclaims, "Winter is past, the rain is over and gone." She seems relaxed and even lethargic, perhaps symbolic of the Christian soul still enthralled in the sleep of deep contemplation. In this state, the bride might be tempted, like Elizabeth Ann Seton, to a quiet life of retirement. But the bridegroom calls her to "arise and come away," and she seems ready to respond to his invitation.

He invites her to come and bear fruit, symbolized by "the fig tree" which "puts forth its figs" and "the vines" which "are in blossom," giving forth their fragrance. Like Elizabeth Ann Seton, the bride must put aside her own desire for ease and comfort and respond generously to the Lord's call to labor and toil for his kingdom.

We all look to dedicate our lives to a cause, to give our lives for a mission, since it is in our very nature to desire to fulfill our purpose in life. In the Spiritual Exercises, Saint Ignatius invites us to consider a cause worth fighting for in his meditation titled "The Call of the King." He first has us consider the call of an earthly king who has a great cause. For Saint Ignatius this inspirational cause might have been the memory of the Crusades or the *Reconquista* of Spain. These battles had inspired many of Saint Ignatius' own people to undertake fierce adventures and make heroic sacrifices. Saint Ignatius has us imagine a noble king who offers a compelling speech: "It is my will to conquer all the lands of the infidel. Therefore, whoever wishes to join with me in this enterprise must be content with the same food, drink, clothing, etc., as mine. So, too, he must work with me by day, and watch with me by night, etc., that as he has had a share in the toil with me, afterwards, he may share in the victory with me" (SpEx 91). For his noble cause the king invites others to share a way of life as a companion in his mission.

As we attempt this meditation, we might have trouble envisioning a leader in our own day worthy of being followed. It might be even more difficult to imagine a just and noble king, since the office of king is so rare in today's world. To overcome this obstacle, we could admire the holy King Saint Louis IX of France, an inspiring leader who was close to his people. His forty-four-year reign is still considered the golden age of France.

Saint Louis led an exemplary life of virtue, not seeking to satisfy himself but bringing God's goodness to his people. He spent long hours in prayer, fasting, and penance without his subjects knowing of it. The administration of justice was dear to Louis' heart. Daily he would attend Mass and go outside under the Oak of Vincennes to hear the complaints and cases of the common people. He established a court of justice consisting of competent experts and judicial commissions to render decisions quickly and fairly. Because Louis felt God was always present to him, he always desired to be available to his people. King Louis was renowned for his charity, sometimes inviting to dinner homeless people whose filth and stench disgusted even the soldiers of his guard. Daily he fed over 100 poor people, walking through the streets of his cities distributing alms by the handful. He would enter hospitals and homes for the dying and nurse the worst cases himself, even embracing those suffering from leprosy. As a patron of architecture, Saint Louis commissioned the lovely Sainte Chappelle. Under his patronage the College of the Sorbonne was founded and became renowned for its theological faculty. Saint Ignatius has in mind an earthly king of the caliber of King Louis as one who might motivate us to follow his call and mission.

Considering the call of an earthly king prepares us to contemplate an infinitely greater and more noble call, the call of Christ our Lord and eternal King. Christ summons us to his more crucial mission: "It is my will to conquer the whole world and all my enemies, and thus to enter into the glory of my Father. Therefore, whoever wishes to join me in this enterprise must be willing to labor with me, that by following me in suffering, he may follow me in glory" (SpEx 95). Jesus desires to conquer the whole world by his love.

In the preceding verse of the Song of Songs (2:4), the bride states that the bridegroom's "intention toward me was love," which is sometimes translated as his "banner over me is love." The Hebrew term *degel* is more accurately translated "army," and the phrase is better rendered "his army against me is love."[78] The bride is overwhelmed, even wounded, by the Bridegroom's love. As we now ponder Christ our eternal King and Bridegroom, we understand that he does not conquer by physical force but only through the power of his love. Christ has conquered us by his love and invites us to labor at his side in his mission to conquer the world with the same love. We do not merely labor for Christ, we labor with him in love, and we are invited to share in the sufferings of Christ so as to share in his victory.

Saint Ignatius wants to show us that Christ not only leads us into battle but also fights alongside us. In the history of combat we find two different ways of commanding soldiers. The first method was used by Napoleon, who would oversee the battle from a high place, encircle himself with envoys, and command his troops by sending messengers to the brigade captains. The second method was exemplified by Alexander the Great, who would command from the very center of the encampment. In battle Alexander would climb his horse and head the charge in the forefront of his troops, putting his own life on the line along with his soldiers. Alexander aroused not only admiration

---

78. See Arminjon, *The Cantata of Love*, 152.

and reverence among his followers, but also love. He was not simply the leader of his men but also their brother in arms. Like Alexander, Jesus is the one who has "lived among us," which in Greek means literally "pitched his tent among us" (see Jn 1:14). Jesus calls us to fight alongside him in his mission. Saint Ignatius shows us how Christ inspires in us not only awe and respect, but also love.

Saint Ignatius illustrates how great leaders with magnetic appeal can inspire us to do things we might not think we can do. It is the charismatic person, not a set of ideas, who motivates us. Our Christian faith is more than a series of propositions to believe; it is a person whom we trust: Jesus Christ. Jesus speaks to our hearts with his truth and love and moves us to action. His word is accomplished in our lives if we are willing to listen and follow.

When Jesus called his apostles they immediately followed him. In the Song of Songs, the Bridegroom calls to his bride, "Arise . . . and come away," and by his power she does so. Similarly, when Jesus calls us, he gives us the power to follow him and to do far greater things than we could imagine. Jesus gives us the power of his Holy Spirit dwelling within us to bring about his will. We must accept his invitation, but even that hinges on God's grace. Saint Augustine asks the Lord to inspire him in his thoughts about God, to teach him words by which to invoke God, and to give him the works with which to please God.[79] He knows he is weak and has to rely on Christ to have any good thought or deed, or he might fail to respond to the Lord's promptings.

Resistance

When Jesus calls us to the great adventure of advancing his kingdom, we can resist in countless ways. We see this in the parable about a man who gave a great banquet and invited many. When the banquet was ready, he sent his servant to call those who had been invited. "But they all alike began to make excuses. The first said to him, 'I have bought a piece of land, and I must go out and see it; please accept my regrets.' Another said, 'I have bought

---

79. See Saint Augustine, Meditations, Ch. 2 cited by Juan Gonzales Arintero, O.P., *The Song of Songs, a Mystical Interpretation*, trans. James Valander and Jose L. Morales (Cincinnati: Monastery of the Holy Name, 1974), 255.

five yoke of oxen, and I am going to try them out; please accept my regrets.' Another said, 'I have just been married, and therefore I cannot come'" (Lk 14:18–20).

We can easily come up with excuses when Jesus calls us to follow him, just as those three people in the parable did. We might protest that such a call is impractical. We have many attachments and possessions we'd rather not leave behind. Or we might see ourselves inferior, not up to the task; we aren't as smart, as well-spoken, or as brave as others. Jeremiah complained that he was too young and inexperienced to speak God's word (see Jer 1:6). Isaiah protested that he was a man of unclean lips living among an unclean people (see Is 6:5). But the Lord purified and equipped them both to be his prophets. We may also feel insufficient and bury our gifts in the ground out of fear, like the unprofitable servant in Jesus' parable of the talents. But Jesus will help us to be like the servants who made a profit from the talents God gave them (see Mt 25:14–30). Jesus exhorts us to let our light shine so that others will see the good we do in order to glorify God (see Mt 5:16).

Saint Juan Diego is a good example of how God overcomes our fears and reluctance to serve him. Our Lady of Guadalupe helped Juan Diego to build the church God wanted in Tepayec to convert the Aztecs to Christianity. She appeared to the poor and humble Juan and told him to go to the bishop with her message about the church. After his first attempt failed to convince the bishop, Juan was frustrated. Mary told him to go back and try again. But because he wanted to help his seriously ill uncle, he tried to avoid her. She appeared on his path once more, however, and informed him that his uncle was cured. When Juan protested that he couldn't persuade the bishop and urged Mary to send a person better known and respected, she replied: "Listen to me, my youngest and dearest son; know for sure that I do not lack servants and messengers to whom I can give the task of carrying out my words, who will carry out my will. But it is very necessary that you plead my cause and, with your help and through your mediation, that my will be fulfilled."[80] In her message to Juan Diego, Mary told him how important he was to this cause, one of love. Even the term she uses for him—youngest of my sons—indicates her love, for it is a translation of an

---

80. Franciscan Friars of the Immaculate, *A Handbook on Guadalupe* (Fall River: Academy of the Immaculate, 1997), 196.

Aztec idiom: favorite son. Inspired and enabled by her love, Juan accomplished the daunting task of convincing the bishop. Juan shows us that even the humblest person with simple faith has an important role in advancing God's kingdom.

Aware of the human tendency to make excuses, Saint Ignatius points us in the opposite direction. In the Call of the King meditation, he has us "ask of our Lord the grace not to be deaf to His call, but prompt and diligent to accomplish His most Holy Will" (SpEx 91). Saint Matthew, for example, was sitting at the tax office when Jesus approached him and said, "Follow me." Matthew "got up, left everything, and followed him" (Lk 5:27–28). This kind of instant response and radical detachment was possible only by God's grace, in cooperation with a willing human spirit. As a typical tax collector, Matthew was probably attached to wealth. His own people would have despised him for collaborating with the hated Romans and, they assumed, for practicing extortion. Matthew may have even feared rejection from Jesus' own inner circle of apostles. The Lord's love and acceptance of Matthew must have given him solace and courage to effectively respond to Jesus' invitation.

A beautiful painting by the great baroque artist Caravaggio, "The Calling of Saint Matthew," illustrates this dramatic scene. The painting shows us how Christ's call overcomes our fears, making us a new creation. The rich and cosmopolitan Matthew is sitting at a table with his partners as they count money. Across the room Jesus stands facing them, holding out his right hand toward Matthew, whose face reflects his utter astonishment. Caravaggio's masterpiece harkens back to Michelangelo's "Creation of Adam" in the way Jesus reaches out to Matthew. Jesus' posture is a replica of God the Creator reaching out to Adam. As Caravaggio's painting tells us, when Christ beckons us to follow him unreservedly, we become a new creation, filled with new life, energy, and purpose.

The bride in the Song of Songs experiences the same vitality in hearing her bridegroom call her: "Arise, my love, my fair one, and come away." Though she is lethargic in her sleep and reluctant to follow, her bridegroom's words fill her with life; she arises to follow him. She is not deaf to his call but responds wholeheartedly in love. The bride now becomes a new creation raised up in union with her bridegroom. Correspondingly, in the Call of the King meditation, God gives the grace to each one of us to respond immediately and wholeheartedly to his call (see SpEx 91).

Saint Ignatius closes his meditation with a prayer of self-offering that he invites us to say in response to the call of the eternal King. He has us consider that anyone of good judgment will offer oneself entirely to such a mission. Even more, Saint Ignatius suggests that any person who wants to devote oneself so as to excel in serving his or her King will not only offer oneself entirely but also act against one's own selfishness, comfort, and worldly love. Such a person will make a greater offering and say:

> Eternal Lord of all things . . . it is my earnest desire and my deliberate choice, provided only it is for Thy greater service and praise, to imitate Thee in bearing all wrongs and all abuse and all poverty, both actual and spiritual, should Thy most holy majesty desire to choose and admit me to such a state and way of life. (SpEx 98)

Such a radical self-offering reminds us that to be a Christian fundamentally means to take up one's cross and follow Christ by working for his kingdom, suffering, and being raised up. The bride of the Song of Songs is similarly invited to come away and share the bridegroom's life, to deny her own sensuality and desire for comfort, and to follow him. Later in the Song of Songs, she will willingly suffer injuries and abuse for the sake of her beloved.

When we desire to undertake a great work in service of our Lord, it will inevitably involve suffering. While we don't look for suffering, we realize that in following Jesus we are bound to experience persecution and poverty. Saint Ignatius invites us to ponder our willingness to experience actual poverty, which should not be considered lightly, especially if we have to provide for a family. We might consider whether we are willing and able to earn less or live in less comfortable circumstances in order to follow the Lord's call.

Saint Ignatius shows us how to make our self-offering to Christ in a commitment to take up our cross and follow him in labor. Such a radical self-offering is seen in the life of Saint Damien of Moloka'i.

In the 1850s, Hawaiian authorities established a colony on the remote island of Moloka'i for those suffering from leprosy (now known as Hansen's disease). Victims were exiled there in hopes of containing the disease, which was poorly understood. Lepers would be snatched by force from their families and sent to this island to perish. Moved by their terrible predicament, a young Belgian priest, Damien De Veuster, asked to minister to them. The bishop had arranged for priests to visit for three months at a time, but when

Father Damien saw the people's misery, he committed to stay and work on Moloka'i.

Damien had grown up on a farm and knew how to use his hands to serve and animate the community. He begged for lumber and nails to construct hundreds of small homes to supplant the dismal shacks on Moloka'i. The pipes he laid drew fresh water from inland springs. He buried the dead with dignity in hand-built coffins, placing them to rest in a cemetery instead of the shallow mass graves previously used. Damien taught residents to farm in plots of land and raise livestock. He constructed health clinics and chapels, teaching the people to sing and play music in a choir and orchestra. Barehanded he cared for the sores of their leprosy.

Damien restored enthusiasm and hope to the sick throngs who poured into the colony. For eleven years he labored vigorously, transforming the settlement from one of misery to one of joy. Then, one Sunday morning in June during his twelfth year in Moloka'i, Father Damien approached the pulpit to read the Gospel. He looked out over his crowded assembly in the Church they had built together and began his homily with these words: "We lepers." The people were stunned. Damien related that he too had been infected with the terrible malady. The people immediately embraced him and took him to their hearts as one of their own. He continued toiling for four more years as his body decayed, until the Lord granted him eternal rest.[81]

Father Damien offered his life as a holocaust for Christ by laboring for his kingdom among the sick. He was not deaf to the Lord's call. As a Christian Damien could not remain a mere spectator; he had to involve himself as a participant in carrying his cross for Christ. As in the Call of the King meditation, Damien desired to be with Christ by sharing his lifestyle and embracing outcasts. When we join with Christ and his mission, the Lord gives us the inspiration and we labor with the perspiration—the sweat, blood, and tears it will entail to follow him. In giving us the Call of the King exercise, Saint Ignatius helps us to overcome our self-indulgent tendencies, roll up our sleeves, and get to work in serving Christ. Like the bride of the Song of Songs, we are called to "arise and come away" with Christ, bearing fruit in our work for his kingdom.

---

81. See Jan de Volder, *The Spirit of Father Damien* (San Francisco: Saint Ignatius Press, 2010), 108–109.

Questions for Reflection and Discussion

1. Are you drawn more to the romantic call of Christ the Bridegroom in the Song of Songs (2:10–13) or to Saint Ignatius' more militaristic Call of the King (SpEx 91–97)? How can you harmonize the two?

2. Where do you feel called to serve more generously? Like Elizabeth Ann Seton, is there anything you feel reluctant to do as a Christian but sense the Lord calling you to do anyway?

3. Do you feel enthusiastic about following the Lord in labor and toil, sharing in his sufferings in order to share in his glory? Why or why not?

4. How has Christ's call made you a new creation? How does Carravaggio's painting of the Calling of Saint Matthew speak to you in this regard?

5. What are your fears, resistances, and excuses about following the call of Christ?

6. How do you feel you are living your Christian calling each day?

Prayer Exercises

1. Pray with Song of Songs 2:10–13, along with Psalm 45, and ask for the grace to experience joy at the Lord's call to you personally.

2. Imagine an earthly king like Saint Louis of France (pp. 125–126), his call to labor in a great cause, and how you might respond. Then imagine Christ the King and his call to conquer the world with his love (p. 126). Ask for the grace not to be deaf to his call, but to respond with the prayer of self-offering (p. 130).

3. Reflect on the battle strategy of Alexander the Great (p. 127). Pray with Matthew 16:21–28, and ask for the grace to be willing to suffer with Christ in order to share in his glory.

4. Reflect on the story of Juan Diego (p. 128). Pray with Luke 14:15–24, and ask for the grace to overcome fears and excuses in following the Lord's call.

5. Pray with Luke 14:25–33, and ask for the grace to respond to Jesus' call as a true and wholehearted follower.

6. Ponder the story of Saint Damien and his service to the sick exiled on Moloka'i (pp. 130–131). Consider the ways you have been able to serve the Lord by his grace. Reflect on Matthew 25:14–30, and ask for the grace to rejoice in his reward and overcome sloth.

7. Make a repetition on any of the above contemplations, returning to the places of greater interior movement.

CHAPTER 12

Surely Chosen

[G] The flowers appear on the earth;
    the time of singing has come,
and the voice of the turtledove
    is heard in our land.
The fig tree puts forth its figs,
    and the vines are in blossom;
    they give forth fragrance.
Arise, my love, my fair one,
    and come away. (Song 2:12–13)

[There are] three times when a good and correct choice of a way of life may
be made.

First Time. When God our Lord so moves and attracts the will that a
devout soul without hesitation, or the possibility of hesitation, follows what
has been manifested to it. . . .

Second Time. When much light and understanding are derived through
experience of desolations and consolations and discernment of diverse
spirits.

Third Time. This is a time of tranquility . . . when the soul is not agitated
by different spirits, and has free and peaceful use of its natural powers. (SpEx
175–177)

The call of the bride leads us to consider the Lord's desire with respect to our vocation to a state in life and many other important life choices. The question often arises in discernment: "How do I know I'm doing God's will?" Describing his vocational discernment as a young adult, the Benedictine priest Phillip Bennett speaks to this question. On a retreat he met a monk named Benedict who patiently listened to his desire to find God's plan for his life. After Bennett poured out his confused questioning, Brother Benedict suggested to him that his image of God's will resembled a tape recorder full of instructions to be followed. It was like the tape recorder was playing in the next room and Bennett could not hear all the words in order to accurately know God's will. Then Benedict suggested an alternative image. He asked Bennett to consider God sitting in the chair right next to him, wanting to be with Bennett, delighting in his presence. He instructed Bennett not to have an agenda or to try to hear that tape recorder, but instead to let God love him, then to see what would transpire. Eventually, Bennett did experience that divine Presence embracing and sustaining him, loving him in wordless peace. This presence felt like a power both within and without him—a great inexhaustible strength, yet one intimately close and gentle. In pursuit, the Lord desired to first pull Bennett nearer in cherished love before engaging him in the choice of his vocation.[82]

How many of us have an image of God's will like the one Bennett had before he met Brother Benedict? We think God has elaborate and precise instructions for us to follow. We imagine God as the master architect with a blueprint for our lives, and that we are called to follow God's rigid specifications. The plan easily becomes a burden, one that rewards me if I get it right or blames me if I get it wrong. So we look for God to reveal it to us in an instant with great clarity, to speak to us with a loud voice from heaven. Some people claim that God speaks to them, and he certainly may in some way, either audibly or inaudibly. Still, desiring that kind of clarity might be dangerous since we can easily mistake our own voice for God's. How often people report that they are certain God wants this or that, only to discover that God has changed his mind.

The Lord does have plans for us and he wants our free cooperation in choosing them. God is not locked into a fixed way of doing things or a fixed

---

82. See Phillip Bennett, *Let Yourself Be Loved* (Mahwah: Paulist Press, 1997), 1–2.

plan for each of his children. The psalmist tells us that God is supremely free to do as he chooses; "he does whatever he pleases" (Ps 115:3). God can adapt to our unique needs and situations. Saint Paul reminds us that God often manifests his will through any measure of desire that he places in our hearts (see Phil 2:13). Our job is to discover our deepest desire. We can only do so, however, after we first become aware that the Lord loves us freely, embraces us, and wants us to be in the shadow of his presence. Once we know that God holds us dear and we are at peace in his embrace, we will experience moments of clarity—some stronger than others—about what he has in store for us.

God reassures us through Jeremiah, "For surely I know the plans I have for you, says the LORD, plans for your welfare and not for harm, to give you a future with hope. Then when you call upon me and come and pray to me, I will hear you. When you search for me, you will find me; if you seek me with all your heart" (Jer 29:11–13). Our foundation should be this trust that God does have our welfare in mind, and he has plans for our lives. Once we are seeking God, secure in his love, we can receive his guidance through his loving Providence.

In the Song of Songs, the bride rests securely in her bridegroom's loving embrace as he calls her to arise and come away with him. Any fears about where he might be taking her simply dissolve because he will be leading and accompanying her. Aware of his loving presence, she can trust in his plans for her good.

Since God's plans are for our good and not evil, discernment must be about matters of fundamental goodness; we cannot discern whether or not to do evil (see SpEx 170). For example, we would not discern whether or not to rob a bank in order to provide for our family. God's law and commandments are clear on these matters. In such situations we can only pray that we might listen to our upright consciences and have the courage to do what is right. Saint Ignatius even counsels that to be ready to make choices for Christ, we should be willing to die for our faith rather than commit sin (SpEx 165–168, *Three Kinds of Humility*).

Saint Thomas More gave heroic witness to this kind of commitment to Christ. He was the chancellor to King Henry VIII in the sixteenth century. When the king divorced his wife to marry Anne Boleyn, he wanted Thomas More to sign a document attesting that the new marriage was valid. Facing tremendous pressure from the king and his colleagues, More resolved to be faithful to the teachings of the Church even if that meant death. Refusing to sign, he died with integrity, a sign of contradiction to the world and its values. As a martyr for the faith, he strengthened other Christians in their witness to Christ. Thomas More shows us what Saint Ignatius insists on—that we may never make up our mind to commit a sin.

Apart from matters of sin, our calls, though perhaps less dramatic, are important matters for discernment. We may make choices about whether to volunteer for a Church project or to run for a local government office. Other choices might entail whether to go back to school for further education or stay in our current career. We might pray about whether to take a job with a higher salary to better provide for our families. Our decision might entail moving to another city or state with the upheaval that would involve, perhaps making it more difficult to raise children in a good environment. We consider these factors in discerning what is best in God's eyes for ourselves and others. Some decisions will require more time for deliberation than others, depending on how weighty they are. A discernment regarding one's state in life is a major decision that would require more time. When discerning whether to remain single, marry, or pursue religious life or the priesthood, one should be prepared to invest time and energy to discern well. For those who have already chosen a state in life or have made other important long-term decisions, Saint Ignatius recommends praying about reforming oneself in one's vocation (SpEx 189).

Saint Ignatius wants us to have a high degree of indifference even toward good options in order to be free to choose what will best glorify God and contribute to our own good. If we cling to what we think is best and right, we may not be open to what God has in store for us. Then we might miss God's attempts to show us his desires.

My first assignment as a priest was in Saint Andrew's parish in New Jersey. After a few years, I was hitting my stride, involved in all kinds of ministries to prisoners, the handicapped, the poor, and others. Then came the news: our provincial rector wanted me to go to Boston to become novice master and eventually rector of the seminary. "Are you interested?" he asked. Novitiate is the most important year of intensive spiritual formation for shaping future priests in our congregation. Facing such a weighty choice, I thought it over for a while before deciding that I did not want this change in assignment. I wrote a five-page protest letter (which I never sent) listing the reasons why I was hardly qualified for the position. I had little experience as a priest; I was a terrible teacher; I saw myself as having a weak intellect and too many character flaws. Besides, as I pointed out, I was very happy at Saint Andrew's. I loved the people and the ministry, and couldn't see myself leaving to return to that dreaded place I had spent seven years waiting to escape. I was very closed to the idea, and writing the letter helped me realize my obstinacy. Eventually the official request came from the provincial council. I trembled as I took the request to prayer, only able to think of Mary and her "fiat." By God's grace, all my fears were lifted and my objections cleared away. We may not be able to ignore what we feel attached to. But we can pray for independence from the attachment and for the grace of indifference so that we can freely follow God's call.

The First Way God Calls Us

In the Spiritual Exercises, Saint Ignatius identifies three major "times" or ways in which God calls us. The first, he says, is "when God our Lord so moves and attracts the will that a devout soul without hesitation, or the possibility of hesitation, follows what has been manifested to it" (SpEx 175). Saint Paul exemplifies this first way in his dramatic conversion and instant choice to follow Jesus. The previously discussed call of Saint Matthew and his immediate response to follow Jesus is another good example. The first type of calling includes God's direct, clear action and results in our own certainty beyond doubt that the call is from God. It also includes our immediate willingness, brought about by God's grace, to follow his invitation. God enlightens our minds and conditions our will to choose in true freedom to accept his invitation.

An example of this type of discernment can also be found in the life of Pope Francis. Just before his seventeenth birthday, he was walking to meet his girlfriend and other friends to honor National Students' Day. As he was walking past the Basilica of Saint Joseph, where he often went to pray, he felt inspired to enter and something amazing happened:

> I looked, it was dark, it was a morning in September, maybe 9:00 a.m., and I saw a priest walking, I didn't know him, he wasn't one of the parish clergy. And he sits down in one of the confessionals, the last confessional as you're looking down the left side at the altar. I don't quite know what happened next, I felt like someone grabbed me from inside and took me to the confessional. Obviously I told him my things, I confessed . . . but I don't know what happened.

When I finished my confession I asked the priest where he was from because I didn't know him and he told me: "I'm from Corrientes and I'm living here close by, in the priests' home. I come to celebrate Mass here now and then." He had cancer—leukemia—and died the following year.

Right there I knew I had to be a priest; I was totally certain. Instead of going out with the others, I went back home because I was overwhelmed. Afterward I carried on at school and with everything, but knowing now where I was headed.[83]

Pope Francis experienced the characteristics of the first mode of God's election. God so moved and attracted his will that he could not hesitate in following the divine call to priesthood. He was overwhelmed by God's grace in calling him and was totally certain about what he had to do. His will was completely docile in following God's call.

Similarly, a woman whom we will call Pauline describes her very clear calling to follow Christ in religious life. She had previously experienced at times what she describes as "touches" from God. In her latest prayer experience she clearly perceived the Lord's call to her:

I was alone in the kitchen of my parents' home, finishing up the supper dishes, when again the "sudden something" took hold of me. I wish I could describe it, but I cannot. I remember being so affected by it that I had to grab the sink with one hand and the stove with the other. Again tears. This time I knew the change had happened—that it was permanent and unmistakable. I could not doubt the "message" of the encounter even if I wanted to. I don't know how this knowledge was so certain; but as soon as I "recovered," I called my sister long distance to inform her, "I have a vocation." . . . The conviction of God's call to me did not go away and has remained to this moment.[84]

Pauline was later accepted into a contemplative religious community. Her experience illustrates Saint Ignatius' first mode of election. With a direct intervention, God takes hold of Pauline. She has certainty, beyond the shadow of a doubt, that God has seized her very being. She is also certain

---

83. Austen Ivereigh, *The Great Reformer, Francis and the Making of a Radical Pope* (New York: Henry Holt and Company, 2014), Chapter 1, Kindle Edition.

84. Jules J. Toner, S.J., *What Is Your Will, O God? A Casebook for Studying Discernment of God's Will* (St. Louis: The Institute of Jesuit Sources, 1995), 76.

that God is calling her to religious life. Finally, Pauline responds with a wholehearted willingness to follow the Lord's call and decides to enter religious life. Her conviction about God's calling remains with her for the rest of her life. God so moved her soul that she did not hesitate to follow what he manifested to her (see SpEx 175). Pauline's beautiful experience of God's calling reminds us of the bridegroom's invitation to the bride: "Arise, my love, my fair one, and come away."

The Second Way

The second method Saint Ignatius recommends for discerning one's call is to pay attention to the movements of spirit within. He asks us to take note of the times "when much light and understanding are derived through experience of desolations and consolations and discernment of diverse spirits" (SpEx 176). Spiritual consolation and desolation are guideposts by which to gauge our choices. The Lord moves us with deep affective attraction toward himself and toward the choice that he desires for us.

The enemy spirit may also be at work to instill desolations and sabotage God's call. As discussed in Chapter 6, these desolations often involve feelings of fear, sadness, discouragement, and the like. The enemy spirit might also propose deceptive consolations that would divert us from the true path God desires for us (see Chapter 16). It is important for us to be aware of the consolations and desolations and what they signify as we consider possible choices. A helpful practice is to discuss these movements of the heart with a spiritual director familiar with Saint Ignatius' teaching on discernment of spirits to arrive at greater clarity in finding God's will for our lives.

During my thirty-day spiritual exercises as a religious novice, I was making the "election" or choice of a state of life according to Saint Ignatius' second way. I was already two years into my seminary training and very sure of God's call to me. While contemplating the storm on the Sea of Galilee, I experienced my own storm, a huge surge of fear that I might be making the wrong choice. Before joining the seminary, I'd been involved with a Catholic lay group. Other group members had told me that I was called to join their movement as a lifetime member. I had never felt an attraction toward that particular vocation, but felt external pressure from certain members of the group. In my retreat the enemy used that episode from the past to stir up confusion and fear of making the wrong choice. I experienced a crisis of faith and despair regarding my salvation. Maybe I was running away from what God really wanted. Being a member of this movement rather than a priest seemed to me the more difficult choice. I mistakenly considered that God probably wanted me to do what I found least attractive and most difficult.

When I continued to pray with the Gospel mystery, I put myself in the place of Peter as he walked on the water. Jesus stood before me. He gave me the spiritual consolation of courage and confidence to continue my walk toward him despite these fears and doubt. When I kept my eyes fixed on Jesus, the consolation remained. The wind and the waves of spiritual desolation no longer affected me. When I took my eyes off him, though, the wind howled and the waves threatened to drown me. With my eyes diverted from Jesus, I could easily slip into spiritual desolation.

Through days of agonizing back and forth movements of spirit, with my director's help I discerned that the fear and doubts regarding my vocation were spiritual desolations stirred up by the enemy spirit. The peace and growing confidence about my call was spiritual consolation given by the Spirit of God. During spiritual desolation the enemy spirit was using fear, doubt, and despair to counsel me away from God's call (see SpEx 316). Once exposed, the spiritual desolation brought about by the enemy spirit became further evidence of my true call to follow the Lord in religious life and priesthood.

A Third Way of Discernment

Saint Ignatius recommends a third way of making a decision, which we shall call the deliberative method. It is simply the use of our human reason guided by faith. As he describes it, "One considers first for what purpose man is born, that is, for the praise of God our Lord and for the salvation of his soul. With the desire to attain this before his mind, he chooses as a means to this end a kind of life or state within the bounds of the Church that will be a help in the service of his Lord and for the salvation of his soul" (SpEx 177).

For the deliberative method, Saint Ignatius recommends listing the advantages and disadvantages of any decision and its consequences, especially with eternal life as one's primary goal. He recommends weighing the different criteria for the decision based on their relative importance. For instance, in deciding whether or not to marry a person, one might place a heavier weight upon the criterion of the future spouse's religious conviction than on his or her ability to provide a high standard of living for the family.

In this deliberative method of making a choice, supernatural prudence—a knowledge of reality that is enlightened by faith—will play an important role. Supernatural prudence will help us to know what is good and right according to revelation and universal principles such as the Ten Commandments, the Beatitudes, the theological and cardinal virtues, and our moral values and principles. We must also be in touch with reality, what is actually happening in our concrete situations. Ideals are important, but we have to be realistic about whether we can achieve them. Current experiences and memories of past experiences will play an important role in gauging our abilities and future outcomes. We will also want to place our ideas and proposals before the judicious views of friends, authorities, and associates. They may be able to direct us to other sources of information, wisdom, and proficiency. They may know our strengths, weaknesses, and potential pitfalls better than we do. Finally, we need to recognize the role God's providence may play in the future, having the foresight to estimate future events and effects. Jesus speaks of the wise man desiring to build a tower who first figures out how much it will cost and if he has enough resources to complete the project. Similarly, Jesus uses the analogy of a king who considers whether he has enough men in his army to engage a rival in battle (see Lk 14:28–32). Clearly, Jesus wants us to use our rational powers along with his gift of supernatural prudence.

Saint Ignatius demonstrated how to use the deliberative method in his discernment of the kind of poverty he and his companions would choose for their new religious institute, the Society of Jesus. They might choose a lesser form of poverty, whereby they would accept fixed revenues such as salaries or any regular stream of income. Or they could choose a more radical form of poverty without any fixed income and rely on the donations of benefactors. Saint Ignatius entered into forty days of discernment about the matter and kept a record of his feelings and thought processes in his *Spiritual Journal*.[85] He first listed eight advantages to having fixed income, such as:

- The Society will be better supported and preserved.
- They will avoid irritating others by begging.

---

85. See *The Spiritual Journal of Saint Ignatius of Loyola: February 1544 to 1545*, trans. William Young, S.J. (Woodstock : Woodstock College Press, 1958), 61-63 .

- ◉ The Society will be able to pray in a more orderly fashion with greater serenity at the proper time.

- ◉ The time that would be spent in begging alms could be spent preaching, hearing confessions, and performing other good works.

- ◉ The members of the Society will have more time for study and by this means be able to edify their neighbors.

Clearly, Saint Ignatius identified some strong reasons in favor of having a fixed income. He then listed seventeen advantages to not having any fixed income, such as:

- ◉ With a revenue the members would not be so diligent in helping the neighbor, nor so ready to go on journeys and endure adversity. Moreover, they could not so well persuade the neighbor to true poverty and self-abnegation in all things.

- ◉ The Society will more closely imitate Jesus Christ who was poor and thereby gain greater spiritual power, sharing his hardship. It will have greater spiritual strength and greater devotion by a closer resemblance to the Son of the Virgin, our Creator and Lord, who lived in such great poverty and hardship.

- ◉ By not seeking regular revenues, the members will in no way be greedy. All worldly greed will more readily be put to flight.

- ◉ If the members are united in having nothing and if they look to the poverty of Christ in the Holy Eucharist, the Society will be united to the Church in greater love.

- ◉ They would find greater facility in hoping for everything from God by renouncing all that belongs to the world.

Saint Ignatius recognized a much greater number of advantages to maintaining the more radical form of poverty, but he also placed greater weight upon many of these criteria. He ultimately decided for the deeper-seated form of poverty by rejecting a fixed income.

Saint Ignatius is also concerned that in making a decision we consider those criteria that will lead to the perfection of our soul (see SpEx 185). Perfection does not mean having no flaws but fulfilling the purpose for which God made me, according to my unique personality and character. The choices I make for the greater praise and service of God are likely to be the activities

I excel at, which fulfill my purpose in life. Saint Irenaeus affirmed that "the glory of God is a man fully alive." The more truly alive I feel in using my talents in God's service, the more it will be to God's praise and the good of my neighbor.

Continuing with discernment regarding important life decisions, Saint Ignatius proposes two practical methods that will help us maintain objectivity. First, he suggests the action of representing to myself "a man whom I have never seen or known, and whom I would like to see practice all perfection. Then I should consider what I would tell him to do and choose for the greater glory of God our Lord and the greater perfection of his soul. I will do the same, and keep the rule I propose to others" (SpEx 185). Based upon the advice I would give to a person like myself in a situation like my own, I will hold to my own counsel. By doing this I gain a more impartial perspective about a person like myself, free from my subjective biases and attachments that might interfere with a sound choice.

Second, he proposes "to consider what procedure and norm of action I would wish to have followed in making the present choice if I were at the moment of death. I will guide myself by this and make my decision entirely in conformity with it" (SpEx 186). This objectivity of such a deathbed perspective will help to inform my choice. Saint Ignatius continues, "Let me picture and consider myself as standing in the presence of my judge on the last day, and reflect what decision in the present matter I would then wish to have made. I will choose now the rule of life that I would then wish to have observed, that on the day of judgment I may be filled with happiness and joy" (SpEx 187). By imagining my advice to another person and my standing before the Lord as my judge, Saint Ignatius helps me to remain unbiased and objective about my choice.

We have seen how Saint Ignatius offers three fundamental ways of recognizing and responding to the Lord's call. Throughout the process of discernment, the Lord speaks to us at the level of the heart through consolation and desolation, and at the level of the head through supernatural prudence and a rational decision-making process. The bride in the Song of Songs is motivated at the levels of both the heart and the head. At the heart level her desire for the bridegroom irresistibly moves her to a greater confidence to "come away" with him. At the head level she is also convinced by the bridegroom's rational appeal to the greater fruitfulness of such a choice, as he shows her the fertility of nature blossoming around them. The bride's choice to accept the bridegroom's invitation will result in greater union and abundance of life.

Questions for Reflection and Discussion

1. How do you understand God's will and the way he manifests it to you? Can you think of some images that help describe it?

2. How much is God's will already clear to you from the teaching of Christ and his Church? How challenging is it for you to live up to this?

3. Have you ever experienced God asking you what you wanted to choose? Have you ever felt as though God was imposing his will on you? How did you handle that?

4. Are you facing any important decisions right now in your life? Which of Saint Ignatius' guidelines do you find helpful?

5. Which do you tend to favor as a basis for decisions: movements of spirit (consolation and desolation) in the heart, or rational, prudential judgment in the head?

6. What aspects of the supernatural virtue of prudence (p. 143) do you find most helpful and tend to practice well? Which aspects could you improve upon?

7. How well does your choice of vocation or career satisfy the criterion laid out by Saint Ignatius?

8. Have you ever tried Saint Ignatius' method of objectivity (p. 145) in making decisions? If so, have you found it helpful?

Prayer Exercises

1. Ponder the story of Phillip Bennet (p. 136). Pray with Matthew 15:21–28, and ask for the grace to express to the Lord what you desire.

2. Reflect on Thomas More's choice to be faithful to God (p. 137). Pray with Matthew 5:17–48, and ask for the grace to observe God's commands in all your choices.

3. Pray about any decision you have to make using Matthew 14:22–33. Notice any movements of consolation or desolation that pertain to the Scripture account or the decision itself.

4. Pray about any decision you have to make using Luke 16:1–13. Use Saint Ignatius' deliberative method (p. 142), and ask for the gift of supernatural prudence.

5. Reflect on the phrase of Saint Irenaeus that the glory of God is man fully alive (p. 145). Pray with Luke 5:1–11, and ask for the grace to know God's call and respond courageously.

6. Pray about any decision you have to make using Saint Ignatius' method of objectivity (p. 145). Pray with Luke 13:22–30, and ask for the grace to be faithful to the Lord as your judge.

7. Make a repetition on any of the above passages and decisions, paying attention to the places of greater movement of spirit.

Chapter 13

Called by Name

[B] My beloved speaks and says to me:
[G] "Arise, my love, my fair one,
    and come away;
for now the winter is past,
    the rain is over and gone.
The flowers appear on the earth;
    the time of singing has come,
and the voice of the turtledove
    is heard in our land.
The fig tree puts forth its figs,
    and the vines are in blossom;
    they give forth fragrance.
Arise, my love, my fair one,
    and come away." (Song 2:10–13)

I call it consolation when an interior movement is aroused in the soul, by which it is inflamed with love of its Creator and Lord, and as a consequence, can love no creature on the face of the earth for its own sake, but only in the Creator of them all. (SpEx 316)

We continue our discussion of Christ's call in the Spiritual Exercises in the context of the bridegroom's personal call to his bride. He calls her my love, my fair one; she belongs uniquely to him. In the same way, each of us belongs exceptionally to the Lord, who calls to each one of us in a matchless way. The Lord has made every person uniquely for himself and desires one and all in a special manner. We are also meant to manifest to others the unique graces God has given us. An old Christian tradition says that God sends each person into this world with a special message to deliver, a special song to sing, and a special act of love to bestow. No one else can speak my message, sing my song, or offer my act of love. These are entrusted only to me.[86]

Such a unique call from the Lord came to a young man named David, who, at the age of sixteen, traveled with his father to India. Leaving the train station in Bombay, David stumbled over a woman and her child, who were sleeping in the mud. As he looked at them, David had a strange feeling that his true self and his purpose in life would involve helping the homeless. Over the next several years, however, David held many jobs that didn't allow him to follow his desire to serve the poor. When his dream to help the homeless was met with discouragement and ridicule by others, David fell into depression. Eventually, he made the Spiritual Exercises, and his director asked if he had ever experienced God's grace in a more intense way. David recalled his experience at the train station in Bombay, when he felt most himself. He then discerned during the retreat to be faithful to this foundational grace, risking everything to leave his job and invest what he had in an organization to help the homeless. Soon he experienced great fulfillment and was winning awards for his work on the local and state levels.[87]

David discovered his calling in life by paying attention to a moment of profound grace and insight, when he had felt whole and enlivened by the Holy Spirit. In this case, David's love for the homeless was not just a vocation to a state in life such as marriage or priesthood, nor was it a career choice. David was being called uniquely and personally by God; he was given what

---

86. See Brian Cavanaugh, T.O.R., "You Have a Special Message to Deliver," *Sower's Seeds Aplenty: Fourth Planting* (Mahwah: Paulist Press, 1996), 32.

87. See Matthew Linn and Sheila Fabricant, Foreword, in Herbert Alphonso, *The Personal Vocation* (Mahwah: Paulist Press, 2001), x–xi.

we will call a "personal vocation." David discovered his unique way of living his call to love the homeless, though he realized his personal vocation was first a way of being before God and only secondarily a mode of doing something. David's ministry of helping the homeless flowed out of his fundamental union with God.

As we contemplate the life of Jesus in the Spiritual Exercises, we see that he had a personal vocation. From an early age, Jesus was aware of his unique relationship as the Son of his heavenly Father. In the Exercises, we contemplate the Lord's finding in the Temple at Passover, when he asked Mary and Joseph why they had been seeking him anxiously. Then he added, "Did you not know that I must be in my Father's house?" (Lk 2:49). This shows he was aware of his special calling.

Saint Ignatius then has us consider Jesus at the beginning of his public ministry. The Father's voice revealed Jesus to John the Baptist and to Israel: "This is my Son, the Beloved, with whom I am well pleased" (Mt 3:17). Jesus' self-understanding was and is to be the Son of the Father. From all eternity Jesus is the Son. Being the eternal Son of the Father is central to his identity and shapes all his actions. Jesus, the Son of God by nature, make us sons and daughters of God by adoption. "And because you are children, God has sent the Spirit of his Son into our hearts, crying, 'Abba! Father!'" (Gal 4:6). The common thread throughout Jesus' life and ministry is his personal vocation as the Son of the Father.

Discovering Our Personal Vocation

We often discover our personal vocation through a pattern of God's grace we perceive at work in our lives—an exceptional way God gets through to us as individuals. As we look back over time, we may discover clues to our personal calling based on what we valued or found profoundly captivating. Perhaps one has a fascination with an activity or the words of someone who had a deep impact on one's life. A person could experience an image of God, such as the Good Shepherd, that spoke profoundly to one's heart.

For example, Dorothy Day recalled certain incidents that gave her clues from an early age that her life's work would involve solidarity with and service to the poor. Once when she was seven years old she spoke with her mother while they ate donuts. Dorothy's mother told her about people in the world who were dying because they didn't have enough to eat. Dorothy asked why, and her mother replied that the world was just like that—some people had things and others didn't. Seeing the sadness in her mother's face, Dorothy then asked if she could give her donut to these people, but her mother said she couldn't because they lived far away. So Dorothy left her donut on the table without eating it and kept asking her mother to give it to someone who needed it. Later, Dorothy recalled walking past beggars with her father, who wasn't in the mood to stop and help. Dorothy often wondered what God thought about situations of injustice in the world and would pray about them while in bed at night. She would daydream and talk to herself about what her future life would be like. Eventually she realized her personal vocation involved dedicating her life to serving the poor, and she gave herself entirely to this mission with heroic charity. Shortly before her death, Dorothy said that in many ways she was the same person then that she had been at seven years old.[88]

These episodes show us that God plants the seeds of our personal vocation at an early age. Looking back at our own lives, we might notice a pattern of how God reveals himself to us in a unique way and discover clues about God's special call to each of us.

The lives of the saints show us the reality of the personal vocation, the special way in which God calls each of us. The angel calls Mary not by her given name but by a new name, full of grace. The form of the noun suggests she was, is, and always will be full of grace. Mary was always growing in her capacity to receive God's grace in its fullness. From her place in heaven she continues to overflow with God's grace, and as mother, she cooperates in bringing this grace into our lives.

The apostles similarly experienced unique calls. After his confession of faith, Peter was called the "rock" upon whom Christ would build his Church. Christ fortified Peter to be a rock of faith, and he fulfilled his role to strengthen the faithful throughout his life and ministry. Saint Paul knew himself as an apostle, even though Jesus did not appear to him until after his resurrection. Saint Paul would later remember his calling as an apostle and assert it when people questioned his credentials. He became the greatest of messengers, bearing great fruit for the Gospel in his missionary journeys and

---

88. See Robert Coles, *The Spiritual Life of Children* (Boston: Houghton Mifflin, 1994), 327–329.

fulfilling his personal vocation as apostle. John the Baptist realized his personal vocation as the "voice crying out in the wilderness" to prepare the way of the Lord as a prophet and forerunner. Saint Teresa of Ávila referred to her personal vocation as a relationship with "God alone" who was sufficient for her every need. The words *Ad Maiorem Dei Gloriam* or "for the greater glory of God" characterized the life and personal vocation of Saint Ignatius. His greatest weakness before his conversion was vainglory. The Lord's grace came to Saint Ignatius precisely where he was weak. The Lord called each of these saints by a name, word, or phrase that characterized a special and unique grace or way of relating to God.

In the Book of Revelation, Jesus promises that he will give to each of his faithful "a white stone, and on the white stone [will be] written a new name that no one knows except the one who receives it" (Rev 2:17). Here, Jesus clearly states that, as Christians, he will give each of us a special name known only to ourselves. Herbert Alphonso, author of *The Personal Vocation*, makes clear that this new name is meant to reflect something of the face or person of Christ.[89] As members of his Body, we are called to be an *alter Christus* or other Christs. We are all meant to put on the Lord Jesus Christ (see Rom 13:14) and to be clothed with him in a uniquely personal way. Each of us is called to be conformed to the image of Christ (see Rom 8:29), "until all of us come to the unity of the faith and of the knowledge of the Son of God, to maturity, to the measure of the full stature of Christ" (Eph 4:13). Christ manifests himself exceptionally to each of us as members of his Body so that we might grow to greater spiritual maturity and manifest him uniquely to others.

The personal vocation of the bride in the Song of Songs seems to be to reflect in a powerful way the beauty of her bridegroom, who represents Christ. He calls her beautiful, and she calls him beautiful in response. He continues to call her beautiful throughout the Song of Songs. The bridegroom repeats this name eight times, more than any other name he gives her, as she is made beautiful in the image of God. She is redeemed from her past history of sin and restored to her beautiful state, able to proclaim her own beauty. The two lovers contemplate one another as beautiful, and now the bridegroom calls her in her beauty, "Arise, my love, my fair one." Her growth in grace and beauty parallels the dynamics of God's grace in the Spiritual

---

89. See Alphonso, *The Personal Vocation*, 23.

Exercises, wherein one becomes aware of one's own goodness and beauty in being created, redeemed, gazed upon, and called by Christ.

The personal vocation is the secret to unifying the many, apparently disparate aspects of our lives, as exemplified by Jesus' encounter with Martha and Mary of Bethany. Martha is anxious about many things: her household tasks and the details of hospitality, which are important matters. Jesus tells her that only one thing is necessary, and that her sister, Mary, "has chosen the better part." As she sits at the feet of Jesus, gazing at him and listening intently to his words, Mary is a model of contemplative prayer (see Lk 10:38–42). This suggests to us that we can discover our personal vocation and the key to unifying our lives in prayer. As we play many roles and juggle many aspects of our lives, the personal vocation is the "one thing necessary" to remember in order to remain with the Lord faithfully.

Saint Thérèse of Lisieux unified the many different aspects of her life as a religious sister through her experience of her personal vocation to prayer. Thérèse's vocation as a Carmelite nun encompassed being the Lord's spouse and, by grace, a mother of souls. She still felt other vocations within, namely that of warrior, priest, apostle, doctor, and martyr. In these roles she felt the need and desire of carrying out the most heroic deeds for Jesus and wondered how she could combine them all. During her meditation, she was at first frustrated and looked to Saint Paul's epistles to find some answer. She opened First Corinthians, chapters 12 and 13, and read that all cannot be apostles, prophets, doctors, etc., that the Church is composed of different members. The eye could not be the hand, for instance. Without becoming discouraged, she continued her reading and was consoled by the sentence, "But strive for the greater gifts. And I will show you a still more excellent way" (1 Cor 12:31). In her *Story of a Soul*, Thérèse recounts her breakthrough experience: "And the Apostle explains how all the most perfect gifts are nothing without love. That Charity is the excellent way that leads most surely to God. I finally had rest. Considering the mystical body of the Church, I had not recognized myself in any of the members described by Saint Paul, or rather I had desired to see myself in them all. Charity gave me the key to my vocation."[90]

---

90. Saint Thérèse of Lisieux, *Story of a Soul: The Autobiography of St. Thérèse of Lisieux*, trans. John Clarke, O.C.D. (Washington, D.C.: ICS Publications, 1996), 193–195.

Thérèse understood that in the body of the Church, the heart was the most important of the parts; love was the expression of the heart and motivated all the other members to act. This love comprised all vocations, and in love's eternity it embraced all times and places. In her joy, Thérèse exclaimed: "O Jesus, my Love . . . my vocation, at last I have found it . . . my vocation is love! . . . Thus I shall be everything, and thus my dream will be realized. . . . I know how to reach you, I have found the secret of possessing your flame."[91]

Saint Thérèse's personal vocation to love unified all aspects of her life. All her other roles: Carmelite, spouse, mother—and all her desires: to be warrior, priest, apostle, doctor, and martyr—were summed up in the word love.

God revealed Saint Thérèse's personal vocation to her through prayer, just as he will do with us. Often, this call comes through Scripture. Sometimes a word or phrase can penetrate our hearts and awaken the personal vocation within us, just as Saint Thérèse recognized her vocation in the word "love" as she read First Corinthians.

It does not have to be a scriptural word that touches us so deeply, however, for God can use any words to get through to us. For example, a phrase such as "my only love" or "faithful forever" are examples of a deeply personal and meaningful relationship with the Lord known only to the receiver. The French theologian Jean Mouroux notes that "the grace given by God is at once personal and personalizing; personal, because it is directed to an individual soul in its own determined situation; personalizing, because it is destined to make the individual soul realize its own unique vocation."[92] As the Lord endears himself to us in a unique and individual way, we become aware of our special calling. Our attentiveness to God's consolations (see SpEx 316) can help us refine our awareness of the personal vocation.

Call within a Call

As Saint Thérèse did, we too may experience the personal vocation as "a call within a call." Though she was already a Carmelite religious sister, she

---

91. Ibid.

92. Abbe Jean Mouroux, *I Believe: The Personal Structure of Faith*, trans. Michael Turner (New York: Sheed & Ward, 1959). Reproduced by kind permission of Continuum International Publishing Group, a Bloomsbury Company.

heard a further call, one more personal and deep, that emerged in her identification with the love of Christ.

We also see this "call within a call" in the life of Saint Teresa of Calcutta. When she received her call to serve the poor, she was already a religious sister teaching affluent girls at a school in Calcutta. Walking the streets of the city, she was disturbed at the sight of the abandoned and dying, and she wanted to do something to help them. Later, going to a retreat in the mountains, she encountered a dying man at the train station in Calcutta. As Teresa later reflected on the experience, she interiorly heard the Lord speak to her the words "I thirst." She understood these words to mean that Jesus himself was thirsting for her love in and through this person who needed love. In ministering to this man, Teresa realized she was ministering to Christ. Serving the abandoned poor, sick, and dying became her fundamental way of knowing Christ and relating to him throughout her life and ministry. She was given permission to leave her congregation, the Sisters of Loreto, to begin a new congregation dedicated to loving the poor, the sick, and the dying. The Missionaries of Charity would be characterized by sisters who understood the meaning of the words "I thirst." A large crucifix with the words "I thirst" beneath it can be found in the chapel of each of their convents. Within Saint Teresa's more general call to be a religious sister was a more specific call to quench the thirst of Jesus with her love.

Just as Jesus can speak into our hearts our personal vocations, a spiritual director can help us arrive at greater clarity about who God is for us in our lives. As we articulate our experience of God, the spiritual director can help us to unpack the graces we receive in prayer and daily life, so that we can perceive things we might otherwise miss. The director can offer wisdom to help us better seek God and better know ourselves.

Herbert Alphonso tells the story of a fellow, middle-aged Jesuit who told him that for many years he had struggled to maintain a regular prayer life. When he did pray, he felt present only bodily, for his mind and soul were somewhere else. He didn't feel like he was actually praying. Sensing the man was at an impasse in prayer, Alphonso asked him if he had ever felt spontaneously close to God. His confrere quickly said yes, that when he looked back at his past life and saw how good God had been to him, he felt immediately in touch with God. Since the priest seemed to come alive with great feeling and his eyes sparkled as he spoke, Alphonso proposed that he pray about the goodness of God. His friend was reluctant and defensive, suggesting that he would quickly tire of praying about that. Alphonso insisted he try, and the man agreed. Three weeks later Alphonso's friend burst into his room, exclaiming that he could always pray on the goodness of God. Months later, he could still pray with this theme and shared in stirring detail all that God's goodness meant to him. It became the key to his prayer, ministry, relationships, leisure, and recreation. As the man finished, Alphonso, profoundly moved, congratulated his confrere for having discovered his personal vocation, the goodness of God.[93] The process of spiritual guidance was instrumental in this priest's discovery of his personal vocation. Alphonso asked questions that helped him pay attention to the consolations he had already received. By encouraging his confrere to pray with the theme of God's goodness, Alphonso helped him overcome his resistance and affirmed God's work in him, enabling him to realize his personal vocation. Discovery of his personal vocation reinvigorated the man's life and ministry. Likewise, the more we discover God's unique plan for our lives, the more fulfilled we become as Christians, with a greater sense of purpose in doing God's will.

As Herbert Alphonso's experience indicates, a life of sustained prayer can help us discern our personal vocation. Saint Teresa of Calcutta's example indicates that we should add to our prayer a discernment of God's voice in our daily lives. To these fine methods, we can add paying attention to the qualities we admire in particular individuals we look up to. Elisha, for example, discovered his call to be a prophet through his encounter with Elijah, which led Elisha to follow the prophet as an apprentice.

Another possible way of finding our personal vocation is through an inspiration that motivates and sustains us in difficult times of crisis or trial. When Archbishop Van Thuan was put into solitary confinement by the Vietnamese regime, he suffered a personal crisis of meaning. He heard a voice from God reminding him that he had chosen God alone, not his works. Those words gave him lasting strength and peace, helping him to surmount extremely painful moments in prison.

As we contemplate Christ in his mysteries in the Spiritual Exercises, we notice his personal vocation and its impact on his life. Praying with these mysteries, we discover the unique features of our relationship with him. We become aware of the unique and personal way in which the Lord speaks to

93. See Alphonso, *The Personal Vocation*, 11–14.

our hearts, calling each of us by name. We imitate the bride in receiving her intimate call from the bridegroom as his "fair one," whom he bids to "arise and come away."

Questions for Reflection and Discussion

1. How might the concept of the personal vocation improve your sense of identity and mission?

2. Have you had touchstone experiences that indicate something of your personal vocation? Do you sense a pattern of grace in your personal history?

3. Does any verse or phrase from Sacred Scripture particularly dear to you suggest your personal vocation?

4. Can you recall any beautiful words or images that help to sustain you in difficult times? Does this indicate your personal vocation in any way?

5. How is your personal vocation revealed in your identity? How is it manifested in your actions and mission?

6. The personal vocation of the bride in the Song of Songs is to be beautiful and manifest this beauty to others. In what sense do we all share in her personal vocation?

Prayer Exercises

1. Pray with Song of Songs 2:10–13, and ask for the grace to be aware of the Lord's unique call to you.

2. Reflect on David's and Dorothy Day's experiences (p. 150 and p. 151) and consider whether you have had any "touchstone" events in your life that point toward your personal vocation. Pray with John 6:1–15, and ask for the grace to offer to the Lord all you are and do in love and service.

3. Ponder the personal vocation of Jesus and the saints. Pray with Matthew 16:13–20, and ask for the grace to realize your own unique call and gifts.

4. Consider Herbert Alphonso's story (p. 153) and the image of the white stone with the name of the faithful on it (Rev 2:17). Pray with Matthew 17:1–13, and ask for the grace to understand Jesus' personal vocation as Son of the Father.

5. Reflect on the "call within a call" of Mother Teresa (p. 156). Pray with Matthew 10:1–15, and ask for the grace to reflect God's grace to others in your life.

6. Pray with Matthew 26:1–13, and ask for the grace to be generous in giving yourself to the Lord in your personal vocation.

7. Make a repetition on any of the above contemplations, returning to wherever you felt greater movement of spirit.

CHAPTER 14

My True Self

[G] O my dove, in the clefts of the rock,
    in the covert of the cliff,
let me see your face,
    let me hear your voice;
for your voice is sweet,
    and your face is lovely. (Song 2:14)

This is to ask for what I desire. Here it will be to ask for a knowledge of the deceits of the rebel chief and help to guard myself against them; and also to ask for a knowledge of the true life exemplified in the sovereign and true Commander, and the grace to imitate him. (SpEx 139)

The bridegroom is intent on seeing the bride face to face. He wants to see her as she is, to see her in her authenticity, without any mask. God calls us to the same authenticity, the same unmasking. Still, we feel the strong pull of the temptation to pretend we're something we're not. Out of false humility we may deny our true selves, daring not to venture to meet the Lord as we are. The bride hides herself from the bridegroom and others, unwilling to expose her true self.

On the other hand, we can put on airs and become an insincere self, seeking to impress ourselves and others. At the instigation of Satan, Adam and Eve strove pridefully to be what they were not: gods knowing good and evil, disobedient to the one God. Moving to correct that human tendency toward pride, Jesus lived a life of humility. Saint Paul tells us that Jesus, "though he was in the form of God, did not regard equality with God as something to be exploited" (Phil 2:6–7). Rather he emptied himself of his claim to divinity in order to assume our humanity and redeem it, becoming as a servant to us. In doing so, he shows us what it means to be authentically human—to live a life of humility and service.

To inspire us to remain true to our authentic selves, Saint Ignatius introduces *A Meditation on Two Standards* (see SpEx 136–147). Here "standard" refers to a battle flag, suggesting spiritual warfare. First he describes the standard of Lucifer—his strategy. From his terrifying chair of fire and smoke, the horrible Lucifer summons his demons and sends them forth to ensnare human beings. Saint Ignatius has us consider how Lucifer addresses the demons, how he prods them on to lay traps for humans and bind them with chains: "First they are to tempt them to covet riches (as Satan himself is accustomed to do in most cases) that they may the more easily attain the empty honors of this world, and then come to overweening pride. . . . From these three steps the evil one leads to all other vices" (SpEx 142).

In contrast we are to ponder Jesus, our true and supreme captain, who stands humbly on a field of Jerusalem. Appearing beautiful, he summons his apostles and sends them forth to spread his sacred teaching to the world, recommending that they seek to help all, "first by attracting them to the highest spiritual poverty . . . even to actual poverty. Secondly, they should lead them to a desire for insults and contempt, for from these springs humility. . . . From these three steps, let them lead men to all other virtues" (SpEx 146).

The two standards, then, are intended to help us understand the methods of the evil one as they contrast with those of Christ. Saint Ignatius wants us to unmask the devil's deceits and understand his strategy so we can reject it. The devil tempts us with riches, which lead first to worldly honor and then to self-sufficiency and self-glorification apart from God. Saint Ignatius wants us to see the contrasting and opposing strategy of Jesus, so that we will be attracted to follow him. Jesus invites us to poverty and to face contempt from the world, resulting in true humility and dependence on God. Saint Ignatius then exhorts us to implore that God will receive us under the standard of

Jesus, so that we may imitate him in the highest spiritual poverty and willingness to bear insults. In this way, we will be more disposed to be true to Christ and our authentic selves. Likewise, the bridegroom wants to see the bride according to her true nature, in all spiritual poverty. He wants her to emerge from her place of hiding and follow him in complete dependence.

The Gospel mystery that most typifies this lesson of complete spiritual poverty and dependence on God is the temptation of Jesus in the desert (see Lk 4:1–13). Immediately before it, at his baptism Jesus had been confirmed in his identity as Son of the Father. The Father's voice was heard, "You are my Son, the Beloved; with you I am well pleased" (Lk 3:22). Satan attempts to dissuade Jesus from his true character as Son, proposing three temptations that correspond to three false associations we make as human beings: to base our identities on our abilities, our possessions, and our reputation.

In the first temptation, the devil says to Jesus, "If you are the Son of God, command this stone to become a loaf of bread" (v. 3). This temptation represents the false concept that our human identity must be based on what we can do. Jesus knew this inclination well but, unlike us, he did not give into it. Yes, he worked miracles, but he didn't enter our world to be a miracle worker. Instead, he wanted to share in and redeem our human condition so he could teach us dependence on God—rather than ourselves—for our needs. With this goal in mind, Jesus refuses Satan's suggestion: "It is written, 'One does not live by bread alone.'" Jesus asserts what he knows to be true from experience, that we live on every word that comes from the mouth of God; we depend on him. Jesus clung to his own poverty of spirit in his humanity, showing that what we do is unimportant in the face of what God does. In his classic book, *Poverty of Spirit*, Johannes Metz explains that to assume humanity means being poor, having nothing at all, no reason to boast before the divine.[94] Saint Paul spoke of Jesus' absolute poverty in this way: "For you know the generous act of our Lord Jesus Christ, that though he was rich, yet for your sakes he became poor, so that by his poverty you might become rich" (2 Cor 8:9). Jesus preferred to assert his total dependence on his Father and to completely surrender his life into the Father's hands. Jesus was later faced with this same temptation—to do something

---

94. See Johannes Metz, *Poverty of Spirit*, trans. John Drury (New York: Paulist Press, 1968), 14.

miraculous—when the crowds ask him, "What sign are you going to give us then, so that we may see it and believe you? What work are you performing?" (see Jn 6:30–35). They want him to make bread, the same bread from heaven that Moses had given them. In response, Jesus explains that he is the true bread from heaven, asserting, "I *am* the bread of life." He emphasizes *who* he is, not *what* he can do.

By luring us away from our essential poverty of spirit as human beings, this first temptation appeals to our need for power and control over our lives and environment. Of course we have a certain legitimate need to achieve, from our simplest accomplishments as children to our greatest triumphs as adults. These feats give us a feeling of self-confidence and command. We need the ability to create in order to survive and flourish. But danger arises when we base our identity and self-worth on this ability rather than on our inherent dignity and worth as human beings. We might try to earn the approval of God, self, and others based on our achievements.

One advertising executive described his colleague Bill as someone who is constantly looking for success even though he's already achieved it. Bill always looks for triumphs even though the contest is finished and the team is victorious. He is very diligent and accomplished, but remains unfulfilled and hungry for more success. There is always another treasure to be discovered, another mountain to climb and conquer.[95] Although Bill had many impressive achievements, they couldn't give him any lasting satisfaction in life. His continual need to achieve prevented him from realizing his true poverty of spirit and dependence on God. Like Bill, we can lose sight of who we are if we pursue a false self based on our achievements. Jesus warns us, "For what will it profit them to gain the whole world and forfeit their life?" (Mk 8:36). And to counter our tendency toward pride based on the good works we do, he exhorts us to say, "We are worthless slaves; we have done only what we ought to have done!" (Lk 17:10). Jesus wants us to cling to our real spiritual poverty, the same spiritual poverty Saint Ignatius has us beg for in the meditation on the two standards. Similarly, the bridegroom is not interested in the bride's achievements but simply desires her presence; he only wants to see her face and hear her voice.

---

95. See Charlie Brower, *Me and Other Advertising Geniuses* (New York: Doubleday, 1974), 36.

The Second Temptation

The devil's first temptation points to man's tendency to worship his abilities. In the second temptation the devil tempts Jesus—just as he tempts man—to identify himself with what he possesses. Satan shows Jesus all the kingdoms of the world, saying, "To you I will give their glory and all this authority; for it has been given over to me, and I give it to anyone I please. If you, then, will worship me, it will all be yours" (Lk 4:6–7). This temptation represents our proclivity as fallen human beings to identify ourselves with what we have.

Most of us realize the dangerous pull of material goods, yet we still fall into the trap of equating our possessions with our worth. As far as we know, Jesus possessed nothing materially. He had no home: "the Son of Man has nowhere to lay his head" (Lk 9:58). He seemed to have no money, for when asked whether to pay the tribute to Caesar or not, he said "show me one of your coins." Along with his disciples, Jesus gleaned leftover wheat from the fields, which was to be left for the poor after the harvest. Jesus even died naked on the cross and was laid in a borrowed tomb. His lack of possessions and utter detachment from them spoke to his complete identification not with what he owned but with his Father's love. Jesus was all about giving, not about taking or having for himself.

Though we strive to emulate Christ's example, we can easily fall into the trap of identifying ourselves based on what we own. Like our achievements, our possessions are not bad in themselves. They are essential to our survival and our need for safety and security. As children we cling to our blankets and toys as though our lives depended on them. As adults we worry about finances and getting ahead, since providing for ourselves and our families is good and necessary. But again we tend to go beyond necessity and identify ourselves with what we have, basing our self-worth on our cars or homes. Once we have these things, we may also become obsessed with the danger of losing them to theft or financial ruin. Saint Paul warns us: "For the love of money is a root of all kinds of evil, and in their eagerness to be rich some have wandered away from the faith and pierced themselves with many pains" (1 Tim 6:10). It is not the possessions themselves but inordinate love of them and the false security they provide that leads to all other vices.

Our possessions are not limited to the material but also extend to psychological and spiritual goods. Intellectually, Jesus had an outstanding mind. We will never fully understand how his divine knowledge translated into his human intellect. But we can reasonably assume that he had at least the infused knowledge of the prophets and awareness of the divine. Yet Jesus admitted to not knowing certain things, such as the day and the hour of the end times, as this information was reserved to the Father. It seems he relied on only the knowledge necessary for the present moment, knowledge supplied by his Father. He did not define himself based upon his possession of knowledge or divine omniscience. Even spiritually he did not cling to his divinity, but emptied himself in order to assume our full humanity.

We also have psychological possessions in the realm of intellect and will. Knowledge is good but can easily become a source of pride. If we know more than another person, it gives us an edge in the game of comparison. Having all the facts, inside information, or good advice to offer others gives us self-satisfaction and an exalted image of ourselves. We hang our degrees on the wall and display our credentials and titles.

Even our spiritual possession—our abilities and the graces we've received—can become a means by which we elevate our self-worth. Jesus saved his harshest criticism for the Pharisees, who in their arrogance considered themselves exceptional in God's sight and acted condescendingly toward those they considered morally inferior. In addition, Saint Paul upbraided the Corinthians for their rivalries over who had the greatest spiritual gifts and a right to the highest position in the Church. He reminded them, "What do you have that you did not receive? And if you received it, why do you boast as if it were not a gift?" (1 Cor 4:7).

We tend to cling even to the gifts that are most obviously of God as though they were ours to possess. The greater the gifts, the greater should be our humility in receiving them and putting them at the service of the community. In the face of this tendency, Saint Ignatius counsels us in the meditation on two standards: to ask for the grace of highest spiritual poverty and to realize that our identity and self-worth are not to be found in possessions of any kind. In the same way, the bride, in her poverty of spirit, depends only on the love of her bridegroom, who utterly possesses her, and she him: "I am my beloved's and my beloved is mine" (Song 6:3).

The Third Temptation

In the third temptation, the devil tries to entice Jesus to identify himself with what other people think of him, a danger we can easily fall prey to. From the pinnacle of the temple, the devil challenges Jesus, "If you are the Son of God, throw yourself down from here, for it is written, 'He will command his angels concerning you, to protect you,' and 'On their hands they will bear you up, so that you will not dash your foot against a stone'" (Lk 4:9).

This temptation represents our all-too-human tendency to seek the esteem and affection of others. In Jesus' case, the spectacular feat of falling from the Temple's height into the arms of the angels would impress everyone. The people would love Jesus and hold him in high regard. Jesus, however, never performed miracles to glorify himself but for the sake of those who were hurting or in need. Often, when he miraculously healed people, he ordered them not to speak about it to anyone, for Jesus didn't want people to follow him out of sensationalist motives. Far from sensationalizing, Jesus warned his followers that they would have to take up their cross and follow him, that they would be persecuted and put to death. Even if we are not called to suffer martyrdom, we might suffer the pain of being ignored, of being considered irrelevant.

It is good to be loved and esteemed. Children need basic affirmation in order to flourish, and this need does not diminish in adulthood. It is good to honor people for who they are and for their achievements. The danger lies in acting in certain ways in order to receive admiration. When we do so, performing in order to gain human respect, we can go to the extreme of basing our identity and self-worth upon whether people notice or compliment us, or out of a fear of rejection. But if we are rooted in God's love for us as his sons and daughters, and the love of one another in the Church, we will be free of the need to act to gain recognition and praise.

In Hollywood, movie producers vie for honor by practicing "power seating." A person's place in the industry is reflected in the prominent position he or she occupies at banquets and important events. Some movie studios employ publicity personnel whose sole job is to secure first-place seating for its executives. One television producer confirms his place before an event, and graciously makes known that if his seat isn't in the right place, he won't attend. Another producer explains that information is leverage. He doesn't want to be associated with people with no influence because that diminishes his prestige and he gains nothing in return.[96] How different from Jesus'

---

96. For this example see Father Joseph Pellegrino, Homily for 22nd Sunday in Ordinary Time, Year C, http://frjoeshomilies.net/09-01-13.html.

exhortation, "When you are invited by someone to a wedding banquet, do not sit down at the place of honor. . . . But when you are invited, go and sit down at the lowest place, so that when your host comes, he may say to you, 'Friend, move up higher'; then you will be honored in the presence of all who sit at the table with you. For all who exalt themselves will be humbled, and those who humble themselves will be exalted" (Lk 14:8, 10–11). Jesus invites us to act against our tendency to seek the exalted place by moving in the opposite direction, seeking the lower place in humility. In the Song of Songs, the bride, because of her humility, desires to be hidden "in the clefts of the rock, in the covert of the cliff." The bridegroom has to call her out of hiding in order to see her face and hear her voice.

Saint Ignatius instructs us to "act against" (*agere contra*) our disordered desires for possessions, achievements, and affection by praying for the grace to receive their opposites. He exhorts us to ask for the grace "to be received under His standard, first in the highest spiritual poverty . . . in bearing insults and wrongs, thereby to imitate Him better" (SpEx 147), leading to humility. Because of our temptation to identify ourselves with these goods extrinsic to ourselves, we must forcefully and decisively resist the temptation by acting against them. In this highest spiritual poverty we find our true selves.

Humility means being honest about who we really are, knowing that we depend on God alone. We are stripped of the false self, which develops from the temptations to riches, honor, and pride. The bride has come to the place of highest spiritual poverty and total dependence on her bridegroom. She is humbly hiding from praise "in the clefts of the rock." She has no possessions; rather, her bridegroom is her sole possession and she depends on him alone.

Questions for Reflection and Discussion

1. Do you notice the battle of Saint Ignatius' two standards being fought in our world today? Do you notice it being fought within your own heart? In what ways?

2. How do you fall into the trap of defining yourself by what you can do? What achievements do you cling to? How do you handle failure?

3. Do you ever define yourself by what you possess? What material, psychological, and spiritual gifts do you cling to?

4. In what ways do you define yourself by what others think of you? How are you influenced by other peoples' opinions of you?

5. When have you felt loved and appreciated by God and others for being truly yourself? How does it impact your life and behavior?

Prayer Exercises

1. Pray with Saint Ignatius' Two Standards meditation (p. 162), and ask for the grace to unmask the deceits of Satan.

2. Consider the story of Bill, the successful advertising executive (p. 164). Pray with Luke 4:1–13, and ask for the grace to avoid the temptation to define yourself by what you achieve.

3. Pray with Luke 4:1–13, and ask for the grace to avoid the temptation to define yourself by what you possess materially, psychologically, or spiritually.

4. Recall the story of the Hollywood "power seating" (p. 167). Pray with Luke 4:1–13, and ask for the grace to overcome the temptation to define yourself based on what other people think of you.

5. Pray with Philippians 3:4–11, and ask for the grace to count all as loss in comparison with the surpassing worth of Jesus Christ.

6. Pray with Song of Songs 2:14, and ask for the grace to know that the Lord sees you and rejoices in your true self.

7. Make a repetition on any of the above passages, dwelling in those places of greater movement of spirit.

CHAPTER 15

Spiritual Vigilance

[B] Catch us the foxes,
   the little foxes,
that ruin the vineyards—
   for our vineyards are in blossom. (Song 2:15)

Method of Making the General Examination of Conscience
   1. ... to give thanks to God our Lord for the favors received.
   2. ... to ask for grace to know my sins and to rid myself of them.
   3. ... to demand an account of my soul from the time of rising up to the present examination.
   4. ... to ask pardon of God our Lord for my faults.
   5. ... to resolve to amend with the grace of God. (SpEx 43)

The bridegroom exhorts his bride to watchfulness, that together they may guard against the foxes ruining the vineyards and work to capture them. What do the foxes symbolize? Literature consistently portrays the fox as wily and devious. Similarly, Jesus referred to the wicked and conniving

Herod as a fox. Highly intelligent, the fox uses its cunning to ensnare its prey and so represents the scheming of enemy spirits, the devils, which would attempt to harm the bride and her union with God. Since as fallen human beings we can easily deceive ourselves, the foxes could also represent those movements of the bride's heart that go against her union with the Bridegroom. If we do not pay attention to the subtle movements of our hearts that lead us away from God, we could gradually fall away from him.

To counter this danger and avoid growing lazy in the spiritual life, we need to develop a constant attitude of being attentive to the Lord. If we are not vigilant, we can easily grow negligent, distance ourselves from God, and even fall into sin. Usually we drift away from God not deliberately but by growing careless. Although we have been redeemed, we can still fall back into the subtle influences of the deadly sins. Therefore, we must keep watch over our hearts to guard against such a relapse. Saint Paul warns those who seemingly stand secure in the faith to take care not to fall. They should have "faith and a good conscience" (1 Tim 1:19). By listening to our conscience and following it, we can avoid falling away from the Lord. Moreover, we gain a more intimate knowledge of Christ in order to love him more and follow him more closely (see SpEx 104).

In the Spiritual Exercises Saint Ignatius offers the general examination of conscience (see SpEx 32–43 [examen prayer]) to maintain this vigilance of heart.[97] The examen is a way of praying over our life experience in order to orient our hearts toward God's presence. The examen can be made at any point during the day, as often as one finds it profitable. It has five steps: gratitude for blessings, prayer for enlightenment, review of life, forgiveness, and amendment of life.

Though many see the examen as a simple inventory of faults and failings, it has a much wider and richer application. The Latin word *conscientia* means not only "conscience," which judges the rightness or wrongness of our actions,

---

97. While Saint Ignatius offers the examen earlier in the Exercises (in the first week), it is meant to be an abiding practice throughout the retreat and in daily life. Although he initially offers the examen for the purgation of past sins, even for one's whole life, he wants us to continue to use it to advance toward perfection in the life of illumination characterized by the second week of the Exercises. I treat the examen here because of its relation to the theme of vigilance in the Song of Songs (2:15).

but also "consciousness," which is an awareness of all that is going on in my heart. Beyond a moral application, it can lead us to become grateful for the many blessings God bestows on us each day. The examen can also serve as a tool for discernment of spirits as we become more sensitive to spiritual movements of consolation and desolation in our relationship with God.

The first important habit to acquire in making the examen prayer is that of interior listening, which involves reflection on oneself and one's relationship with God. Because life often distracts us from such healthy introspection, we need to turn inward and hear God communicating with us in the depths of our consciousness. The bride in the Song of Songs is keenly aware of her inner life and the deep movements of her heart in response to the presence of her bridegroom. She knows he is her heart's desire and asks to be drawn after him. Though a sinner, she experiences his mercy. The bride knows herself to be beautiful in her bridegroom's sight and expresses admiration for his beauty. She is sensitive to her bridegroom's approach over the hills, his peering at her through the lattices, and his call to come away. The bride's attentiveness symbolizes how our growing habit of interior listening results in greater perception and responsiveness to the Lord's promptings.

When we pray the examen prayer, we should first call to mind the ways in which God has blessed us that day. This helps us cultivate a consistent spirit of gratitude. Gratitude is a positive virtue that brings us a sense of wellness at being blessed by God and results in feelings of peace and joy. Gratitude correlates with our capacity to love. As we realize in our thanksgiving how much God loves us in bestowing his many blessings upon us, we are moved to love God, neighbor, and self. Therefore, Saint Ignatius wants us to consider the many gifts God has bestowed upon us each day, gifts of grace and nature, in order to love God more. We only have to look to discover so many gifts and offer thanks.

Our tendency is to focus on what is wrong with our lives or what is missing from them. By only focusing on the negative events in life, we can be blinded to the more fundamental goodness we experience. Gratitude is an antidote to negative thinking and complaining, which sucks the joy out of our lives. For example, one father writes that he is grateful for the taxes he pays, because it means that he is employed. He is thankful for the lawn that needs mowing, the windows that need cleaning, and the gutters that need fixing, because that means he has a home. He is grateful for the teenager who complains about doing dishes, because that means the child is at home, not on the streets. Taking time to focus on gratitude for God's blessings contributes to our feelings of love and well-being and enables us to serve more faithfully.

The experience of a young adult named Inigo illustrates the value of gratitude in this first step of the examen. One summer, Inigo volunteered to go to Nicaragua with a medical mission team, which vaccinated the poor villagers against various diseases. Some of the children had already contracted the dreaded diseases and were turned away, leaving Inigo feeling heartbroken and even guilty. He wondered whose fault it was and how God could permit such suffering. One night, while stargazing with a friend, Inigo became aware of the beauty of creation all around him and realized how great God's gifts were to him. Waking the next morning, he walked through the woods to bathe in the river, enjoying the sounds of singing birds and running water. Again he experienced gratitude for all God's gifts to him. At that moment Inigo felt wonderful, and everything fell into place. Never before had he felt so thankful for all that God had given him. Never before had he felt so loved. As he helped vaccinate the villagers that day, Inigo had such a big smile on his face that his cheeks hurt.[98] He had been so focused on all the negative aspects of the people's suffering that he failed to recognize the more fundamental goodness of creation. Once Inigo took the time to notice God's gifts in the beauty all around him, gratitude flooded over him. This gratitude in turn gave him a desire to love and serve God's people in response to God's love for him.

In contrast to the spirit of gratitude, Saint Ignatius was convinced that ingratitude was the worst of sins. In his letter to a confrere he wrote: "Ingratitude ... should be detested in the sight of our Creator and Lord by all of His creatures who are capable of enjoying His divine and everlasting glory, for it is a forgetting of the graces, benefits, and blessings received. As such, it is the cause, beginning, and origin of all sins and misfortunes."[99] We might take God's gifts for granted and fail to count them, only noticing them if they are withheld momentarily. So we lack gratitude. Sometimes we are so distracted that we fail to recognize our dependence upon God and don't appreciate his continuous gifts and blessings.

---

98. See Mark Link, *Staygreat* web site: http://www.staygreat.com/staygreat.aspx.

99. Saint Ignatius of Loyola, Letter to Simon Rodrigues, in *Letters of Saint Ignatius of Loyola*, trans. William J. Young (Chicago: Loyola University Press, 1959), 55.

Several years ago a magazine ran a story about a man who decided late one night to go fishing in a bay. Everything was quiet as he sat in his rowboat until he suddenly heard a man hollering from the deck of a nearby yacht. The fisherman tried to ignore the noise. Then he saw the man tumble from his yacht into the water with a loud splash. At once the fisherman tore off his coat, dove into the bay, and swam over to help the man. After a monumental effort, he managed to drag the man back onto his yacht. The fisherman gave artificial respiration to the lifeless man until he was breathing normally again. Once the fisherman was sure the man was fine, he put him to bed and swam back to his own rowboat. The next morning the fisherman returned to the yacht to check on the man. But the man was brusque and obnoxious. The fisherman reminded him that he had risked his own life to save his. Rather than thanking the fisherman, the man yelled at him and demanded he get off his yacht. The fisherman rowed away in tears. He couldn't believe how badly he had just been treated. He looked up and told God that he now understood how Jesus had saved us and how we, like the man on the yacht, demand that God leave us alone. The man now understood how Jesus must feel, and it broke his heart.[100] The fisherman was given insight into the heart of Christ, wounded by so much ingratitude for the gift of salvation he offers. Gratitude, by contrast, counteracts our tendency toward egoism, selfishness, and over-indulgence by reminding us that all we have comes from God.

Movements of Spirit

After we reflect with gratitude in the examen, we ask for light to be aware of the movements of spirit during our day. Where have I felt consolation leading me closer to God, and where have I experienced desolation leading me away from God? Of course, our own faults often contribute to our spiritual desolation, a truth we should ponder in relation to our day. We are often blind to our faults and can only see them with God's enlightenment. John Paul II reminds us that "only in the divine light which is revealed in Christ and which lives in the Church can we clearly detect our faults."[101]

---

100. See Link, *Illustrated Sunday Homilies*, Series II, Ordinary Time 28C, 115.

101. John Paul II, General Audience, March 14, 1984, *The Teachings of Pope John Paul II*, CD-Rom (Harmony Media, 1998).

Although we must make some efforts to recall our life experiences, we should rely primarily on God's grace. For this second step of the examen, we might simply petition, "Lord, let me see my day as you see it," or "Lord, show me the events of my day that you want me to see." With such a petition, we trust that God will show us whatever we need to see and to understand our life experience. At other times, we may come to the examen prayer with an event or relationship already weighing on our hearts. In these cases, we could seek enlightenment from the Lord for his perspective on our situation.

Having prayed for enlightenment, in the third step of the examen we review our day. We may discover moments of spiritual consolation where we felt close to God, or we may notice negative experiences where we felt distant from God. We need courage to face these more painful experiences, but we can feel secure in God's presence, knowing he wants to help us. Perhaps we have sinned, or maybe others have hurt us and we reacted in certain ways. It is important to pay attention to all these experiences.

While Saint Ignatius has us notice our sins, we don't need to catalogue them. We can, however, pay attention to the few that stand out, perhaps small neglects or failures, or sins of omission where we could have performed a charitable act but didn't. The struggle to overcome ourselves in little things will enable us to be faithful in greater and keep us from backsliding into more serious faults.

Saint Francis de Sales explains our need for vigilance in overcoming small temptations that arise throughout the day: "While it is not a hard thing to abstain from murder . . . it is very difficult to avoid all-passing fits of anger, which assail us at every moment. . . . While it is easy to keep from stealing another man's goods, it is often difficult to resist coveting them."[102] In the same way, the bride is called to be vigilant about even the little foxes that could eat the flowers and destroy the vineyard, symbolizing the destructiveness of sin. If the flowers do not grow, neither will the fruit. The bride must be vigilant about any slight evil, represented by the little foxes, that would interfere with her relationship with her lover.

Once we have reviewed our day, we take our experiences to the Lord for a moment of graced encounter. If we have experienced spiritual consolation,

---

102. Saint Francis de Sales, *Introduction to the Devout Life* (Christian Classics Ethereal Library), http://www.ccel.org/ccel/desales/devout_life.vi.viii.html, part 4, ch. 8.

we might rejoice with the Lord and unpack its meaning in order to grow in faith, hope, and love. If we have experienced spiritual desolation, we can express our negative feelings to the Lord, like the disciples on the road to Emmaus, trusting that he hears us and will lead us to greater understanding. With God's grace we could also resist the desolation and make acts of trust in the Lord. If we have sinned, we can now bring our faults to God so he may forgive us. God is waiting for us, like the father awaiting the prodigal son, in order to show us his mercy.

Confessing our sins and asking for forgiveness now becomes a moment of graced encounter with Jesus. Rather than distancing us from the Lord, our sinfulness can draw us closer to him. Our relationship to God is like a cord that binds us together, broken by sin and retied in forgiveness, which reduces the length of the cord and the distance between us. We actually draw closer to God in the process of reconciliation. Practicing this step of asking forgiveness in the examen helps us develop a greater awareness that the Lord's mercy is constantly bestowed upon us.

Though we tend to put limits on God's mercy, he is always steadfastly faithful to us, always forgiving when we repent. Brother Lawrence describes his experience of confessing his sins and asking for forgiveness: "The King, full of mercy and goodness, very far from chastising me, embraces me with love, makes me eat at His table, serves me with His own hands, gives me the key of His treasures; He converses and delights Himself with me incessantly, in a thousand ways, and treats me in all respects as his favorite."[103]

With reverence for the Lord his King, Brother Lawrence approaches him as a sinner. He realizes that God forgives, loves, and accepts him. Jesus even becomes a servant to Brother Lawrence, just as he assumed the role of a slave and washed the feet of his disciples, cleansing them from sin. In being forgiven, Brother Lawrence experiences the truth of his own existence as a loved sinner called into friendship with Christ.

The final step of the examen prayer is to propose amendment of our lives, relying on the grace of God. In the previous steps we may have discovered a particular pattern of sin, a place where conversion has to take place. This

---

103. Brother Lawrence of the Resurrection, *The Practice of the Presence of God: The Best Rule of a Holy Life*, Second Letter (New York, Fleming H. Revell Company, 1895), 25-26. https://archive.org/details/brotherlawrencep00lawr.

awareness could develop over a period of days or weeks and may become the focus of our ongoing conversion in life. Saint Ignatius once had an awareness of a movement of heart that was opposed to his spiritual growth. As soon as he realized his disposition was contrary to what God wanted, he observed it and actively pursued what he perceived as God's will.[104] Saint Ignatius countered his tendency toward vice by moving in the contrary direction toward the opposite virtue.

A man named Tom Anderson once rented an ocean cottage for a two-week vacation with his family on the New Jersey shore Before he began to drive there with his wife, Tom thought about how he had recently been living his role as a husband and father, and realized he could improve. He decided to commit to being attentive and caring toward his family for the next two weeks. Tom stopped contacting his office or any clients while he was at home. He caught himself before speaking any harsh words. For those two weeks he was considerate, loving, and caring. Everything was going great until the last night of the vacation. Tom noticed that his wife was looking at him with a grave countenance as though something were seriously wrong. Tom looked at her with wonder and asked her what was wrong. She began to cry, asking Tom if he knew something that she didn't. He honestly replied that he didn't. She went on to explain, "Last week I went to the doctor for a checkup. You've been so kind to me, Tom. Tell me the truth. Did the doctor tell you I had cancer? Did he say I'm going to die? Is that why you've been so good to me, Tom?"

At first Tom was stunned by her concerns and then he laughed and hugged his wife, saying, "No, honey, you're not going to die. It's just that I'm just starting to live."[105]

Tom ended his review of life, his examen, by resolving to improve his marriage with God's help. His wife's reaction to the change suggests that he had, in fact, sorely neglected her. Tom's change of heart reveals the renewal of life that results from practicing the fifth step of the examen prayer, amendment of life. This step helps us to move beyond our past mistakes and face the future with restored vision and sensitivity to God's grace. The pruning of destructive tendencies of the past stimulates new shoots of growth for the

---

104. See *Spiritual Journal* , par. 382.
105. See Link, *Illustrated Sunday Homilies*, Series II, Advent 1B, 2.

future. The bride likewise is exhorted to watchfulness and cooperation with the bridegroom in catching the foxes that threaten to destroy the vineyard. By practicing the examen prayer, we grow in our vigilance in recognizing the Lord's blessings, in checking our heart's subtle tendencies toward sin, and in seeking opportunities to practice virtue.

Questions for Reflection and Discussion

1. What has been your experience of praying any form of an examination of conscience? What was emphasized? How well have you persevered in it?

2. What do you find attractive about the examen prayer? Do you conceive of it differently than before? How might this method of prayer renew your spiritual life?

3. How well do you practice gratitude for God's blessings each day? How can you do so better?

4. Do you seek God's enlightenment about your spiritual state of being and sinfulness? Do you notice a difference when you do?

5. Would you find it helpful to use the examen prayer for discernment of spirits, noticing movements of consolation and desolation and then taking action?

6. Do you experience God's forgiveness daily?

7. What new spiritual energy do you notice as you face the future in the final step of amendment of life in the examen?

Prayer Exercises

1. Pray with Second Corinthians 1:5–19, and ask for the grace of a greater awareness of your conscience and the courage to follow it.

2. Choose a time daily to practice the examen prayer for 10–15 minutes, using Saint Ignatius' five steps: gratitude for blessings, prayer for enlightenment, review of life, forgiveness, and amendment of life.

3. Read the story of the fisherman who saved a man from drowning (p. 175). Pray with Luke 17:11–19, and ask for the grace to have a grateful heart for all the spiritual and material blessings of your life.

4. Read Saint John Paul II's quote on praying for enlightenment (p. 175). Pray with John 4:14–26, and ask for the grace that God reveal your sins, faults, and neglects to you.

5. Reflect on Saint Francis de Sales' quote (p. 176). Pray with Song of Songs 2:15 and Second Corinthians 10:5, and ask for the grace to take captive every thought, word, and deed for Christ.

6. Read Brother Lawrence's quote (p. 177). Pray with Luke 18:35–43, and ask for the grace of a renewed sense of God's mercy toward you.

7. Ponder the story of Tom Anderson (p. 178). Pray with Luke 19:1–10, and ask for the grace of greater hope and renewed energy in Christ's service.

Chapter 16

The Foxes of Deception

[B] Catch us the foxes,
   the little foxes,
that ruin the vineyards—
   for our vineyards are in blossom. (Song 2:15)

It is a mark of the evil spirit to assume the appearance of an angel of light. He begins by suggesting thoughts that are suited to a devout soul, and ends by suggesting his own. For example, he will suggest holy and pious thoughts that are wholly in conformity with the sanctity of the soul. Afterwards, he will endeavor little by little to end by drawing the soul into his hidden snares and evil designs. (SpEx 332)

Symbolizing cunning and deceit, the fox is a good image for Satan, "for he is a liar and the father of lies" (Jn 8:44). In the second week of the Spiritual Exercises, Saint Ignatius gives us tools to unmask the deceits of the devil in the *Rules for Discernment of Spirits*. During the first week of the Exercises, we saw that Satan uses spiritual desolation as the primary tool to discourage us and attack our faith, hope, and love. As we grow wiser and learn to see through his tactics, Satan changes his strategy. He now tries to deceive us by using spiritual consolation. So that we won't languish in consolation that misleads, Saint Ignatius offers another set of rules to help us deal with such deception.

Deceit is the hallmark of the enemy's methodology: "It is characteristic of the evil one," as Saint Ignatius explains, "to fight against such happiness and consolation [from God] by proposing fallacious reasonings, subtleties, and continual deceptions" (SpEx 329). Saint Ignatius then describes the nature of the enemy's falsehood and deceit, how he appears as an angel of light as described earlier. Satan the fox seeks to destroy the vineyard of the Lord in the souls of his beloved ones by appealing even to our intentions of doing good. By suggesting apparent goods that seem in harmony with God's designs but ultimately are not, the enemy leads us astray from the right path.

Saint Ignatius warns us that the evil spirit works to sow seeds of destruction even in holy souls. Satan would like nothing better than to thwart the progress of anyone seeking greater union with God and the growth of his kingdom. We see this dynamic in the life of Saint John Vianney, the Curé of Ars, a simple man of great faith. When he was assigned to the rural parish of Ars in southeastern France, Vianney's preaching, catechesis, and pastoral availability transformed the parish. It became a center for spiritual renewal for Ars and all of France, drawing countless pilgrims to encounter God's mercy through the holy Curé. Ironically, at the pinnacle of his pastoral success, John Vianney often desired to leave his parish and enter a Trappist or Carthusian monastery to dedicate himself fully to prayer and penance. Following this allurement, three times he fled the parish and sought to join the monastery. Each time, he returned to his parish either by popular demand or obedience to his bishop. Over time, he refused to give in to and eventually conquered his escapist tendencies. Although he still felt a desire for the monastic life, Vianney revealed them to his spiritual directors. They helped him to recognize the devil's hand and to see the tremendous good he was doing. Vianney realized that a life of solitude, no matter how good in itself, was not God's will for him. We can understand how Vianney might instinctively have desired to escape from such a heavy burden of pastoral care. Nevertheless, he himself realized that something about the desire was not of God, and that the enemy—that is, the devil—was trying to tempt him through it.[106]

---

106. See Francis Trochu, *The Curé D'Ars, St. Jean-Marie-Baptiste Vianney (1786–1859) According to the Acts of the Process of Canonization and numerous hitherto unpublished documents* (London: Burns Oates & Washbourne, 1951), 339–361.

We can see from these episodes how the enemy, like a fox, sought to destroy the fruitful vineyard of the Lord. Dealing with someone at this stage of spiritual maturity, John Vianney's enemy changed tactics. Instead of the usual means of spiritual desolation: he proposed an apparent good—to go away and join a monastery. Who would argue that a life of prayer, penance, and solitude in the pursuit of union with God is not a good thing? How attractive it must have seemed to John Vianney in the midst of his trials and labor in parish work. The enemy began by suggesting good and pious thoughts to a holy soul, and ended with his own suggestions. Those suggestions probably attracted Vianney because he was living an unbalanced life, often spending eighteen hours a day in the confessional without leisure time. Satan attacked him at his weakest point and almost succeeded in derailing Vianney from God's will for his life. Over time, through the benefit of his spiritual directors, he learned to recognize the deception and to fight against it.

In the Song of Songs, the bride faces similar temptations under the guise of good. In 2:14, she is tempted to hide in solitude in the clefts of the rock when the bridegroom calls to her so that he can see her face and hear her voice. Later, in 5:2–6, the bride chooses to remain complacently on her bed when the bridegroom knocks and seeks to enter. She mistakenly decides to remain retired for the night and so misses her opportunity to welcome the bridegroom.

Discernment

In his landmark work *Discernment of Spirits*, Jules Toner offers some modern images and situations that can help us to understand the subtle and deceptive workings of the enemy.[107] Some televangelists, for example, may be good and trustworthy, but others preach inspiring thoughts to disarm listeners and draw them into a counterfeit plea for generosity—or even worse, to lead them into a perverse cult. Another relevant image that mirrors the evil one's tactics is that of a seducer who appeals to a woman's wholesome religious sentiments, while his ultimate purpose is to calmly and cleverly snare her into unchaste behavior. We could also imagine a card shark who allows

---

107. See Jules Toner, *A Commentary on Saint Ignatius' Rules for the Discernment of Spirits* (St. Louis: The Institute for Jesuit Sources, 1982), 229.

his unsuspecting prey to win a few hands, getting well ahead, before plundering his victim when the stakes are high. In all these cases, the deceitful person begins with good suggestions and outcomes that appeal to the victim's good intentions in order to lure his prey into an evil result.

As we seek God and his will, we listen for the inspiration of the Holy Spirit. The enemy will also attempt to mimic the Spirit's work. But the enemy inspires us toward what is ultimately evil, under the guise of doing good. The inspiration might be toward something objectively good but not subjectively good or appropriate for the person at that moment. In discerning we should ask: Does this course of action fit this particular person? Toner offers examples of persons who are led astray. A zealous person at early stages of conversion may have impulsive desires to undertake great things for God, great things beyond the scope of his or her talents, spiritual endowment, or preparation. Or the evil one may corrupt an originally good inspiration that came from God and was put into practice. For instance, someone with great commercial acumen who initially wanted to help others to acquire wealth might later become obsessed with making money at the expense of others. Or an introverted person may love contemplation and the pursuit of God in prayer. The introvert might extol the value of prayer but use it to avoid real contact with others or challenging opportunities to serve. By contrast, the enemy can easily suggest an imbalance of activism to people who love to work for good causes, suggesting that prayer is a waste of time. Eventually the person might experience burn-out and no longer desire to serve God and others. Or, if the activist's cause does not turn out according to his or her agenda, he or she may experience a weakened commitment to the good cause, discouragement, or bitterness. In each case, the enemy goes along with the weakness or extreme tendency of the person under the guise of good in order to lead toward his wicked result.

Discernment is often a long and delicate process that requires patience and vigilance. We cannot be rash in our judgment or impetuous in our desire to pursue goals. Instead, we must test our desires and objectives throughout the discernment process to insure that our disordered attractions or fallacious reasonings do not lead us astray. If anything is wrong with a part of the inspiration, course of action, or consequences, it will affect the goodness of the whole. Saint Ignatius advises us to "carefully observe the whole course of our thoughts" (SpEx 333) in the discernment process. If the whole course of thoughts is entirely good and oriented toward what is completely right, that indicates they are from the Spirit of God. But if the course of thoughts ends in what troubles the person, ruining one's previous peace and harmony, that might divert us from a greater good we had chosen before. Saint Ignatius tells us these signs clearly indicate that "the thoughts are proceeding from the evil spirit, the enemy of our progress and eternal salvation" (SpEx 333).

For Saint Ignatius the process of discernment of spirits means that the head and the heart agree on the rightness of a particular course of action. We should judge our thoughts to see what is right and wrong in them. We should also pay attention to our deep feelings to see if we are at peace or if anything disturbs us. If we find anything evil in our thoughts and affections that might taint the overall good, we must reject that evil.

We can see Saint Ignatius' rule illustrated in the life of David, a religious priest in his mid-forties who is pastor of a large parish and school.[108] The parishioners greatly admire David for his preaching, and because of his skill, he teaches homiletics at the seminary. He is often called upon to give retreats due to his wise insight into the spiritual life. When David prays, he feels consolation resulting from his work in teaching and giving retreats, which are not his primary ministry. Still, the fruits are negative: tensions abound in the parish and in David's religious community; he suffers in trying to hold it all together. When his associate pastor has the courage to call David's attention to the problems, David becomes angry. He feels insulted at the suggestion that his consolation-filled work could be wrong. Prayer becomes difficult and unattractive, and David is unable to find God as present as before. On the brink of abandoning parish work, a major vocational mistake, he makes a retreat. There he discovers that his desire to abandon his ministry results from a heart overly weighed down by his many labors. With his director's help, he pares down his non-essential commitments into something more manageable and restores the balance in his life.

Looking more closely at David's discernment, we notice warning signs evident at the beginning, middle, and end of the process. David felt excitement at his many gifts being used in so many diverse ways, not only in the parish but also in retreat work and teaching homiletics. At this early stage, he

---

108. See Timothy Gallagher, *Spiritual Consolation*, 66–69.

could have examined his spiritual consolation and realized the difficulty in giving himself fully to parish work and to the other ministries. In the middle of his discernment process, as tensions arose in the parish, David could have noticed that his being away from the parish did not bear good fruit. The parish suffers and, as Saint Ignatius warns, now something less good happens. Finally, at the end of the discernment process, David becomes aware of his frustration and deep disquiet. He is tempted to abandon his parish ministry in disobedience to his religious superior. With his director's help he realizes this course of action is clearly evil. David now understands that his desire to give up is coming from a feeling of heaviness of heart, and he resists giving in to the temptation to leave. We see from David's example the importance of observing "the whole course of our thoughts and actions" to ensure that we are striving to do what is entirely right and good at each stage of discernment.

A Special Kind of Consolation

Saint Ignatius recognizes only one experience as clearly coming from God without any possibility of the enemy's deception. He refers to this experience as "consolation without previous cause." He writes: "God alone can give consolation to the soul without any previous cause. It belongs solely to the Creator to come into a soul, to leave it, to act upon it, to draw it wholly to the love of His Divine Majesty" (SpEx 330).

Most of the spiritual consolations we receive have some preceding cause: some spiritual activity, understanding, or object of our attention that we experience immediately before the consolation occurs. Such a preceding cause could be a reflection on Sacred Scripture, an awareness of the beauty of creation, or a recollection of God's favors in my life. In these cases the spiritual consolation is derived in some way from our faculties of understanding and will. While we can trust the vast majority of spiritual consolations, in these the possibility of deception still remains, for the enemy can influence our intellect and will through suggestions to our mind and heart. By contrast, no experience precipitates a consolation without preceding cause. The spiritual consolation comes from out of the blue, so to speak. The enemy cannot twist any preceding cause or experience to his purposes.

Saint Ignatius describes a couple of instances in which he received the gift of spiritual consolation without preceding cause, such as one he recounts in his *Spiritual Journal*. He came into the chapel and was flooded with total love for the Holy Trinity, growing in devotion and shedding tears.[109] In this case, Saint Ignatius was not meditating or contemplating but rather doing something very routine when the consolation occurred. We notice how Saint Ignatius is entirely caught up in God's love, in an experience that touches his whole person. This experience is disproportionately intense and beyond the ordinary ways of experiencing God's love. Because the effect is far beyond the cause, it could only have come from God.

A few days later, Saint Ignatius had a similar experience of consolation without preceding cause. One day as he reflected that he would be offering the Mass of the Holy Trinity, his heart was totally consumed with love for the divine Persons and he was moved to tears and sobbed.[110] Saint Ignatius experienced consolation without preceding cause according to his own definition of being drawn "wholly to the love of His Divine Majesty" (SpEx 330).

When we receive a consolation without preceding cause, we should pay close attention to it. Because they are certainly from God, these consolations will have some important meaning to us. The experience may tell us something significant about our relationship with God. Perhaps it will indicate a special calling from God and help us to understand his will for our lives.

Recall the story of Pauline in chapter 12 and her definitive experience of her vocational call. Two years before that, she'd had an experience that began to prepare her for her eventual call. Pauline describes the experience:

> I was in our living room scanning our Catholic weekly newspaper when I came across the prayer of Saint Ignatius, the *Suscipe*. Interestingly, I was doing this only because there was nothing else to do at the time. When I got to the words of the prayer, "Give me your love . . . with that I am rich enough," an interior command seemed to take hold of me, one which I can only try to describe in this way. I heard no words, but I seemed to know what I was to do: Stand up, fold the newspaper, go to my room. This I did. When I got to my room, the interior command continued: Shut the door, kneel down. When I did this, my soul was invaded by an onrush of a power I could never describe. Something was poured into me that brought on a torrent of tears; and I just said, "Give me your love, give me your love," over and over again.[111]

---

109. *See Spiritual Journal*, pars. 99–100.
110. Ibid., par. 130
111. Toner, *What Is Your Will, O God?*, 75.

It was important for Pauline to pay attention to this encounter because it was one of several experiences that eventually led her to receive a call to vowed religious life. We can see in her experience an instance of consolation without preceding cause.

The time immediately following any spiritual consolation should be distinguished from the actual moment of the consolation. In this time afterward, Saint Ignatius explains, the person is still enthusiastic, experiencing the consequences of the consolation that has ended. Saint Ignatius warns that afterward "the soul frequently forms various resolutions and plans which are not granted directly by God our Lord. They may come from our own reasoning on the relations of our concepts and on the consequences of our judgments, or they may come from the good or evil spirit. Hence, they must be carefully examined before they are given full approval and put into execution" (SpEx 336).

The time immediately following a spiritual consolation could be called an "afterglow" experience. After the consolation, we continue to linger in the delightful feelings and memory of the encounter. In many respects, however, this afterglow is distinct from the consolation, as Saint Ignatius points out. During the actual moment of consolation, we are under the immediate influence of God, while in the afterglow we are not. Here we may introduce our own thoughts or be open to the influence of the evil one, all the while thinking the influence remains God's. We can only be sure about the feelings and ideas revealed during the consolation itself. If we blur our consolations with our afterglows, then we can easily make the mistake of assuming that God sanctions all our opinions and plans.

Consider Saint Peter's experience atop Mount Tabor. He saw the Lord transfigured—radiant, dazzling—and heard the Father's voice, "This is my Beloved Son, with whom I am well pleased, listen to him" (see Lk 9:28–36). Falling on their faces in awe, Peter and the others certainly experienced great consolation. This experience was intended to show Peter, James, and John who Jesus really was and to strengthen them for his impending passion, death, and resurrection. In the moment of afterglow, Peter missed the point of the revelation and introduced his own inspiration and plans. He exclaimed, "Master, it is good for us to be here; let us make three dwellings, one for you, one for Moses, and one for Elijah." Luke adds that he was "not knowing what he said," to show that after the experience Peter misinterpreted its meaning. Jesus explains to Peter that he was not given the experience in order to remain on the mountaintop in ecstasy but so that he would have the courage to descend into the valley of suffering. Then Peter remonstrates with Jesus that he should not have to suffer. Jesus tells Peter, "Get behind me, Satan! You are a stumbling block to me; for you are setting your mind not on divine things but on human things" (Mt 16:23). In the afterglow of the consolation, Peter offered his own interpretation of the event, which was clearly mistaken.

Throughout the Song of Songs, the bride is tested in her desires and in judgments to discern the bridegroom's presence and call. Early in the poem, she determines that he is the only one she seeks, not the mere sensual delights of wine and perfume. As a lost shepherdess, she begs for the wisdom to discern how to pasture her flock in the right path, learning to follow in the tracks of her shepherd. She perceives the bridegroom coming as a gazelle over the hills and discerns his presence, peering at her through the lattice. Discerning the true voice of her bridegroom, the bride follows his call to come away. Now the bridegroom warns her about the danger of the cunning foxes that could destroy the fruit of their vineyard. As we listen for the voice of God and labor in his vineyard, we too must be careful to distinguish his consolations from those of the wily enemy who seeks only to destroy.

Questions for Reflection and Discussion

1. Have you ever fallen victim to deceptions by the enemy spirit? How did it come about? When did you recognize it? How were you able to change course and return to God?

2. Like Saint John Vianney, do you tend to be vulnerable to a particular deception? How can you better defend against it?

3. Have you ever experienced an inspiration that seemed to be legitimate, except for one or two things that were not quite right? How did you discover it and deal with it?

4. How do you fall victim to the deception to do too many things in God's service, or things beyond your talent, spiritual endowment, or preparation?

5. Do you ever succumb to the temptation to do too little out of fear or desire to remain in your comfort zone? How do you recognize this and overcome it?

6. Have you ever experienced what Saint Ignatius calls "consolation without preceding cause"? When you examine the consolation, can you find a message of particular importance about God's relationship with you and his will for your life?

7. Have you ever had to distinguish between a moment of consolation and the afterglow experience?

Prayer Exercises

1. Reflect on the story of Saint John Vianney (p. 182). Pray with Genesis 3:1–7, and ask for the grace to be aware of the fallacious reasoning, subtleties, and continual deception of the enemy.

2. Ponder Rule 329 (p. 182) of Saint Ignatius' Spiritual Exercises. Pray with Matthew 13:24–30, and ask for the grace of knowledge of the discernment of spirits.

3. Read Saint Ignatius' rule 333 (p. 184) and David's experience (p. 185). Pray with Matthew 7:16–20 and Galatians 5:22, and ask for the grace to know the authenticity of consolation by its fruit.

4. Read Saint Ignatius' description of "consolation without preceding cause" (p. 186). Consider the story of Pauline (p. 187). Pray with Luke 1:26–38, and ask for the grace to be open and attentive to the Lord's gifts.

5. Read Saint Ignatius' description of the afterglow experience (SpEx 336, p. 188). Pray with Luke 9:28–36, and ask for the grace to remain faithful to the Lord's actual consolation and not mistake your own ideas and plans for his.

6. Pray with 1 John 4:1–6, and ask for the grace to test the spirits and discern well between true and false prophets in the world and in your life.

7. Make a repetition on any of the above contemplations, returning especially to the place of greater movement of spirit (consolation or desolation).

CHAPTER 17

The Night of Absence

[B] Upon my bed by night
I sought him whom my soul loves;
I sought him, but found him not;
    I called him, but he gave no answer.
"I will rise now and go about the city,
    in the streets and in the squares;
I will seek him whom my soul loves."
    I sought him, but found him not.
The sentinels found me,
    as they went about in the city.
"Have you seen him whom my soul loves?"
Scarcely had I passed them,
    when I found him whom my soul loves.
I held him, and would not let him go
until I brought him into my mother's house,
    and into the chamber of her that conceived me.
I adjure you, O daughters of Jerusalem,
    by the gazelles or the wild does:
do not stir up or awaken love
    until it is ready! (Song 3:1–5)

Consider what Christ our Lord suffers in His human nature, or according to
the passage contemplated, what He desires to suffer. Then I will begin with
great effort to strive to grieve, be sad, and weep.... Consider how the divinity
hides itself; for example, it could destroy its enemies and does not do so, but

leaves the most sacred humanity to suffer so cruelly. . . . Consider that Christ suffers all this for my sins, and what I ought to do and suffer for Him. (SpEx 195–197)

Throughout the first two chapters of the Song of Songs, the bride has been seeking her bridegroom with passionate desire and readily finds him in spiritual consolation. He has taken her into his chambers to enjoy the wine of spiritual ecstasy. She has rested in his shadow, held in his embrace. Now a most sacred moment in the Jewish wedding ritual arrives: the moment to consummate the marriage, when the bridegroom comes to the bridal chamber. But suddenly the bridegroom disappears. We see here a veiled reference to the crucifixion. Jesus had said that when the bridegroom would be taken away, then the disciples would fast (see Mt 9:15). The bride now painfully experiences her bridegroom's absence in the dark night. She is on her bed expecting him, but he does not appear. The bride's friend is lost and she cannot find him. All the pleasant experiences have now passed: the scent of the flowers, the richness of the fruits, and the fragrance of the vines. Now she is bereft, left in sadness and grief.

Like the bride, in the spiritual life we go through many "dark nights," figuratively speaking. In these difficult moments of purification it seems impossible to find God. Sometimes smaller dark nights occur in the early stages of our spiritual journey, as we are being purified from sin and egoism. We need this because none of us is fully conformed to Christ. Even the bride must be purified. Though she is conformed to Christ, she still has places of self-centeredness, symbolized richly by her bed of comfort. The bride on her bed at night also suggests dreams and places in the unconscious depths of self, where the Gospel has not yet penetrated. Maloney describes how, as we make progress in the spiritual life, we come to realize what these nights mean:

> Such purification is a call to go deeper into your "heart," the scriptural symbol of deepest consciousness, in self-surrendering love to Christ as your supreme lover. Beyond all preconditioning of your false self, your past training, thought patterns, even sins, you are called by Christ to enter deeper and deeper into your consciousness and to claim new areas of conquest in the

dark recesses of your unconscious. You push in prayerful encounter with Christ through the various strata of emotions and affections, beyond the confinement of fixity arranged comfortably into a status quo of heredity, social relationships, and former prayer experiences.[112]

The bride has become comfortable and complacent, satisfied with the status quo in her relationship with the bridegroom, symbolized by her resting on her bed. We too can grow self-satisfied in our spiritual life and ignore the need for ongoing conversion and growth in our relationship with the Lord. The experience of darkness invites us to open our hearts to God's deep work of renovation.

Beginners in the spiritual journey are often led swiftly and easily to their desired goal of union with God. Eventually, however, they hit patches of dryness that may even develop into dark nights that test their faith and perseverance. This dynamic is analogous to that of married couples. The early days of a marriage are blissful. It is easy for the couple to love one another, as the spouses can see only the other's goodness. Over time, however, the romance fades and each one's faults and weaknesses become more obvious. Even the qualities that once attracted one partner to the other might now irritate them, and they grow disillusioned. At this crucial point in the marriage the couple must make a decision to love, with a love no longer based on pleasant feelings. Each spouse should will the good of the other, despite the lack of feeling or the cost to self. This decision to love invigorates the marriage and leads to true joy.

In the divine romance, God refines our love in a similar way. So far in our spiritual lives it has been easy to seek God and enjoy his presence and delights in prayer. But what happens when he withdraws his gift? Will we continue to seek only his consolations? Or will we move beyond mere good feelings to God himself? The bride has to move out of her comfortable bed to seek her bridegroom in the night. She no longer experiences the good feelings associated with his presence, but must choose to seek him in the night of absence.

The drama of the bridegroom's presence and absence, woven through the Song of Songs, serves as a clear paradigm for our spiritual lives. Experiencing the Lord close to us strengthens our union with him, while experiencing his distance tests our faithfulness and desire for him. The seeming absence of

---

112. Maloney, *Singers of the New Song*, 59.

God is perhaps the most tortuous of all trials in the spiritual life. The martyrs could fervently offer their sufferings to Christ while he seemed near, but even they found the Lord's apparent absence a greater trial, where their sufferings didn't seem as meaningful.

Christ experienced everything we do, including this feeling of abandonment during his passion. His cry from the cross, "My God, my God, why have you forsaken me?" (Mt 27:46) expresses this abandonment, his perceived forsakenness.

At this moment of the Song of Songs, the bride experiences seeming abandonment in the disappearance of her lover. The losing/finding dynamic continues to happen in the lives of contemporary Christians. Saint Teresa of Calcutta was granted ecstasies in prayer for a time, leading to her call to serve the poor and to found a new religious congregation. When those experiences were withdrawn, she was led into a long period of darkness. Somehow she managed to be cheerful in the face of her great trials. In anguish she surmised this might be the consequence of Jesus' express desire for her to share in his passion. She quietly and lovingly accepted his invitation to bear his cross.[113] Others could perceive Mother Teresa's closeness to God in her serenity and enthusiasm to serve others, even while she didn't feel God's presence. Nevertheless, she constantly went out of herself to seek the suffering Christ by serving the poor and downtrodden.

Contemplating the Passion and Death of Jesus

In the next phase of the Spiritual Exercises (the third week), Saint Ignatius has us seek the suffering Christ by contemplating his passion and death. Jesus' death is the apostles' night of absence, the moment when they lose Jesus. Jesus spoke of himself as the Bridegroom who would be taken away from his followers (see Mt 9:15). The bride's experience of losing the bridegroom corresponds to this loss of Jesus in his passion and death. She is compelled to go out and search for him. Saint Ignatius leads us to seek Christ, even as he is taken away from us in his passion. We descend deeply into participation with Christ in his suffering, into union with him here. To this end, we are to ask for sorrow with the sorrowing and brokenhearted Christ, tears

113. See Brian Kolodiejchuk, M.C., *Come Be My Light* (New York: Doubleday, 2007), 188.

and interior suffering for the suffering Christ, painfully aware of the suffering he endured for us (see SpEx 197). Deeply grieved at the loss of her bridegroom, the bride searches for him in anguish. The bride suffers the most precisely at this moment of loss.

In chapter 5 of the Song of Songs, the bride expresses similar grief over the loss of her beloved. Again she runs out to pursue him. She searches but fails to find him, but she is found by the watchmen, who mistreat her: "They beat me, they wounded me, they took away my mantle, those sentinels of the walls" (Song 5:7). She not only searches for her bridegroom, but she also shares in his suffering, being beaten and wounded with him. She suffers not only the loss of the bridegroom's presence, but also the harshness and cruelty of men, adding to her agony. The very people whom she used to consult for help and comfort now persecute her. Despite this abuse and betrayal, the bride still single-mindedly pursues the bridegroom. In fact, the torture only increases her desire for him. She seeks him even more ardently, without complaining about her sufferings.

Saint Ignatius ushers us into this same participation with Christ suffering as we come to greater union with him. Christ bears all this for our sins, so we are to consider what we "ought to do and suffer for Him" (SpEx 197). In light of Christ's sufferings, we ask God for the grace of "sorrow with Christ in sorrow, anguish with Christ in anguish, tears and deep grief because of the great affliction Christ endures for me" (SpEx 203). A lover desires to share the experience of the beloved, even to the point of suffering with him.

We begin the journey with Christ to Calvary by contemplating the Last Supper and the institution of the Holy Eucharist, Christ's supreme self-offering. His oblation is continued and completed through his passion and death on the cross. Saint Ignatius wants each of us to accept this self-offering of Christ "for me" (SpEx 203) in a very personal way. In return for Christ's total self-gift to us, we are invited to offer ourselves to the Father through, with, and in Christ. In these contemplations of the passion, we weep with Christ and consider what we ought to suffer for him in return. We make this same self-offering as we share in Christ's self-offering in the celebration of the Holy Eucharist. The theologian Bertrand de Margerie remarks:

> Communion is a participation in a sacrifice. To receive Communion is to become one victim with Christ for the glory of the Father and for the salvation of the world. Communion is not only to receive the present of the

ineffable Presence, but to unite myself, to associate myself most intimately to the action of this Presence, and even to his Passion, and so to commit myself to transform my whole life in a holocaust in which selfishness is ever consumed in the flames of charity.[114]

Christ is not sacrificed to dispense me from offering myself, but to give me the strength to do so happily and persistently. The Lord's passion does not give me a free pass to avoid suffering; it invites and strengthens me to willingly share his sacrifice and enter more deeply into union with him. The bride, beaten and wounded by the sentinels, is willing to offer herself in sacrifice in her desire for her beloved (5:7). In receiving Christ's sacrifice, we are brought to offer ourselves in sacrifice for others. As members of Christ's Body, and by his power, we are broken like bread and given to each other for sustenance and life.

In 1987 the film *Babette's Feast* won the Academy Award for the best foreign language film. This story shows the transforming power of a sacrificial meal. Babette is an exquisite chef who has fled to Denmark to escape civil turmoil in France. She seeks work as a cook for two women, the daughters of the now deceased austere pastor. They can't afford to pay Babette, so she offers to forego any wages. They agree, but they never allow her to cook extravagantly. Years later she wins the lottery and offers to cook a dinner to honor the memory of the pastor. After spending days in preparation, Babette serves the meal to the women and members of their congregation. They all are delighted as they dine, remembering the old pastor. Many divisions in the congregation are healed during the banquet as they confess their transgressions, forgive one another, and are reconciled. By the end of the meal, everyone is transformed, savoring the moment provided by this amazing chef. Afterward, the two sisters thank Babette and ask her where she will be moving, now that she has won the lottery. She tells them that she is going nowhere, because she couldn't afford to move. She spent all her money on the feast. The sisters are stunned that Babette spent all she had in order to make something beautiful for others. The complete sacrifice of her gift of self recalls Jesus' self-giving to us in the Last Supper. He gave himself totally, holding nothing back: "This is my body, given for you. . . . This is my blood, poured out for you" (see

---

114. Bertrand de Margerie, *Theological Retreat, with Some Ignatian Spiritual Exercises* (Chicago: Franciscan Herald Press, 1976), 177.

Lk 22:19–20). Just as the congregation is reconciled with each other during the meal, Jesus' sacrifice reconciles us to God and to one another. Just as Babette's feast transformed her guests, the Lord's banquet transforms us. Babette remained hidden during the meal; Jesus remains hidden in the Holy Eucharist. Babette chose to remain as their cook; Jesus chooses to remain with us always in the Holy Eucharist as a poor servant.

The Agony in the Garden

After contemplating the Last Supper, we contemplate Jesus' agony in the garden. In his agony Jesus models perseverance in prayer, despite the darkness and desolation we can suffer in the spiritual life. The author of Hebrews explains how Jesus suffered the same anguish we do: "In the days of his flesh, Jesus offered up prayers and supplications, with loud cries and tears, to him who was able to save him from death, and he was heard for his godly fear" (Heb 5:7–8). Christ shows us the way to peace by persevering in prayer even in the midst of anguish. This perseverance is often experienced as a battle within—against the flesh and against the evil of Satan. Christ wins the battle over evil precisely through faithfulness to prayer and surrender to the Father's will. At this moment Jesus exhorts his disciples to "stay awake and pray that you may not come into the time of trial; the spirit indeed is willing, but the flesh is weak" (Mt 26:41). When we face suffering, darkness, or turmoil, we are most tempted to give up on prayer or see it as useless. Peter, James, and John fall asleep despite Jesus' exhortation, symbolizing the weakness of our fallen nature and the danger of sloth in our spiritual lives. Jesus exhorts us to "watch and pray," to maintain a life of prayer and vigilance. This fortifies us against the attacks of the evil one who suggests that prayer is useless, that many other occupations would be more useful and urgent. Prayer is often a battle. Despite being prone to dryness, distraction, lack of faith, and sloth, by God's grace we can resist the temptation to avoid prayer.[115] We are challenged to persevere in prayer and to keep watch with Christ in his passion. By his passion Christ strengthens us to remain faithful in prayer.

Saint Ignatius reminds us that Jesus suffered greatly for our sins (see SpEx 197). He felt their weight in the garden of Gethsemane: "In his anguish

---

115. See *Catechism of the Catholic Church*, 2725–2745.

he prayed more earnestly, and his sweat became like great drops of blood falling down on the ground" (Lk 22:43–44). A gethsemane was a huge stone column used in the laborious process of extracting olive oil. The cracked olives were scooped into burlap bags, which were then stacked beneath the gethsemane. The enormous weight of the stone forced the precious oil to drip from the fruit into a groove and then into a pit at the base of the olive press. When Jesus knelt in the garden, he began to experience the full weight of sin laid upon him like a gethsemane, a weight so incredibly heavy that it squeezed his own precious blood out of him.

As we pray over Jesus' agony, Saint Ignatius instructs us ask for the grace of compassion, "sorrow with Christ in sorrow, anguish with Christ in anguish" (SpEx 203) for the great affliction he endures for us. We might also feel anger at the mistreatment he endured and desire to defend him from the insults and torture. That happened to the Frankish king Clovis when Christian missionaries came to his court and told the story of Christ's passion. As they spoke, the old king reached for his sword and shouted that if he and his army of Franks had been there, they would have stormed Calvary and rescued him from his enemies. Perhaps Saint Peter felt the same way as he used his sword to cut off the ear of Malchus at the arrest of Jesus. Mother Teresa shows us a better approach of concern, addressing Christ in her Lenten prayer with the words of the *Stabat Mater*, asking him to make her feel what he had felt and to share his pain.[116] This empathy is a very important way of accessing the inner feeling of Christ as he suffers for us. Our compassion for Jesus becomes our point of connection with his humanity and enables us to share his inner experience. The bride desires to feel what her bridegroom has felt, sharing his pain by allowing herself to be beaten and wounded (5:7). She is unfazed by the violence she suffers and desires only his presence.

Instead of experiencing intense emotion, at times we may feel almost numb as we pray with our Lord's passion. This is a natural reaction and doesn't mean that we lack understanding or compassion. John Cassidy, an Ignatian retreat master, remarks that "in fact, feeling anesthetized, deadened, paralyzed, tired, frustrated, edgy, angry, depressed—all these may well be signs that a retreatant is actually very present to the reality of the passion,

---

116. See Mother Teresa of Calcutta, Letter to Father Neuner, quoted in Kolodiejchuk, M.C., *Come Be My Light*, 242.

even to Jesus' own experience. Encouragement to stay with Jesus is perhaps all they can be given and all they really need."[117] While we would desire to experience pain and deep sorrow for Jesus' suffering, it may be a greater sacrifice and expression of love to remain with the Lord in the absence of such feelings. Mother Teresa lamented her own experience of numbness in prayer during Holy Week. Jesus' sufferings did not affect her interiorly and her prayer seemed meaningless, even as she persevered in prayer.[118]

God sometimes permits us to be dry and desolate, without consolation, and unable to shed tears for Christ's passion because he wishes us to understand that "it is not within our power to acquire and attain great devotion, intense love, tears, or any other spiritual consolation" (SpEx 322). Our weakness in being unable to feel what we desire in prayer is similar to Jesus' powerlessness in his passion, his inability to feel consolation. These moments of weakness test our faithfulness to God in prayer. As a model of faithfulness for us, the bride perseveres in her search for the bridegroom amid loss and distress. She resolutely desires him even if she lacks feeling. She is willing to suffer with him, beaten and wounded in her search (5:7). Like the bride who is drawn out of herself in her compassionate search for the bridegroom, Saint Ignatius draws us out of ourselves into compassion for Christ suffering in his passion and death.

Finally, we ponder Jesus' death on the cross as the consummation of his marriage to his bride, the Church. In the beginning, the first man, Adam, was cast into a deep sleep. God removed a rib from his side to form his wife, Eve, who became mother of all the living. Now as Christ, the new Man, sleeps in death on the cross, his side is opened and his bride, the Church, is formed as the blood and water flow forth. The water symbolizes Baptism, by which new members of the Church are formed and incorporated into Christ. The blood symbolizes the Holy Eucharist, by which Christ nourishes the members of his Body, the Church. As Jesus tastes the sour wine of the final cup of the Passover meal on the cross, he exclaims, "It is consummated" (see Jn 19:30). His union with his bride, the Church, is accomplished on the marriage bed of the cross. Saint Augustine explains, "Christ proceeded like a bridegroom

---

117. John Cassidy, S.J., "Directing the Third Week," *Ignatian Exercises: Contemporary Annotations*, ed. David Fleming, S.J. (St. Louis: Review for Religious, 1996), 269.

118. See Mother Teresa, Letter to Father Neuner, quoted in *Come Be My Light*, 242.

coming forth from his bridal chamber ... and when he arrived at the marriage bed of the cross, he ascended it and consummated his marriage. When he heard the gasping sighs of the creature, with loving devotion he gave himself up to the pains in place of his bride . . . and united himself to her forever."[119]

Christ disappears from the wedding feast of the Last Supper in order to consummate the marriage to his bride, not on a bed of pleasure but of pain. The bride symbolizes the Church that is born from Christ's side, is joined to him in marriage, and is fruitful in bearing spiritual children. Mary, as the new Eve, the "woman" (Gen 2:22; John 2:4, 19:26), becomes the new mother of the living (see Gen 3:20; Jn 19:27; Rev 12:2). She represents the bride, the Church, who becomes fruitful in giving birth to many children.

Questions for Reflection and Discussion

1. How have you experienced "losing God" in your prayer and in your life? How often does it happen? When it does, what are your feelings, thoughts, and actions?

2. How is the dark night and the desert of prayer a positive experience for you, leading to growth in the Spirit?

3. Has your life of prayer progressed beyond the beginner stage of mostly consoling experiences? Did you accurately perceive what was happening? How did you deal with this?

4. How have you experienced praying with the passion of Jesus? How do you find Christ suffering in hidden ways in your own life and the lives of others?

5. Are you able to remain with Christ compassionately in his passion? How do you identify with him?

6. How are you tempted to abandon prayer in the face of dryness, distraction, lack of faith, or sloth? What helps you persevere?

---

119. Saint Augustine, *Sermon on the Lord's Nativity*, numbered 120, 8 in the appendix, *Patrologia Latina*, Migne, vol. 39, p. 1987.

Prayer Exercises

1. Ponder the words from Maloney (p. 192). Pray with Song of Songs 3:1–5, and ask for the grace of courage to enter the experience of darkness and suffering with Christ.

2. Read the section about Mother Teresa's interior darkness (p. 194). Pray with Luke 2:41–51, and ask for the grace to seek Christ in suffering.

3. Read the quote from de Margerie (p. 195) and consider the story of *Babette's Feast* (p. 196). Pray with Matthew 26:17–29, and ask for the grace of gratitude for Jesus' self-sacrifice and the desire to imitate him.

4. Pray with John 13. Ask for the grace of grief and confusion as the Lord goes to his passion for our sins.

5. Pray with Matthew 26:30–46. Ask the grace of grief with Christ in grief, anguish with Christ in anguish, tears and interior pain at the great pain Christ suffered for us.

6. Pray with Matthew 26:59–75. Ask for the grace of perseverance in prayer and the courage to remain faithful to Jesus.

7. Make a repetition on any of the above contemplations, returning to the places of greater movement of spirit (consolation or desolation).

CHAPTER 18

The Love That Suffers

[B] Upon my bed by night
I sought him whom my soul loves;
I sought him, but found him not;
    I called him, but he gave no answer.
"I will rise now and go about the city,
    in the streets and in the squares;
I will seek him whom my soul loves."
    I sought him, but found him not.
The sentinels found me,
    as they went about in the city.
"Have you seen him whom my soul loves?"
Scarcely had I passed them,
    when I found him whom my soul loves.
I held him, and would not let him go
    until I brought him into my mother's house,
    and into the chamber of her that conceived me. (Song 3:1–4)

Consider that Christ suffers all this for my sins, and what I ought to do and suffer for Him. . . . In the Passion it is proper to ask for sorrow with Christ in sorrow, anguish with Christ in anguish, tears and deep grief because of the great affliction Christ endures for me. (SpEx 197, 203)

We continue with the bride's suffering in search of her lost beloved, which parallels losing Christ in his passion and death. In praying with our Lord's passion, we might focus so much on the physical sufferings of Jesus that we fail to understand his interior feelings of sorrow and rejection, which wounded his heart more deeply. The meaning of the passion is more about Christ's extreme love for us, which enabled him to willingly endure his sufferings. The passion is not about a God whose unrelenting justice and wrath necessitates human sacrifice to pay for our sins. Such a message would obscure the fundamental truth that "God so loved the world that he gave his only Son" (Jn 3:16). Joseph Ratzinger explains that "the cross is not a part of a mechanism of injured right, but the reverse; it is the expression of the radical nature of the love that gives itself completely . . . the expression of a life that is completely being for others."[120] The Father is not exacting atonement in demanding that one man die for the sins of many, but so loves the world that he is giving his only Son. In his passion, Jesus suffered willingly for my sins out of love, not merely to satisfy the demands of justice.

The love Jesus has for us is illustrated in a science-fiction novel by Richard Matheson called *The Traveller*. The story is about a scientist named Paul Jairus, who is part of a research team that has developed an energy screen to permit people to travel back into time. The first trip is scheduled to take place, and Jairus has been elected to make the trip. He chooses to go back to the crucifixion of Jesus on Calvary. Jairus is a non-believer and anticipates finding the crucifixion different from the way the Bible describes it. When the historic moment comes, Jairus steps into the energy screen and soon finds himself soaring back in time 2,000 years. He touches down on target and finds Calvary swarming with people whose attention is focused on three men nailed to crosses about 100 feet away. Immediately Jairus asks the command center for permission to move closer to the crosses. They grant it but tell him to stay inside the energy screen. Jairus moves closer and, as he does, his eyes rest on Jesus. Suddenly something remarkable begins to happen. Jairus feels magnetically drawn to Jesus. He is deeply moved by the love radiating from Jesus, a love Jairus had never experienced before. Contrary to all his expectations, the events on Calvary begin to unfold exactly as the Gospel describes

---

120. Joseph Ratzinger, *Introduction to Christianity* (San Francisco: Saint Ignatius Press, 1990), 281–282.

them. Jairus is visibly shaken. The command center realizes this and fears he's becoming emotionally involved. They tell him to prepare for immediate return to the twentieth century. Jairus protests, but to no avail. The trip back goes smoothly, but when Jairus steps from the energy screen, he's a changed man.[121] This story makes the point that Jesus endured such great physical sufferings for us because of his tremendous love. Once we are aware of the love of Jesus shining through his sufferings, we are powerfully moved to accept his gift of redemption and love him mightily in response.

Saint Margaret Mary received a privileged manifestation of the madly intense love of Jesus that drove him to endure his passion for us. On the eve of the octave of Corpus Christi, 1674, she was praying with great devotion before the Lord exposed in the Blessed Sacrament. Jesus Christ appeared to her, resplendent with glory, his five wounds shining like five suns, flames darting from every part of his human form. His heart seemed to be an open furnace, revealing to her the marvels of his pure love and to what excess it had driven him out of love for men and women, from whom he received only ingratitude. He said to her: *"This is more grievous to me than all that I endured in my passion. If they would only give me some return of love, I should not reckon all that I have done for them, and I would do yet more if possible. But they have only coldness and contempt for all my endeavors to do them good. You, at least, can give me the happiness of making up for their ingratitude, as much as you can."*[122] Jesus reveals his overriding motivation and interest in his passion: love. We do well to focus on that love in contemplating his sufferings. He regards his sufferings as little in comparison to their intended effect— that we love him in return.

Saint Ignatius wants us to be aware of the profoundly personal nature of Christ's passion and death. He reminds us "to consider that Christ suffers all this for my sins" (SpEx 197). My sins put Jesus on the cross. Jesus lovingly offers himself in suffering the punishment that is due to us as a consequence of our sins. Saint Paul tells us that it is unlikely that a man would give his life for another man, but while we were yet sinners, Jesus gave his life for us (see Rom 5:8). It is important to realize that Jesus does this

---

121. See Link, *Illustrated Sunday Homilies*, Series I, Palm Sunday Year A, 29.

122. The Divine Mercy Library, Dr. Robert Stackpole, S.T.D., St. Margaret Mary and the Sacred Heart, Feb. 24, 2006, http://www.thedivinemercy.org/library/article.php?NID=2265.

not just for humanity as a whole, but *for me* personally. Any one of us could imagine being the individual person before Christ in the following imaginary dialogue (words of Christ in italics):

I say, "Oh yes, Lord, I know that you saw me, but what am I in the crowd of this world? And you looked at so many others besides me."

And Jesus answers, "*I saw you alone.*"

"Then no doubt, Lord, you saw me with a distant look in your eyes, like a vision that vanishes among thousands of others. Tell me the moment when you had that thought."

"*I've always had it.*"

"Lord, tell me this too. During those hours, from what did you suffer most?"

"*From you.*"

"Ah, Jesus, you bore the sins of all. Their weight was increasing. But tell me, with what thorn did I pierce your forehead?"

"*With all of them.*"

"What, Lord? Is it I, too, who scourged you? And I who nailed you and killed you, too? Then, Lord, what did the others do?"

"*You are my passion.*"

"Then, Savior, your soul was distressed and afraid. Tell me, what did you fear most?"

"*To lose you.*"

"Oh yes, Lord, I know the loss would make your passion useless, but tell me, are there many who get lost? Is it true that their number is greater than that of the elect?"

"*If I lose you, I lose all.*"

"But again, Lord, what did you want? What did you desire most at that last moment?"

"*To save you.*"

"You were dying for all mankind, and you thirsted to save them all. When you wanted all people so ardently, could one alone quench your thirst?"

"*I thirst for you.*"

"Lord, how mysterious this is. How is it that I alone, if I am lost, make your passion useless? And if I am saved, I take from you all regret for having suffered. But what share did the others bring to your victory?"

"*You are my victory.*"[123]

---

123. William J. Bausch, *A World of Stories for Preachers and Teachers* (Mystic: Twenty-Third Publications, 1998), 224–225.

As the above dialogue shows, once we realize that Christ suffered "for me" personally, out of gratitude we will want to share and imitate the life of so great a friend. By praying with the passion, we will more effectively recognize the cross as an aspect of our lives and the decisions we have made for Christ— even to desire to suffer for Christ and embrace our cross. This leads to greater union with Jesus and growth in holiness and virtue.

In one of his letters Saint Ignatius writes that the trials we endure are a sign that God desires us to attain great holiness: "The flame of divine love never rises higher than when fed with the wood of the cross, which the infinite charity of the Savior uses to finish his sacrifice. All the pleasures of the world are nothing compared with the sweetness found in the gall and vinegar offered to Jesus Christ, that is, hard and painful things endured for Jesus Christ and with Jesus Christ."[124] Suffering has great value in leading us to greater charity in union with the Lord, who suffered for us in his tremendous love. While we ought not ask for sufferings out of mere Christian duty, self-loathing, or as an endurance test, we can desire them in imitation of our Savior and out of gratitude for such great love shown to us.

Sufferings willingly endured will purify our hearts in love and bring us to greater identification with Jesus. Once, as a group of women studied the Book of Malachi, they were puzzled by this verse: "He will sit as a refiner and purifier of silver" (Mal 3:3). They wondered what this statement meant about the character and nature of God. One of the women offered to do some research about the process of refining silver and get back to the group at their next Bible study. That week the woman made an appointment with a silversmith to watch him at work. As she watched, he held a piece of silver over the fire and let it heat up. He explained he had to hold it in the hottest part of the fire so the flames could burn away all the impurities. The woman thought about how God holds us in such a hot spot—then she thought again about the verse, that he sits as a refiner of silver. She asked the silversmith if he had to sit in front of the fire the whole time the silver was being refined. The man answered yes, he not only had to sit there holding the silver, but he also had to keep his eyes on the silver the entire time because if he left the silver in the flames even a moment too long, it would be destroyed. The woman was silent for a moment, then she asked the silversmith how he knew when the silver

---

124. Attributed to Saint Ignatius of Loyola.

was fully refined. He smiled at her and answered, "Oh, that's the easy part. When I see my image reflected in it." Like the silversmith, God never takes his eyes off of us in our suffering but remains close to us. Just as the silversmith would not allow the silver to remain in the fire too long, so God never allows us to suffer beyond our capacity and strengthens us to endure it gracefully. We become more like Christ in our sufferings offered in union with him. Once we are purified by suffering, the Father sees Jesus' image in us, just as the silversmith saw his own image reflected in the finished silver.

Saint John Paul II affirms that "*in suffering there is concealed* a particular *power that draws a person interiorly close to Christ,* a special grace. . . . He becomes a completely new person. He discovers a new dimension, as it were, of *his entire life and vocation.*"[125] We discover in our own afflictions the value of pain endured in union with Jesus, which awakens us to a new dimension of our existence and reveals the evangelizing power of suffering.

One of the evangelizing effects of our embracing the cross will be greater love and life-giving power for other human beings. Christ died for us all so that we might live for Christ and others (see 2 Cor 5:14–15). Joseph Grassi notes that associating one's sufferings with those of Jesus brings about an outpouring of vitality, force, and love that flows to others for their edification.[126] Imitation of Christ's suffering and death in one's body brings about an outflow of life for others. Saint Paul describes how his sufferings, in union with Jesus, help to bring about Christ's life in others: We are "always carrying in the body the death of Jesus, so that the life of Jesus may also be made visible in our bodies. For while we live, we are always being given up to death for Jesus' sake, so that the life of Jesus may be made visible in our mortal flesh. So death is at work in us, but life in you" (2 Cor 4:10–12). If we willingly bear the cross in imitation of Christ, we can extend the forgiveness of Christ and truly help others.

The Power of Sacrificial Love

Paradoxically, God taught his wisdom to Saint Paul through the ordeals that frustrated his plans. When Saint Paul's way failed, the divine plan was

---

125. John Paul II, *Salvifici Doloris* (Boston: Pauline Books & Media), no. 26.
126. See Joseph Grassi, *The Secret of Paul the Apostle* (Maryknoll: Orbis, 1978), 102–103.

manifested in a surprising way. So Saint Paul would repeatedly tell his followers to rejoice in trials and persecution, because they would then be more open to God's ways. Saint Paul and his companions became more conformed to Christ and his cross, which became the means of revealing his glory.[127] Saint Paul desires each of us to do the same: "and you became imitators of us and of the Lord, for in spite of persecution you received the word with joy inspired by the Holy Spirit" (1 Thes 1:6). Understanding this teaching, we learn surrender to Christ and his will in trials, just as Christ learned obedience through what he suffered. We cannot avoid the cross; it is a fact of human existence and especially of Christian life. We are always tempted to avoid the cross and suffering, but that only leads to greater suffering. If we embrace the cross, we will know the joy of Christ and his followers. Benedict XVI affirms, "It is not by sidestepping or fleeing from suffering that we are healed, but rather by our capacity for accepting it, maturing through it, and finding meaning through union with Christ, who suffered with infinite love."[128] Jesus took our human suffering on himself and transformed it into his love. When we accept suffering in love, in union with Christ, our suffering is also changed into love.

Prayer in the midst of suffering opens us to the presence of Christ and to God's consolation. Saint Paul tells the Corinthians that God "consoles us in all our affliction, so that we may be able to console those who are in any affliction with the consolation with which we ourselves are consoled by God. For just as the sufferings of Christ are abundant for us, so also our consolation is abundant through Christ" (2 Cor 1:3–5).

Saint Paul's ministry brought him many trials and afflictions. He was harassed by Gentiles, persecuted by his fellow Jews, falsely accused, beaten, stoned, thrown in prison, and shipwrecked. He had to deal with internal disputes in the churches and among leaders of the larger Church, feeling the daily pressure of his anxiety for all the churches (see 2 Cor 11:28). Far from avoiding these trials, Saint Paul even found reason to rejoice in them. He shared them with the Lord and found meaning in them as an opportunity to share in Christ's suffering. He found Christ present in his trials and realized how efficacious they were in bringing God's salvation to others.

---

127. See Grassi, *The Secret of Paul the Apostle,* 104–105.

128. Benedict XVI, *Spe Salvi* (Boston: Pauline Books & Media, 2007), no. 37.

As we too share in Christ's sufferings, we come to identify with him in his sacrifice as Saint Paul did, "always carrying in the body the death of Jesus" (2 Cor 4:10). Filled with our love for God, we suffer at seeing a world that has no regard for God. Jean Danielou comments on how the Lord invites us to share in this burden in his passion. Jesus was torn apart, bearing within himself the strife and opposition between a godless world and the love of the holy Trinity. Remaining in the heart of the Trinity, he plummets to the depths of human misery and fills up all the space between. The extension of Christ on the cross in four directions is the hidden meaning of our own being stretched and rent asunder with Christ.[129]

Christ bears within himself the gap between God and a world hostile to God. His love makes him willing to be broken and so open the floodgates of his grace to the world, to reconcile us to the Father. Our lives are now drawn into Christ's sacrifice, which saves us and keeps us in existence. The sacrifice of others has brought us into being and nurtured us, and we need to accept that sacrifice in gratitude and poverty of spirit. We can't earn the immense love of Christ, but we can only accept it as a complete gift.[130] Only then can we participate in his sacrifice and share it with others.

On January 28, 1945, Russian soldiers set free the prisoners of a Nazi concentration camp in Hassak, Poland. One of these women, Edith Zirer, had been imprisoned for almost three years and forced to work in a munitions factory. She didn't know that she was the only member of her family to survive the Nazi massacre. She was alone, confused, and sick—almost at the point of death—when she was shipped off by train. Two days later she arrived at a small train station between Czestochowa and Krakow. She was convinced that she was at the end of her journey. She fell on the ground in a corner of the large hall where dozens of refugees were gathering, most of whom were still wearing their numbered uniforms from concentration camps. A young priest saw Edith. He came with a big cup of tea, the first hot beverage she had drunk in weeks. Afterward, he brought by a little bit of cheese with black Polish bread. She was so tired that she didn't even want to eat, but the priest gently urged her. Then he picked Edith up in his arms and carried

---

129. See Jean Danielou, S.J., *The Lord of History: Reflections on the Inner Meaning of History*, trans. Nigel Abercrombi (Cleveland: Meridian Books, 1958), 340.

130. See Ratzinger, *Introduction to Christianity*, 266–269.

her outside for a long way, despite the falling snow. Later she would remember his brown jacket and his tranquil voice as he told her of the death of his parents and his brother, of the loneliness he felt, and of the need to accept suffering and fight to live. They finally met the convoy that would take the refugees West, and after assuring that she had passage, the priest bid her goodbye.

Thirty three years later, when Edith heard the name of the newly elected Pope, Karol Wojtyla, she instantly recognized him as the young priest who had helped her. Karol had suffered under the heel of the Nazi and Russian regimes in Krakow. As a child he experienced the terrible loss of his mother. As a young man he experienced the loneliness of losing his father and brother. His suffering was a participation in the cross of Jesus Christ and led him to compassionate sacrifice on behalf of Edith and many others.

On the cross Jesus experienced the greatest of all sufferings: abandonment. As he was dying, he cried out to his Father, "My God, why have you abandoned me?" Jesus felt the rejection of his own people whom he loved dearly. Following his Father's will in being crucified for our salvation, he felt abandoned by God himself. Though sinless, Jesus took upon himself our own experience of separation from God due to sin, our own feeling of alienation. He transformed that suffering into love through his sacrifice. By uttering the first line of Psalm 22, "My God, why have you forsaken me?" Jesus implied the entire psalm, as was the Hebrew custom. It goes on to say that God is not far off and hastens to our aid, and is to be praised in the vast assembly (see vv. 22, 25). While feeling abandoned humanly, Jesus affirms his ultimate trust in the Father, abandoning himself to him: "Father, into your hands I commend my spirit" (Lk 23:46). Even though Jesus felt forsaken by the Father, he is immediately aware of the Father's presence and intimate love, as he completely surrenders himself.

The bride enters into Christ's abandonment, feeling forsaken by her bridegroom as he disappears. She dies to her own will in giving up the comfort of her bedchamber while awaiting the pleasurable experience of her bridegroom. She has consented to accept suffering in searching the streets for her beloved (3:1–3). She is willing to be struck and bear insults for his sake, and now discovers him in a new and more profound way (3:4).

If we are willing to accept being forsaken like Jesus, experiencing rejection and affliction for his sake, we will encounter the Lord in a more penetrating way. He will transform our suffering into love.

Questions for Reflection and Discussion

1. Have you ever focused so much on the sufferings of Christ as the price he paid that you lost sight of the love behind the sufferings?

2. To what extent do you realize the personal nature of Christ's sufferings "for me" as Saint Ignatius notes?

3. In what sense do you experience purification in love through your sufferings in union with Christ?

4. How do you sense that your sufferings in union with Christ are efficacious in evangelizing others?

5. What is your experience of the cross as the agony of bearing with a world alienated from the holy Trinity, a gap that Danielou speaks of (i.e., our hearts cannot simultaneously love the most holy Trinity and love a world alienated from the Trinity)?

6. How do you experience the cross as the sacrifice of your own will in obedience to Christ? Where does this sacrifice occur the most in your life?

Prayer Exercises

1. Read the words of Jesus to Saint Margaret Mary (p. 205). Pray with Matthew 27:1–13, and ask for the grace to accompany Jesus in love throughout his passion.

2. Ponder the story of the woman's visit to the silversmith (p. 207). Pray with Matthew 27:15–31, and ask for the grace to remain united to Christ in his sufferings.

3. Pray with Matthew 27:32–44, and ask for the grace to imitate Christ in the surrender of his will to that of the Father.

4. Consider the story of *The Traveller* (p. 204). Pray with Matthew 27:45–56, and ask for the grace to know Christ's love in undergoing his passion for you personally.

5. Read Jean Danielou's thoughts about the cross (p. 210). Pray with John 19:17–30, and ask for the grace to share in Christ's sacrifice for the sake of others.

6. Ponder the story of Saint John Paul II and Edith Zirer. Pray with Song of Songs 5:6–8, and ask for the grace to be willing to suffer with Christ out of love.

7. Make a repetition on any of the above contemplations, returning to those places of greater movement of spirit (consolation or desolation).

CHAPTER 19

Keeping Vigil for the Beloved

[B] Upon my bed by night
I sought him whom my soul loves;
I sought him, but found him not;
    I called him, but he gave no answer.
"I will rise now and go about the city,
    in the streets and in the squares;
I will seek him whom my soul loves."
    I sought him, but found him not.
The sentinels found me,
    as they went about in the city.
"Have you seen him whom my soul loves?"
Scarcely had I passed them,
    when I found him whom my soul loves.
I held him, and would not let him go
    until I brought him into my mother's house,
    and into the chamber of her that conceived me.
I adjure you, O daughters of Jerusalem,
    by the gazelles or the wild does:
do not stir up or awaken love
    until it is ready! (Song 3:1–5)

He was taken down from the cross by Joseph and Nicodemus in the presence of His sorrowful mother. . . . The body was borne to the sepulcher, and anointed, and buried . . . Guards were stationed. (SpEx 298)

215

One should consider . . . that the most Sacred Body of Christ our Lord remained separated from the soul, and the place and manner of burial. Let him consider, likewise, the desolation of our Lady, her great sorrow and weariness, and also that of the disciples. (SpEx 208)

The passion of the Lord ends with his death and burial (see SpEx 208). As Jesus experienced a real separation of his soul from his body, a real death, we grieve him. We grieve the loss of Jesus our brother who gave his life for our sins. We keep vigil over Christ at the tomb and ponder the meaning of death, which Christ desired to share in taking on our humanity.

The bride too grieves the loss of her beloved. Experiencing deep loneliness, she desperately searches for but does not immediately find him (Song 3:1–3). She calls to her beloved but he does not answer her (Song 5:6). The bride reminds us of Mary Magdalene searching for Jesus at his tomb, looking to anoint his dead body and distressed that someone may have taken him away (see Jn 20:11–18).

In choosing to die for us, Jesus enters into the complete loneliness we experience as human beings when we die. The central core of Jesus' passion consists not only of physical pain, but also the excruciating experience of radical loneliness and complete abandonment. Because we are social beings who need the company of others, we experience loneliness with a visceral dread. Joseph Ratzinger explains how severe loneliness is experienced as a kind of hell that we fear in death: "If a state of abandonment were to arise that was so deep that no 'You' could reach into it any more, then we should have real, total loneliness and dreadfulness, what theology calls 'hell.' . . . Thus hell, despair, would dwell at the very bottom of our existence, in the shape of that loneliness that is as inescapable as it is dreadful."[131] Human beings fear loneliness, which death and the tomb represent in its ultimate form. But in his passion and death Christ enters into our loneliness; we are not abandoned but consoled.

---

131. Ratzinger, *Introduction to Christianity*, 300.

When loved ones die, we feel their loss and desire to remain close to their bodies, the last vestiges of their earthly existence. As Jesus lies dead in the tomb, we desire to remain close to him, keeping vigil with him in his death and loneliness. We are filled with grief, but we also have tremendous reverence for the body of Jesus and what he has suffered for us. This sense of reverence for the dead was once reinforced for me by the breathtaking experience of observing the changing of the guard at the Tomb of the Unknown Soldier. I later learned that the guards not only display reverence by performing painstakingly awed rituals, but by living their lives in a way that respects their fallen heroes. Since the sentinels are held to such a high standard, if they ever do anything that is deemed unbecoming behavior for a tomb guard or brings dishonor upon the tomb, their honor badges may be revoked, even if they are no longer in the military. During the first six months of duty a sentinel must undergo rigorous training, including several hours a day of marching, rifle drill, and uniform preparation. Every tomb sentinel is expected to be completely versed in the history of the tomb and of Arlington National Cemetery.

In 2003, as the deadly Hurricane Isabelle roared toward Washington, D.C., the tomb guards were given permission to suspend their assignment. They respectfully declined the offer. Soaked to the skin, marching in the pelting rain, they remarked that guarding the tomb was not just an assignment but the highest honor they could receive. The respect they displayed for the fallen soldiers is the same kind of reverence we should desire to have for the body of Jesus as he lies in the tomb. Aware of what he has sacrificed for our salvation, we want to pledge our very lives for him, to live each day in gratitude and devotion, and to make sacrifices on his behalf. Saint Ignatius reminds us "to consider that Christ suffers all this for my sins, and what I ought to do and suffer for Him" (SpEx 197). We have seen that the bride is willing to bear injuries in her search for her lost Beloved (Song 5:7). She allows herself to feel the depths of grief and distress at his loss, for she is "lovesick" (5:8) without him.

Watching at the Tomb

We stand watch at the burial place grieving the loss of Jesus, in reverence for what he has done for us. We ponder the meaning of Jesus' death and his body being laid in the sepulcher. The tomb may be a sign of death and mourning, perhaps reminding us of defeat and despair. Interiorly, the tomb symbolizes the empty place of our hearts wherein we frequently experience death. The desert visionary Saint Macarius of Egypt wrote of the human heart as a tomb: "When you hear that at that time the Lord delivered the souls from hell and darkness, and went down to hell, and did a glorious work, do not imagine that these things are so very far from your own soul.... When you hear of sepulchers, do not think only of visible ones; your own heart is a sepulcher and a tomb."[132] Within this tomb of the heart we experience death to sin and selfishness. There we die to ourselves in sacrifice for others. We may also experience the death of our illusory hopes and unrealized dreams. In this place of dying we might feel miserable and hopeless. But, ironically, the tomb can also be a "womb" of sorts. The womb, like the tomb, is an empty, dark place, but also a place that breeds and fosters new life.

In Christ's resurrection, the tomb becomes the place of his new life and ours too. Christ generates life in those places of emptiness, darkness, and dying. Caryll Houselander writes of the importance of trusting God in our experiences of emptiness and dying, during moments when we encounter no delight, no relief, no noticeable indication of the nearness and expansion of Christ in us. These most important circumstances are those in which Christ does in actuality mature to his flourishing within us. There is by all accounts nothing that we can do during these moments to exalt God, just as it is true that on our own we can do nothing (see Jn 15:5). Abiding in Christ, we can act like him, staying discreetly in the tomb, rest, and find a sense of content-ment. We can trust God when he is ready to stir us to a spring time of Christ, to a sudden enlivening and blooming and fresh experience of the life of Christ in our souls.[133]

We remain with Christ in the tomb in our grief and emptiness, in his dying and in our many smaller deaths. At the same time, we trust that he remains with us in the tomb of our own hearts, desiring to lead us to the new life of his resurrection. Similarly, after her ordeal of losing her bridegroom and searching for him, the bride remains resting, waiting for her lover to

---

132. Macarius the Egyptian: *Spiritual Homily* 11, 10–11, trans. A. J. Mason, D.D., https://archive.org/stream/fiftyspiritualho00pseuuoft/fiftyspiritualho00pseuuoft_djvu.txt.

133. See Caryll Houselander, *The Way of the Cross* (Liguori: Liguori Publications, 2002), Ch. 14, Kindle Edition.

awaken her love (3:5). She is patient in her waiting, advising none of the bridesmaids to awaken love until it is pleased to do so.

We patiently remain in the empty, dark tomb of our hearts in hope of the new life of Christ that will emerge. While a pregnant woman is aware of her child alive and growing within her, she remains in hope, as her child reaches full development, to meet him or her. Conscious that the promise of her pregnancy will be fulfilled, she awaits her child's birth with anticipation, preparing herself in every way possible. Giving birth is a painful process, but a woman's pain pales in comparison to her joy in seeing and holding her child. A mother may perhaps grieve her loss of carrying the child in the womb as she experiences the child's presence in a new way. Likewise, the bride has experienced the loss of her lover and must search in the empty darkness to discover his presence in a new way.

Once the bride finds her bridegroom again, she will not let him go. She leads him to her mother's house, "into the chamber of her that conceived me" (3:4). In her new relationship with her lover, in some way she wants to be maternally conceived and begotten again. Arminjon describes the bride's desire for regeneration: "She feels quite keenly that in order to be fully his, to be truly one with him, she must be reborn from him, not only to link her life with him but to receive her very life from him."[134] Figuratively speaking, just as she received natural life from her biological mother, she desires to receive supernatural life from her lover. We recall how Jesus told Nicodemus that he had to be born anew from on high, not from his mother's womb but from Christ himself by water and the Spirit (see Jn 3:1–12). The bride is the figure of the Church of God, born anew from Christ in his death and resurrection. The Church Fathers used the image of the Church as the bride being born from the side of Christ. Just as Adam was cast into a deep sleep and Eve was formed from one of his ribs, so Christ, the New Adam, slept the sleep of death on the cross, and from his side his bride, the Church, was formed. The Church as the New Eve is "mother of the living" in Christ, who generates life in her from on high. Similarly, the bride in the Song of Songs now desires to receive this new formation of her being from her bridegroom in her mother's house.

For such a rebirth the tomb represents a place of waiting, which is essential in the spiritual life. Prayer is an act of waiting on the Lord—waiting for

---

134. Arminjon, *The Cantata of Love*, 191.

his presence, his promises, his transformative power. During this time of waiting we often grow impatient and question. Keenly feeling the uncertainty of our situation, we feel anxious and hesitant in prayer. Waiting sometimes means remaining immobile when we would prefer to be working, a great challenge for us. I experienced this challenge waiting at the hospital during my father's heart bypass surgery. Eager to remain busy to stave off anxiety, my brothers and I brought work to do while we waited. We sought distraction because we were not getting the information we craved about our father's status. We often seek distraction while waiting. But we are called to stay in the present moment, uncomfortable though it might be, to accept the present reality and simply wait. We must remain in what may feel to be an unnatural patience and supernatural trust. In this vein, Saint James reminds us: "Be patient, therefore, beloved, until the coming of the Lord. The farmer waits for the precious crop from the earth, being patient with it until it receives the early and the late rains. You also must be patient. Strengthen your hearts, for the coming of the Lord is near" (Jas 5:7–8).

We are called to wait in patience and in trust that the Lord will fulfill his promises to us. The prophet Habakkuk takes his stand as a watchman who is vigilant for the Lord's response to his hopes that Israel would be restored. The Lord answers by exhorting Habakkuk to patience and trust: "Write the vision; make it plain on tablets, so that a runner may read it. For there is still a vision for the appointed time; it speaks of the end, and does not lie. If it seems to tarry, wait for it; it will surely come, it will not delay" (Hab 2:2–3). We grow impatient waiting for the Lord to fulfill his plan for our lives. The Lord calls us to trust his plans for our good, that he will reveal them to us and fulfill them.

God revealed his plans to a vigilant trucker named Ron Lantz in 2002, when the D.C. sniper, John Allen Muhammed, and his partner were terrorizing Washington, D.C. Fifty Christian truckers gathered to pray that the sniper would be caught. Lantz was only passing through the area but joined in the prayer. He had a strange inkling not only that God would answer their prayers, but also that God would use him to catch the sniper. Lantz told this to his friends. A few days later he was listening to the radio as he drove through the area again. He felt compelled to pull off the highway into a rest stop, just a few miles from where the prayer meeting had taken place. As he pulled in, he was shocked to see a car similar to the one described on the radio. He carefully tried to read the license plate, and a chill went up his spine as the numbers matched. Lantz quickly called 911 and remained there until the police arrived for what he described as the longest fifteen minutes of his life. He pulled his truck across the exit to block any escape for the elusive murderers. The police finally came and took the criminals into custody without incident. God did have a plan for Lantz's life, to use him as an instrument to catch the vicious sniper. Like Habbakuk, Lantz was aware that God had a vision for him, that he was called to wait for the vision, and that it would be fulfilled. Lantz exercised vigilance and received the inspiration in prayer. He also expressed his trust in God's promise, telling others of his confidence that he would be the one to find the sniper. Lantz's testimony shows the power of prayer and the importance of vigilance and listening in order to be attuned to God's plan.

We are also called to be patient in our waiting on the Lord. To be patient means to be willing to act and even to suffer in order to remain faithful. Henri Nouwen explains the challenge of living the virtue of patience. Patience is not mere passivity and lack of control over events that happen to me, but rather an active and growing engagement with God's work. We wait with a sense of promise for something to be received with our cooperation. The farmer waits patiently for the seed to sprout and eventually bear fruit. A mother waits for her child to be formed in her womb and to be born. We enter into the experience of the present moment, even if it involves pain, with a trusting attitude that God is at work. In our anxiety, the temptation is to run away from the place we are rather than remain steadfast. We hope according to God's promise, not just for our specific wishes, but according to his will.[135]

In times of waiting we are called beyond mere passivity into activity, working for the kingdom and the goals God has put before us. Scripture gives us other examples. Saint Paul warned the Thessalonians not to sit back in idleness while awaiting the Lord's second coming, but to actively perform virtuous works to prepare for that coming. While Mary was awaiting the birth of her Son, she ventured out in charity to her cousin Elizabeth who

---

135. See Henri Nouwen, *Bread for the Journey, A Daybook of Wisdom and Faith,* January 5 (HarperCollins e-books, EPub Ed., 2007).

needed help. John the Baptist prepared the way of the Lord through preaching and baptism as he awaited Christ's manifestation.

In the Spiritual Exercises we are called to actively participate in the mystery of Christ's passion and death. We are to sorrow with Christ sorrowing, to be willing to suffer pain and trials for his sake. In prayer we remain vigilant in compassion for our dear Savior, attending to his needs. Christ's death and burial present us with a great challenge to remain with him in grief, loneliness, and reverence. Keeping watch with Jesus in compassion will be our fundamental act of love. Think of the love shown by Joseph of Arimathea in providing a tomb for the Lord, and by Mary Magdalene in her desire to anoint the dead body of Jesus.

As we conclude the third week of the Spiritual Exercises with Christ's long Sabbath rest in the tomb, we remain in a spirit of reverence and vigilance, anticipating the new life and love that will emerge. To do so will require a great deal of patience. The bridegroom exhorts the observers of the bride to patience: "I adjure you, O daughters of Jerusalem, by the gazelles or the wild does: do not stir up or awaken love until it is ready!" (3:5). The maidens await the bride's awakening in love to the glory of her bridegroom. Having patiently endured his passion, death, and burial, Christ awakens to his own glorious resurrection. Having kept vigil with the Lord in his death and burial, we will soon be awakened to his grandeur. As we prepare for Christ's resurrection, we await the eternal glory to be revealed in us at our own resurrection from the dead.

Questions for Reflection and Discussion

1. How do you experience the loneliness symbolized by death as a kind of hell from which to be saved?

2. How do you imagine Christ dead and in the tomb? What kind of reverence do you feel for Christ in his death?

3. What is your experience of being around those who die—before, during, and after their death?

4. What moments of dying in life have led to moments of new life—from "tomb" to "womb?"

5. How do you deal with "waiting" in life? How does waiting factor into your life of prayer and waiting on the Lord?

Prayer Exercises

1. Read Joseph Ratzinger's thoughts on loneliness (p. 216). Pray with Matthew 27:45–55, and ask for the grace of gratitude to Jesus for dying to save you from utter loneliness.

2. Read the story of the guards at the Tomb of the Unknown Soldier (p. 217). Pray with John 19:31–42, and ask for the grace to reverence the death of the Lord

3. Read the thoughts about trusting God even regarding the reality of death (p. 218). Pray with Matthew 27:57–66, and ask for the grace to see death and the tomb as a place of hope and new life.

4. Read the thoughts about patience (p. 220). Pray with Song of Songs 3:1–5, and ask for the grace to actively seek the Lord in your waiting upon him.

5. Pray with Habbakuk 3:1–4 or James 5:7–11, and ask for the grace of patience and trust in the Lord's promises to you.

6. Ponder the story of Ron Lantz (p. 220). Pray with Matthew 27:57–66, and pray for the grace to be vigilant in keeping watch with Christ.

7. Make a repetition on any of the above contemplations, returning to those places of greater movement of spirit (consolation or desolation).

CHAPTER 20

Dawn of Glory

[D] What is that coming up from the wilderness,
   like a column of smoke,
perfumed with myrrh and frankincense,
   with all the fragrant powders of the merchant?
Look, it is the litter of Solomon!
Around it are sixty mighty men
   of the mighty men of Israel,
all equipped with swords
   and expert in war,
each with his sword at his thigh
   because of alarms by night.
King Solomon made himself a palanquin
   from the wood of Lebanon.
He made its posts of silver,
   its back of gold, its seat of purple;
its interior was inlaid with love.
Daughters of Jerusalem, come out.
Look, O daughters of Zion,
   at King Solomon, at the crown with which his mother crowned him
   on the day of his wedding,
   on the day of the gladness of his heart. (Song 3:6–11)

Ask for the grace to be glad and rejoice intensely because of the great joy and
the glory of Christ our Lord.... Consider the divinity, which seemed to hide
itself during the passion, now appearing and manifesting itself so

miraculously in the most holy Resurrection in its true and most sacred effects. Consider the office of consoler that Christ our Lord exercises, and compare it with the way in which friends are wont to console each other. (SpEx 221–224)

❀❧❀❧❀

Having journeyed with the Lord through his passion and death in the Spiritual Exercises, we now begin to contemplate Christ in his risen glory. In this corresponding passage from the Song of Songs, the bridegroom appears in all his glory, rising up from the wilderness. For the first time he is referred to as King Solomon, who reigned during Israel's brief period of glory and foreshadowed the coming of Christ our true King. Solomon was renowned for his wisdom, and Christ is Wisdom Incarnate. Jesus said of himself, "See, something greater than Solomon is here" (Mt 12:42). Christ reigns as King of the universe not only from the cross but especially in his risen glory, having conquered the enemy: death.

The Song of Song's description of the king surrounded by clouds of incense hearkens back to Israel's exodus, led through the desert by the Lord, mysteriously present in a cloud of smoke by day and a pillar of fire by night. The Exodus is also connected to the mystery of the Lord's resurrection. During the Easter vigil, the giant Easter candle recalls the pillar of fire by night and symbolizes the risen Christ as our light in the darkness. The resurrection is the new Exodus from the land of sin and slavery into the promised land of everlasting life.

The column of smoke in this passage of the Song of Songs recalls the divine theophany when the Lord revealed himself as a consuming fire, wrapping Mount Sinai in smoke that "went up like the smoke of a kiln, while the whole mountain shook violently" (Ex 19:18). Similarly, when Isaiah was called, he had a vision of smoke filling the Temple. "The pivots on the thresholds shook at the voices of those who called, and the house filled with smoke" (Is 6:4). Arminjon explains how the significance of an aromatic smoke yielding perfumes is "precisely linked to the Temple in the liturgy, myrrh and frankincense . . . radiating from the presence of him who is at the same time

King of his people, King of all the foreign nations, and 'beyond every-thing.'"[136] Christ our King is truly divine and beyond everything we could imagine. As we begin to ponder Christ's most glorious moment, his resurrec-tion from the dead, Saint Ignatius has us ponder how Christ's divinity, hidden during his passion and death, now manifests itself in glory. The divinity of Christ is "now appearing and manifesting itself so miraculously in the most holy Resurrection in its true and most sacred effects" (SpEx 223). Christ's grandeur radiates from his glorious body, which now reveals his divinity.

Christ's resurrection is also symbolized in King's Solomon's throne, con-structed of wood from Lebanon, silver pillars, a gold canopy, and a purple seat with its back inlaid with ebony. Maloney describes the materials of the throne as an image of the risen Lord: "The throne is Christ himself in his risen glory, which becomes the nuptial seat for the bride and him now one in transform-ing union."[137] Wood from Lebanon was considered to be everlasting: "Christ's risen body is now incorruptible, and we Christians are called to share in his incorruptible body."[138] The silver pillars depict the humanity through which he redeemed us. Thus the strength of these pillars consists in "not only Christ's humanity, but that humanity exalted in glory and made one with his divinity so that we who are totally human can be given a share in his divinity through his redemption."[139] The gold canopy symbolizes that Christ is divine, of the same substance with the Father, yet he shared our humanity in order to redeem us: "Our redemption stands on the fundamental reality that God in the humanity of Christ suffered and died. We are saved by God's infinite love poured out on the cross, God truly dying for us."[140] His purple seat signifies royalty: "Christ through his resurrection has been raised up by the Father in glory and been given the name of *Kyrios*, Lord of the universe. He rules over all. He is the *Pantocrator*, the one who is almighty over every kingdom, including the kingdom of sin and death."[141] The back of the throne is inlaid with love: "this love goes out for the daughters of Jerusalem, for

136. Arminjon, *The Cantata of Love*, 202.
137. Maloney, *Singers of the New Song*, 67–68.
138. Ibid.
139. Ibid.
140. Ibid.
141. Ibid.

Christ's bride, his church, for the individual Christian to whom he wishes to wed himself."[142] Everything about the throne symbolizes the divinity that Christ our true King manifests in his resurrection and desires to impart to us. The bride will share the King's throne and be transformed to share in his divinity and incorruptibility.

Saint Ignatius has us begin our contemplation of Jesus' resurrection by pondering the mystery of the empty tomb. The vacant tomb doesn't prove Christ's resurrection from the dead, but it is an important piece of evidence in our believing he is risen. We should approach our inspection of the tomb in a new and perhaps unusual way—as detectives. In prayer we can observe clues the evangelists left for us, contemplate them, and ask God to connect the dots for us to lead us to the risen Lord.

The 1944 movie *Laura* presented the story of a New York City detective named McPherson, who attempts to solve the murder of a young woman named Laura. Apparently the murderer had knocked at the apartment door and then, when she had answered it, fired a shotgun into her face. During his investigation, the detective begins to examine Laura's apartment, combing through all her belongings—clothes, books, records, photographs. He even reads her letters and personal diaries in his search for clues that might lead to the perpetrator. Then something strange begins to happen. McPherson becomes infatuated with Laura. He begins to fall in love with her, even though she is dead! One night, while sitting in the apartment sorting through the evidence and his feelings for Laura, McPherson hears a key turning in the lock. The door opens and the detective is incredulous because Laura is standing before him. When she demands to know why he is in her apartment, McPherson explains everything. He finds out that Laura had gone to the country for a few days to get away and has had no access to any news. The detective discovers that the murdered woman was a friend who was using the apartment during Laura's absence. The story ends with Laura and the detective falling in love and marrying.[143]

The search for Jesus on Easter morning is similar to the detective's search for Laura. Those who loved Jesus search for him—Mary Magdalene and the

---

142. Ibid.

143. See Link, *Illustrated Sunday Homilies*, Series I, 4th Sunday of Easter Year C, 37.

holy women, Peter, and John the beloved disciple. Seeing the empty tomb, like detectives they search for the evidence they need to help them to understand the mystery. In John's Gospel, Mary Magdalene is the first to arrive at the tomb (see Jn 20:1–18). Seeing the stone rolled away, she realizes something is wrong. Have they stolen the body? After all that has happened to Jesus, this would be the ultimate indignity. She hurries to tell Peter, who runs to the tomb with John. The detective work begins as John inspects the tomb and finds the linen shroud lying in the place where it covered Jesus. It is not thrown in a heap as robbers would leave it, but draped and folded the same way as when it covered Jesus' body. It looks as though Jesus had passed right through it. John also finds the headdress folded up like a napkin in the corner of the tomb, again not how a grave robber might leave it. The beloved disciple sees this evidence and right away he believes. He felt the flame of faith already burning in his heart and knew Jesus was alive. John loved Jesus and this, together with some small pieces of evidence, was all he needed to believe. Love helped him to interpret the facts. As we contemplate the empty tomb, we not only examine the evidence, but we also begin to intuit in love that Jesus is risen from the dead. Believing, we are filled with awe.

After we have pondered the empty tomb, Saint Ignatius has us contemplate the Lord's resurrection appearances to his disciples. Although it is a historical event, the moment when Christ rose from the dead transcends history. It enters into the eternal, beyond the detection of human senses and the grasp of the mind. Perhaps because we find it hard to conceptualize the resurrection, Saint Ignatius does not ask us to contemplate the actual moment of resurrection but only Jesus' appearances.

The Resurrection Appearances

After the resurrection Jesus first appears to Mary, his mother. Though this appearance is not recorded, Scripture does tell us that Jesus appeared to many others (see Lk 24:44–49; 1 Cor 15:7). It would be highly unlikely for the Lord to ignore his own mother, who, as the perfect disciple, would have instinctively believed in his resurrection. Christian writers and thinkers over the centuries, including Saint Ignatius of Antioch, Saint Ambrose, and Saint Anselm wrote in favor of this. A fourteenth-century Carthusian monk, Ludolph of Saxony, included it in his popular *Life of Christ*, which Saint Ignatius read as he recovered from his battle wounds. At the Lord's burial,

Saint Ignatius has us ponder "the desolation of our Lady, her great sorrow and weariness" (SpEx 208).

In the Middle Ages, Bishop Amadeus of Lausanne wrote eloquently of how our Lady's grief was turned to joy at the resurrection appearance of her Son.[144] As Jesus emerged, her soul revived, arising as though from a profound sleep. She found in the rays of dawn the daystar of righteousness and the beams of his rising. Mary also became more aware of her own destiny for eternal glory, gazing upon the rising first light. The glorious body of the risen Lord delighted Mary's eyes, and her heart perceived the glory of his divinity, so that, immersed in it, she drank in the nourishment of genuine and eternal delight. In faith and self-forgetfulness Mary abandoned herself to God, giving him her entire self, completely engulfed in his great love. Mary received her risen Son with complete faith and gave herself to him completely in return.

Mary is the perfect disciple because of her practice of faith in the Lord. Mary "believed that there would be a fulfillment of what was spoken to her by the Lord" (Lk 1:45). She also believed in Jesus' prediction that he would rise from the dead. In fact, Mary does not go to the tomb to anoint the dead body of her Son on Easter morning because she knows he is risen. The apparition of Christ to his mother is the foundation for the resurrection exercises and the upcoming mysteries of Christ's appearances to his disciples. The other disciples were unbelieving at first—the Lord even rebukes them for their unbelief (see Mk 16:14)—but Mary always believed in her Son's resurrection. She represents the full faith of the Church in her essential act of belief in Jesus. Giles Cusson explains that Mary represents a new and transformed humanity in its ability to accept the reality and fullness of Christ in his risen glory: "In his victorious love Christ could not offer his life immediately to those whose faith had not yet overcome the final obstacles. Mary alone awaited the divine manifestation; in her, the daughter of Sion, the new 'mother of the Living,' the risen Christ appeared to all of the new creation, to the universal Church born on that day."[145] Because of her faith, only Mary, as

---

144. See Bishop Amadeus of Lausanne, *Eight Homilies on the Praises of Blessed Mary, Cistercian Fathers Series: Number Eighteen B*, trans. Grace Perigo (Kalamazoo: Cistercian Publications, 1979), 50.

145. Giles Cusson, *Biblical Theology and Spiritual Exercises* (St. Louis: Institute of Jesuits Sources, 1988), 306.

representative of the human race, had the capacity to fully receive the revelation of the risen Christ.

Mary's exalted position as representative of the human race reaches its pinnacle in her role as queen, sharing in Christ's kingly rule. The Song of Songs contains a reference to King Solomon wearing "the crown with which his mother crowned him on the day of his wedding" (3:11). In Hebrew tradition, the queen is the king's mother, reigns with him on a throne set beside him. Her role extends to offering advice to the king on matters of state and also interceding on others' behalf with requests to the king. Mary as mother of Christ our King is exalted as Queen in his kingdom. She shares in his kingly rule and intercedes on our behalf before the King. At Christ's resurrection, "the day of the gladness of his heart," she is the one to crown him as King of the universe.

Rising on his throne in the wilderness, King Solomon enjoys his wedding as "the day of the gladness of his heart" (Song 3:11). We contemplate Jesus our true King rising in glory and united with his bride the Church; we can imagine the tremendous joy he feels. Saint Ignatius has us desire "to be glad and rejoice intensely because of the great joy and the glory of Christ Our Lord" (SpEx 221). It isn't easy to "rejoice with those who rejoice" (Rom 12:15), because we often celebrate only if we receive something. We are called to go outside of ourselves and share in compassionate joy for Jesus as he experiences his resurrection, not just for ourselves and our own hope of resurrection. Why should we rejoice for Jesus' sake? The Father confirms Jesus in his very person, works, and teachings after he was rejected by those who opposed him. In his transformed humanity Jesus now experiences the fullness of life and extends his love in a transcendent way to the whole universe. He offers his grace to all of us sacramentally, especially through Baptism and Eucharist. The risen Christ is now wedded to his bride, the Church; like King Solomon on his wedding day, he truly experiences gladness of heart.

Saint Ignatius instructs us to notice how the risen Lord assumes the office of consoler. He comforts and encourages his disciples, sharing his peace and joy with them. In the Scriptures we contemplate here, the people who see Jesus are distressed when he first appears. They feel sadness, fear, grief, or desolation. Mary Magdalene weeps at Jesus' tomb, thinking someone has stolen his body. Jesus appears to her but she doesn't recognize him right away. When she does, she rejoices and even tries to grab hold of him. The disciples on the road to Emmaus are running away from Jerusalem, feeling downcast over Jesus' death. They had thought he was the great prophet who would restore Israel to political greatness. Jesus walks alongside them but they don't recognize him even as he explains the Scriptures. They eventually recognize him in the breaking of the bread and recall how he made their hearts burn with love. The apostles locked in the Upper Room tremble in fear when Jesus appears to them. They mistake him for a ghost, perhaps even fearing retribution for the way they abandoned him. Jesus instead blesses them with peace, convincing them of his bodily presence, and they end up rejoicing. In each appearance we see how the risen Jesus brings his followers from desolation to consolation, to an experience of greater faith, hope, and love.

Just as Jesus consoles his disciples, he will also console us. As we ponder the Lord's resurrection, we open our hearts to receive his consoling presence, peace, and joy. Each retreatant emerging from the third week's contemplation of the passion and death of Jesus likely feels grief and fatigue at the painful loss, but each also will likely be brought to great joy at Jesus' resurrection. Saint Ignatius here emphasizes spiritual consolation as a fountain of grace that renews life in a person's heart, extending one's spirit in the delight of Christ. Spiritual consolation impels a person toward Christ and his service.[146] The spiritual consolation that Christ offers in the mystery of his resurrection expands our hearts to receive the fire of his love. Like the disciples, our hearts burn with love for our Creator and Lord, such that we can love no created thing apart from him. We are ignited with zeal for the Lord's kingdom and filled with energy for our apostolic works. The gladness that King Solomon experienced on his day of glory is the gladness of Christ in the glory of his resurrection, which has in turn become our gladness.

Questions for Reflection and Discussion

1. How do you see the divinity of Christ reflected in this passage from the Song of Songs and in the liturgy we celebrate, especially at Easter?

2. What significance does the empty tomb have for you, even before Christ appears to anyone?

3. How do you imagine the actual moment of Jesus' resurrection?

4. How do you imagine the physical body of Jesus risen from the dead?

---

146. See Coathalem, *Ignatian Insights*, 211.

5. To what extent can you imagine Jesus' own joy and rejoice with him for his own sake?

6. How would you imagine Jesus appearing to his mother? What would each say and do?

7. What does it mean to you that the risen Lord assumes the "office of the consoler"?

Prayer Exercises

1. Ponder the scenes from the movie *Laura* (p. 228). Pray with John 20:1–10, and ask for the grace of greater faith in the resurrection of the Lord, even without seeing him.

2. Read Giles Cusson's words (p. 230) about Mary's receptivity to the truth of the resurrection. Using your imagination, pray about the moment the Risen Jesus appeared to his mother. Ask for the grace to rejoice and be glad at the great glory and joy of Christ our Lord.

3. Read about the meaning of Christ's resurrection (p. 227). Pray with Mark 16:1–8, and ask for the grace to rejoice and be glad in the gift of eternal life won for us by Christ our Lord.

4. Consider how Jesus' divinity, which seemed to hide itself in the passion, now appears and shows itself so marvelously in the resurrection. Pray with Matthew 28:1–10, and ask for the grace to appreciate the gift of Jesus' resurrection.

5. Pray with Matthew 28:1–10 and 16–20, and ask for the grace to rejoice and share the good news of Jesus' risen life in some form of evangelization.

6. Pray with Luke 24:13–35. Consider the office of consoling that Christ our Lord bears, and compare it with the way friends console each other. Ask for the grace to be aware of the consolation of Jesus' risen presence.

7. Read Maloney's words about the resurrection of Jesus (p. 227). Pray with Song of Songs 3:6–11, and ask for the grace to know the presence of the risen Lord.

8. Make a repetition on any of the above passages, dwelling on those points where you feel greater movement of spirit (consolation or desolation).

CHAPTER 21

Vibrant Life

[G] How beautiful you are, my love,
    how very beautiful!
Your eyes are doves
    behind your veil.
Your hair is like a flock of goats,
    moving down the slopes of Gilead.
Your teeth are like a flock of shorn ewes
    that have come up from the washing,
all of which bear twins,
    and not one among them is bereaved.
Your lips are like a crimson thread,
    and your mouth is lovely.
Your cheeks are like halves of a pomegranate
    behind your veil.
Your neck is like the tower of David,
    built in courses;
on it hang a thousand bucklers,
    all of them shields of warriors.
Your two breasts are like two fawns,
    twins of a gazelle,
        that feed among the lilies.
Until the day breathes
    and the shadows flee,
I will hasten to the mountain of myrrh
    and the hill of frankincense.

You are altogether beautiful, my love;
there is no flaw in you. (Song 4:1–7)

Ask for the grace to be glad and rejoice intensely because of the great joy and
the glory of Christ our Lord.... Consider the divinity, which seemed to hide
itself during the passion, now appearing and manifesting itself so miraculously in the most holy Resurrection in its true and most sacred effects....
Consider the office of consoler that Christ our Lord exercises, and compare
it with the way in which friends are wont to console each other. (SpEx
221–224)

The king has arrived at his palace for the wedding feast and now extols
the loveliness of his bride, "How beautiful you are, my love, how very
beautiful!" Up to this point his kingship, power, and authority have been
emphasized and we now await his enthronement speech, in which he would
likely assert his dominion over his people. But as Arminjon notes, "to our
great astonishment, all his discourse is far from being an act of government:
it is a love declaration, an endless praise of his dearly beloved bride, a song of
passionate admiration for her who is always present to his heart."[147] The
king is so overwhelmed by the bride's beauty that he can only utter his love
for her. He now speaks of her many beautiful features—her eyes, teeth, lips,
cheeks, neck, and breasts—comparing them to the attributes of nature in the
Holy Land. The Hebrews thought that external beauty reflected some interior quality that could only be revealed by comparing it to something
outwardly beautiful.[148] The bride's many beautiful physical features represent and manifest her interior spiritual beauty.

In the last chapter we pondered how King Solomon prefigured the glory
of the risen Christ, our true King. Now we consider how Christ our King
confers the beauty of his risen life on his bride, the Church, through his gift
of the Holy Spirit. In the Song of Songs, the king first notices the bride's eyes,

---

147. Arminjon, *The Cantata of Love*, 208.
148. See Maloney, *Singers of the New Song*, 71.

comparing them to living doves. We can think of doves as a symbol of the Holy Spirit, who imbues the Christian with faith. Of these divine things, faith in the resurrection, the cornerstone of our faith, is especially necessary for the Christian. Saint Paul reminds the Corinthians of the essential importance of their belief in Christ's resurrection: "If Christ has not been raised, then our proclamation has been in vain and your faith has been in vain. . . . But in fact Christ has been raised from the dead, the first fruits of those who have died" (1 Cor 15:14, 20). Christ is alive and present to us through the mode of his resurrection. As members of his Body, we are united with the risen Jesus and receive our supernatural life from him, which will lead to our own resurrection. We are called to believe in Christ risen and to let the resurrection transform us into his risen life, as the following story illustrates:

> One day a mother conceived twins. One child was a girl, the other a boy. Months passed, and they developed. As they grew, they sang with joy, "Isn't it great to be alive!"
>
> Together they explored their mother's womb. They found the life cord. "How great is our mother's love that she shares her own life with us!"
>
> Soon the twins began to change drastically. "What does this mean?" asked the boy.
>
> "It means that our life in the womb is coming to an end," said the girl.
>
> "But I don't want to leave the womb," said the boy, "I want to stay here forever."
>
> "We have no choice," said the girl, "but maybe there is life after birth."
>
> "How can there be?" asked the boy. "We will shed our mother's cord, and how is life possible without it? Besides, there's evidence in the womb that others were here before us, and none of them ever came back to tell us that there is life after birth. No, this is the end."
>
> So the boy fell into despair, saying, "If life in the womb ends in death, what is its purpose, what is its meaning? Maybe we don't even have a mother. Maybe we made her up just to feel good."
>
> "But we must have a mother," said girl. "How else did we get here? How else do we stay alive?"
>
> And so the last days in the womb were filled with deep questioning and fear. Finally, the moment of birth arrived. When the twins opened their eyes, they cried for joy.
>
> What they saw exceeded their wildest dreams.[149]

---

149. Link, *Illustrated Sunday Homilies*, Series II, Ordinary Time, Week 32 C, 125.

This analogy helps us see that life in the womb, which leads to life outside the womb, compares to life in this world, which leads to life beyond this world. Though we don't see the one who sustains our life as we grow in the womb, we are aware of a mother who does sustain us, and even begin to bond with her. Though we don't see God, we are aware of his invisible presence and begin to bond with him. The infant is attached to the comfort and security of the womb and doesn't want to leave it, just as we adults are very attached to the comfort and security of the world and don't want to depart. The infant spends a relatively short nine months in the womb compared to a long lifetime outside of it. Similarly, we spend a relatively short life in the world compared to an eternity beyond it. For a human being, birth is perhaps the most traumatic of experiences, yet this tremendous moment transforms us. We find a new way of being outside the womb, in which we grow to our full adult stature and potential. We often fear death as a traumatic experience. Yet it is the most dynamic moment that transforms us from life in this world to eternal life, where we grow to our full stature and potential as human beings.

Like life outside the womb, eternal life will give us a whole new world to experience and enjoy, as Saint Paul says: "What no eye has seen, nor ear heard, nor the human heart conceived, what God has prepared for those who love him" (1 Cor 2:9). Just as infants open their eyes to finally see their mothers who gave them life at birth, so we will see the face of Christ who gives us eternal life in the beatific vision. In heaven, our joy will be to gaze on the loving face of our Creator and Redeemer in the beatific vision. We will experience his loving embrace in the very heart of our being. All our questions about life will be answered and our desire for infinite love and knowledge will be fulfilled. We can look to the paradigm of Christ's resurrection to understand what our own risen life will be like, as Saint John explains, "Beloved, we are God's children now; . . . we will be like him, for we will see him as he is" (1 Jn 3:2). Eternal life will be a full communion, soul and body, with the risen Christ, a sharing of his glory and joy.

Throughout the fourth week's contemplations on the resurrection of Jesus, Saint Ignatius instructs us to "call to mind and think on what causes pleasure, happiness, and spiritual joy, for instance, the glory of heaven" (SpEx 229). As in all the other mysteries of the life of Christ, he does all these things "for us," so that we may participate in the mystery of his resurrection. Pondering eternal life disposes us to receive the Lord's consolation and joy.

Saint Paul reminds us that by grace we have already been raised up with Christ, so we should "set [our] minds on things that are above" (Col 3:2), where Christ has been raised. As Christ is revealed in the glory of his resurrection, so too shall we be revealed with him in glory (see Col 3:4). By fixing our thoughts on our own resurrection and heavenly things, we will experience happiness and spiritual joy.

In his resurrection, Christ as Bridegroom prepares an everlasting home for us as his bride, the Church. When the disciples are distraught at his impending departure, wondering where he is going and how to follow him, Jesus reassures them: "In my Father's house there are many dwelling places. If it were not so, would I have told you that I go to prepare a place for you? And if I go and prepare a place for you, I will come again and will take you to myself, so that where I am, there you may be also" (Jn 14:2–3). Jesus goes before us to heaven, to his Father's house. He promises to prepare a place for us and to return in order to take us with him.

The design of ancient homes in Israel can shed light on this. Families lived close to each other, only a few doors down, and shared a courtyard. After a bridegroom declared his intent to marry, he would begin building the home he would share with his future bride. The new home was built in a space directly adjoining his family's home. Excitement grew as the building progressed, for when the house was ready the wedding could begin.

Jesus went before us to prepare a place for us as his bride, the Church. Christ the Bridegroom has come to take us with him, by giving us a share in his own resurrection.

Just as Jesus promises the disciples that he will go to prepare a place for them in eternity, he promises them—and us—that he will show us the way to eternal life. The Letter to the Hebrews uses the Greek word *prodromos*, meaning "forerunner," to refer to Jesus (6:20). He has gone before us into the land of eternity, blazing the trail for us so that we might follow him.

Hiking the Appalachian Trail helped me to understand the importance of trail blazers. As my friends and I trudged along, I noticed rocks embedded in the trail. I almost tripped several times and the path seemed treacherous to me. It took a lot of concentration to walk and keep one's balance. But I came to appreciate the rocks, because they helped me gain leverage and push off, especially going uphill. They also kept the path from eroding. Walking on the rocks was less slippery than walking on mud and leaves. The steep uphill paths marked out by the trail committee were challenging, and they could not have taken a more circuitous routes. I asked myself, "Couldn't these people make it a little easier? Are they sadistic? Do they want me to suffer in walking their trail?" But as I reached the highest points of the trail and walked along the ridge provided with breathtaking views, I came to appreciate the challenge and the routes those trailblazers had chosen.

At one point my confreres and I followed a wide swath that looked like the trail and went downhill, even though we still had an uphill climb to make on the mountain. The descent seemed appealing and we took it, but after a while, we realized it had none of the white crosses that marked the actual trail. This wide, easy way had taken us off track, and eventually we had to double back, losing time and energy.

This incident speaks to me of the challenges leading to Jesus' risen glory. Like the trailblazers of the Appalachian Trail, Jesus did not choose an easy way, a wide and flat path, to eternal life. He exhorts us: "Enter through the narrow gate; for the gate is wide and the road is easy that leads to destruction, and there are many who take it. For the gate is narrow and the road is hard that leads to life, and there are few who find it" (Mt 7:13–14). Jesus chose the narrow, difficult way of suffering. But his way is solid and sure; it is based on the certitude of his promises and leads to a most beautiful vision. Jesus is the rock of our salvation, guiding our feet in his paths lest we stumble.

So we have our forerunner in Jesus, a trail map and markers in the Scriptures, and the destination: heaven. But we still need a guide for our journey. Jesus is that guide, telling us not only that he goes to prepare a place for us but also that he will come and take us there. Jesus not only shows us the way; he *is* the way. What does that mean? Compare the experience of receiving direction and then trudging off alone and getting lost, with the experience of receiving direction from someone who accompanies you every step of the way. In the latter case, in a sense you could say that *person is the way*.

The way along the Appalachian Trail was challenging for the three of us who had never hiked it. And I had never been on a hiking *and* camping trip before, so I had no idea what to bring, what to expect, or where to go. I totally depended on the help of my friend Tom, who was familiar with the trail. He knew how to read the trail map, where to stop and camp, where to find fresh water, how to cook over a campfire, and, most importantly, how to scare off a hungry bear. I had new hiking shoes that weren't broken in, so I got large red blisters after the first day of hiking. Tom had the right remedy—"moleskin" patches—so I could continue. Tom reminded me of Jesus. Jesus not only goes before us as a trailblazer; he walks alongside us as a companion and guide, knowing every step of the way and caring for us throughout the journey.

As we approached our final destination on the Appalachian Trail, we stopped for lunch on a mountain summit. It was the last mountain of the hike and we had conquered the highest peak. While we ate lunch together, we laughed about the journey and all its trials—the blisters, the bug bites, the bear that invaded our camp, and the harsh weather. As painful as the experience was, it felt very worthwhile. The pains were nothing compared to those glorious moments spent together, which spoke to me of eternal life.

Pope Benedict XVI describes eternity as "not an unending succession of days in the calendar, but something more like the supreme moment of satisfaction, in which totality embraces us and we embrace totality."[150] When eternity holds us, we experience fullness of life and satisfaction, and we wish to remain in the moment. Eternal life is like that moment we wish will never end, and—unlike all the moments of happiness in this life—it actually never will end! It reminds me of the words of the hymn "Amazing Grace: "When we've been there 10,000 years, bright shining as the sun, we've no less days to sing God's praise than when we've first begun."

Eternal life is not something we experience only at our death and resurrection, but also in the here and now. We need to be attentive to and understand personal experiences of dying and rising in the present moment. One might go through the dying process of confronting a friend with a hurt, leading to the resurrection experience of forgiveness and healing in the relationship. Some people experience dying in the failures of life that lead to resurrection when they ultimately succeed.

A nun tells the inspiring story of a family who experienced dying and rising in the wake of a terrible tragedy. A few weeks before Easter, the father of one the convent school's students accidently got caught in a fire while burning brush in his backyard. Sadly, he died from the burns. For weeks following the incident, the man's family grieved deeply as they daily lived in the very place of the catastrophe. In her distress, his wife could not even look at the garden. On Easter Sunday afternoon, the nun visited the family again. She anticipated continued sadness but was astonished to discover a change in the atmosphere as she entered the house. She experienced a lightness of spirit

---

150. Benedict XVI, *Spe Salvi*, no. 12.

and told the mother that she could sense something was different. The mother replied that early in the day her sister and a neighbor came to visit her. They requested that she get out into nature and enjoy her garden. She thought she would go crazy at the possibility of going out there. Still they persisted and persuaded her that it would be helpful, so she finally did accompany them. Gradually they strolled down to where the fire had occurred. As they arrived at the place, her whole body was overcome with trembling. Out of the blue, she heard the words of the Gospel "Why do you seek the living among the dead? He is not here but has risen." And right then and there it was as though she was freed from an overwhelming burden, and an incredible feeling of serenity and delight washed over her.[151]

That mother received a concrete experience of the risen Lord that impacted her life in a profound way. The risen Jesus exercises his "office of consoler" (SpEx 224), leading those in grief and disbelief into an experience of peace and joy.

In the Song of Songs, the king beholds his bride in an eternal moment of admiration at the new life she manifests through their union. He describes the bride's beauty and liveliness, using images that speak to us of the fullness of risen life and joy that both await us and that begin even now in this life. The bride's long, freely flowing hair is like a "flock of goats moving down the slopes" and speaks of the freedom of her spirit in relation to her bridegroom. Her pure white teeth can chew the word of God for her supernatural nourishment. Her crimson lips speak enchanting words in imitation of her bridegroom, of whom it is written, "grace is poured upon your lips" (Ps 45:2). Her neck is a "tower" on which "hang a thousand bucklers, all of them shields of warriors," displaying her new power for spiritual warfare. Her breasts, symbol of the heart, are "two fawns," evenly balanced in exercising faith and love. The fawns "feed among the lilies," symbolizing the purity of the bride's conscience, as she returns the bridegroom's love in pure innocence.[152] The fullness of life, love, and beauty experienced by the bride corresponds to our experience of the risen life bestowed upon us by the Lord.

---

151. See Flor McCarthy, *New Sunday and Holy Day Liturgies, Year A*, Easter Sunday, Year A, 103–104.

152. See Maloney, *Singers of the New Song,* 71–73.

Questions for Reflection and Discussion

1. How do you look forward to your own resurrection and sharing in Christ's glory? How have you already experienced the new life of resurrection breaking in upon you?

2. Do you ever imagine this life as a prelude to birth to a new and exciting eternal life to come? Can you see parallels to life in the womb preceding natural birth?

3. Where are you "dying" in sinfulness or brokenness and need to experience the power of Christ's resurrection?

4. In what way do you experience the trials of this life as nothing compared to the life to be revealed within you?

5. When have you felt the hope of resurrection to be a help in difficult or sorrowful times?

6. How does Christ not only mark out the path for you to travel to heaven but accompany you as well?

7. When have you had feelings of being the most alive? How were they related to Christ in his resurrection and his gift of risen life to you?

Prayer Exercises

1. Ponder the story of the infants in the womb (p. 237). Pray with John 20:19–24 and 1 John 3:2–3. Ask for the grace to rejoice in the mercy and transformation promised to you.

2. Pray with Song of Songs 4:1–7, and ask for the grace to rejoice in the transformation and fullness of life promised to you.

3. Pray with John 20:25–30, and ask for the grace to recognize any areas of pain or death where you need to experience the Lord's risen life.

4. Reflect on the journey of the Appalachian Trail (p. 239). Pray with John 21:1–14, and ask for the grace to follow the risen Jesus as the Way, Truth, and Life in order to experience eternal life.

5. Consider the trail guide (p. 240). Pray with John 21:15–19, and ask for the grace to know the risen Lord as your companion and guide along the path to eternal life.

6. Ponder the story of the widow on Easter morning (p. 241). Pray with Luke 24:36–42, and ask for the grace of having your burdens lifted by the risen Lord in order to experience his joy and peace.

7. Make a repetition on any of the above contemplations, returning to places of greater movement of spirit (consolation or desolation).

CHAPTER 22

Soaring Above

[G] Come with me from Lebanon, my bride;
    come with me from Lebanon.
Depart from the peak of Amana,
    from the peak of Senir and Hermon,
from the dens of lions,
    from the mountains of leopards.
You have ravished my heart, my sister, my bride,
    you have ravished my heart with a glance of your eyes,
with one jewel of your necklace.
How sweet is your love, my sister, my bride!
    how much better is your love than wine,
    and the fragrance of your oils than any spice!
Your lips distill nectar, my bride;
    honey and milk are under your tongue;
    the scent of your garments is like the scent of Lebanon.
A garden locked is my sister, my bride,
    a garden locked, a fountain sealed.
Your channel is an orchard of pomegranates
    with all choicest fruits,
    henna with nard,
    nard and saffron, calamus and cinnamon,
    with all trees of frankincense,
myrrh and aloes,
    with all chief spices—
a garden fountain, a well of living water,
    and flowing streams from Lebanon. (Song 4:8–15)

He led them to Mount Olivet and He was lifted up before their eyes and a cloud received Him out of their sight. . . . While they were gazing up into heaven, the angels said to them: "Men of Galilee, why do you stand looking up into heaven? This Jesus who has been taken up from you into heaven will come after the same manner wherein you have beheld him going up into heaven." (SpEx 312)

Toward the end of the Spiritual Exercises, Saint Ignatius has us move from the contemplation of Christ's resurrection to his ascension in glory (see SpEx 312). In the passage from the Song of Songs (4:8–15), the bridegroom commands the bride to depart with him from Lebanon, from the peaks of Amana, Senir, and Hermon. Those were dangerous rugged mountains where lions hunted and leopards prowled. The bridegroom's departure corresponds to Christ's ascension from this world to his Father's right hand in glory. Just as the bridegroom came over the mountains (2:8) from heaven to earth, symbolizing the Lord's incarnation, now he departs from the mountains, from earth to heaven, symbolizing the ascension of the Lord to heaven in glory. The bride Israel is called to accompany the Lord as he departs. But the world in which she lives remains perilous. Northern invaders from Canaan could tear her apart like lions and leopards. These hazardous places symbolize the world as a place of temptation. While God created the world good, the effects of men's sins put the world as a whole in a sinful condition, as John's Gospel describes: "the sin of the world" (Jn 1:29). The bride is called to rise above such corrupting influences, to rise above the "dens of lions," and ascend with her bridegroom. Like the eagle that rises higher as it flies into strong headwinds, so the temptations the bride faces can lead her to soar higher in union with her ascending bridegroom.

Like the bride ascending with the bridegroom, so we are to ascend with Christ. How can this happen? How are we to go with Christ in his ascension, since Jesus left his disciples behind? Following the rule of "*lex orandi, lex credendi,*" or "as the Church prays, so she believes," the prayers from the Mass of the Ascension enlighten us. The Collect prayer reminds us that the ascension of Christ is our elevation to eternal life, and where Christ the Head has gone before in magnificence, we as his Body expect to follow. The Prayer over the

Offerings implores that the Lord's gifts help us rise with him to the joys of heaven. The exchange mentioned in this prayer is Christ's divinity for our humanity, in which our humanity is taken up into his divinity. And the Prayer after Communion makes supplication that Christ might draw us in hope to the heavenly realms where our humanity is united with him. While even now we ascend spiritually with Christ, we hope for our eventual bodily ascension in union with Christ.

All these prayers confirm that we are united to Christ in his ascension and "go with him" spiritually in unitive prayer, just as we will eventually go bodily in our risen state to his place at the right hand of the Father. In fact, Christ never really departs from his bride, the Church, even in his ascension. He even says before he leaves, "I am with you always, to the end of the age" (Mt 28:20). Pope Benedict explains, "Because Jesus is with the Father, he has not gone away but remains close to us. Now he is no longer in one particular place in the world as he had been before the ascension: now, through his power over space, he is present and accessible to all—throughout history and in every place."[153] Christ doesn't leave us; through his ascension he draws closer and helps us transcend worldly realities through the grace of his abiding presence. When Jesus led his earthly life, he was confined to the limitations of space and time and could not reach the minds and hearts of people everywhere. We see Christ's presence reflected in the bridegroom of the Song of Songs, who is present to his bride as she is called to depart from the mountaintops in union with him.

In the splendor of his ascension, Christ reveals his role as the High Priest and mediator with the Father. The priest's role is to unite God and his people through sacrifice and intercession as a mediator between God and man. Christ is the one Priest of the new and eternal covenant as he enters the Father's sanctuary. The author of Hebrews explains the mystery of our Lord's ascension, "For Christ did not enter a sanctuary made by human hands . . . but he entered into heaven itself, now to appear in the presence of God on our behalf" (Heb 9:24), to intercede for us before the Father. By this intercession Christ is able "to save those who approach God through him" (Heb 7:25), because of the blood he shed in giving his life for us.

---

153. Benedict XVI, *Jesus of Nazareth: Holy Week* (San Francisco: Saint Ignatius Press, 2011), 284.

The shedding of blood was a necessary component of the covenant between God and Israel. Essentially a covenant is a bond and exchange of persons. Blood symbolizes a person's very life pulsing through his or her veins. The blood of the old covenant symbolized the very life of God given to man; for this reason the blood of the animal sacrifice was sprinkled on the altar of God. The blood also symbolized the very life of man given to God, and so the blood was sprinkled on the people in turn.

Additionally blood symbolized death, in that if one were to break the covenant with God by sinning, one would become like the sacrificed animal, cut in two. By sinning, one breaks oneself against the covenant and chooses death. In order to expiate the guilt of sins, one must be purified by sacrificial blood (see Heb 9:22). The temple sacrifice in Jerusalem involved the priests slaughtering animals and spilling their blood, sprinkling it on the people to expiate their sin.

The priest was more important than both the king and the prophet because he offered the sacrifice of blood to remove the people's guilt and regain God's favor. Joseph Ratzinger explains the spiritual meaning behind the offering of blood by Jesus, our great High Priest: "When Hebrews says that Jesus accomplished the expiation through his blood (9:12), this blood is again not to be understood as a material gift, a quantitatively measurable means of expiation; it is simply the concrete expression of a love of which it is said that it extends "to the end" (Jn 13:1). It is the expression of the totality of his surrender and of his service; an embodiment of the fact that he offers no more and no less than himself."[154]

Christ truly loved us to the end in dying for us on the cross, having nothing greater to give us than his very self in sacrifice. As the soldier lanced his heart, the last ounces of his blood poured forth, the blood of the new and everlasting covenant with us. In the bridegroom's marriage covenant with the bride he exclaims, "You have ravished my heart" (Song 4:9). By her beauty and her glance, the Church as bride has seized her Lover's heart and driven him to mad excess, to the point of suffering his passion and death, with his heart totally poured out for us.

Jesus presents this act of total self-giving to us in sacrifice as a gift pleasing to the Father. We are called to imitate Christ in his self-offering. Jesus

---

154. Ratzinger, *Introduction to Christianity*, 287.

tells us: "No one has greater love than this, to lay down one's life for one's friends" (Jn 15:13).

In his book *Written in Blood*,[155] Robert Coleman uses a powerful story to illustrate this total self-giving in imitation of Jesus. A six-year-old girl, Mary, had a life-threatening disease and needed a blood transfusion. Her only hope of recovering would be to received blood from someone who had already overcome the disease. This meant her brother, who had made a remarkable recovery the year before. And sharing Mary's blood type, he was the ideal donor. The doctor asked Johnny if he would like to give his blood to Mary. Johnny thought for a moment while his lower lip quivered. He then replied yes, he would do it for his sister.

Soon the two kids were wheeled into the operating room—Mary, pale and thin, and Johnny, robust and healthy. Neither of them spoke, but when their eyes met, Johnny grinned. A nurse inserted a needle into his arm, and as he watched his blood flowing through the tube into Mary's body, Johnny's smile faded. He watched as his blood seemed to bring new life into Mary's frail body. When the ordeal was over, Johnny's shaky voice broke the silence. He quietly asked the doctor when he would die.

The doctor then realized why Johnny had hesitated when he had been asked to donate his blood. Johnny had believed that giving his blood to his sister meant giving up his own life. In his mind, he had agreed to die so that his sister would live, just as Jesus gave his life to save us. Johnny's gift of blood symbolized giving all he had, his very life. In interceding before the Father, Jesus presents the blood, his very life, as a complete self-offering, poured out for our salvation.

As Jesus gave his life for us, so we are to give our lives for others in order to bring them the salvation Jesus offers. The mystery of the ascension has apostolic implications. We are to go out to others to extend Jesus' kingdom of love. Just before he ascends, Jesus tells his disciples to go into the whole world and proclaim the Gospel to every creature (see Mk 16:15–20). He commands them: "Go therefore and make disciples of all nations, baptizing them in the name of the Father and of the Son and of the Holy Spirit, and

---

155. See Robert Emerson Coleman, *Written in Blood: A Devotional Bible Study of the Blood of Christ* (Old Tappan, NJ: Fleming H. Revell Co., 1972), 35–36. Originally told by Myron L. Morris, M.D., in *Coronet*, November 1948.

teaching them to obey everything that I have commanded you. And remember, I am with you always, to the end of the age" (Mt 28:18–20). Jesus gave his followers the task of completing his work by preaching the Gospel to the whole world.

Saint Ignatius has us ponder the ascension for the third point of his contemplation (see SpEx 312). The apostles are looking up at heaven, where Jesus has just ascended. Angels say to them, "Men of Galilee, why do you stand looking up into heaven?" Instead of staring up at the sky, they should be rolling up their sleeves and getting to work proclaiming the kingdom of God, which they eventually do as seen in the Acts of the Apostles. With this contemplation Saint Ignatius wants us to not only ponder the meaning of Christ's entry into glory at the right hand of the Father, but also to do the work of extending Christ's reign.

Although grieved at Jesus' departure, the apostles were overjoyed at receiving a mission to proclaim the good news, a mission that gave their lives meaning and purpose. The great work Jesus had accomplished would not die but would spread to the ends of the earth. Jesus needed the apostles' efforts, and they felt privileged to be chosen to participate in such a great work.

Jesus depends upon us to finish his work, as illustrated in an ancient legend about his ascension into heaven. According to the legend, when Jesus entered paradise, his body still displayed the marks of his wounds: nail prints on his hands and feet, the scar on his side, lash marks on his back, and the marks where the thorns had pierced his head. When those in paradise saw these wounds, they fell down to adore Jesus. They were dumbfounded to realize how much he had endured. At that point the blessed messenger Gabriel stood and said to Jesus, "Lord, how much agony you endured on earth! Does everyone on earth know and acknowledge how much you endured for them and how much you cherish them?"

Jesus answered, "No, just at few people in Palestine understand that. The rest haven't known about me. They don't know my identity. They don't know anything I endured, or the extent of my love for them."

Gabriel couldn't believe this. He said to Jesus, "How will everyone else come to know of your affliction and how much you love them?

Jesus explained, "Just before I ascended, I told Peter, James, John, and some of their companions to speak to others on my behalf. They'll tell just as many people as possible, who will in turn tell other people. Thus, the entire world will in the end find out how much I love them."

But Gabriel seemed confounded. He knew how untrustworthy, careless, and suspicious people can be. So he told Jesus, "Be that as it may, Lord, imagine a scenario where Peter, James, and John become weary or discouraged. Imagine if they disregard you or grow uncertain about you. Don't you have a plan B?"

Jesus looked at him and smiled. Then he said, "I did consider your concerns, but I still ruled out any plan B. I only have one strategy: that Peter, James, and John will fulfill their mission—and so will their followers—because I will be with them always."[156]

Jesus had no backup plan. He depended on Peter, James, and John, and they didn't disappoint him. He depended on the people they told, and they didn't disappoint him. Now Jesus depends on each one of us, and hopefully we won't disappoint him.

Like Gabriel, we are deeply moved as we ponder the wounds Jesus suffered in dying for us. We wonder if people really understand how much Jesus loves them. We must be convinced that people need to hear the Gospel. Once we realize our mission to proclaim such good news, Jesus' love will become known and bear fruit in the hearts of those who accept him.

The bride of the Song of Songs displays the qualities of fruitfulness that demonstrate the extension of the kingdom to the entire world. She is first described as a "garden locked" and a "fountain sealed," which symbolize her belonging exclusively to God, especially in the intimacy of prayer and union. But we then hear that the shoots from her garden plants form an orchard of trees exuding pleasant scents. Her fountain not only makes the garden fertile, but also wells up in living water that flows down from Lebanon. Her garden and trees extend beyond the garden enclosure and grow throughout the whole world.

The bride fulfills Isaiah's prophesy that "in days to come Jacob shall take root, Israel shall blossom and put forth shoots, and fill the whole world with fruit" (Is 27:6). As an image of the Church, the bride is "the river of the water of life, bright as crystal, flowing from the throne of God and of the Lamb through the middle of the street of the city. On either side of the river is the tree of life with its twelve kinds of fruit, producing its fruit each month; and the leaves of the tree are for the healing of the nations" (Rev 22:2).

---

156. See Mark Link, *Illustrated Sunday Homilies, Series I*, Ascension, Year C, 43.

United to her bridegroom in a most particular and hidden way—as an enclosed garden and sealed fountain—the bride opens widely to the nations in a fruitful watering of flowing streams and varieties of trees. Her flowing streams and fruitfulness originate in Christ, as Jesus says, "And let the one who believes in me drink. As the Scripture has said, 'Out of the believer's heart shall flow rivers of living water'" (Jn 7:38). And he tells the Samaritan woman that whoever drinks of the water he shall give will never thirst; that "the water that I shall give him will become in him a spring of water welling up to eternal life" (Jn 4:14). Christ is the source of the waters of life within us that eventually flow as streams of life to the world. In the mystery of the ascension, we, like the bride, are rendered exceedingly fruitful by God's grace.

Questions for Reflection and Discussion

1. How do you experience prayer and Christian worship as an ascension with Jesus to the right hand of the Father?

2. How do you perceive Jesus in heaven with the Father and here with you on earth at the same time?

3. When have you felt a homing instinct—a desire to be home and an internal sense of direction about how to get there?

4. What is your understanding of Jesus as the great High Priest and mediator of the covenant in his blood in the mystery of his ascension? How do you share in that offering?

5. How is the ascension a call to evangelization? How do you see Christ ascended to the Father as bringing about his kingdom? To what degree do you sense your own cooperation and fruitfulness in this?

Prayer Exercises

1. Pray with Luke 24:44–53, and ask for the grace to rejoice with Christ ascended into heaven.

2. Consider the petitions that we make in the Mass of the Ascension (p. 246). Pray with Luke 24:44–53, and ask for the grace to spiritually ascend with Jesus to the Father.

3. Pray with Song of Songs 4:6–18, and ask the grace to spiritually transcend the dangers of sin and temptation of this world.

4. Read the quote from Ratzinger (p. 248) and the story of the boy who gave blood for his sister's transfusion (p. 249). Pray with Hebrews 9:11–22, and ask for the grace to share in the High Priesthood of Christ.

5. Pray with John 14:1–7, and ask for the grace to desire to be home with the Lord.

6. Ponder the legend of Christ's arrival in heaven. Pray with Matthew 28:16–20 and Mark 16:15–20, and ask for the grace to be a fervent evangelizer.

7. Make a repetition on any of the above contemplations, returning to the places of greater movement of spirit (consolation or desolation).

CHAPTER 23

Love's Exchange

[G] Awake, O north wind,
    and come, O south wind!
Blow upon my garden,
    that its fragrance may be wafted abroad.
[B] Let my beloved come to his garden,
    and eat its choicest fruits.
[G] I come to my garden, my sister, my bride;
I gather my myrrh with my spice,
I eat my honeycomb with my honey,
I drink my wine with my milk.
[D] Eat, friends, drink,
    and be drunk with love. (Song 4:16—5:1)

Love consists in a mutual sharing of goods, for example, the lover gives and shares with the beloved what he possesses, or something of that which he has or is able to give; and vice versa, the beloved shares with the lover. Hence, if one has knowledge, he shares it with the one who does not possess it; and so also if one has honors, or riches. Thus, one always gives to the other. (SpEx 231)

The final prayer experience of the Spiritual Exercises is the Contemplation to Attain Divine Love. This encapsulates the whole retreat experience and provides a foundation to enable the retreatant to move forward into daily life. Saint Ignatius has the retreatant first consider that true love is a mutual sharing of oneself and one's goods with the other: "The lover gives and shares with the beloved what he possesses, or something of that which he has or is able to give; and vice versa, the beloved shares with the lover." Thus, if one has knowledge, honors, or riches, one "shares it with the one who does not possess it" (SpEx 231). This mutual self-giving of being and goods is at the heart of love.

We find ourselves in this mutual sharing as the bride invites the bridegroom to come into her garden and taste its rarest fruits, for what is hers also belongs to him. Accepting her invitation, the bridegroom enters her garden and gathers what he now describes as his myrrh and spice, honeycomb and honey, and wine and milk (see Song 5:1). The bridegroom recognizes that what belongs to his bride also belongs to him in their mutual sharing of goods, characteristic of true love.

Union with the Lord in love means sharing our whole lives with his. The goal of this contemplation is to help us find God present in all aspects of our daily lives and ordinary activities. To achieve this goal, Saint Ignatius offers us four points to ponder, corresponding to one week of the Exercises.

The First Point: Gratitude for God's Blessings

In the first point of the contemplation, Saint Ignatius has us consider all that God has bestowed upon us, to "recall to mind the blessings of creation and redemption, and the special favors I have received." He has us ponder with great affection "how much God our Lord has done for me, how much He has given me of what He possesses," and finally how much the same Lord "desires to give Himself to me" (SpEx 234). In the first week of the Exercises we pondered the tremendous blessings of creation and redemption. We have received our whole inheritance from God in being created and redeemed. This point pertains of course to the whole human race, but more particularly, to me individually. Saint Paul writes of this love and sacrifice of Christ for me personally: "who loved me and gave himself *for me*" (Gal 2:20, italics added). Saint Ignatius also has us ponder the particular gifts given to each person: our unique personal histories, personalities, character, and talents.

Mary Lou Williams, the great jazz pianist, is a good example of a person endowed with wonderful gifts of nature and grace. One noteworthy grace was the great conversion she had that led to her immersion in God's redemptive love.

Mary Lou Williams grew up abused, neglected, and lonely in an environment of poverty and alcoholism. She taught herself piano at age five and soon began performing at tea parties, galas, and churches throughout Pittsburgh. Leaving home as a teenager, she began her life as a jazz artist and quickly came to be recognized as a "musician's musician" and a composer. In the male-dominated world of big band, Williams arranged music for stars like Duke Ellington and Benny Goodman. Like so many talented jazz musicians of her era, Williams was often destitute and rarely collected royalties for her work. She had the added tribulation of suffering at the hands of crooked managers and drunken lovers and husbands. Eventually, following years of living on the road and generally demoralized by ill treatment, Williams found herself at rock bottom. Stranded in Europe with no money and no means to return to the United States, she was befriended by a wealthy American patron. This devout Catholic introduced her to a quiet church in Paris with a walled garden. When Williams returned to the garden alone, she experienced a stirring vision of the Virgin Mary. This was the most powerful supernatural experience of her life. Shortly thereafter, Williams took instruction in Catholicism and entered the Church in 1957, finally experiencing peace of heart.

After becoming Catholic, Williams wrote and arranged a jazz Mass and many liturgical works, including one commissioned by the Vatican. Williams said that jazz was healing to her soul, that she felt herself praying through her fingers when she played.[157] She experienced God's presence not only in her moments of prayer, but also in the midst of her performances. God bestowed tremendous talent upon her and made her performance a participation in his grace.

As the bride in the Song of Songs shares her gifts with the bridegroom and experiences his delight, so Mary Lou Williams shared her life with Jesus

---

157. See Deanna Witkowski, *Mary Lou's Sacred Jazz*, Urbanfaith web site, April 20, 2010, http://www.urbanfaith.com/2010/04/mary-lous-sacred-jazz.html/, last accessed October 14, 2016.

and received his delight as she played. Williams' life is a testimony to the conversion and transformation we experience in the first point of the contemplation as we consider our own creation and salvation by God.

Now that we are overwhelmed with so many blessings of nature and the outpouring of God's grace, Saint Ignatius invites us in this contemplation to express immense gratitude to God. We have seen in the examen prayer how gratitude to God is at the heart of Saint Ignatius' spirituality. One way of finding God in all things throughout our day is to constantly notice God's blessings and acknowledge them with thanks. Saint Paul urges the Ephesians to give "thanks to God the Father at all times and for everything in the name of our Lord Jesus Christ" (Eph 5:20).

Gratitude for such blessings can take the form of outspoken praise to the Lord, but it can also take the form of a strong willingness to serve him. With this in mind, Saint Ignatius invites us to make a prayer of self-offering to Jesus with much feeling, saying: "Take, Lord, and receive all my liberty, my memory, my understanding, and my entire will, all that I have and possess. Thou hast given all to me. To Thee, O Lord, I return it. All is Thine, dispose of it wholly according to Thy will. Give me Thy love and Thy grace, for this is sufficient for me" (SpEx 234). Here we offer our entire being and all the powers we have as human persons, even our freedom, in love and service to Christ our Lord. Our faculties of memory, intellect, and will have been exercised in prayer with the Lord throughout the retreat. Now we offer these faculties entirely to the Lord for his service in all that we do.

Saint Ignatius also reminds us that "love ought to manifest itself in deeds rather than in words" (SpEx 230). While it is important for us to express our heartfelt love for the Lord in prayer, we must concretize our love in deeds. The bride not only articulates her affection for her bridegroom, but she conveys it with her actions. She shares all she has in her garden—her spices, honey, wine, and milk—with her beloved so that it all becomes his.

The Second Point: How God Dwells in Creatures

From thanksgiving and self-offering we move to the next point of the contemplation, with Saint Ignatius guiding us to reflect on how God dwells in creatures: "in the elements giving them existence, in the plants giving them life, in the animals conferring upon them sensation, in man bestowing understanding." Saint Ignatius has us ponder God's dwelling with each of us: God "gives me being, life, sensation, intelligence; and makes a temple of me, since I am created in the likeness and image of the Divine Majesty" (SpEx 235). Here Saint Ignatius emphasizes that God is present in his creation. He's dwelling in all things, a point that finds its origin and summit in God's indwelling in man through the incarnation of Jesus Christ. The theologian Michael Buckley explains:

> The second point of the contemplation considers how God does not remain outside of his creation but dwells within creatures, effecting them to be what they are by this presence. The meaning and worth of things come out of the presence of God, ranging from his presence within sub-life until the divine indwelling that makes a man into his temple. For such a consideration, the incarnation becomes the highest instance of presence, but it does not exhaust it. What God has done in Christ is indicative of what he has done to man as his temple. What he has done in man is in itself indicative of what his presence is in animals and things.[158]

Saint Ignatius emphasizes how God dwells in all things. The incarnation is the peak of God's indwelling in creatures; God assumes our very human nature. In his incarnation, Christ is the very Sacrament of God, the revelation of God himself, and the mediator between God and his creation. Through the incarnation of Jesus Christ, God is able to come to dwell in man by grace. Saint Paul asks, "Do you not know that you are God's temple and that God's Spirit dwells in you?" (1 Cor 3:16). God has made us in his image and likeness so that he can live in us. By grace he has made us partakers of the divine nature (see 2 Pet 1:4).

God is in everything by his essence, presence, and power. God's essence is to exist and his being sustains all creation in existence. Saint Paul reminds us that "in him we live and move and have our being" (Acts 17:28). God is everywhere, seeing all reality, by his presence in each particular place in the here and now. Saint Paul reflects on the truth that "before him no creature is hidden, but all are naked and laid bare to the eyes of the one to whom we must render an account" (Heb 4:13). God is everywhere in the world by his power because everything is subject to him as revealed through the psalmist: "If I

---

158. Michael Buckley, S.J., "The Contemplation to Attain Love," *Supplement to The Way* 24 (Spring 1975), 101.

ascend to heaven, you are there . . . If I take the wings of the morning and settle at the farthest limits of the sea, even there your hand shall lead me" (Ps 139:8–10). God is present to us in every aspect of our lives.

In his book *The Golden String*, the Benedictine monk Bede Griffiths describes a remarkable episode of encounter with the ever-present Lord. As a schoolboy, Griffiths was walking outside alone one summer evening at sunset. Strolling along, he became aware of how beautiful was the sound of the birds singing and wondered why he had not heard them singing like that before. As he continued walking, he came upon some lovely hawthorn trees in bloom, which emitted the sweetest fragrance. Griffiths wondered why he had never noticed their beauty or aroma before. He felt as if he had been inserted into the Garden of Eden to see and smell its wonders and to hear its choir of angels singing. Coming upon some playing fields, he noticed the stillness all around him as dusk began to settle. He fell on his knees, feeling God's presence in an almost tangible way. "Now that I look back on it," wrote Griffiths, "it seems to me it was one of the decisive events of my life."[159] Until then he had been a normal schoolboy, content with the world as he found it. He was suddenly made aware of another world of beauty and mystery he had never imagined existed, except in poetry. Griffiths experienced God present in nature, like a return to the Garden of Eden. Likewise, the bride experiences her bridegroom visiting her garden, which becomes a paradise with his presence. As she shares all that she is and has with him, she experiences his delight with her.

After explaining how God dwells in the natural world, Saint Ignatius highlights how God dwells within each one of us and "gives me being, life, sensation, intelligence; and makes a temple of me, since I am created in the likeness and image of the Divine Majesty" (SpEx 235). God continually creates me. He gives me a human soul with sensation, intellect, and will. Because I am made in his image with my powers of the soul, I am able to be a temple in which God can more fully dwell. Jean-Pierre de Caussade helps us to understand how we experience God's indwelling existentially:

> All things are intended to guide, raise, and support you, and are in the hand
> of God whose action is vaster and more present than the elements of earth,

---

159. Bede Griffiths, *The Golden String* (Springfield: Templegate Publishers, 1980), 9–10.

air, and water. Even by means of the senses God will enter, provided they are used only as he ordains, because everything contrary to his will must be resisted. There is not a single atom that goes to form part of your being, even to the marrow of the bones, that is not formed by the divine power. From it all things proceed, by it all things are made. Your very life-blood flows through your veins by the movement this power imparts to it, and all the fluctuations that exist between strength and weakness, languor and liveliness, life and death, are divine instruments put in motion to effect your sanctification. Under its influence all bodily states become operations of grace. From this invisible hand come all your opinions, all your ideas on whatever subject they may be formed. What this action will effect in you, you will learn by successive experiences, for there is no created heart or mind that can teach it to you. Your life flows on uninterruptedly in this unsounded abyss, in which each present moment contains all that is best for you and as such must be loved and esteemed. It is necessary to have a perfect confidence in this action which of itself can do nothing but what is good.[160]

De Caussade describes how God's presence springs up from within us and surges through our very being and life. The Lord also communicates his presence to us from without. All situations can lead us to union with God; persons, places, events, and circumstances are opportunities to experience his presence. We need to be more accepting of God's presence and allow him to conduct our lives, which are in his hands.

Stephane-Joseph Piat, O.F.M., details God's presence in the beauty of the human person of Celine, the older sister of Saint Thérèse of Lisieux. Celine's example shows us how we can radiate Christ to others in and through our very being.

Celine was a vibrant, charming woman. She had a great love for life, was intelligent and endowed with many talents. Even as a Carmelite nun she had a great interest in science and read widely in that field as well as in philosophy. Her conversation sparkled with vivacity and humor, even in her final and intensely painful illness at almost ninety years of age.[161] God created Celine

---

160. Jean Pierre de Caussade, S.J., *Abandonment to Divine Providence*, (Exeter, England, The Catholic Herald Press, 1921), 32. Internet Archive https://archive.org/details/divine providence00causuoft.

161. See Stephane-Joseph Piat, O.F.M., *Celine* (San Francisco: Saint Ignatius Press, 1997), *passim*, esp. 14–15, 33–43, 52, 101–119, 142–192.

with magnificent interior beauty and a tremendous capacity to receive his presence. As her gifts developed, God's presence so imbued her personality and character that she luminously radiated Christ to others. We can imagine how much God enjoys dwelling in and sharing his life with such a person, like the bridegroom in the Song of Songs who delights in the garden of his bride, admiring her flowers and consuming her fruit as his own.

Just as Christ is present to us and manifests himself to us through all that exists, we are called to manifest his presence to others. Christ makes us vessels of his presence to others. The more we share Christ's likeness, the more transparent we become in revealing his presence to others. As we imitate Christ in the use of our faculties, in thinking according to his perspective and choosing according to his values, we will become more Christ-like in charity toward others. This means allowing Christ to reign in our inner lives. We surrender our lives and our powers to him as Saint Ignatius suggests in his *Suscipe* prayer in the contemplation: "Take, Lord, and receive all my liberty, my memory, my understanding, and my entire will" (SpEx 234). Such a prayer represents our total surrender and self-giving to the Lord in freedom in order to allow him to take up his dwelling within us, manifesting his life in and through us.

Caryll Houselander imagines how the Blessed Virgin Mary opened her heart to fully receive Christ, nurture his life, and manifest his presence in giving birth to him. She wanted to give Jesus the very substance of her bones, each cell of her physique, the surging of her blood. It would not have been enough to merely be present to her Son. She desired to be his nourishment in order to be part of his very physical being. She gave of herself physically in each brief instant of life, in her speech, in her labor, in her eating and drinking, in distress or euphoria—in order to communicate her very self and her bounteous life.[162]

Mary gave herself totally to Christ in becoming his dwelling place for his incarnation. As Christ continues to dwell in us, we want to imitate Mary in giving the Lord full reign over our lives, sharing ourselves totally with him, as Saint Ignatius suggests in the Contemplation to Attain Love. Like the bride speaking to her bridegroom, we want to say to Christ, "Let my beloved come

---

162. See Caryll Houselander, *Lift Up Your Hearts* (New York: Arena Lettres, 1978), 32–33.

to his garden, and eat its choicest fruits" (4:16). We want to hear Christ say to us, like the bridegroom speaks to his bride, "I come to my garden, my sister, my bride. I gather my myrrh with my spice, I eat my honeycomb with my honey, I drink my wine with my milk" (5:1). As the bridegroom shares in the garden and in the fruits of the bride as his own, so Christ shares in the garden of our souls as his unique possession. Saint Ignatius insists that love shares one's gifts, indeed one's very self, with the beloved.

Questions for Reflection and Discussion

1. How do you sense the Lord sharing his gifts with you? How do you share your gifts with him in return?

2. What is your sense of gratitude to the Lord for all you have received? How well do you notice those gifts and express gratitude?

3. What are the specific gifts of your being created? How do you sense God present in you through them by his presence and power?

4. In what ways are you aware of how all creation mediates God's presence to you?

5. What is your sense of God's indwelling presence in you? Do you have any awareness of radiating Christ in this?

6. How is Christ's becoming incarnate in Mary a paradigm for how he wants to make his dwelling in you?

Prayer Exercises

1. Reflect on Saint Ignatius' words that love consists in a mutual sharing of goods (p. 255). Pray with Song of Songs 4:16—5:1, and ask the Lord to share whatever you have to offer him.

2. Consider the first point of Saint Ignatius' Contemplation to Attain Love (p. 256). Pray with 1 John 4:7—5:4, and ask for the grace to recognize and be grateful for all the gifts of nature and grace you have received. Close with Saint Ignatius' prayer of self-offering (p. 258).

3. Consider the story of Mary Lou Williams (p. 257). Pray with Colossians 1:3–14, and ask for the grace to recognize and be grateful for all the gifts of nature and grace you have received.

4. Reflect on the second point of the contemplation about God dwelling in all things (p. 259). Pray with Ephesians 3:14–21, and ask for the grace to know Christ's indwelling in you and in all things.

5. Ponder the second point of the contemplation and the quote from de Caussade (p. 260). Pray with John 15:1–11, and ask to know the indwelling presence of the Lord by grace and to radiate his presence. Close with Saint Ignatius' prayer of self-offering (p. 258).

6. Consider the second point of the contemplation and thought about Mary from Caryll Houselander (p. 262). Pray with Colossians 3:12–17, and ask for the grace to offer yourself totally to Christ in loving union and service.

7. Make a repetition on any of the above contemplations, returning to the places of greater movement of spirit (consolation or desolation).

Chapter 24

Enduring Love

[B] I opened to my beloved,
    but my beloved had turned and was gone.
My soul failed me when he spoke.
I sought him, but did not find him;
    I called him, but he gave no answer.
Making their rounds in the city
    the sentinels found me;
they beat me, they wounded me,
     they took away my mantle,
     those sentinels of the walls.
I adjure you, O daughters of Jerusalem,
    if you find my beloved,
tell him this:
    I am faint with love. (Song 5:6–8)

Consider how God works and labors for me in all creatures upon the face of the earth, that is, He conducts Himself as one who labors. Thus, in the heavens, the elements, the plants, the fruits, the cattle, etc., He gives being, conserves them, confers life and sensation, etc. (SpEx 236)

The Third Point: The Great Work of Salvation

We continue to ponder Saint Ignatius' Contemplation to Attain Love, which encapsulates the four weeks of the Exercises in four points for prayer. In the third point, which summarizes the Lord's passion in the third week, Saint Ignatius invites us to "consider how God works and labors for me in all creatures upon the face of the earth, that is, He conducts Himself as one who labors. Thus, in the heavens, the elements, the plants, the fruits, the cattle, etc., He gives being, conserves them, confers life and sensation, etc." (SpEx 236). This labor corresponds to the Lord's toil in his passion and death for us, accomplishing the great "work" of our salvation. We are called to suffer in union with Christ in labor as a share in his passion and death in order to bring about his work of salvation. In chapter 5 of the Song of Songs, the bride willingly chooses to suffer in searching for her bridegroom, saying, "they beat me, they wounded me, they took away my mantle." In her compassion for her suffering bridegroom, she desires to share in his afflictions.

In the third point of the contemplation, we consider the Lord's active laboring for our benefit in all creation and in every gift, as Jesus reminds us: "My Father is still working, and I also am working" (Jn 5:17). Jesus and the Father are always working for our salvation, and Jesus invites us to share in his work. Saint Ignatius highlights the importance of the lover sharing everything with the beloved; and in this case, Christ shares his work with us. Hopefully we desire to participate in his work even to the point of sharing in his sufferings, which are part of his work. Buckley explains how in the third point of the contemplation the labors of Christ intersect with our world of work: "This theme of the third week is resumed now as the work of God in all things, the work of which the passion of Christ is paradigmatic, and in which all things, whether cosmos or the subatomic, are seen as events and moments in which he labors. Again the internal development is obvious: God who gives, God who indwells—now God who works out the salvation of men within all things."[163]

God labors on our behalf as he continually creates our world, keeping the galaxies and our planet in motion, giving life to all things on earth. In

---

163. Michael Buckley, S.J., "The Contemplation to Attain Love," *Supplement to The Way* 24 (Spring 1975), 102.

becoming man, Jesus Christ shared in our labors as a carpenter, an itinerant preacher, and a healer of bodies and souls. He labored in his passion and death for our salvation. Now the Lord continues his labor for us in all the persons, events, and circumstances of our lives.

If God is already at work in the world, we should discern his presence and activity as we seek to cooperate in his labors. Discernment becomes a matter of noticing that God is active, already at work in our lives and our daily routines. It is not so much a question of inviting God to be with us in our labors as realizing the privilege of being called to share in God's labor for us and the world. We are co-creators with a God who is already busy bringing about the salvation of the world in love.

Saint Ignatius has us contemplate God's primary and fundamental work in our immediate environment. Once we are more aware of his ongoing activity, we can join ourselves to him as cooperators in this work. Discerning God's activity is a far cry from having our own agenda and enlisting God to carry out what we have envisioned. It means getting in tune with God's desire for our lives in our concrete situation, and then having the detachment and freedom to follow his will.

Jim Johnson was a hotel manager who was asked to save a failing hotel. Other managers had tried but failed, and the hotel was in a do-or-die situation. Because Jim was prayerfully in tune with God's plan and activity, he decided to try a new approach. Instead of focusing all his energies on new budgets and protocols, Jim focused on prayer. Each night he drove to the top of the hill overlooking the hotel and the city, and he prayed for the hotel guests resting in their rooms, for his employees and their families, and for his business associates. Finally, he prayed for the city and its people. He did this night after night, and, not coincidentally, the hotel's dire situation soon started to improve. Confidence began to radiate from its employees. Each guest was welcomed and greeted with new warmth. The hotel began to operate with a new spirit. These signs marked the hotel's experience of a remarkable rebirth, a rebirth Jim rightly attributed to God's action through his nightly prayer.[164] Clearly Jim was open to God's desire for the hotel, not by producing his own agenda and asking God to bless it. Instead, through prayer he became aligned to God's will, which concerned the welfare of the hotel's

---

164. See Link, *Illustrated Sunday Homilies*, Series II, Ordinary Time 17C, 85.

guests and its staff. God produced the work and, through prayer and discernment, Jim became a willing instrument in helping God bring it about.

Our engagement with God's labor will entail sacrifice and suffering. Each sacrifice in our work consecrates to God something of our time, strength, and material good. Work temporarily depletes human strength, even our very selves, as we grow weary laboring with the sweat of our brow. Jesus grew weary in his travels, preaching, and healing. We see him tired as he speaks to the Samaritan woman, groaning as he heals the woman with the hemorrhage, and asleep in the boat during the storm at sea. In his passion and death, Jesus experienced the destruction of his body and the brokenness of his spirit brought about by his sacrificial work. As we share in Christ's labors, we will suffer similar pains and losses in trial. Saint John Paul II said that our sweat and toil is a loving participation in the passion of Christ for the salvation of others: "Th[e] work of salvation came about through suffering and death on a cross. By enduring the toil of work in union with Christ crucified for us, man in a way collaborates with the Son of God for the redemption of humanity. He shows himself a true disciple of Christ by carrying the cross in his turn every day in the activity that he is called upon to perform."[165]

By our toil, stress, and pain we share in the sufferings of Christ and participate in his redemptive activity. We are privileged to share in Christ's work of salvation and can develop a willingness to suffer for it. Similarly, the bride has been laboring in her garden to produce the fruits that delight her lover (4:16). She is then beaten and wounded by the watchmen as she searches for her beloved through the streets (5:7). She is so consumed in the labor of seeking and finding him that she doesn't seem to mind the pain of the blows. In her love she seems very willing to suffer through her labors because her only end is to seek her beloved. Far from complaining about her suffering, she seeks her beloved all the more intensely. If our goal is Christ, we will labor and not count the cost.[166]

The third point of Saint Ignatius' contemplation helps us to remain united in prayer to Christ in the hardship of our work, as we consider him

---

165. John Paul II, *Laborem Exercens* (Boston: Pauline Books & Media, 1981), no. 27.

166. The prayer of generosity attributed to Saint Ignatius expresses this sentiment: "Lord, teach me to be generous. Teach me to serve you as you deserve; to give and not to count the cost, to fight and not to heed the wounds, to toil and not to seek for rest, to labor and not to ask for reward, save that of knowing that I do your will."

laboring with suffering for our salvation. We start working with the best of intentions, but the hardship of work sometimes kills our joy. Various difficulties, failures, and opposition may arise as we labor, disturbing our equilibrium and upsetting our inner peace.

Author and retreat master David Fleming notes how we can overcome these difficulties with a change in attitude. Instead of becoming upset, we can let every unforeseen circumstances that disrupt our prearranged plans or schedule be received in a spirit of supernatural submission, as did Christ.[167]

Walter Ciszek, a Jesuit priest and missionary to Russia, was captured by the communist authorities and sentenced to fourteen years in Siberia's labor camps. He is an example of a person willing to suffer in order to serve Christ and his mission of evangelization. In Cisezk's book *He Leadeth Me*, he describes how he was assigned to the lowest work and the roughest brigades during his years of forced labor. He did the most difficult and dirtiest jobs: digging foundations by hand, shoveling long sewer trenches through the frozen ground, loading heavy construction materials with his bare hands and brute strength, and crawling in damp, dark spaces to dig new mines where death was always one careless step away. Ciszek came to know work at its worst: ugly, demeaning, and dehumanizing. His efforts offered little in which he could take pride or feel fulfilled. It was the commonest, roughest labor, requiring little skill or thought, only brute strength. Yet Ciszek writes that he did take pride in his work for supernatural reasons:

> I did each job as best I could. I worked to the limit of my strength each day and did as much as my health and endurance under the circumstances made possible. Why? Because I saw this work as the will of God for me. I didn't build a new city in Siberia because Joseph Stalin or Nikita Khrushchev wanted it, but because God wanted it. The labor I did was not a punishment but a way of working out my salvation in fear and trembling. Work was not a curse, even the brutish grunt work I was doing, but a way to God—and perhaps even a way to help others to God. I could not, therefore, look upon this work as degrading. It was ennobling, for it came to me from the hand of God himself. It was his will for me.[168]

---

167. See David L. Fleming, "Finding a Busy God," in *A Spirituality for Contemporary Life* (St. Louis: Review for Religious, 1991), 21–23.

168. Ciszek, S.J., *He Leadeth Me*, 100–101.

With amazing fortitude, Ciszek turned the curse of forced labor into love and service of God. He realized the dignity of human work, that it ennobled him as a person. His attitude toward work as the will of God helped him to perform it with devotion. As he suffered, Ciszek remained united to Christ and participated in his saving work. This courageous priest shows us how to be heroic in everyday, ordinary things, by persevering in the smallest, dullest duties and drudgery of one's state in life.

Sharing in Joy

For a Christian, labor is not all suffering and toil, however, but also a share in the joy of the resurrection. Saint John Paul II comments on our participation in Jesus' resurrection through work: "In work, thanks to the light that penetrates us from the resurrection of Christ, we always find a glimmer of new life, of the new good, as if it were an announcement of 'the new heavens and the new earth' in which man and the world participate precisely through the toil that goes with work."[169]

Just as Jesus' suffering and death led to resurrection, so the struggle of work leads to our happiness. When our work enables us to be creative and accomplish things as we collaborate with others, we can enjoy it as we share in the joy of Jesus' resurrection.

The technological achievements of the monks of the Middle Ages give us a good example of how our work can produce good things for the world.[170] Manual labor played a central role in monastic life. Often the monks freely embraced difficult work, viewing it as a channel of grace and a way of mortifying the flesh. This was certainly true as they cleared and reclaimed lands. They built dikes and drained swamps, turning a source of disease into fertile agricultural land. Their expertise in mining, metallurgy, and other technology spread industry and economic development throughout Europe. They built a better world on earth in preparation for the life to come. They anticipated the coming of "a new heaven and a new earth" (Rev 21:1) by creating a more productive and prosperous life for the people of their time.

---

169. John Paul II, *Laborem Exercens*, no. 27.

170. See Thomas Woods, *How the Catholic Church Built Western Civilization* (Washington, D.C.: Regnery, 2005), 28–35.

Our labor too should be inspired by supernatural motivation, and it will be if we keep Christ before our eyes as the goal of all our actions. Saint Paul exhorts us: "And whatever you do, in word or deed, do everything in the name of the Lord Jesus" (Col 3:17). Our work is not for vainglory or a selfish desire to get ahead of others. United to Christ, we act to serve him so as to permeate this world with his values.

A story from the Middle Ages shows us the importance of working for God with a supernatural motive. At a building site in France a construction manager went out to ask some laborers how they felt about their work. He asked the first worker, "What are you doing?"

"What, are you blind?" the worker snapped back. "I'm cutting these impossible boulders with primitive tools and putting them together the way the boss tells me. I'm sweating under this blazing sun. This back-breaking work is boring me to death."

The manager quickly backed off and approached a second worker. He asked the same question, "What are you doing?"

The worker replied, "I'm shaping these boulders into usable forms, which are then assembled according to the architect's plans. It's hard work and sometimes it gets boring, but I earn five francs a week and that supports my wife and kids. It's a job. Could be worse, too."

Somewhat encouraged, the manager went on to a third worker. "And what are you doing?" he asked.

"Why, can't you see?" said the worker as he lifted his arm to the sky. "I'm building a cathedral!"

The first worker complained because he was focused on the mere toil and suffering involved in his work. The second worker had a sense of his work's value in providing a living for his family, but not much beyond that. The third worker profoundly understood the purpose of his labors because he realized the beauty of the end result. His attitude corresponds to our having a supernatural motive in realizing that all our work can build up the Lord's kingdom in love.

As we ponder God's work in the third point of Saint Ignatius' Contemplation to Attain Love, we unite our work to his in love. We can perform any task out of love for God, whether it be cooking a meal at home, studying at school, or selling a product in the marketplace. In these acts of love we exercise our creativity. Caryll Houselander ponders how we can improve our attitude about our work: do it first and foremost out of love. She observes that we use the expression "make love" in only one sense. But the entire existence of each laborer ought to be about making love, because labor is creative. The person who is a contemplative in action discovers the delight of adoring the Holy Trinity in the midst of his work through his personal experience in his very heart, wherein Christ is discovered. He experiences the unspeakable secret of God's delight in creating a new earth capable of holding Christ.[171]

When we contemplate the Lord's labors on our behalf, in our creation and redemption, we are filled with his love. We desire to respond in love, uniting our efforts to God's and laboring on his behalf to build a better world in which God can more readily dwell. Saint Ignatius invites us to contemplate God's work in order to attain his love, sharing in Christ's labor and suffering. In the same way, all that the bride suffers she endures out of love, having only the higher motive of seeking her bridegroom. She will not rest until she has found him.

Questions for Reflection and Discussion

1. In what way is your work a participation in the suffering and death of Christ? What are the greatest trials you face in your work?

2. How do you experience work as a sacrifice and a destruction of yourself and energy?

3. To what degree can you experience union with Christ in the midst of your labors? What helps to foster this? What hinders it?

4. In what sense is your work a sharing in the resurrection of Christ and a foreshadowing of the "new heavens and new earth" to come?

5. How well do you organize yourself in your work? How is this a share in God's ordering of the universe?

6. How much can you exercise creativity in your work? What does it mean to you? How is it a means of self-expression?

7. How well do you work as an expression of love of God? How do you maintain a supernatural motive?

---

171. See Caryll Houselander, *The Risen Christ* (New Rochelle: Scepter Publishers, 2007), 72–73.

Prayer Exercises

1. Read Saint Ignatius' third point of the Contemplation to Attain Love and the quote from Michael Buckley (p. 266). Pray with John 5:1–29, and ask for the grace to know Christ in his laboring to heal you.

2. Ponder the story of Jim Johnson (p. 267). Pray with Matthew 11:25–30, and ask for the grace to consecrate your work to the Lord and know his peace.

3. Consider the quote from Saint John Paul II (p. 268) and the story of Walter Ciszek (p. 269). Pray with Song of Songs 5:6–8, and ask for the grace to labor with Christ in suffering and to share in his sacrifice.

4. Read the quote of Saint John Paul II (p. 270). Pray with Luke 19:12–28, and ask for the grace to enjoy your work and to be industrious and productive in it.

5. Reflect on the story of the cathedral building project (p. 271). Pray with Genesis 1:1—2:3, 15, and ask for the grace to maintain a supernatural motive of love of God in your work.

6. Read Caryll Houselander's observation about creative work (p. 271). Pray with Luke 10:38–42, and ask for the grace to exercise creativity and love of God in your work.

7. Make a repetition on any of the above contemplations, paying greater attention to those places of greater movement of spirit (consolation and desolation).

CHAPTER 25

Love's Descent

[D] What is your beloved more than another beloved,
　　O fairest among women?
What is your beloved more than another beloved,
　　that you thus adjure us?
[B] My beloved is all radiant and ruddy,
　　distinguished among ten thousand.
His head is the finest gold;
　　his locks are wavy,
　　black as a raven.
His eyes are like doves
　　beside springs of water,
bathed in milk,
　　fitly set.
His cheeks are like beds of spices,
　　yielding fragrance.
His lips are lilies,
　　distilling liquid myrrh.
His arms are rounded gold,
　　set with jewels.
His body is ivory work,
　　encrusted with sapphires.
His legs are alabaster columns,
　　set upon bases of gold.
His appearance is like Lebanon,
　　choice as the cedars.
His speech is most sweet,

and he is altogether desirable.
This is my beloved and this is my friend,
O daughters of Jerusalem.
[D] Where has your beloved gone,
    O fairest among women?
Which way has your beloved turned,
    that we may seek him with you?
[B] My beloved has gone down to his garden,
    to the beds of spices,
to pasture his flock in the gardens,
    and to gather lilies.
I am my beloved's and my beloved is mine;
    he pastures his flock among the lilies. (Song 5:9—6:3)

Consider all blessings and gifts as descending from above. Thus, my limited power comes from the supreme and infinite power above, and so, too, justice, goodness, mercy, etc., descend from above as the rays of light descend from the sun, and as the waters flow from their fountains, etc. (SpEx 237)

The Fourth Point: God as the Source of All Good

So far in the first three points of the Contemplation to Attain Love, we have considered God *conferring* his gifts on us, God *present* in his gifts, and God *working* for us in his gifts. We now arrive at the fourth point of the contemplation, in which Saint Ignatius has us consider God as the *origin* of his gifts. We are to ponder how all the good things and gifts descend from above, how our limited power as human beings comes from God's infinite and supreme power on high. So also our human virtues such as justice, goodness, and mercy descend from God above, as "the rays of light descend from the sun, and as the waters flow from their fountains" (SpEx 237).

In this fourth point of the contemplation we shift our focus from the manifestations of God to their origin in him as the source of all that is good. All the goodness we have as human beings has its source in God and speaks of divine goodness bestowed upon us, like water streaming from a fountain or light shining from the sun. Michael Buckley explains that this fourth point of the contemplation encapsulates the experience of the risen Christ, which we contemplate in the fourth week of the Exercises: "As the risen Christ is the source of consolation, that is, of the Holy Spirit, so God is the source of all that is. All things descend and they speak out the 'above' from which they move. What is found through them is not only a moment of blessing, and the enduring love behind it. What is found is any moment of created goodness and the God whom it resembles."[172]

Christ, risen and ascended, continues to bestow the consolation of his Holy Spirit upon us. Each reality of our lives reminds us of God, the source and origin of all that is good, present to us in and through these realities. We encounter the person of the risen Christ, who gives these gifts in abundance.

The Song of Songs now parallels the movement of the fourth point of the Contemplation to Attain Love as the bridegroom descends from above to be present to his bride in his gifts. When asked where her bridegroom is, the bride replies, "My beloved has gone down to his garden . . . to pasture his flock in the gardens" (Song 6:2). This "going down" from the hills of Jerusalem to the bride's garden represents the descent of grace from God to human beings. Because all gifts come from above, from Christ and his divinity, all reality can be seen in relation to God and in Christ. For the bride, all the precious materials of the universe are seen in her bridegroom and are part of him, just as we see all reality in Christ. The bride uses the most precious worldly materials to describe her beloved: gold, jewels, ivory, alabaster, cedar, beds of spices, and aromatic perfumes. These substances evoke the Temple of Jerusalem in its construction and decoration, representing symbols of divinity. God shines forth in these precious materials as their divine source. This sheds some light on why Jesus compared himself to the Temple (see Jn 2:19–22). After he threw out the money changers, Jesus said, "Destroy this temple, and in three days I will raise it up." Though the people thought he meant the building, John says, "He was speaking of the temple of his body." Christ would be put to death and his body would be raised up in his resurrection. The bride's description of the valuable materials in the

---

172. Buckley, "The Contemplation to Attain Love," 103.

Temple therefore evokes Christ in his resurrection and all his goodness streaming "from above" (SpEx 237).

We will now consider how the precious substances of the Temple, applied to the bridegroom in the Song of Songs, manifest the risen Christ in his divinity. The bridegroom's head is of gold, the symbol of divinity in the Scriptures. The Holy of Holies, at the "head" of the Temple, was covered with fine gold. The cedar altar in front of it was overlaid with gold and contained the gold placed there by King Solomon (see 1 Kgs 6:20). The black palm fronds of the bridegroom's hair resemble the palms decorating the gates of the Holy of Holies. Black symbolizes the eternal youthfulness of the risen Christ (contrasted with the white hair of old age). The bridegroom's eyes that are doves recall the doves that adorned the Temple, and remind us of the Holy Spirit, who is associated with the gift of the risen Christ. The pool of water recalls the water basin that was the bronze sea of the Temple. The waters symbolize the cleansing power of the Bridegroom in Baptism and the rivers of life flowing from him, just as living waters of grace flow from the heart of Christ (see Jn 7:38). The bridegroom's hands are golden, rounded, and set with jewels of Tarshish, symbolizing Christ's hands that reach out to us and his actions flowing out from his divinity to others. The rare jewel of Tarshish was the beryl stone set in gold on the breastplate of the high priest, whose role was mediator between God and Israel (see Ex 28:20). The risen Christ is the one mediator between God and man, the great High Priest who intercedes for us. The bridegroom's belly is a block of ivory covered with sapphires, symbolizing the "bowels" or depths of his being as the source of life from which flow love and compassion. Jesus felt compassion in the very depths of his divine being, moved with the deepest emotions (see Jn 11:33–35). The sapphires of the bridegroom's body remind us of the blue color of heaven, reflecting Christ's perfect heavenly virtues. The alabaster legs of the bridegroom, representing the humanity of Christ, are set into his sockets of pure gold, representing the divinity of Christ. The bride concludes her adulation of the bridegroom by comparing him to Lebanon and its towering cedars. The cedars bring to mind the transcendence of Christ's divinity, which shines forth in his resurrection as the source of all spiritual gifts "from above" (SpEx 237).[173]

---

173. See Maloney, *Singers of the New Song*, 107–113.

Following the bride's praise of the bridegroom, she then mentions how he has "gone down to his garden . . . to pasture his flock in the gardens" (Song 6:2). The bridegroom reminds us of Christ, who, though exalted in heaven, descends "from above" to be with his beloved friends, to accompany and pasture them. From heaven the risen Christ does not leave us bereft but comes down to comfort us, especially in the midst of trials.

This is exemplified in the story of a woman named Irene. An attorney, Irene worked for a legal-aid society that was on the brink of collapse due to lack of funds. Because the office was understaffed, Irene was overworked in trying to find basic housing for the elderly poor. She arrived at an Ignatian retreat exhausted, welcoming the respite. After several days of rest, Irene began to pray with John 1 ("come and see"). In her prayer, she was soon given a sense of "seeing" Jesus present and fully alive. She saw no pictures or images, but felt a compelling sense that nothing restricted Jesus' presence to the world. Irene realized that all limitation was in the world, in its sinfulness, brokenness, fear, and rage. She stayed with that sense of Christ's presence. Jesus strongly consoled her, and she gradually became aware that his resurrection meant an unrestricted presence to all the experiences of anguish and suffering crucifixions in the world (ironically as her legal and social work was being defeated). This gave Irene an awareness of strength as she faced the possible demise of the society. Though she still felt angry about it, she experienced her uncertain future as borne in some way by the Risen One.[174] The consolation of Jesus did not lead Irene away from her work and fundamental commitment, but instead strengthened her in the midst of her struggles. Just as the bridegroom came down to his garden to pasture and comfort his flock, so the risen Christ descended into Irene's difficult life situation to accompany and encourage her to remain faithful to his work.

Saint Ignatius keeps us focused on the realities of our relationships and work as a place where we meet our Creator and Lord. Any spirituality that would remove us from our basic life commitments would be suspect, for God is to be found in the midst of our sensing, thinking, choosing, and acting. He is in our conversations and relationships. We are called to be contemplatives

---

174. See Brian McDermott, S.J., *With Him, in Him: The Graces of the Spiritual Exercises, Studies in the Spirituality of the Jesuits*, no. 4, September 1986 (St. Louis, The American Assistancy Seminar on Jesuit Spirituality, 1986), 20.

in action, prayerfully reflecting on Christ's presence to us in every situation. Caryll Houselander's description of a mystical experience on a crowded subway train reflects this principle of contemplation in action. Houselander saw all sorts of people jostled together, sitting and strap-hanging, workers going home at the end of the day. Then an amazing thing happened. Suddenly in her imagination she saw Christ in each and every person on the train. Christ dwelled within each person, living, dying, and rising in them. Because of his presence, he shared in their sorrow and their joy. Those people on the train symbolized the presence of the entire world—not just the people of that time and place, but people of every time and place, past, present and future. After leaving the train station she strolled for quite a while among the people hurrying through the streets. Houselander experienced the same phenomenon all around her, in each bystander, all over the place—she saw the presence of Christ in and among those people.[175]

In the midst of an ordinary human activity, Houselander was open to Christ's presence in each and every person she saw. Even though they were strangers, Christ manifested himself through them in a very personal way. Through his risen presence, Christ was living and dying in them, through their joys and sorrows. With Christ, Houselander felt a presence of the whole world, of people from every nation, time, and place in a universal solidarity. Christ was indeed pasturing his flock (see Song 6:3), through his presence and life within these people and the whole human race. Houselander's life in the world did not take her away from contemplating Jesus, but brought her into greater awareness of his presence. She shows us the potential to become contemplatives in the midst of our activities.

The intended effect of Saint Ignatius' Contemplation to Attain Love is to seek and find God in all things. This attitude is a hallmark of Ignatian spirituality and a full flowering of the Principle and Foundation that we examined at the beginning of the retreat. The goal of the Principle and Foundation is to use all things insofar as they lead us to God. In the Contemplation to Attain Love we discover that the persons, places, events, and objects of everyday existence do, in fact, lead us to God. Our life situations are the occasion of meeting God and experiencing mutual love between ourselves and God.

---

175. See Caryll Houselander as quoted in Maisie Ward, *The Divine Eccentric* (London: Sheed and Ward, 1943), 74.

Contemplation fosters an awareness that all things at every moment are not hindrances but ways of meeting God.[176]

We often think that our life and activities in the world distract us and take us away from God, sapping our divine energy. Far from that, our active life in the world is meant to be the very place of our encounter with God. Jean Pierre de Caussade writes of his very positive experience of divine grace in the world: "I should die of thirst rushing like this from one fountain to another, from one stream to another when there is a sea at hand, the waters of which encompass me on every side. All that happens to me therefore will be food for my nourishment, water for my cleansing, fire for my purification, and a channel of grace for all my needs. That which I might endeavor to find in other ways seeks me incessantly and gives itself to me through all creatures."[177] We do not have to go far to discover God's presence, since God is very close and engulfs us like an ocean with his presence. It is not so much we who seek God but God who seeks us at every moment. God is communicating himself to us in each and every situation; we need to open our hearts to be aware of his presence in and through his creatures.

Saint Ignatius aimed to find God in all things. Though he was certainly a man of great mystical prayer, Saint Ignatius did not find God only in prayer. He learned to discern God's presence in the midst of persons, places, and events. Saint Ignatius knew that being attuned to the divine will in charity and obedience was more important than one's own prayer agenda. For instance, one might be interrupted in the midst of seeking Christ in prayer to help Christ in one's neighbor in need. Christ is as much present in one's neighbor as he is in one's experience of prayer.

As General of the Society of Jesus, Saint Ignatius realized the importance of finding God in his activities. Once, at the Jesuit school at Coimbra, two scholastics had decided on their own, without the superior's permission, to undertake additional penances and devotions beyond the community rule. Saint Ignatius responded by writing the rector of the school and explaining that, given the importance of their studies, the scholastics should not be giving themselves to prolonged prayer periods. Beyond their assigned time of

---

176. See Micheal Ivens, *Understanding the Spiritual Exercises* (Trowbridge, Wiltshire: Cromwell Press, 1998), 169–170.

177. De Caussade, *Abandonment*, 32.

prayer, they were to "practice the seeking of God's presence in all things, in their conversations, their walks, in all that they see, taste, hear, understand, in all their actions, since His Divine Majesty is truly in all things by His presence, power and essence."[178] Saint Ignatius considered this kind of reflection on God in all things to be easier than meditation on more abstract divine truths; they prepared one for "great visitations of our Lord," even in abbreviated moments of prayer. The scholastics were also counseled to find God in their study of divine truths, offering the sacrifices of their demanding efforts to God in his service.

Saint Ignatius recognized the tendency of the scholastics to allow their own agenda of prayer and acts of piety to take them away from their ordinary life and duty. In this case, prayer had become an escape from the demands of discipleship, because our call to be disciples is first a call to live and serve in the ordinary circumstances of our lives. While prayer is necessary for recollection, it should also foster seeking God in one's daily routine.

In the fourth point of the Contemplation to Attain Love we have seen how God is present as the source of his gifts, which descend from above. The bridegroom descends from his exalted place in the Temple to dwell with his bride in the garden, to pasture his flock. Christ is also to be found not only in his exalted place in heaven, but with his bride, the Church, whom he pastures with care. Christ gives his very self as gift and we surrender ourselves to him in return, such that he belongs to us and we belong to him. The bride has similarly arrived at deep communion with her lover and can exclaim, "I am my beloved's and my beloved is mine" (6:3).

Questions for Reflection and Discussion

1. How aware are you of all God's gifts coming *from above* and from the heart of God himself?

2. To what degree do you see all created things as participating in the Author of life?

3. How do you imagine and understand the risen Christ? How does the imagery in this passage of the Song of Songs help or augment your understanding?

---

178. Saint Ignatius of Loyola, Letter to Father Anthony Brandeo, June 1, 1551, in *Letters*, 240–241.

4. Are you aware of the presence of the risen Christ? Is it vivid in your imagination or more obscure, yet real?

5. To what extent are you aware of Christ present in all things—in the persons, places, and events of your life?

6. Do you tend to find God more in prayer or in activity? Is there any correlation between these two aspects of your life?

Prayer Exercises

1. Read Saint Ignatius' fourth point of the Contemplation to Attain Love (p. 276). Pray with Ephesians 1:1–15, and ask for the grace to know all God's gifts descended from above in Christ.

2. Reflect on the quote from Buckley (p. 277). Pray with Ephesians 1:16–23, and ask for the grace of an interior awareness and strength of the risen Lord's presence.

3. Ponder the meaning of the description of the bridegroom (p. 278). Pray with Song of Songs 5:9—6:3, and ask for a greater awareness and appreciation of the beauty of the risen Lord.

4. Consider the woman who made the Ignatian retreat (p. 279). Pray with Colossians 1:9–23, and ask for the grace of a profound awareness of the presence of Christ in you and in his Church.

5. Reflect on Caryll Houselander's experience on a train (p. 280). Pray with Revelation 21, and ask for the grace to know Christ's presence in all things.

6. Read the quote from de Caussade (p. 281) and from Saint Ignatius (p. 282). Pray with Revelation 22, and ask for the grace to know Christ's presence in all things.

7. Make a repetition on any of the above contemplations, paying greater attention to those places of greater movement of spirit (consolation or desolation).

CHAPTER 26

The Bride's Theophany

[G] You are beautiful as Tirzah, my love,
  comely as Jerusalem,
    terrible as an army with banners.
Turn away your eyes from me,
  for they overwhelm me!
Your hair is like a flock of goats,
  moving down the slopes of Gilead.
Your teeth are like a flock of ewes,
  that have come up from the washing,
all of them bear twins,
  and not one among them is bereaved.
Your cheeks are like halves of a pomegranate
  behind your veil.
There are sixty queens and eighty concubines,
  and maidens without number.
My dove, my perfect one, is the only one,
  the darling of her mother,
    flawless to her that bore her.
The maidens saw her and called her happy;
  the queens and concubines also,
    and they praised her.
"Who is this that looks forth like the dawn,
fair as the moon, bright as the sun,
  terrible as an army with banners?"
[B] I went down to the nut orchard,
  to look at the blossoms of the valley,

to see whether the vines had budded,
>   whether the pomegranates were in bloom.
Before I was aware, my fancy set me
>   in a chariot beside my prince. (Song 6:4–12)

Consider all blessings and gifts as descending from above. (SpEx 237)

After He had manifested Himself for forty days to the Apostles, and had given them many proofs, and worked many miracles, and had spoken to them of the kingdom of God, He commanded them to await in Jerusalem the promise of the Holy Spirit. (SpEx 312)

The bridegroom continues to praise the bride's increasing beauty, which symbolizes the presence and transforming power of the indwelling Holy Spirit in the individual soul. As the bride becomes more and more like her bridegroom, so we become more like Christ through the Holy Spirit's power. The bride is now "beautiful as Tirzah" and "comely as Jerusalem" (Song 6:4), the capital cities of Israel, symbolizing Israel in her glory. She is "terrible as an army with banners" ready for battle. Just as the king had arrived surrounded by his warriors (Song 3:8), she now resembles him as a formidable army in the intensity of her presence, before which he is filled with awe. He tells her to "turn away your eyes from me," for her beautiful Spirit-filled eyes assault him. The bride's energetic and vivacious presence corresponds to the Holy Spirit's life-giving presence. In fact, we call the Spirit the "Lord and giver of life" in the Nicene Creed. The bride's hair, the glory of a woman (see 1 Cor 11:15), is an energetic flock of goats frisking down the slopes. Her teeth are a "flock of ewes" that each "bear twins," another sign of the abundance of life given by the Spirit.

In the Spiritual Exercises, the Contemplation to Attain Love (see SpEx 234–237) initiates us into the experience of life in the Holy Spirit. Having pondered the life of Christ throughout the Exercises, we now culminate the retreat in the Contemplation by considering the Spirit's action in our lives.

The bridegroom evokes the image of the Holy Spirit as he calls his bride "my dove, my perfect one." The dove reminds us of Baptism, during which the Spirit descends upon the baptized believer with the gift of supernatural life. The Holy Spirit was seen as a dove at Jesus' baptism. He was anointed with the Holy Spirit and his mission was a joint one with the Spirit, the two remaining distinct but inseparable. The Spirit reveals Christ as the visible image of the invisible God. When the risen Christ is glorified, he in turn sends the Spirit to us believers in order to conform us to himself, that we might resemble him as other Christs. The bride now resembles her warrior king in her glory. Just as he emerged in the wilderness surrounded by a great number of skilled swordsmen (Song 3:8), she appears as an army in battle array, surrounded by queens, concubines, and maidens without number. She so resembles the bridegroom in her beauty that he goes so far as to call her "my perfect one" who is flawless. Insofar as we are baptized and receive supernatural life, washed from our sins, we resemble Christ and share in his perfection.

Mary is perfectly filled with the love of God in the Holy Spirit. She is flawless in never having contracted the slightest stain of sin and in always following God's will. United to the Holy Spirit as his spouse, Mary is one with God in a perfect way beyond any other human being. The bride represents Mary as the flawless and perfect bride, beloved of the Bridegroom. The Church is called to imitate Mary as the spotless bride of Christ. The Church is holy and perfect in her essence as the spotless bride purified by Christ in his gift of salvation (see Eph 5:27), though she always needs purification in her individual members, who journey toward perfection in imitation of Mary. Filled with the Holy Spirit, Mary, as the flawless dove, is transparent to the Spirit's presence. We perceive, admire, and love the Spirit, which is so radiant within her. The Holy Spirit shines through her perfect humanity.

Just as the Spirit manifests the Son of God in Mary, here in the Song of Songs the Spirit manifests God through the bride in a kind of "theophany" or visible exhibition of the divine. "Mary is the burning bush of the definitive theophany. Filled with the Holy Spirit, she makes the Word visible in the humility of his flesh."[179]

---

179. CCC 724.

Occurring throughout the Scriptures, theophanies consist of elements that are both luminous and obscure; they reveal something of God while shrouding his divine existence. In the Old Testament book of Exodus, God revealed himself in the burning bush and in the cloud and pillar of fire in the desert. When Moses went up on Mount Sinai, the cloud and thunder signified that God was revealing himself to Moses and Israel in giving the Ten Commandments. Solomon experienced the Spirit of God in majesty before his throne at the dedication of the Temple (see 1 Kgs 8:10–12).

In the New Testament, the Holy Spirit is manifested in many similarly powerful ways. The Holy Spirit overshadows Mary at the annunciation. At the transfiguration the Spirit comes in the cloud and overshadows Jesus and the apostles. The cloud of the Spirit lifts Jesus into the heavens at his ascension, and a similar cloud will reveal him as the Son of man finally coming in glory. The moment of Pentecost is also a theophany of the Spirit, who is manifest in flames of tongues over Mary and the apostles, and who enables them to speak different languages. At Pentecost, we see the fulfillment of Jesus' promise to send the Holy Spirit as fire upon the earth (see Lk 12:49).

These awesome revelations of God leave the participants and observers quaking in holy fear. Similarly, the queens, maidens, and concubines witness the bride as the dawn rising, "fair as the moon, bright as the sun." Her emergence strikes fear into their hearts as they describe her as "terrible as an army with banners" (Song 6:10). The Holy Spirit is manifested through the bride, just as the Spirit fills the whole Church and the individual Christian, making her beautiful, radiant, and awesome to behold.

The Lord gives his Holy Spirit throughout the Spiritual Exercises to help us conform our lives to his. The Holy Spirit's dynamic presence is revealed in the personal salvation history of the person seeking God. The retreatant is immersed into the life of the Spirit in prayer and daily life, coming to greater awareness of the Spirit's presence and understanding better the Spirit's movements as he or she seeks to advance the kingdom of God.

The grace of the fourth week of the Exercises is closely related to the grace of Pentecost and life in the Spirit. In the mysteries of the fourth week, the risen Lord exercises his office of consoler (see SpEx 224). At Pentecost the Holy Spirit, the Consoler, does the same work. Easter and Pentecost are two complementary moments in the one mystery of the outpouring of the Holy Spirit. As part of the Easter mystery, Jesus breathes the Holy Spirit upon the apostles on the evening of Easter Sunday. In fact, John's Gospel has no reference to the descent of the Holy Spirit, because the Spirit is given at Easter. Coming at the end of the retreat, the fourth week is the ideal time to begin to pray on the mysteries of the Holy Spirit. This will help the retreatant make a good transition back into the world with a sense of being led now by the Spirit and imbued with his gifts.

The Exercises are an experience of Pentecost and serve as the launching point for a new life in the Spirit as we move into daily living. In this transition it is helpful to review the Contemplation to Attain Love insofar as it relates to life in the Spirit. The theologian Joseph Bracken asserts that the final reflection of the Exercises, the Contemplation to Attain Love, is a particular realization of God's presence in the person of the Holy Spirit, which "corresponds to what the disciples in the upper room experienced through the coming of the Holy Spirit on Pentecost Sunday . . . the concluding contemplation of the Spiritual Exercises could be said to send the retreatant forth into the world like the disciples at Pentecost, with a new sense of purpose in life."[180]

The first point of the Contemplation shows how God bestows his gifts upon us through the Holy Spirit, who hovered over the waters at creation and continues to create each of us in God's image. God is present in and through his creation, especially in human beings, through his gift of the Spirit who dwells within us, as emphasized in the second point. In the third point, we ponder God as the Spirit who labors for us to give us his gifts (see 1 Cor 12:11) and works to bring forth his fruit in the lives of believers (see Gal 5:22–23). God sends forth his Spirit who descends "from above" (SpEx 237) as God's gift of himself within his many gifts, which is highlighted in the fourth point. The retreatant has experienced all these dynamics of the Spirit in each of the four weeks of the retreat and now emerges, imbued with the Spirit, to manifest the Holy Spirit and his gifts in the Church.

The Spirit descends upon the Church in order to make her one with her Bridegroom, Christ. Saint Paul speaks of the Church as the bride for which Christ gave himself, the place where the Holy Spirit dwells and wherein we know the Spirit. In the Song of Songs, the bride increasingly resembles her bridegroom, just as the Church as bride resembles her Bridegroom, Christ.

---

180. Joseph Bracken, The Contemplation to Attain Love As an Experience of Pentecost, Theological Implications, *The Way Magazine*, 52/4 (October 2013).

The bride in the Song of Songs manifests the same glory as her bridegroom, as an "army with banners." By the Spirit's power the army of saints in the Church resembles Christ, manifesting his holiness and continuing his work of salvation. The retinue of countless queens, concubines, and maidens alongside the bride points to the Spirit present in the manifold charisms and ministries that build up Church. The glory of the bride is described as the moon, reflecting the sun, just as the Church reflects the Spirit in the inspired Scriptures, in the tradition of the Fathers, and in the Magisterium, which the Spirit aids. This theophany of the bride united to her bridegroom in her glorious wedding ritual resembles the Spirit's presence in the sacramental liturgy, which, through its words and symbols, puts us in communion with Christ. Finally, the Spirit intercedes for us in our individual moments of prayer (see Rom 8:26–27). The entire experience of personal prayer in the Spiritual Exercises is an experience of the Spirit that makes us resemble Christ and espouses us with him as our Bridegroom.

The Holy Spirit is fruitful in the life of the Church, just as the bride is fruitful. The bride's "garden brings forth blossoms" and her "vines bud with fruit," reminding us of the fruits of the Holy Spirit such as peace, love, joy, and forbearance. The gifts of the Holy Spirit are given to the Church as the bride of Christ in order to unite her more intimately with her Lord.

The bride now exclaims: "Before I was aware, my fancy set me in a chariot beside my prince" (6:12). She has been united with her king in his chariot, which will move them swiftly together. This swift movement in unison with her bridegroom reminds us of the youthful vigor of the Spirit. Our spiritual fountain of youth is the Holy Spirit, the one who renews us in youthful vitality. "By the power of the Gospel he makes the Church keep the freshness of youth. Uninterruptedly he renews it and leads it to perfect union with its Spouse."[181] The Spirit renews us interiorly, rejuvenates us, and makes us young in spirit. He restores us to our youthful innocence, cleansing us from sin at Baptism and in the sacrament of Penance. By his grace, the Spirit strengthens and enlivens us, so we can say with Isaiah that we will run and not grow weary (see Is 40:31).

In her responsiveness to grace, Mary typifies the youthful vitality of the Church renewed by the Holy Spirit. Mary is always available to God, always

---

181. *Lumen Gentium*, no. 4.

fulfilling his will swiftly and with vigor. She immediately responds to the angel's proposal as the Lord's humble maidservant: "Let it be with me according to your word" (Lk 1:38). She journeys promptly to Ein Karem to visit her cousin Elizabeth in her need. At Cana, she notices even before her Son that the guests have no wine and intercedes on their behalf.

In *The Diary of a Country Priest*, the young dying priest is counseled by his older mentor to turn to Mary: "The eyes of Our Lady are the only real child-eyes that have been raised to our shame and sorrow ... eyes with something that makes her younger than sin, younger than the race from which she sprang, and though a mother by grace, mother of all graces, our little youngest sister."[182]

Mary's young and vivacious eyes convey the eternal youthfulness of the Spirit who dwells within her. Conceived without sin, she bears no trace of the old man, Adam. The Spirit makes us young and vibrant in Baptism by cleansing us from sin in the old man, Adam, and establishing us in the grace of the new man, Christ.

The life-giving renewal in the Spirit is illustrated by a story that captivated me when I was a teenager in Chicago in 1976. After a horrible traffic accident, emergency room doctors pronounced a twenty-one-year-old man, Peter Saraceno, dead on arrival. But when the doctor re-checked Peter, he found a faint pulse and revived him. Peter was not expected to live through the night and faded into a coma. The doctors advised relatives that if he survived he would likely be completely paralyzed for life.

Peter's fiancée, Linda Fraschalla, hurried to his bedside, spending every spare hour outside of work with him, constantly speaking to him. After four months with absolutely no response from Peter, his toe moved. A few days later his eyelashes fluttered. When Linda observed this, she quit her job to spend all her time at Peter's side. Against the advice of the doctors, she tried to help him recover movement. She massaged his arms and legs and even spent her savings on a swimming pool, hoping the sun and water would help restore motion to his body. Soon he grunted his first word. When he was finally able to speak in sentences, he asked Linda's father for her hand in marriage. Her father told Peter that when he could walk down the aisle, they

---

182. George Bernanos, *The Diary of a Country Priest* (Chicago: McMillan Co., 1937), 211–212.

could marry. Two years later, with the help of a walker, Peter walked down the aisle of Our Lady of Pompeii Church in Chicago and married Linda. They were featured on *NBC Nightly News*; people around the world heard the story and were inspired with Linda's patience and dedication to her fiancé.[183]

The story of Linda and Peter illustrates the life-giving power of the Holy Spirit. Though we are nearly dead and paralyzed by the effects of sin and its wounds in our life, the life-giving Spirit labors over us to bring us to life and motion—just as Linda labored over Peter to bring him back to life and movement. The Spirit communicates his love to us, even though we are barely aware of his presence and message—just as Linda spoke to Peter without any sign that he heard or understood what she was saying.

Saint Paul explains that in our weakness we don't know how to pray as we ought, but the Spirit intercedes for us with inestimable groanings to bring us into union with Jesus Christ and the Father (see Rom 8:26). The Holy Spirit empowers us to love like Jesus, even to the point of laying down our lives for our loved ones. The same Spirit empowered Linda to dedicate her entire life to reviving her beloved Peter.

The bride in the Song of Songs, fierce in her love, inspires awe, terrible as an army in battle array, resembling her bridegroom and his warriors. Linda's love in action inspired awe in all who observed her. Imbued with the Holy Spirit we too resemble our Bridegroom, Christ, in being transformed into fierce lovers. As the bride mounts the chariot with her bridegroom, so we are united in the Spirit with Christ our Bridegroom, moving swiftly toward our goal of eternal life.

Questions for Reflection and Discussion

1. How do you experience the Holy Spirit as the Lord and Giver of Life? What is life-giving about the Spirit?

2. How do you understand the significance of the dove as a symbol of the Holy Spirit?

---

183. See "Fiancée Who Never Lost Hope, Is Married to 1976 Crash Victim," by Nathaniel Sheppard Jr.; July 17, 1978, Section A, p. 13.

3. In what sense do you see the Holy Spirit manifested in the Bride in the Song of Songs, and also in the life of Mary and the Church?

4. What is your favorite image of the Holy Spirit? In what ways do you perceive his presence to you?

5. How do you feel perpetually renewed in youthful vigor by the Holy Spirit?

Prayer Exercises

1. Pray with Song of Songs 6:4–12, and ask for the grace to be aware of the Spirit's life-giving presence with you. Pray with Luke 3:21–22, and ask for the grace to receive the Holy Spirit and to be a beloved son or daughter with whom the Father is well pleased.

2. Pray with Luke 3:15–17, and ask for the grace to experience the fire of being baptized with the Holy Spirit.

3. Pray with John 7:37–39, and ask for the grace to drink fully of the Holy Spirit and to experience the rivers of living water flowing out of your own heart.

4. Pray with Galatians 4:1–7, and ask for the grace to realize that you are a son or daughter of your heavenly Father by the grace of adoption.

5. Consider the role of theophanies in God's revelation (p. 288). Pray with Luke 9:28–36, and ask for greater awareness of the presence of God in the overshadowing of the cloud of the Holy Spirit.

6. Make a repetition on any of the previous contemplations, returning to the places of greater movement of spirit (consolation or desolation).

CHAPTER 27

Spirit Dance

[D] Return, return, O Shulammite!
    Return, return, that we may look upon you.
[B] Why should you look upon the Shulammite,
    as upon a dance before two armies? (Song 6:13)

Consider all blessings and gifts as descending from above. (SpEx 237)

After He had manifested Himself for forty days to the Apostles, and had given them many proofs, and worked many miracles, and had spoken to them of the kingdom of God, He commanded them to await in Jerusalem the promise of the Holy Spirit. (SpEx 312)

As previously discussed, the Contemplation to Attain Divine Love (see SpEx 230–237) is an experience of life in the Spirit to help the retreatant move forward from the Spiritual Exercises into daily routine. In this chapter we will continue to ponder the action of the Holy Spirit in our lives as reflected in the experience of the bride in the Song of Songs. The chorus of nations now calls the Bride a Shulammite or maid of Solomon, whose name is based upon the Hebrew word "shalom," meaning "peace." The bride bears the name and characteristics of her husband, King Solomon, who is the epitome of peace. She returns to him in order to be more accessible to him and his divine gift of peace. As the bride draws close to the bridegroom, his love changes her into a person alive with the fullness of God's grace and victorious peace. As a result, the bride demonstrates the dynamic vitality of the Holy Spirit, mediating the Spirit's presence.

The bride's energy in the Spirit is expressed in a dance that reconciles two army camps, bringing them peace. The two camps represent the Jews, who were divided into the two rival territories of Judah and Israel from the time of the Davidic dynasty until after the exile. This passage's reference to the dancing of armies points to Jeremiah 31, a joyful description of the post-exilic reunion of the two kingdoms into a single kingdom and a new covenant: "Again I will build you, and you shall be built, O virgin Israel! Again you shall take your tambourines, and go forth in the dance of the merrymakers. . . . Then shall the young women rejoice in the dance, and the young men and the old shall be merry. I will turn their mourning into joy, I will comfort them, and give them gladness for sorrow" (Jer 31:4, 13). The dream of the Jews had been reunion, a changing of the rival camps into a double troupe of dancers—a dream that is now realized in and through the bride's dance. Scripture scholar Andre Chouraqui eloquently describes the effects of the Shulammite's mesmerizing movement:

> The chorus contemplates in the bride the dance, i.e., the dynamic harmony of reconciled opposites. The two camps that were enemies yesterday—with the hardships of separation and exile—are now reconciled in the reflection of triumphant love. . . . Love reconciles the opposites, resolves them in its cosmic dance, reflected by the maid of Shulam returning from exile and being wed again. . . . She must appear in the contemplation of a reconciled universe, re-created to the image of the couple who is triumphant in the unity of love. Yes, a dance and no more a war of the two camps. . . . The maid of Shulam continues to bear in her womb two camps that are now pacified in the new rhythm of their cosmic dance.[184]

The bride reconciles the two rival camps by the beauty of her movement. As the people of Judah returned from the foreign lands of their exile, the

---

184. Andre Chouraqui, *Le Cantique des Cantiques*, in Arminjon, *The Cantata of Love*, 303.

prophets dreamed they would be reunited in the gestures of rebuilding the Temple and reading the Law. They would coordinate their movements in working together to reconstruct the Temple and be more faithful in adhering to the Lord. Despite the prophets' dreams, the northern tribes and the Samaritans were not included in the project of rebuilding the Temple. Eventually, even Jews and Gentiles would be united in Christ, who came to reconcile all peoples in himself by the blood of his cross (see Col 1:20). At Pentecost we see all nations being gathered together in the Church by the Holy Spirit. The bride as a symbol of the Spirit-guided Church similarly draws opposing peoples and nations to herself in her gesture of reconciliation and gathering.

The Holy Spirit is the gift of God's communion to us, and his action brings about that communion in our lives. Just as the Father and Son share their lives in union and total self-giving to one another, so they desire for us to share in their communion. As the bond of unity between the Father and Son, the Holy Spirit, who is given to us, unites us to the Trinity in love. Participation in the unity of God brings about unity between human beings and God, and among human beings themselves. In our world where individuals and communities suffer from a lack of unity and cohesion, the Spirit brings about peace and reconciliation.

During the vigil Mass of the Feast of Pentecost, the first reading from Genesis speaks about the debacle of Babel, wherein the city's men decide—in their arrogance—to build a tower reaching to heaven, to make a name for themselves without reference to God. Or perhaps they build the tower in an attempt to get God's attention so that, in their twisted pride, they can manipulate him to their purposes. Because of their arrogance, God confuses their language, preventing them from communicating. This sends them into such disarray that they scatter to the ends of the earth, leaving the tower in ruins (see Gen 11:1–9). Here we see the misunderstanding and rupture caused by a breakdown in language, a massive disintegration.

At Pentecost, however, the reverse happens. Instead of one language diverging into many tongues, many languages converge into one faith, one hope, one baptism. Whereas Babel results from human pride and initiative, Pentecost happens through the Holy Spirit's initiative. While Babel results in confusion and misunderstanding, Pentecost results in restored communication, understanding, and unity. Here people of various tribes and nations—Parthians, Medes, Elamites—who could not communicate before, now hear and understand the divine message in their own languages. Babel ended in dividing the human race into rival peoples and nations, but Pentecost gathered them together and re-integrated them into one universal family.

At Pentecost the Holy Spirit descended from above as a divine gift from God. Before Jesus ascended to the right hand of the Father in heaven, he promised they would send their Spirit as a gift from above. Saint Ignatius has us consider in the Contemplation to Attain Love how God's gifts descend like light or as a fountain from above (see SpEx 237). The gift of God is first and foremost God himself, in the person of the Holy Spirit poured out on us as an endless spring. As primordial gift in himself, the Holy Spirit pours out gifts upon us—wisdom, understanding, knowledge, etc.—in order to lead us to all truth in Jesus Christ and continue his mission of salvation.

Even before Pentecost, Jesus breathes the Holy Spirit upon the disciples in order to complete his mission. He tells them, "As the Father has sent me, so I send you. . . . 'Receive the Holy Spirit. If you forgive the sins of any, they are forgiven them'" (Jn 20:21–23). The disciples are given the Holy Spirit to continue Jesus' mission of reconciliation.

A wonderful illustration of this principle is the story of the great Italian composer Giacomo Puccini,[185] who wrote a number of famous operas. In 1922, the sixty-four-year-old Puccini was stricken with cancer. Despite the disease, Puccini was determined to complete his final and greatest opera, *Turandot*. He worked on it day and night. Many urged him to rest, thinking he couldn't possibly finish it. When his sickness worsened, Puccini said to his disciples, "If I don't finish *Turandot*, I want you to finish it for me." Then came the sad day in 1924 when Puccini was taken to Brussels for an operation, and he died two days after surgery. Puccini's disciples in Italy gathered the various scores from *Turandot*, studied them carefully, and completed the opera. In 1926 the world premiere was performed in Milan's magnificent *La Scala* opera house, directed by Puccini's favorite student, Arturo Toscanini. Everything went beautifully until the opera reached that point where death had forced Puccini to put down his pen. Tears streaming down his face, Toscanini stopped the music, put down his baton, turned to the audience, and cried out, "Thus far the Master wrote, but he died." Silence filled the Milan opera house. No one moved; no one spoke. After a couple of minutes,

---

185. See Link, *Illustrated Sunday Homilies*, Series I, Easter 7C, 45.

Toscanini picked up the baton again. He turned to the audience, smiling through his tears, and cried out, "But the disciples finished his work." When *Turandot* ended, the audience broke into thunderous applause. No one there ever forgot that moment of beautiful tribute of Puccini's disciples to their master.

The story of Puccini's disciples finishing *Turandot* resembles the story of the apostles finishing the work that Jesus came to do. They too had been taught by the divine Master, Jesus. They lived and worked alongside him, absorbing his love and vision for humanity. Before Jesus died, he asked his disciples to finish the work he had begun. Jesus' tremendous vision was seemingly impossible to complete, at least through mere human means. Yet Jesus had told the apostles, "Very truly, I tell you, the one who believes in me will also do the works that I do and, in fact, will do greater works than these" (Jn 14:12). How would they know what to say and do? Jesus had promised them: "the Advocate, the Holy Spirit, whom the Father will send in my name, will teach you everything" (Jn 14:26).

Jesus also said that the Spirit "will take what is mine and declare it to you" (Jn 16:14). Sharing in the very mind of Christ, the Holy Spirit would be the living memory of Christ for his disciples and would be their Advocate. "Do not worry about how you are to defend yourselves or what you are to say; for the Holy Spirit will teach you at that very hour what you ought to say" (Lk 12:11–12). Just as a lawyer advises a client how to speak in court, so the Spirit would guide the disciples in their witness to Jesus before governors and kings. The Spirit gave them the courage to overcome their fears of proclaiming Christ to a hostile world. Puccini's disciples remembered all he taught them, finished his musical score, and boldly performed his opera. By the power of the Spirit, Jesus' disciples remembered his teaching and boldly proclaimed it.

The Harmony of the Dance

Through her dance, the bride brings together differing camps, enabling them to work together. The Holy Spirit enables us, as human beings with different supernatural gifts, talents, characters, and temperaments, to unite as one in Christ. The Holy Spirit could be likened to a composer of music for a symphony orchestra, with dozens of musicians playing various instruments. The musicians focus their attention on the conductor, the unifying force and mover of the orchestra. Yet the true origin of the music is the composer, not the conductor. The musical score brings together all the minds of the musicians and synchronizes their efforts as they play beautiful, flowing melodies. Great virtuosos though they might be, the musicians do not take credit for the beauty of the music. They play it as best they can and pay tribute to the composer. Likewise we might think of ourselves as musicians called to play in God's symphony, doing our best to learn to play virtuously. We try to stay faithful to the Spirit's musical score and play according to his vision and promptings toward holiness. We each possess many gifts and talents. Though we play many different melodies and rhythms, they all come together in a marvelous harmony as we seek to stay true to the composer of the music. Thus the Holy Spirit ensures unity among diverse peoples in the profession and practice of our faith.

By the Holy Spirit's power, Christians seek the renewal of the Church in unity. Saint Ignatius of Antioch wrote to the Ephesians on the importance of harmony: "Therefore in your concord and harmonious love, Jesus Christ is sung. And man by man become a choir, that being harmonious in love, and taking up the song of God in unison, you may with one voice sing to the Father through Jesus Christ."[186] Members of a choir sing with different voices and notes, yet they all focus on the one song and sound as one harmonious voice. The outpouring of the Holy Spirit will gather people of every tribe, nation, and language into one people in order to sing one song by professing one faith.

The Spirit's gift and mission of unity is brought to completion in the Church, the Body of Christ and the Temple of the Spirit. In her whole being and in all her members, the Church is sent to announce, bear witness, make present, and spread the mystery of the communion of the Holy Trinity.[187] Saint Cyril of Jerusalem writes that all of us who have received the same Spirit are "blended together with one another and with God."[188] The gift

---

186. Adapted from Saint Ignatius of Antioch, *Letter to the Ephesians*, Chapter IV, trans. Alexander Roberts and James Donaldson. From *Ante-Nicene Fathers*, vol. 1, eds. Alexander Roberts, James Donaldson, and A. Cleveland Coxe (Buffalo, NY: Christian Literature Publishing Co., 1885).

187. CCC 737.

188. Saint Cyril of Alexandria, *Commentary on the Gospel According to St. John*, eds. and trans. P. E. Pusey (v. 1) and T. Randell (v. 2), *A Library of Fathers of the Holy Catholic Church*, vol. 48 (London: W. Smith, 1885), 543.

"from above" (SpEx 237), the one indwelling Spirit of God, leads us to spiritual unity in the one Church of God. The bride of the Song of Songs, in her dance unifying the people of Israel, foreshadows the Church, imbued with the Spirit, uniting all peoples.

Questions for Reflection and Discussion

1. Reflecting on the Tower of Babel story in Genesis, how do you experience fractures in the world and within the Church?

2. How can you focus on Christ and the Holy Spirit to bring about reconciliation and unity? How have you concretely experienced this?

3. How do you perceive the Holy Spirit in the Church as finishing the work Christ came to do?

4. Do you sense a call to be faithful to the Spirit instead of your own agenda in order to bring about greater communion?

5. Are you daunted by the task of being the representative of Christ in finishing his work? How does the Spirit give you confidence?

Prayer Exercises

1. Ponder the words of Chouraqui (p. 296). Pray with Song of Songs 6:13 and Ephesians 4:1–13, and ask for the grace to know the reconciling and unifying power of the Holy Spirit in your life.

2. Consider the tragedy of the story of the Tower of Babel (p. 297). Pray with Acts 2:1–13, and ask for the grace of greater unity, communication, and understanding.

3. Ponder the story of Puccini's disciples (p. 298). Pray with Acts 2:14–36, and ask for the grace of courage in your mission and that of the Church to finish Jesus' work in spreading his kingdom.

4. Consider the image of the symphony orchestra (p. 299). Pray with John 14:15–27, and ask for the grace to be faithful to the Holy Spirit's mission in harmony with the Church.

5. Pray with John 16:1–16 and Mark 13:9–11, and ask for the grace to overcome your fear in serving the Church and her mission.

6. Make a repetition on any of the above contemplations, paying greater attention to those places of greater movement of spirit (consolation or desolation).

CHAPTER 28

Mesmerizing Maiden

[D] Return, return, O Shulammite!
  Return, return, that we may look upon you.
[B] Why should you look upon the Shulammite,
  as upon a dance before two armies?
[G] How graceful are your feet in sandals,
  O queenly maiden!
Your rounded thighs are like jewels,
  the work of a master hand.
Your navel is a rounded bowl
  that never lacks mixed wine.
Your belly is a heap of wheat,
  encircled with lilies.
Your two breasts are like two fawns,
  twins of a gazelle.
Your neck is like an ivory tower.
Your eyes are pools in Heshbon,
  by the gate of Bath-rabbim.
Your nose is like a tower of Lebanon,
  overlooking Damascus.
Your head crowns you like Carmel,
  and your flowing locks are like purple;
  a king is held captive in the tresses.
How fair and pleasant you are,
  O loved one, delectable maiden! (Song 6:13–7:6)

Consider all blessings and gifts as descending from above. (SpEx 237)

Ask for the virtues or graces which one sees one needs most. (SpEx 257)

As we have seen, the Contemplation to Attain Love at the end of the Spiritual Exercises speaks of the gifts of God that come "from above" (SpEx 237), referring to the Holy Spirit, who descends from above. The Holy Spirit is the gift of God himself, who bestows gifts upon his beloved people. The presence and gifts of the Holy Spirit are now reflected in the bride, whom the bridegroom in the Song of Songs beholds in her glory. As she continues her dance (6:13), he observes her graceful movement and extols her body from head to toe. These very carnal images symbolize her beauty and maturation in the Spirit. Arminjon suggests that the progressive description of the bride from feet to head suggests the Spirit's building up of the Body of Christ in the Church: "Offered as a dance, this new celebration of the bride starts quite naturally, this time with the feet, and rises progressively to the full light and royalty of the face. Thus is revealed little by little the beauty of a woman in an entire land—rather in the entire cosmos—working progressively to build the whole body until the latter finds its perfect accomplishment and achievement in the head."[189]

The bride's progressive development in grace and beauty reminds us of Saint Paul's description of how the Spirit builds up the Body of Christ in love to a mature person, to the stature of the fullness of Christ (see Eph 4:13). The bride of the Song of Songs, in her well-proportioned development, prefigures the evolution of the Church.[190]

The bridegroom marvels at the grace and loveliness of the bride's body. Her feet are beautiful in their sandals, reminding us of Isaiah's praise: "How beautiful upon the mountains are the feet of the messenger who announces peace, who brings good news, who announces salvation" (Is 52:7). The Church

---

189. Arminjon, *The Cantata of Love*, 304–305.
190. See ibid., 305

as the bride of Christ is ready to go about announcing the good news of salvation to the nations. We think of the apostles and missionaries of the early Church, who went to the ends of the earth to plant the seed of the faith. The bridegroom continues to extol the bride's thighs and legs, which are perfectly curved and athletically suited to the dance, suggesting the Church's fitness for the work of carrying the good news. The bride's navel is the well-rounded drinking bowl filled with wine and her belly is a heap of wheat, indicating her fruitfulness and ability to nourish others. The bread and wine have Eucharistic overtones that point to the Church's nourishment of the faithful in the sacraments. The bride's breasts are like twin fawns, which suggest the dual virtues of love of God and love of neighbor that Christ commands his Church to practice. An added symbol of twin gazelles suggests her swiftness in obeying God's commands. The bride's neck is compared to the tower of David, and conveys the Church's strength and courage in her Lord. Her eyes, like the deep, clear pools of Heshbon, suggest the Church's penetrating insight into the depths of God and things spiritual. The bride's nose is like Mount Hermon as a sentinel facing and challenging its enemies, just as the Church militant defends the flock against evil. The bridegroom is captivated by the beauty of her tresses of hair. Her flowing locks are like purple, the color of royalty and divinity. The Church, by her marriage to Christ, the Bridegroom, has become divinized with the Holy Spirit and now shares in his royal reign.[191]

The Gifts of the Spirit

In being built up to mature stature, the bride symbolizes the mature Christian built up with the gifts of the Holy Spirit. The bride's glorious transformation and tremendous beauty image the splendor of Christian holiness in the Spirit. The seven gifts of the Spirit are given to each of us to perfect us in faith, hope, love, and all virtue, making us strong and beautiful in Christ. The same gifts poured out on the Messiah in Isaiah 11 are bestowed upon each member of the Body of Christ: "The Spirit of the LORD shall rest on him, the spirit of wisdom and understanding, the spirit of counsel and might, the spirit of knowledge and the fear of the LORD" (Is 11:2).

---

191. Maloney, *Singers of the New Song*, 130–136.

Acting in unison, the gifts of the Spirit perfect our human faculties of intellect and will, making them more Godlike in their operation. Four of these gifts (wisdom, understanding, counsel, and knowledge) direct the intellect, while the other three gifts (fortitude, piety, and fear of the Lord) direct the will toward God. The gifts operate through our faculties, making the soul act in a divine way, with a divine intuition. The soul's activity is to accept and assent to God's activity, the mind yielding to the divine intuition implanted in it through the gifts. In short, the human way of acting is transformed by the divine. The Dominican theologians Farrell and Hughes describe the activity of the gifts as follows: "The Holy Spirit never impels to action without at the same time enlightening the soul. In every act of any of the gifts there is both a sudden illumination and a swift surge of love. . . . The Holy Spirit unites in due measure science and sanctity, truth, and love, a complete sanctification in truth. His movement, moreover, imparts certitude and security since it has not natural or human norms, but divine knowledge and action as its measure and rule."[192]

The Spirit overtakes the human mind with divine enlightenment and the human will with divine love. We are guided to truth transcending natural knowledge and confirmed in love surpassing mere human affection.

The Holy Spirit's operation through his gifts is illustrated in Saint John XXIII's description of the inspirational grace he received to call the Second Vatican Council:

> The decision to hold an ecumenical council came to us in the first instance in a sudden flash of inspiration. We communicated this decision, without elaboration, to the Sacred College of Cardinals. The response was immediate. It was as though some ray of supernatural light had entered the minds of all present; it was reflected in their faces; it shone from their eyes. At once the world was swept by a wave of enthusiasm, and men everywhere began to wait eagerly for the celebration of this Council.[193]

The Spirit was operating in the minds of the Holy Father and the cardinals, bringing them great clarity and certainty about holding an ecumenical

---

192. Walter Farrell, O.P. and Dominic Hughes, O.P., *Swift Victory* (New York: Sheed and Ward, 1955), 18.

193. John XXIII, *Address at the Opening of Vatican Council II*, October 11, 1962.

council. Saint John XXIII and the cardinals were docile to the Spirit's action in choosing to call the council. As the bishops around the world were informed, they too were enlightened and accepted the Pope's decision. The Holy Spirit' work continued in a profound way throughout the council to bring the participants to unity in belief and charity in divine love, despite the inevitable debates.

The Virtues and the Gifts

We operate in a divine way with supernatural motives through both the infused virtues and the gifts of the Holy Spirit. The infused virtues are faith, hope, charity, prudence, justice, fortitude, and temperance. God gives us these supernatural virtues to guide us to our eternal destiny. But even with these virtues we sometimes fail, out of weakness, to do the good we intend. We do the evil we do not wish to do, as Saint Paul said (see Rom 7:14–25). In other words, these virtues do not suffice in all circumstances. Therefore, the Holy Spirit himself prompts our actions at critical moments through his gifts, which perfect the seven infused virtues. In these moments, the gifts make the faculties of the soul compliant and inclined to respond more swiftly and effortlessly to the concrete graces the Holy Spirit offers.

When the Holy Spirit takes over the direction of our action through his gifts, he makes us simple instruments in his hands: "Let your good spirit lead me on a level path" (Ps 143:10). Here, no longer in control, we are disposed to readily obey the Spirit; we simply consent in freedom to the Lord's work, willing to give up our desire to control when and how the Spirit will act. Jesus points out this dynamic of the Spirit: "The wind blows where it chooses, and you hear the sound of it, but you do not know where it comes from or where it goes. So it is with everyone who is born of the Spirit" (Jn 3:8). Our role is to prepare to receive the gifts by remaining pure of heart, removing obstacles, and focusing on the things of God. We can seek to purify our hearts from sin and dispose our hearts to God's will in order to receive the Spirit.[194]

When the Holy Spirit leads us by means of his gifts, his action overcomes our human weakness. We accomplish the task with great ease and exercise the infused virtues more perfectly because the Holy Spirit leads us. In some

---

194. See Farrell and Hughes, *Swift Victory*, 20.

respects, the gifts are similar to the infused virtues. But a key distinction is that the virtues operate under the impetus of human reason (prompted by grace), whereas the gifts operate under the impetus of the Holy Spirit. The virtues can be used when one wishes, but the gifts operate only when the Holy Spirit wishes. These two ways of acting can be likened to advancing by rowing a boat and sailing, respectively.[195] In rowing, which corresponds to our exercising the virtues, we maintain control and steer the boat. But that requires more work and produces slow movement. In contrast, sailing with strong winds, which corresponds to the Holy Spirit's gifts, enables us to move quickly.

We can also understand the connection between the supernatural virtues and the gifts of the Holy Spirit by an analogy with our physical senses. Imagine a person born blind who undergoes surgery that restores his sight. His new ability to see would be like the supernatural virtues God has given us—faith, hope, love, and the cardinal virtues—to pursue divine things. But if his vision remained blurred even after the surgery, his doctor would prescribe glasses. His sharpened eyesight would be like the Holy Spirit's gifts, such as understanding more clearly and deeply the truths of the faith, or having the courage to offer one's life in martyrdom. Suppose a scientist now gives him a telescope to see the grandeur of the stars, or a proton microscope to study subatomic particles and the structure of an atom. He now has a power way beyond his ordinary sight. The Holy Spirit operates in our lives through this extraordinary vision and love. The experience is beyond our own capabilities, even beyond our usual faith experience. Under the influence of the gifts of the Spirit, the soul is equipped and strengthened so that it more easily and promptly obeys his voice and impulse. These gifts are so effective that they lead the well-disposed person to the highest point of sanctity. When the Holy Spirit finds the soul prepared, he takes it over and leads it along the paths of deep prayer.

Throughout the Spiritual Exercises, the retreatant has been disposing his or herself to receive the Holy Spirit's gift of deep prayer. At the end of the Exercises: Saint Ignatius offers three methods of prayer (see SpEx 238–260), which include meditations on the bodily senses and the three powers of the soul: the memory, the intellect, and the will. During the colloquy or

---

195. See Father Paul A. Duffner, O.P., *The Infused Virtues and the Gifts of the Holy Spirit*, http://copiosa.org/virtue/virtues_infused.htm.

conversation with God at the end of the meditation, he recommends turning, in a few words, to the Lord and asking "for the virtues or graces which he sees he needs most" (see SpEx 257).

It is good for us to meditate on the virtues and gifts of the Holy Spirit, as Saint Paul suggests, "Finally, beloved, whatever is true, whatever is honorable, whatever is just, whatever is pure, whatever is pleasing, whatever is commendable, if there is any excellence and if there is anything worthy of praise, think about these things" (Phil 4:8). As we understand these gifts and become more aware of our own weaknesses, we ask the Lord to grant us these gifts in greater abundance.

We now seek to understand more fully the gifts of the Spirit through the lens of the life of the Blessed Virgin Mary, who was filled with the Spirit and demonstrates his gifts. Built up in virtue through the gifts of the Spirit, Mary is prefigured in the well-formed bride of the Song of Songs. In the following reflections on the gifts of the Holy Spirit, we will consider how Mary is our model in receiving these gifts.

The Seven Gifts of the Holy Spirit

The Spirit's gift of understanding gives us a deeper insight and penetration of divine truths held by faith, not as a momentary enlightenment but as a permanent intuition. The gift of understanding perfects our speculative reason so that we can better understand the truth. Understanding is the gift whereby self-evident principles are known, a kind of spiritual common sense. When Jesus' mother and brothers were outside waiting to see him, he responded, "Who are my mother and my brothers?" And looking at those who sat around him, he said, "Here are my mother and my brothers!" (Mk 3:33–34). Yes, Mary is literally Jesus' mother, but she is also the one who hears and obeys God's word, keeping it perfectly. Mary truly understood Christ's words and she put them into practice.[196]

The gift of knowledge enables us to judge rightly concerning the truths of faith in accordance with their proper causes and the principles of revealed truth. Knowledge perfects a person's reason in matters of judgment about the

---

196. See Peter John Cameron, O.P., *The Gifts of the Holy Spirit, According to St. Thomas Aquinas* (New Haven: Knights of Columbus Supreme Council, New Haven, CT), 39–40.

truth. When Mary uttered her Magnificat, she knew that almighty God had done great things for her and that his name was holy. She knew God as the source of justice and mercy, who had remembered his people Israel. By the gift of knowledge, we believe in God and all that he has said and revealed to us, freely committing our entire selves to God. Elizabeth exclaims of Mary, "Blessed is she who believed that there would be a fulfillment of what was spoken to her by the Lord" (Lk 1:45). Believing the angel's message from God, Mary committed her entire life to the Lord.[197]

The *gift of wisdom* helps us to judge and order all things in accordance with God's ways, perfecting our speculative reason in matters of judgment about the truth. When Mary witnessed her Son's tragic and brutal passion and death, she maintained a divine perspective about its eternal value due to the gift of wisdom. Mary realized that Jesus' suffering would lead to his resurrection and our redemption.[198] Through the gift of wisdom, we can have the same supernatural perspective about our own trials and sufferings. Wisdom also helps us to order our many loves by putting love of God first and loving our neighbor and all things within the context of God's love.

The *gift of counsel* renders us docile and receptive to the counsel of God regarding our actions. Counsel perfects our practical reason in understanding truth and allows us to respond prudently. At the wedding feast of Cana, Mary displays the gift of counsel, informing Jesus that the wine has run out. She then prudently directs the servants to "do whatever he tells you" in following Jesus' will. As our mother, Mary also directs us to do what is right in our following of her Son.[199] When Jesus told the servants to fill up the six giant water jars, they may have thought that action didn't make sense, yet they followed his directions. Like the servants at Cana, we may sometimes feel that what we are doing is senseless by worldly standards. In these moments we need to trust in the Holy Spirit through the gift of counsel.

The *gift of piety* enables us to give filial worship to God as our Father and, in justice, to relate with all people as children of the same Father. Piety leads us to be devoted to and care for our family, our country, and the poor and suffering. At the visitation to her cousin Elizabeth, Mary shows pious

---

197. Ibid., 34–35.
198. Ibid., 40–41.
199. Ibid., 37–38.

concern for her relative and serves her because of her particular need. Mary also exclaims her pious joy for God's regard for her native country Israel in uttering her Magnificat: "He has helped his servant Israel, in remembrance of his mercy, according to the promise he made to our ancestors, to Abraham and to his descendants forever" (Lk 1:54–55).[200]

The gift of courage empowers us to overcome difficulties or to endure pain and suffering with the strength and power given us by God. Courage grants us the firmness of mind required both in doing good and in enduring evil, especially when the good is difficult to achieve or the evil is difficult to endure. Mary and Joseph display courage in the episode of the finding of the child Jesus in the Temple. When Jesus was lost, they feared the worst and endured great torment and suffering in their three-day search for him. Courage enables us to conquer fear, even fear of death in facing trials and persecutions. Mary displayed especially great courage in accompanying Jesus throughout his passion, remaining steadfast beneath the cross at the moment of his death.

The gift of the fear of the Lord gives us a deeper reverence and love of God, and so helps us avoid sin and attachment to created things. This gift is not fear of God himself but fear of separation from God. Fear of the Lord is a filial fear—like a child's not wanting to offend his father out of love— rather than a servile fear of punishment. To avoid confusion with servile fear, this gift is often referred to as wonder and awe. This fear also involves knowing God as all-powerful. Mary experienced the fear of the Lord at the annunciation; hers was not a servile fear but a desire to fulfill all that God desired for her. This included a desire for the salvation of the human race. She is filled with wonder and awe at what God is proposing to do through her. As a result, Mary reverences God and offers herself in willing obedience to accomplish his plan.

In the Song of Songs, the bridegroom describes his bride as finely built and well-proportioned in her physical beauty, which is an apt metaphor. Mary's beauty is strongly built in the virtues and gifts of the Holy Spirit. The Church, indeed each individual Christian, grows to the same mature and lovely stature through the gifts of the Holy Spirit.

In the Contemplation to Attain Love, Saint Ignatius has us ponder God the Holy Spirit as the source of these gifts that descend "from above." Moving

---

200. Ibid., 33–34.

beyond the retreat, the Contemplation helps us to have greater sensitivity to the Spirit's very concrete action, through his gifts, in leading us to greater faith, hope, and love in our daily lives.

Questions for Reflection and Discussion

1. In what way do you see the face and body of the bride as an image of the mature Christian?

2. How aware are you of the gifts of the Holy Spirit in your Christian life? Can you distinguish between the gifts and the more active exercise of the infused virtues?

3. How well disposed are you to receive the gifts of the Holy Spirit? What is one gift that you need to ask for now?

4. To what extent can you surrender control to the Holy Spirit in the exercise of his gifts?

5. Have you ever experienced the gifts of the Spirit as if they were eyeglasses or a telescope that increases and perfects your faith vision?

6. Where are you weak in exercising the infused virtues and need to ask for a greater outpouring of the Holy Spirit?

Prayer Exercises

1. Ponder the words of Arminjon (p. 304). Pray with Song of Songs 7:1–6, and ask the grace to grow into full maturity as a Christian moved by the Holy Spirit.

2. Reflect on the symbolism of the face and body of the bride (p. 304). Pray with Ephesians 4:13–16, and ask for the grace to be fully sanctified by the gifts of the Holy Spirit.

3. Consider the inspiration of Saint John XXIII to convoke the Second Vatican Council (p. 306). Pray with John 3:1–13, and ask for the grace of docility to the gifts of the Holy Spirit.

4. Ponder the analogies of the sailboat in the wind and the person receiving eyeglasses and a telescope. Pray with John 7:37–41, and ask for the grace of greater openness to the gifts of the Holy Spirit.

5. Reflect on where you are weak in living virtue and ask for the corresponding gift of the Holy Spirit. Reflect on the life of the Blessed Virgin Mary and pray with the following Scripture passages for each gift:

> Understanding—Mark 3:31–35
> Knowledge—Matthew 12:46–50
> Wisdom—John 19:26–30, also First Corinthians 13:4–7
> Counsel—John 2:1–11
> Piety—Luke 1:39–56
> Fortitude—Luke 2:41–52
> Fear of the Lord—Luke 1:26–38

6. Pray with John 3:1–8. Consider and ask for the gift of the Holy Spirit you most need right now.

7. Make a repetition on any of the above contemplations, returning to the places of greater movement of spirit (consolation or desolation).

CHAPTER 29

Mature in the Spirit

[G] You are stately as a palm tree,
    and your breasts are like its clusters.
I say I will climb the palm tree
    and lay hold of its branches.
O, may your breasts be like clusters of the vine,
    and the scent of your breath like apples,
and your kisses like the best wine
      that goes down smoothly,
      gliding over lips and teeth.
[B] I am my beloved's,
    and his desire is for me.
Come, my beloved,
      let us go forth into the fields,
      and lodge in the villages;
let us go out early to the vineyards,
    and see whether the vines have budded,
whether the grape blossoms have opened
    and the pomegranates are in bloom.
There I will give you my love.
The mandrakes give forth fragrance,
    and over our doors are all choice fruits,
new as well as old,
    which I have laid up for you, O my beloved. (Song 7:7–13)

Consider all blessings and gifts as descending from above. Thus, my limited power comes from the supreme and infinite power above, and so, too, justice, goodness, mercy, etc., descend from above as the rays of light descend from the sun, and as the waters flow from their fountains, etc. (SpEx 237)

In the Contemplation to Attain Love, Saint Ignatius has us consider the gifts and blessings of the Spirit "descending from above" (SpEx 237). These include the many charismatic gifts of the Holy Spirit given to Christians for building up the Church in holiness. In the Song of Songs, the bride is described as "stately as a palm tree," high and rising to the heavens. The towering palm tree symbolizes the mature Christian who has grown and is flourishing with the Holy Spirit and his charisms, maturing in likeness to Christ, as described by Saint Paul: "But each of us was given grace according to the measure of Christ's gift . . . until all of us come to the unity of the faith and of the knowledge of the Son of God, to maturity, to the measure of the full stature of Christ" (Eph 4:7, 13).

The bride is like the stately palm tree grown to maturity, and her "breasts are like its clusters" of fruit of different kinds—dates, grapes, and apples. These fruits represent the many and varied charisms of the Holy Spirit that are given to the Church as a whole and to the individual Christian. The bride's fruitfulness mirrors the Church's fruitfulness in the Spirit. A single, large cluster of dates may produce over a thousand single dates and weigh twenty pounds or more—an appropriate symbol of the enormous fruitfulness of the Church in her charisms. Through them the Church nourishes her children in the sacraments and in virtuous acts of service.

The bride symbolizes the Church filled with the Spirit, docile to his will and activity. The Holy Spirit is the principal agent of the Church's mission.[201] The Church is inseparable from this one Spirit of Life, the fountain of living water (see Jn 7:37–39), who continually sanctifies, unifies, vivifies, and counsels the Church. The Second Vatican Council explains that the Spirit guides the Church in truth and unity of fellowship and service: "He

---

201. For more on this, see Pope John Paul II, *Mission of the Redeemer*, Part III (Boston: Pauline Books & Media, 1990).

both equips and directs [the Church] with hierarchical and charismatic gifts and adorns [her] with his fruits."202

The Spirit bestows hierarchic gifts, found especially in the institutional charisms of the Church's leaders to teach, govern, and sanctify the faithful. The Spirit also pours out charismatic gifts on all the faithful to build up the Church in holiness. Because all the gifts are from the same Spirit and lead to the same union in Christ, they produce a marvelous harmony between the hierarchical structure and the lay members of the Mystical Body of Christ. The Spirit makes the Church grow in a structured way, leading her to maturity as a bride in union with Christ.

The Holy Spirit is essentially the gift of the Father and the Son given to us. The Spirit's mission is to bestow the many gifts of God upon us Christians, including the charismatic gifts. We are to receive these gifts with gratitude and imitate the Spirit in giving our gifts in service to others.

The charisms come to us in different forms to animate and unite the Body of Christ in her various functions. Saint Paul teaches that the whole Body grows through Christ and "as each part is working properly, promotes the body's growth in building itself up in love" (Eph 4:15–16). Through the proper functioning of the Body we are organized to exercise Christ's love within the Church and in the world. Indeed, a local church is alive and healthy when its members exercise their charisms in service to one another.

In the First Letter to the Corinthians, Saint Paul explains that the varieties of charisms have their common source in God and are ordered to unity of the faithful in God: "Now there are varieties of gifts, but the same Spirit; and there are varieties of services, but the same Lord; and there are varieties of activities, but it is the same God who activates all of them in everyone. To each is given the manifestation of the Spirit for the common good" (1 Cor 12:4–7). God inspires the charisms in each of us for the good of others in building up the Church. Saint Paul goes on to identify various charisms: "To one is given through the Spirit the utterance of wisdom, and to another the utterance of knowledge according to the same Spirit, to another faith by the same Spirit, to another gifts of healing by the one Spirit, to another the working of miracles, to another prophecy, to another the discernment of spirits, to another various kinds of tongues, to another the interpretation of

---

202. *Lumen Gentium*, no. 4.

tongues" (1 Cor 12:8–10). The Spirit bestows these widely varying gifts on different individuals in whatever measure he chooses.

Father Gerard E. Welch describes the dynamic character of these tremendous gifts of the Spirit: "The charisms are manifest, creative, love-forging, explosive, divinely bestowed power. The charisms evidently overlap, complement, catalyze, and even seemingly compete with one another. The dynamic, creative breath of God blows where he wills."[203] The Spirit comes in power and love through these divinely bestowed charisms. Although we know that charisms come from the Holy Spirit, we cannot predict when, where, and how they will be manifested in individuals. The power of the charisms cannot be contained, but should be harnessed by individuals and the Church to renew the world in holiness and charity.

As a seminarian in 1991, I was on pastoral assignment at a parish in Los Angeles. I followed an amazingly humorous event involving a truck driver named Larry Walters. This story symbolizes the Holy Spirit's taking us beyond our natural abilities and fulfilling our deepest desires.

Larry had always dreamed of flying, but the Air Force had disqualified him due to his poor eyesight. From his backyard he would watch others fly as he dreamed of the magical experience denied him. One day Larry had a wild idea. He bought several helium tanks and forty-five weather balloons, each four feet in diameter. Using straps, Larry attached the balloons to his lawn chair, anchored the chair to the bumper of his Jeep, and inflated them with helium. He packed a small cooler with sandwiches and a six-pack of beer, and he loaded a pellet gun, figuring he could pop a few balloons when it was time to descend.

Larry's plan was to lazily float up to about 300 feet over his backyard and then float down a few hours later. But things didn't work out that way. When everything was ready, he cut the anchoring cord and shot up like a rocket, leveling off not at 300 feet but at 16,000 feet! Once up that high, Larry couldn't risk deflating the balloons, lest he unbalance the load.

For fourteen hours Larry remained in the stratosphere—cold, frightened, and helpless—until he drifted into LAX airport's primary approach corridor. A pilot immediately spotted Larry and radioed to the tower that a guy in a lawn chair holding a gun was floating into the airport! Disaster

---

203. Gerard E. Welch, *Charisms in the Life of the Church*, August 1997, Renewal Ministries web site, http://www.crmweb.org/publication/misc/charisms.htm.

struck, though, as coastal winds began to change and pushed Larry out to sea. The Navy helicopter dispatched to rescue Larry could not reach him at first, since the propeller's draft pushed him away at every approach. But eventually they succeeded by using a rescue line that hauled Larry back to earth. Once on land, the LAPD immediately rushed in, sirens blaring, and arrested him for violating LAX airspace. As Larry was being led away, a television reporter shouted, "Mr. Walters, why'd you do it?" Larry stopped, eyed the man, and nonchalantly replied, "A man can't just sit around."

Despite his understatement, Larry's misguided sense of adventure spoke to me of our own desire for true adventure in the service of the Lord. Larry knew he was meant to fly but was hindered by natural limitations. In lifting Larry far beyond his human potential, the balloons represent the Holy Spirit's power. Just as Larry was lifted into the stratosphere, the charisms of the Holy Spirit elevate us by the power of God to do divine things. Jesus had promised his disciples they would do even greater things than he had done when he walked the earth—and they did. By the Spirit's power we really do accomplish the works of God.

As we ponder the charisms of the Holy Spirit, we could apply Larry's phrase, "a man can't just sit around." God's gifts aren't given only for us to enjoy, but also to give away to others and build up the Church. We see that the bridegroom and bride don't merely "sit around" and relish one another's presence. Instead they say energetically, "Let us go forth into the fields, and lodge in the villages; let us go out early to the vineyards, and see whether the vines have budded.... There I will give you my love" (Song 7:12). Going into the fields symbolizes the Lord's commission to every Christian to go into the missionary fields of the world to sow the seed of the Gospel and bring forth an abundant harvest. Through our apostolic labors we, like the bride, give the Lord our love, which bears fruit in service. We find that with the power of the charisms the Holy Spirit gives us, we are taken beyond our natural capacity to evangelize. Like the farmer in Jesus' parable of the sower, we plant the seed and watch it grow, not knowing how it increases. We come to realize that the kingdom of God grows by the Spirit's power, which includes our efforts, but transcends them. We are elevated to supernatural levels by the Holy Spirit working in and through us to bring about the kingdom in the Church and renew the face of the earth.

Saint Ignatius leads us through the Spiritual Exercises so that we will become missionaries of Christ to the world. Recall the meditation on the

Call of the King (see SpEx 91–98), wherein Saint Ignatius has us consider Christ's call to labor with him in order to "conquer the world" for Christ. Then in the Meditation on Two Standards (see SpEx 136–147), Saint Ignatius has us consider how the Lord "chooses so many persons, apostles, disciples, etc., and sends them throughout the whole world to spread His sacred doctrine among all men" (SpEx 145). Our mission as Christians is directed toward spreading God's kingdom so that all people might share in Christ's saving redemption; we are to bring the whole world into relationship with Christ. To prepare ourselves for Christ's mission, we will want to take inventory of the charisms and talents with which God has enriched our souls, so that we may exercise the Spirit's gifts more effectively.

Through the charisms, the Holy Spirit lifts us up to do things above and beyond what is humanly achievable. Charisms go beyond our mere natural human talents, though they sometimes are related to them. All of us have innate gifts that we often exercise on a human level. One person, for instance, might be a naturally talented teacher who shares effectively without any reference to God or the spiritual benefit of others. Another person might have a supernatural charism of teaching and uses it in charity for the spiritual good of his or her students. This latter teacher might show extraordinary kindness and concern to struggling students. He or she might try to offer his or her students a wise perspective on life from his or her faith experience. This teacher might also put his or her gifts at the service of the Church in teaching catechism. Through the inspiration of a charism, the Holy Spirit has elevated this person's teaching to a new, supernatural plane to further the kingdom of God.

Sherry Weddell, founder of the Catherine of Siena Institute that teaches Christians to discern their charisms, describes her own experience of teaching as a charismatic gift: "I remember the vivid relief I felt when I was finally able to leave a job for which I was not well-suited and work as a full-time teacher of adults. I realized that one of the reasons I loved teaching was that I could be most freely and exuberantly myself." Sherry describes how exercising a charism helps us to be our most authentic selves: "There is a natural flow and ease about the whole experience. We sense that we 'fit' and that we have found our place, that we can be most truly ourselves and, at the same time, an agent of a Goodness that far exceeds our natural abilities."[204] There

---

204. Sherry Weddell, *The Catholic Spiritual Gifts Inventory*, third edition (Colorado Springs: The Siena Institute Press, 1998), 49.

is a sense of both truly being oneself and of being lifted beyond oneself by God.

Unfortunately, many Christians are not aware of their charismatic gifts. The Church has only recently emphasized that all baptized Christians receive charisms. Many Christians believed that such gifts were reserved for ordained clergy or religious sisters and brothers, beyond the reach of the layperson. The Second Vatican Council, in its *Decree on the Apostolate of the Laity*, raised awareness that all Christians are given charisms and should put them at the service of the Church in freedom.[205] At the same time, charisms should be exercised in communion with the Church's pastors, who test the authenticity of the charisms and order their exercise toward the common good. Though the Church has provided no fully defined or exhaustive list of charisms, the globally recognized *Catherine of Siena Institute* has gathered and defined a list of twenty-six,[206] grouped by seven types that are based on the texts of Sacred Scripture, especially Romans 12, First Corinthians 12, and Ephesians 4.[207] These are the seven types of charisms:

- *Pastoral charisms* are given to nurture individuals and foster communities. Pastoral charisms are pastoring, mercy, encouragement, helps, and hospitality.

- *Organizational charisms* are given to lead and coordinate an organization or group. The organizational charism are administration, leadership, service, and giving.

- *Healing charisms* are given to channel God's love for healing and renewal of mind, body, and spirit.

- *Creative charisms* of craftsmanship, music, and writing are given to bring beauty and order to our physical world.

- *Communication charisms* of evangelism, prophecy, and teaching are given to impact peoples' lives with precision and veracity.

- *Lifestyle charisms* of celibacy, faith, being a missionary, and voluntary poverty are given as ways of living that enable extraordinary ministry.

---

205. See no. 3.

206. For more information about the charisms, please consult *The Catholic Spiritual Gifts Resource Guide* by Sherry Weddell, available from the Catherine of Siena Institute, www.siena.org.

207. Weddell, *The Catholic Spiritual Gifts Inventory*, 24–59.

  ◉ *Understanding charisms* are given in order to comprehend the workings of God and human beings. The understanding charisms are knowledge, wisdom, discernment of spirits, publicly speaking in tongues, and the interpretation of tongues.

Most people have a few charisms. Usually one but sometimes two or three of them stand out most powerfully in a person's life. In the latter case, these charisms might be grouped together in a unique and complementary way. How do we discern which charisms have been given to us? A good first step is to pray for enlightenment. Then it is helpful to learn more about each charism and how it operates. We may notice which gifts we have already used in our lives of faith and apostolic activity. Another clue comes when other people notice the charisms in us and point them out. Through prayer, education, and others' help, we will be able to determine our charisms.[208]

Once we realize our charisms and practice them, they will have great impact on the lives of others, pleasing God to fulfill his will in us. The bride exclaims that she has laid up fruits of the harvest including mandrakes, which "give forth fragrance" pleasing to her bridegroom (Song 7:13). Maloney explains that the bride's self-giving mirrors the Christian's total and continuous giving to Christ in which "she finds that she can always be united in her consciousness with him who is one with her." Far from removing her from her Beloved, Jesus Christ, such activity brings her closer to him. By constantly giving him love in every situation, "the Spirit of love flows over her at all times. She is on fire with love for Christ. The more she loves, the more she burns to love." The more she does out of love for him, the more her love for him increases and she dares to do more for others: "She becomes compassion, like a universal mother to the entire, suffering world."[209] The bride in the Song of Songs has laid up her acts of love as a gift in return for the love of her bridegroom. These acts of love have transformed her into a living flame of love that burns continuously for her lover. In all her actions, she is keenly aware of belonging to him and experiencing

---

208. The Catherine of Siena Institute offers nationwide "Called and Gifted" conferences that help persons understand and discern their charisms. To attend a workshop, visit their web site at http://www.siena.org/Called-Gifted/called-a-gifted.

209. Maloney, *Singers of the New Song*, 148.

his love: "I am my beloved's and his desire is for me" (Song 7:10). As we exercise our charisms in service of the Lord and the Church, we are truly united with the Spirit and belong to him and he to us.

Questions for Reflection and Discussion

1. In what way are you motivated to go forth as an apostolic laborer for the Lord in bringing about his harvest?

2. How have you been lifted up beyond your ordinary human capacity to accomplish works in the Lord's service?

3. As you look over the seven types of charisms of the Holy Spirit (p. 321), which ones do you sense might be given to you? Would you like to discover more about the charisms you have and how they operate?

4. In what way are the charisms unpredictable in your life and the life of the Church?

5. Are your charisms the same or different from your natural talents? In what way?

6. How do you exercise your charisms in harmony with the authority of the Church and her pastors? Do you ever experience a tension with Church leaders in exercising your charisms?

7. Do you perceive the Lord's delight in his gift of your charisms and their fruit?

Prayer Exercises

1. Ponder the symbolism of the palm clusters and the fruitful bride (p. 000). Pray with Song of Songs 7:7–13, and ask for the grace to delight in the charisms of the Holy Spirit.

2. Reflect on the teaching of *Lumen Gentium* (p. 317) Pray with First Corinthians 12:4–11, and ask for the grace to be open to receive the charisms of the Holy Spirit.

3. Pray with Ephesians 4:7–16, and ask for the grace to be lifted beyond your human capacity into the life and ministry of the Spirit.

4. Read about the seven types of charisms of the Holy Spirit (p. 321). Pray with Romans 12, and ask for the gift to be more aware of your charismatic gifts and to put them into practice.

5. Reflect on Weddell's words (p. 320). Pray with First Corinthians 2:1–16, and ask for the grace to be aware of your charismatic gifts as distinguished from your natural gifts.

6. Pray with Romans 12, and ask for the grace to put your gifts into practice.

7. Make a repetition on any of the above contemplations, returning to the places of greater movement of spirit (consolation or desolation).

CHAPTER 30

Mother and Teacher

[B] O that you were like a brother to me,
who nursed at my mother's breast!
If I met you outside, I would kiss you,
    and no one would despise me.
I would lead you and bring you
    into the house of my mother,
      and into the chamber of the one who bore me,
      [and you will teach me].
I would give you spiced wine to drink,
    the juice of my pomegranates. (Song 8:1–2)

To foster the true attitude of mind we ought to have in the Church. . . . We must put aside all judgment of our own, and keep the mind ever ready and prompt to obey in all things the true Spouse of Christ our Lord, our holy Mother, the hierarchical Church. (SpEx 352–353)

At the end of the Spiritual Exercises, Saint Ignatius has the retreatant reflect upon the ecclesial nature of being a Christian; that one belongs to a Church in which a person gives public witness to his or her faith in the company of Christian brothers and sisters.

The bride speaks of her desire to give public witness of her love to the bridegroom; she wants to meet him outside and kiss him and have "no one . . . despise" her. In Hebrew culture it was forbidden for lovers to show affection publicly, even as husband and wife. But it was acceptable for family relatives to display affection and even to kiss. Therefore, the bride exclaims that she wishes her lover was her kin: "O that you were like a brother to me."

The bride is symbolic of the Church as a visible public institution in which one can profess love for Christ the Bridegroom. The monk Anastasius of Sinai helps us to understand the bride's wish that her bridegroom was a brother by nature, as Christ is brother to the Church supernaturally by grace: "You alone are 'blood of the blood' of his steadfastly solid divinity. You are flesh born of flesh of his human nature, harbor of his divine nature. You alone have become the 'help' of man: of God himself who is your help and your protection. In fact, he is your concern; you teach, you proclaim, you baptize, you convert, you procure everything for him since he is the light of men in the darkness and shadow of death."[210]

Christ is divine and he is Head of his Body, the Church, whose members are united with him by grace. The Church is so one with him as his Body that the members share his divine nature by participation. Since Christ has shared our human nature and given us a share in the divine nature through grace, we can truly call Christ our brother.

The bride expresses her desire to lead her beloved into the house of her mother, into the chamber of the one who conceived her. The Hebrews always understood Jerusalem to be their mother, her two hills symbolizing the breasts that nursed her children: "that you may nurse and be satisfied from her consoling breast" (Is 66:11). The house of the bride's mother would symbolize the Temple, the place of public worship and covenantal bond between God and Israel. Jerusalem and the Temple foreshadow the Church of God, the New Jerusalem come down from heaven (see Rev 21:2), which is the new mother of all the faithful, Jews and Gentiles alike. Saint Paul writes, "But the other woman corresponds to the Jerusalem above; she is free, and she is our mother" (Gal 4:26), showing us that the Church, as the new Jerusalem, is essentially our mother in the faith.

---

210. Anastasius of Sinai in Luigi Guissani, *Why the Church?* (McGill-Queen's University Press, 2001), 150.

The bride desires marital union with her bridegroom within her mother's house, "into the chamber of she who conceived me." This symbolizes the individual Christian's desire for union with Christ within the house of holy mother Church. The Church is essentially a mother to all the faithful, conceiving and bearing children for God. Jesus uses the maternal image of being "born again," not from one's biological mother but "from above," of water and the Spirit in the womb of one's spiritual mother, the Church.

Saint Cyprian of Carthage explains that in order to be a child of God, one must be a child in the Church: "He cannot have God for his Father who has not the Church as his Mother."[211] To be a Christian it is essential to be attached to one's mother, the Church of God. Yves Congar, a theologian at the Second Vatican Council, explains that the Church is no longer just the Body of Christ but also the womb that forms and enlivens the Body.[212] The Church not only belongs to Christ as his spouse, but she also conceives and bears children as a mother, and she nourishes the life of her children.

The Church gives supernatural life to her children through the waters of Baptism and continues to nourish that life through the supernatural food of the Holy Eucharist. She gives growth in the Spirit through a greater outpouring of grace in the sacrament of Confirmation. She also nourishes her faithful in divine teaching, helping them to understand and love the person of Jesus Christ and his revelation. Saint John XXIII explains the role of the Church as mother and teacher of all nations in his encyclical *Mater et Magistra*: "To her was entrusted by her holy Founder the twofold task of giving life to her children and of teaching them and guiding them—both as individuals and as nations—with maternal care."[213]

Christ commanded his apostles to make disciples of all nations, giving them supernatural life in Baptism and teaching them to observe all he commanded them (see Mt 28:19). The Church's divine teaching is supernatural nourishment. As newborn children in grace, we cry out for the pure spiritual milk of Christ's teaching given by our mother the Church, so that we may "grow into salvation" (1 Pet 2:2).

---

211. Saint Cyprian, *Treatise on Unity*, 6, quoted in CCC 181.
212. See Yves Congar, *The Mystery of the Church* (Baltimore: Helicon Press, 1965), 70.
213. Saint John XXIII, *Mater et Magistra* (Boston: St. Paul Editions, 1961), par. 1.

Christ's teaching within the house of Mother Church is symbolized by the bride's desire to lead the bridegroom into her mother's house, that he would teach her (see 8:2). In this intimate moment of marital union, the bride desires and receives great enlightenment in love and knowledge through the bridegroom's teaching. As the bridegroom loves his bride he reveals himself more and more to her. The more she loves him, the more she desires to know him—and the more she knows him, the more she desires to love him. She symbolizes the Christian who has been enlightened by Christ in Baptism and has begun a process of ever-deepening love and knowledge, growing into deeper relationship with Jesus. The Christian receives education and guidance in Christ's teaching within the Church's maternal embrace of love.

Saint Ignatius emphasizes the Church's role as mother of the faithful in giving supernatural life to her children and nourishing them by divine teaching. At the end of his Spiritual Exercises, Saint Ignatius includes a section of guidelines "to foster the true attitude of mind we ought to have in the Church" (SpEx 352). A child wants to be taught by his or her mother and, in goodness, desires to respect and obey her. So too, children of the Church ought to desire her teaching and follow her in respect and obedience. Saint Ignatius' guidelines are designed to help us to go forth from the retreat with the realization that we are united as members of the family of God in the Church. As such we are not independent agents in our thinking or practice, but are children under parental authority, teaching, and guidance. We act together with other family members toward a common purpose: unity and salvation in Christ.

Saint Ignatius begins his rules by focusing on the familial images of the Church as bride and mother: "We must put aside all judgment of our own, and keep the mind ever ready and prompt to obey in all things the true Spouse of Christ our Lord, our holy Mother, the hierarchical Church" (SpEx 353). As the spouse, we, the members of the Church, are to think and act in unison with the Bridegroom, to be of one body and mind. Christ loves his bride the Church as his own flesh, and each of us as members of his Body (see Eph 5:29). Spouses will be in ever-greater union if they are of the same mind, sharing vision and purpose. Saint Paul explains that "we have the mind of Christ" (1 Cor 2:16), judging and acting according to his perspective. As we seek to remain united in matters of faith as members of the true spouse of Christ, the Church, we are assured of Christ's guidance in truth.

The Second Vatican Council speaks of the *sensus fidei* or the supernatural sense of the faithful by which they believe the truth of Christ in unison. By the power of the Holy Spirit, the whole body of the faithful "cannot err in matters of belief." Christ's faithful exhibit this supernatural sense when the members—from the bishops to the laity—demonstrate widespread accord in matters of faith and morals. The Holy Spirit guides the sacred teaching authority of the Church and the grasp of that teaching by the faithful. Through the *sensus fidei*, the Church as "... the people of God adheres unwaveringly to the faith given once and for all to the saints (see Jude 3), penetrates it more deeply with right thinking, and applies it more fully in its life."[214] God grants his faithful a supernatural instinct for detecting, understanding, and living the Catholic faith as taught by the Church's pastors.

Saint Ignatius not only calls the Church a true spouse, but a holy mother as well. As Mother Church gives us the supernatural life of grace and virtue by her teaching and her sacraments. Since the Church educates and nourishes our faith, we know and adhere to revelation because of her. The Church exercises her role as mother and teacher especially through her leaders. Saint Paul exemplifies this, even comparing himself to a mother: "But we were gentle among you, like a nurse tenderly caring for her own children. So deeply do we care for you that we are determined to share with you not only the gospel of God but also our own selves, because you have become very dear to us" (1 Thes 2:7–8). Saint Paul uses maternal imagery to express his longing that Christ be formed in his people: "My little children, for whom I am again in the pain of childbirth until Christ is formed in you!" (Gal 4:19). The Apostle experiences his hardship and sufferings in spreading the Gospel as labor pains that bring forth the life of Christ in believers. These two Pauline Scripture passages show us various aspects of motherhood, such as bearing children, teaching, nurturing, and guarding them.

A modern example of Saint Paul can be found in the life of Bishop George Gottwald, an auxiliary bishop of St. Louis who served as apostolic administrator of the archdiocese in 1967. The bishop showed great courage in asserting the teaching of Christ and guarding her children from falsehood. It was a tumultuous time for the Church, with plenty of creative movement prompted by the reforms of the Second Vatican Council. But those confusing times also included a lot of doubt, error, hurt, and confusion, including a crisis in the archdiocesan seminary in St. Louis. The student body was

---

214. *Lumen Gentium*, no. 12.

decimated by the departure of many of the faculty priests, and little sound theology was being taught. The remaining faculty demanded the presence of Bishop Gottwald at a campus demonstration in early spring of 1968, to present him with their list of demands in front of TV cameras. This shy, nervous, and unknown country priest walked into the lion's den. The leader of the faculty and students informed the bishop that, since the whole enterprise of priestly formation and Catholic theology was up for grabs, the seminary should close.

The bishop responded that even with the changes of the Second Vatican Council, the clear and consistent truths of the Catholic faith had to be taught to any future priest. "Hah," the spokesman taunted, "I dare you to tell me what we can possibly teach our students now that has not changed, that will not change, and that can be stated with any amount of conviction at all! I dare you to tell me!" All eyes were on the bishop as microphones clicked on and cameras whirled for a sound bite. His answer was, "I believe in God, the Father Almighty, Creator of heaven and earth, and in Jesus Christ, his only Son, our Lord, who was conceived by the Holy Spirit. . . ."—the very words of the Creed.[215] Facing ridicule and doubt, Bishop Gottwald had the courage to assert and defend the true faith of Catholics. As a bride desires to be true to her husband in fidelity, so the bishop demonstrated fidelity to Christ and the truth of his teaching. As a mother protecting her children from falsehood and vice, the bishop protected his flock from those who would seek to destroy its faith and virtue.

As a faithful spouse, the bride desires to share the truth and vision of her bridegroom. She desires greater enlightenment of love and wisdom, asking for him to teach her (Song 8:3). We seek more illumination from on high in the person of Jesus Christ so that we may grow in truth and love of him. The bride has "spiced wine to drink" (8:2), which symbolizes the wine of the Spirit that intoxicates us and leads us to this deeper understanding of the Lord. The Church as spouse of Christ imbibes the teaching of her husband, putting on the mind and heart of Christ. The bride offers her lover "the juice of my pomegranates" (8:4), the fruit of her own transformation, symbolizing the Church's ability to now transmit her faith in her Lord. Saint John of the

---

215. Timothy Dolan, *Priests for the Third Millennium* (Huntington: Our Sunday Visitor Publishing Division, 2000), 17–18.

Cross asserts that the pomegranates symbolize the mysteries of Christ, the judgments of the wisdom of God, and the virtues and attributes uncovered in the knowledge of these innumerable mysteries and judgments: "Just as pomegranates have many little seeds, formed and sustained within the circular shell, so each of the attributes, mysteries, judgments, and virtues of God, like a round shell of power and mystery, holds and sustains a multitude of marvelous decrees and wondrous effects."[216] The truths of the Catholic faith are like the seeds of the bride's pomegranates, each containing truth, power, sweetness, and the ability to nourish the faithful. Having received her teaching from Christ her Spouse, the Church now offers the fruit of her teaching back to him by transmitting it to all nations, extending the Body of Christ throughout the world. As Saint Ignatius asserts, the Church is faithfully the "true spouse" of Christ and "holy mother" to the children she generates.

Questions for Reflection and Discussion

1. As a member of the Church, how do you experience her as bride to Christ, collectively and individually?

2. In what way do you experience the Church as a mother and teacher? How do you participate in each of those roles?

3. How do you respond to the legitimate role of the Church as teacher of the Christian faith? How do you feel about the call to be obedient in faith?

4. In what ways are you called to stand up in greater fidelity to the Church's teaching?

5. How do you feel called to participate in the motherhood of the Church by handing on the faith to others?

Prayer Exercises

1. Consider the quote from Anastasius of Sinai (p. 326). Pray with Song of Songs 8:1–5, and ask for the grace to understand the deep union of the Church with Christ.

---

216. Saint John of the Cross, *The Spiritual Canticle*, Stanza 37, 7, in *The Collected Works*, 617.

2. Reflect on the quote from *Mater et Magistra* by Saint John XXIII. Pray with First Thessalonians 2:7–8 and Galatians 4:19, and ask for the grace to understand the maternal role of the hierarchy of the Church.

3. Pray with Matthew 12:46–50, and ask for the grace to realize your own role as a mother in the Church.

4. Reflect on Saint Ignatius' first rule (no. 353) for thinking with the Church (p. 325). Pray with Luke 10:1–16, and ask for the grace to be obedient to the teaching of the Church.

5. Consider the quote from *Lumen Gentium* 12 (p. 329). Pray with Ephesians 4:1–13, and ask for an increase of faith and unity among Christians.

6. Ponder the story of Bishop Gottwald (p. 329). Pray with Second Timothy 4:1–8, and ask for the grace to be steadfast in promoting the Christian faith, "in season and out of season."

7. Make a repetition on any of the above contemplations, paying closer attention to those places of greater consolation or desolation.

CHAPTER 31

Surrender in Freedom

[B] I would lead you and bring you
    into the house of my mother,
      and into the chamber of the one who bore me
    [and you would teach me].
I would give you spiced wine to drink,
    the juice of my pomegranates.
O that his left hand were under my head,
    and that his right hand embraced me!
I adjure you, O daughters of Jerusalem,
    do not stir up or awaken love
until it is ready!
[D] Who is that coming up from the wilderness,
    leaning upon her beloved? (Song 8:2–5)

We must put aside all judgment of our own, and keep the mind ever ready and prompt to obey in all things the true Spouse of Christ our Lord, our holy Mother, the hierarchical Church. (SpEx 352)

We should be more ready to approve and praise the orders, recommendations, and way of acting of our superiors than to find fault with them. (SpEx 362)

For I must be convinced that in Christ our Lord, the bridegroom, and in His spouse the Church, only one Spirit holds sway, which governs and rules for the salvation of souls. For it is by the same Spirit and Lord who gave the Ten Commandments that our holy Mother Church is ruled and governed. (SpEx 365)

The bride's desire that her lover would teach her in the house of her mother (see 8:3) corresponds to the Christian's seeking to be taught by Christ in the house of one's mother, the Church. Saint Ignatius exhorts us to docility in receiving the teaching of Christ through the Church (see SpEx 352). In the Creed, we profess that salvation and faith come from God alone, but because we receive the life of faith in and through the Church, she is our mother and teacher in the faith. Saint Ignatius wants us to realize that though faith is a personal act, it is not private or isolated from other people. We can neither live nor believe in isolation from others. We receive our faith from others, as we received our life from others. Since we receive our faith from others and believe within the communion of the Church, we ought to make "every effort to maintain the unity of the Spirit in the bond of peace" (Eph 4:2). Saint Ignatius wants us to be aware of the grace of the Holy Spirit given to unite the Church as true spouse in her fidelity to Christ and his teaching.

Whenever we are inspired to undertake a new work in the Church, we should submit it in faith to our leaders who are charged with testing the authenticity of these inspirations and guiding their appropriate use. Christ reigns in the Church insofar as its members are charismatically gifted by the Holy Spirit to perform various works in building up the body of Christ. Christ also manifests his lordship through the institutional structures of the Church: its official teaching, worship, and government. These are stable and uniform while also allowing for necessary diversity. The charismatic gifts of the faithful are in harmony with the hierarchic leadership and structure of the Church, both originating in God. Some charisms given to the Church are precisely for her administration and leadership in government.

Saint Ignatius emphasizes the virtue of obedience as a means of fostering and maintaining unity in the Church. In the first paragraph of his Rules for Thinking with the Church (see SpEx 353), he includes a new governing "principle and foundation" of obedience for the retreatant going forth into the

Church and the world. Obedience means truly hearing and being ready to believe the Church and her teaching. Christians ought to be submissive to the authority of the Church, which oversees and confirms the charisms and activities of the faithful. Obedience is complementary to freedom of thought and will, and ought to be given to legitimate authority. Some might criticize obedience as mechanical or complain that it stifles originality. But such criticism caricatures obedience as merely doing what one is told without any freedom or creativity. A mature religious person integrates both self-determination and obedience in the experience of freedom. The psychologist Adrian Van Kaam elucidates how human existence is rooted in obedience: "To listen to the demands of being, the claims of reality, the appeal of life, the requirements of the situation, is the very basis of man's realistic standing out into reality, into being. Therefore, the experience of self-determination in the personality is a relaxed and joyful awareness that he himself freely decides to be obedient, to listen, knowing full well that he could decide not to do so."[217]

The truly obedient person is sensitive to the needs of reality and persons. Through obedience the person freely chooses to go out of oneself in love to meet the demands of others.

Obedience to God is rooted in Sacred Scripture and expressed in obedience to religious leaders. The word obedience has as its root "to hear." Jesus said to his apostles, "Whoever listens to you listens to me" (Lk 10:16). Some persons find it difficult to obey fallible, sinful human beings. Even if religious leaders fail to edify us by their example, Jesus tells us to obey them: "Do whatever they teach you and follow it; but do not do as they do, for they do not practice what they teach" (Mt 23:3). Obedience is meant to be tender, loving, and respectful, as that of a son or daughter to a parent. Herve Coathalem explains that such obedience to the Church does not mean maneuvering to avoid constraint. The obedient person freely welcomes the instruction and guidance of the Church.[218]

Many in the Church find ways to avoid obedience and compliance with authority. Saint Ignatius exhorts us to desire obedience in accord with our true nature as human beings subject to and dependent on God. In the

---

217. Adrian Van Kaam, C.S.Sp., *The Religious Personality* (Garden City: Image/Doubleday, 1968), 63.

218. See Coathalem, *Ignatian Insights*, 301–302.

Contemplation to Attain Love, he has us offer to the Lord our most precious gifts of will and intellect, which we have received from him. In the Rules for Thinking with the Church, Saint Ignatius offers a concrete means of expressing the gift of our will and intellect to God in being subject to the Church as Christ's spouse and our mother.

Similarly the bride gives this most precious and cherished gift of her human freedom in obedience and surrender to her bridegroom. Her obedience is her greatest gift and expresses most fully her love and dedication to union with her spouse in doing his will. Arminjon explains how the bride now gives herself in a final, complete way, holding back nothing from her bridegroom: "She did, however, believe in good faith that she had given her all! But there was a part of her soul, unknown to herself until now, that she was not yet able to offer: the last depth of ourselves, that we usually take so long in discovering and thus to be able to offer. It takes years of ripening and listening in the school of the Bridegroom. 'Take my yoke upon you, and learn from me,' Jesus says (Mt 11:29). What the Bride learns in this school are spaces so far unsuspected in the heart of the Bridegroom."[219]

Until now, the bride has maintained something of her own will in the secret places of her heart, where she has not totally surrendered to her bridegroom. As Christians all of us have certain attachments of the heart and self-will that we have not yet given to God in obedience. And yet we must surrender to him, as the bride has learned to give her heart completely to her bridegroom. She is fully embraced by him and leans upon him in total dependence (8:5). In obedience and surrender, she moves in synchronicity with his movements as they emerge together from the wilderness (8:5). She is given his wisdom, symbolized by her head, the place of the intellect, resting in his left hand (8:3).

We find an example of such complete surrender in obedience to the Lord in Sister Floralba Rondi of the Sisters of the "Poverelle," based in Bergamo, Italy. Following her profession of vows, Sister Floralba's first assignment had been to Kikwit, Zaire. After serving there for many years, she returned to Italy. But, when she was seventy-one years old, the order's Mother General asked her to return to Kikwit. And Sister Floralba did so willingly. Shortly after returning to Zaire, she wrote to her Mother General: "Having spent so

---

219. Arminjon, *Cantata of Love*, 332.

many years in Kikwit, no sooner had I arrived than I had the impression of having always been here ... When I saw the hospital, I felt the energy drain out of me.... Yet I said to myself: I did not ask to return here; on the contrary, I never imagined that I would be sent here again since I had been here for twenty-five years. And so I am sure that I am doing the will of God, and this gives me peace and joy."[220] When the Ebola virus broke out in Zaire in 1995, Sister Floralba and five of her sisters heroically gave their lives caring for those who had contracted this highly contagious and deadly disease.

The peace Sister Floralba experienced came from her obedience to the Lord. Having already spent twenty-five years in Zaire, Sister Floralba might have been tempted to refuse the assignment. Instead, she chose in freedom to give herself completely—even to the point of sacrificing her very life—in obedience to the Lord's will, expressed through her religious superior. Sister Floralba is like the bride "leaning on her beloved" (8:5), totally surrendered in obedience to him. The bride is secure and tranquil in his embrace, aware that his left arm is firm and tender under her head and that his right hand embraces her (8:3). In her self-sacrifice of obedience to his will, the bride finds her peace.

Obedience and Difficult Situations

Sometimes pastors, leaders, and other members of the Church cause harm to Christ's faithful people, making it difficult to trust leaders with our obedience. While each of us in the Church is meant to be a bridge to an encounter with Jesus Christ, we sometimes are obstacles due to our character weaknesses and sins.

A woman named Rose Ellen was let go from her job as secretary in an archdiocesan chancery. She felt the priest who fired her did so in an unjust and unkind way. As a result, she gave up her practices of prayer and abandoned her works of evangelization. Where she had once felt close to the Lord, she now felt distant. Years later, Rose Ellen experienced some spiritual counseling and underwent a process of healing and forgiveness. She returned to her practices of prayer and piety and developed an outreach to other women

---

220. From a newsletter of the Sisters of the Poverelle, also found in Timothy Gallagher, *Discerning the Will of God* (New York: Crossroad, 2009), 136.

who had felt alienated from the Church.[221] Rose Ellen regretted her decision to give up on the Church because of the harmful actions of one or a few of its members. God did not abandon her and even used her experience to help heal others who were no longer practicing their faith.

Many of us have experienced similar wounds at the hands of others in the Church. Drawing closer to the Lord in prayer and seeking help from others can heal our pain and alienation.

In his Rules for Thinking with the Church, Saint Ignatius helps us to navigate many elements of the Church's structural life, worship, and doctrine. The issues he mentions as important were flashpoints of his day and not necessarily the contentious matters we face in the Church today. Even if in conscience we have difficulty understanding or accepting certain teachings, practices, or decisions, we must be humble enough to realize that our personal viewpoints do not have as great a weight and authority as the Magisterium (teaching authority) of the Church and her pastors. In such situations we should be more inclined to think that the teaching authority of the Church has greater credibility than we do. While everyone's opinion is valued in the Church, Saint Ignatius suggests that we should subject our own thoughts to the teaching authority of pastors and experts in theology. Christ has given his authority to teach to his apostles and their successors. We are to look to the Church of the living God as the "pillar and bulwark of the truth" (1 Tim 3:15). Saint Ignatius further reminds us that the Holy Spirit guides the Church to all truth and toward salvation. Common belief in the Church's teaching, worship, and governance contributes to greater unity in the Church.

While we hold fast to the teachings of Christ and his Church, we must avoid a fearful or defensive posture that holds us back from proclaiming the Gospel of love. We are bound to face disagreement and opposition to Church teaching both within the Church and outside of it. We are aware of the tensions within the Church and, if we are not careful, misunderstandings and mutual suspicion can lead to painful divisions. Patristics scholar David Meconi describes his experience as a novice entering religious life where other candidates had differing views:

> I became a candidate for religious life two decades ago and then the divisions and tensions within the novitiate were thick. Holding fast to my defenses, I

---

221. See Jules Toner, *What Is Your Will, O God?*, 39.

would dismiss someone just after one conversation. "Well, he's one of them. He's a dissenter." At one level it was so understandable, so natural, yet *so un-Christian*. I see now that in a time of battle I allowed myself the uncharitable sally, the harsh judgment, the one-sided perspective, and then simply chalked it up to the tensions of the day or to the gravity of what was at stake. But how do we witness to the beautiful integrity of Catholic orthodoxy without putting up walls? For I now see how I used the faith, not as a means of building unity, but as a sword of division and as a way of making myself feel satisfied about my own position, my own worked-out systems, my own orthodoxy. Because I was not wholly motivated by love, fear was still present (see 1 Jn 4:18)—fear of looking dim, fear of not knowing more than those who criticized the hierarchy, fear that maybe the way I had learned or had come to explain the tradition was not as unassailable as it could be. How often the truth became a club, a place for my self-complacency and separation built on the implicit creed, "Oh, God, I thank you that I am not like other men—extortionists, the unjust, adulterers, or even like this tax collector" (Lk 18:13).[222]

Meconi learned that we must be willing to dialogue with others and always speak the truth with charity. The truth is not a weapon we wield to destroy those who do not agree with us, but an instrument of healing and enlightenment.

That is why early on in the Spiritual Exercises, Saint Ignatius suggests that we should enter into relationship and dialogue with others with mutual trust and not suspicion regarding the Christian faith. "It is necessary to suppose that every good Christian is more ready to put a good interpretation on another's statement than to condemn it as false. If an orthodox construction cannot be put on a proposition, the one who made it should be asked how he understands it. If he is in error, he should be corrected with all kindness. If this does not suffice, all appropriate means should be used to bring him to a correct interpretation, and so defend the proposition from error" (SpEx 22). Saint Ignatius suggests that we try to understand other peoples' statements in a Catholic way. Sometimes we have to seek to clarify other peoples' meanings to better understand them. Always we respectfully take people where they are in their understanding of the Christian faith and hopefully have the opportunity to lead them to greater truth.

---

222. David Meconi, S.J., *Razing the Bastions, Yet Again*, Homiletic and Pastoral Review, June 1, 2011, http://www.hprweb.com/2011/06/razing-the-bastions-yet-again/.

Saint Ignatius was keenly and painfully aware of the splintering of the unity of faith during the Reformation, knowing that some persons in the Church had contributed to the split with their bad behavior. He wanted to reform the Church from within, desiring his Society of Jesus to be particularly sensitive to Protestant concerns in an effort to win them back to the Catholic faith. He was opposed to persecuting Protestants and preferred the more peaceful and positive approach of preaching and teaching the Catholic faith. Saint Ignatius wrote that everything ought to be done with modesty and Christian charity, that "no injurious statement should be made against [the Protestants], nor any kind of disdain shown toward them, but compassion instead."[223] Saint Ignatius wanted to win back Protestant brothers and sisters to the Catholic faith through the witness of charity and the proclamation of truth, not by antagonism and force.

In his day Saint Ignatius desired to be a force for unity through friendship and charity. So too in our own day we engage in ecumenism in a spirit of fraternity with our separated brethren. In our dialogue with them, we emphasize the greater truths that unite us, such as belief in the Trinity, the incarnation, Baptism, and the Scriptures, our supernatural life of grace, the infused virtues of faith, hope, and love, and the gifts of the Holy Spirit, more than the things that divide us.

Saint Ignatius' Rules for Thinking with the Church cover a broad variety of topics that were controversial in his day. He wanted retreatants to be cautious about how they spoke about these controversial issues in such a tense climate. Today as well, tension may sometimes exist within the Church. Saint John Paul II called for "a sincere effort of permanent and renewed dialogue within the Catholic Church herself. She is aware that, by her nature, she is the sacrament of the universal communion of charity; but she is equally aware of the tensions within her, tensions which risk becoming factors of division."[224]

Christ bestowed unity upon the Church from the beginning as something that subsists and remains—something we can never lose, fundamentally.

---

223. Saint Ignatius of Loyola, in Candido Dalmases, *Saint Ignatius of Loyola: Founder of the Jesuits* (St. Louis, Institute for Jesuit Sources, 1985), 196.

224. John Paul II, Apostolic Exhortation *Reconciliation and Penance* (Boston: Pauline Books & Media, 1984), no. 25.

We hope to work to maintain, reinforce, and increase this unity, making Jesus' prayer for unity our own.[225]

According to the Second Vatican Council, some of the means to bring about an increase in unity among separated Christians are:

- Renewal of the Church in greater fidelity to her vocation.
- Conversion of heart and striving to live holier lives, because lack of faithfulness causes divisions.
- Prayer in common with other Christians, which is the soul of the ecumenical movement.
- Fraternal knowledge of each other as Christians.
- Ecumenical formation of the faithful.
- Dialogue among theologians and meetings among different Christians.
- Collaboration among Christians in various areas of service to all humanity.[226]

As Christians share their common faith in prayer, conversion, and works of charity, they will realize the bond in the Holy Spirit that unites them all in Christ. They will desire increased unity in the heart of Jesus Christ, who prayed that "they may all be one" (Jn 17:21).

Praise and gratitude for the Church that Christ gave us will also foster unity, as opposed to destructive criticism and factions, which causes disintegration. Saint Ignatius insists in exactly half of his Rules for Thinking with the Church (see SpEx 354–362) that "we ought to praise" various Church practices and ecclesial structures. The Rules come out of Saint Ignatius' experience of living in a tumultuous time in Paris, when opponents of the Church spewed vitriolic criticism of Church worship, structure, and devotional practice.

In the Church today we may encounter similar cynicism and denigration. We need to be careful not to fall into the temptation of gossip and negativity, not to divide ourselves into rival camps within the Church, but instead seek reason to praise. If a Church prelate or his pastoral style is not to our liking, we can still find reason to praise him. If a particular Church practice, such as

---

225. See CCC 820.
226. See *Unitatis Redintegratio*, nos. 4–12.

a charismatic prayer service, is not our preferred way of worship, it is still worthy of our praise. Even Saint Ignatius did not adopt every practice he mentions in these rules, such as always praying the Divine Office in common, but he still considered them praiseworthy. As with the attitude of thanksgiving in the examen prayer, an attitude of praise to God for the Church and her teachings and practices will lead to a joyful appreciation of God's gifts, greater apostolic effectiveness, and a bond of unity among Christians.

Questions for Reflection and Discussion

1. How have you been involved in efforts toward Church unity? What has been your experience of ecumenism? Do you feel called to become more involved, and if so, how?

2. Some of the means to greater unity in the Church are renewal in fidelity, conversion of heart, prayer in common, fraternal knowledge, ecumenical formation, and dialogue. How do you exercise these?

3. How well do you dialogue with other Christians about faith and evangelization? Are you good at emphasizing the things that unite us? Are you a good listener, one who hears the heart of the other person?

4. How do you experience obedience to the legitimate authority of the Church in the exercise of your Christian apostolate?

5. Have you felt that your opinions about Church matters have been valued and understood?

6. If you have been hurt by a leader or other member of the Church, how did you respond? Have you sought or experienced healing of these wounds?

7. Have you ever struggled to believe any of the teachings of the Church? How could Saint Ignatius' Rules help you?

8. In what way is the gift of yourself in obedience to God in his Church a greater surrender and sacrifice to Christ as Bridegroom?

Prayer Exercises

1. Reflect on the means to unity outlined in *Unitatis Redintegratio* (p. 341). Reflect on John 7:17–26, and ask to have a greater desire to act for unity in the Church.

2. Pray with Mark 9:38–41, and ask for the grace of greater acceptance and respect for other Christians.

3. Pray with First Corinthians 12:21–25, and pray for the grace to better realize our need for others in the Church.

4. Pray with Luke 14:12–15, and ask for the grace to desire to bring in and include the least and the lost in the kingdom.

5. Ponder the quote from *Reconciliation and Penance* (p. 340). Pray with First Thessalonians 5:12–23, and ask for the grace of awareness of the harmony between the institutional and charismatic elements of the Church.

6. Reflect on the story of Sister Floralba (p. 336). Pray with John 21:18–19 and Romans 13:1–4, and ask for the grace of total surrender in obedience to Christ.

7. Make a repetition on any of the above contemplations, returning to the place of greater movement of spirit (consolation or desolation).

CHAPTER 32

Image and Seal of the Beloved

[D] Who is that coming up from the wilderness,
    leaning upon her beloved?
[B] Under the apple tree I awakened you.
There your mother was in labor with you;
    there she who bore you was in labor.
Set me as a seal upon your heart,
    as a seal upon your arm;
for love is strong as death,
    passion fierce as the grave.
Its flashes are flashes of fire,
    a raging flame.
Many waters cannot quench love,
    neither can floods drown it. (Song 8:5–7a)

We must put aside all judgment of our own, and keep the mind ever ready and prompt to obey in all things the true Spouse of Christ our Lord, our holy Mother, the hierarchical Church. (SpEx 353)

W e continue with our reflection on the Rules for Thinking with the
Church (see SpEx 352–370), in which Saint Ignatius shows us
how the Church as a true spouse is faithful in communicating her Lord's
presence and message. Each Christian, as a spouse of the Bridegroom, Jesus
Christ, is a representative of Christ as a member of his Body, the Church.
We go forth as emissaries of Christ to bring his presence and teaching to the
world, totally dependent on Jesus and his Spirit in accomplishing the work
of evangelization.

The Song of Songs illustrates this dependence as the bride is now seen
"coming up from the wilderness, leaning on her beloved" (8:5). According to
a literal translation of the Hebrew, the bride is leaning on the bridegroom's
very heart,[227] suggesting her utter dependence, complete union, and total
abandonment to her beloved. In the same way, the Church and every Christian
must remain in union with Christ as branches on the vine and depend totally
upon him. Jesus reminds us, "Apart from me you can do nothing" (Jn 15:5).
Apart from the abiding presence of Christ, the Christian will remain inef-
fectual. Only through, with, and in Christ will we bear much fruit.

The bride "under the apple tree" (8:5) is an image of the Christian awakened to the new life of grace, transformation, and ultimately resurrection by
her Bridegroom. Christ is the fruitful apple tree through his life-giving
death and resurrection on the cross, the new Tree of Life (see Rev 22:2).
Saint John of the Cross imagines Jesus addressing similar words to us:
"Beneath the apple tree: there I took you for my own, there I offered you my
hand, and restored you."[228] The tree of Christ's cross, leading to the fruit of
his resurrection, is now the place of union and the marriage of Jesus with his
Church. The crucifixion and death of Jesus was his moment of travail,
shared by his bride, the Church. In the Book of Revelation, the woman,
symbolizing the Church, gives birth to her children in travail, sharing the
labor pains of Christ's sufferings. Similarly, in the Song of Songs the bridegroom awakens his bride under the apple tree, the place where "your mother
was in labor with you" (8:5).

The bride responds to her awakening and espousal with an impassioned
request to her lover: "Set me as a seal upon your heart, as a seal upon your

---

227. See Origen, *The Song of Songs, Commentary and Homilies*, 276.
228. Saint John of the Cross, *Spiritual Canticle*, Stanza 23, in *Collected Works*, 563.

arm" (8:6). The seal comes from a signet ring, which was carried around the bearer's neck. The one who used it had the power to make contracts in the family name. In biblical times an intact seal assured the recipient that the contents were genuine. The seal also indicated ownership since it bore one's legal signature and credentials. Pharaoh gave his signet ring to Joseph to empower him to act as his royal deputy (see Gen 41:42). The Lord chose Zerubbabel and made him like a signet ring (see Hag 2:23). All that Israel would say and do would manifest and commit God himself. In the Song of Songs the bride is expressing her desire to be so completely identified with her husband that she becomes the very character mark and sign of his presence.

The Church is the seal of Christ, her Husband, and as his Body, she is the visible sign and continuation of his presence in the world. Each individual Christian is to be the seal of Christ, manifesting his presence to others. We are sealed with the Holy Spirit as the image of Christ the Bridegroom that the Father engraves on the heart of his faithful ones (see 2 Cor 1:22; Eph 1:13, 4:30). In Revelation, John writes of the seal of the living God imprinted on the forehead of the servants of God (see Rev 7:2–10). We are marked with the character of Christ in Baptism and meant to manifest him to the world.

Through marriage, the bride now belongs to her lover and becomes his character seal. Arminjon explains this new level of union and identification of the bride with the bridegroom in her daring request to be his signet ring: "Since she will be the seal of her bridegroom, she will by this very fact be constantly on his finger or around his neck, on his heart. . . . Her place will now always be on the very heart of her beloved. And thus he will never be able to cease thinking about her. Not only will she not be absent from his memory, but she will always and everywhere be with him."[229]

Similarly, the Lord always remembers and cares for us as the signet ring of his heart. We are to abide as the Lord's special possession in the depths of his being. Arminjon continues to clarify that the bridegroom will accomplish his works through his bride as his seal: "All that he will do in the world throughout the creation and history of men she will also do with him. She will participate in all his works. Without her, he will not do anything anymore. They can work only together. They can be committed only together."[230] In the same way,

---

229. Arminjon, *The Cantata of Love*, 344–345.
230. Ibid.

Christ has chosen to accomplish his works in cooperation with his Church. He makes himself dependent upon our collaboration as his Body. The bride bears her lover's name and identity. She belongs to him and he belongs to her (6:3). Likewise, we are called Christians after the name of Christ, anointed by the same Spirit, belonging to the Lord as his special possession.

A story about Teresa of Ávila relates that the Lord once appeared to her during her early years in the convent and asked her name. Taken aback by the stranger, she replied, "Teresa of Jesus." Wondering who he was, she then asked his name. He replied, "Jesus of Teresa," showing that her name was now his and his name was now hers.[231] Jesus equally identifies himself with each one of us as we bear the name "Christian" and convey Jesus to others by our life and actions.

In calling the Church the true spouse of Christ, Saint Ignatius indicates that we are to identify with Christ as members of his Body. We identify with Christ by thinking in accord with his teaching and choosing according to his ideals and goals. The Church is the extension of the Body of Christ in space and time, as Saint Luke demonstrates in his Gospel and in the Acts of the Apostles. Whatever Jesus does, the Church also does. Jesus preaches, heals the sick, casts out demons, and even raises the dead; so do the apostles. Jesus had prophesied that if he was persecuted, the apostles' would also be persecuted—which did happen. Just as Jesus was arrested, interrogated, and put to death by the Jewish leaders, so too were the apostles. Finally, as Jesus forgave his persecutors on the cross, handing over his spirit to God, Stephen forgave his persecutors and commended his spirit to God. Whatever happens to Christ happens to the Church. From this comparison of biblical texts,[232] it is clear that the Church has become identified with Christ. Everything Christ does, the Church does to accomplish his mission by the power of the Spirit. All that she is and does communicates the character of Christ, imprinting it through her witness and actions in unison with him.

Acting in unison with Jesus Christ will increase our likeness to him. Father Bruno Lanteri explains that we are to cooperate with Christ in our

231. See Joseph Gicquel, *Fioretti* in Arminjon, *The Cantata of Love*, 345.

232. For a complete comparison of Luke and Acts, see Felix Just, S.J., *The Acts of the Apostles*, Electronic New Testament Educational Resources (E.N.T.E.R.), http://catholic-resources. org/Bible/Acts.htm.

actions by "making constant efforts to keep the memory from dissipation, tranquilly fixed in Jesus, accustoming the mind to see and judge everything according to Jesus and keeping the will ever peacefully united to Jesus, conversing with Jesus, ever united with Jesus in our intentions and actions, and becoming a living copy of Jesus."[233]

In thinking with Jesus we will be thinking as the true spouse of Jesus, the Church. We identify more and more with him as our spouse when we remain focused on him and choose according to his will and values. The image of Jesus will be reflected in our being. Saint Teresa of Ávila saw the image of her soul like a brightly polished mirror with Christ at its center.[234] She saw him clearly in every part of her soul. The Lord fully engraved his image on her soul by means of an intensely loving communication so that she became a replica of Christ. Even if we sometimes do a poor job of imitating Jesus, Christ's image is impressed upon our hearts and we can reflect him to others.

As Christians, we are called to deep union and identification with Christ, so that we become the image, likeness, and representatives of Christ in his Church. Saint Paul tells the Corinthians, "You show that you are a letter of Christ" (2 Cor 3:3) and "ambassadors for Christ" (2 Cor 5:20). We are to be agents of Christ, able to mediate his presence to others.

A. J. Cronin's novel *The Keys of the Kingdom* describes the efforts of a missionary, Father Chisholm, to win village people in China to Christianity. After many years of patient work and genuine Christian witness, Father Chisholm starts to perceive steady growth in his congregation. But he seems to have failed to touch Chia, a leading townsman's heart. Even the healing of Chia's son does not convince Chia to convert. Nevertheless, Father Chisholm plods on with works of charity. Eventually Chia approaches Father Chisholm and unexpectedly expresses his desire to become a Christian, saying, "Now it would appear that I have the extraordinary desire to enter by your gate." He explains that it was not the cure of his son that convinced him, but that he has watched the priest and been impressed by his patience, kindness, and

---

233. Ven. Pio Bruno Lanteri, *Directory of the Oblates of the Venerable P. Lanteri*, ed. G. B. Isnardi, O.M.V., Pt. 1, Ch. 1, Art. 1, Sec. 3 (Rome: Tipografia Agostini, 1974), 40–41.

234. *Life*, 40.5. in *The Collected Works of Teresa of Ávila*, trans. Kieran Kavanaugh and Otilio Rodriquez, vol. 1 (Washington, D.C.: Institute of Carmelite Studies, 1976), 278–279.

courage, adding: "The goodness of a religion is best judged by the goodness of its adherents. My friend . . . you have conquered me by example."[235]

Chia was not convinced by the teaching of Christ or even by a miraculous healing, but by the witness of Father Chisholm. Chia was impressed with Father Chisholm's faith put into action, not necessarily expressed in words or books. Often, the only scriptures people will read will be the bible of our life witness, those words of God made flesh in our lives. Saint John Paul II explains that people are usually less interested in theory, placing more confidence in observable lives and deeds: "The witness of a Christian life is the first and irreplaceable form of mission: Christ, whose mission we continue, is the 'witness' par excellence (Rev 1:5; 3:14) and the model of all Christian witness. The Holy Spirit accompanies the Church along her way and associates her with the witness he gives to Christ (see Jn 15:26–27)."[236] Persons are most convinced by the Gospel witness of concern and kindness toward others, especially the poor and suffering. The evangelical witness that the world finds most appealing is that of generous concern for people, and of charity toward the poor, the weak, and those who suffer.

In the bride's final stage of transformation in the Song of Songs, she is so identified with her bridegroom that she becomes his seal or character mark. Because of her oneness with him, anyone who observes or experiences her presence will experience the bridegroom.

An incident in the life of the fourteenth-century mystic Saint Catherine of Siena illustrates the union and surrender of the transformed Christian.[237] Her experience began with a fervent prayer to the Lord, an echo of King David: "Create a clean heart within me, O God, and renew a right spirit within me." She asked him again and again to take her own heart and will from her and replace it with a heart spotless and true. In response, Jesus consoled her with a vision of himself as the Heavenly Bridegroom. As usual, he approached her lovingly, but then did something unusual: he opened her left side, removed her heart, and promptly fled. Catherine suddenly felt that she now existed without her heart. When she told her confessor of her

235. A. J. Cronin, *The Keys of the Kingdom* (New York: Little, Brown, and Co., 1941), 320.

236. John Paul II, *Redemptoris Missio* (Boston: Pauline Books & Media, 1990), no. 42.

237. See Raymond of Capua, *The Life of St. Catherine of Siena*, trans. George Lamb (Rockford: TAN Books and Publishers, 2009), 164–165.

vision he did not believe her, for how could she live without her heart directing blood in her body? In response, she reminded him that nothing is
impossible for God.

Some days later Saint Catherine remained in the church to pray after
everyone else had left. As she rose to leave, a light from heaven suddenly
enveloped her, illuminating the Lord who was holding a human heart in his
holy hands. She fell, trembling at his appearance and wondering at the bright
red, shining heart he held. Approaching her, he placed the heart in her left
side, saying, "Dearest daughter, as I took your heart away from you the other
day, now, you see, I am giving you mine, so that you can go on living with it
forever." He then closed the opening he had made in her side, and left a scar
on her flesh as concrete evidence of the miracle. From that day forward, she
could never entreat the Lord to give her his heart, for he already possessed it
just as she possessed his.

After this exchange of hearts, Saint Catherine experienced an abundance
of graces pouring forth from her. She saw many things beyond the physical
senses, especially at Holy Communion. When she participated in the Mass
or received Holy Communion, she would be overjoyed, and her heart would
often throb in her chest so loudly that even her companions could hear it. She
felt changed into a different person, transformed into Christ. Saint Catherine's
soul felt inflamed and renewed in purity, humility, and youthfulness. She was
ablaze with love for her brothers and sisters and a desire to lay down her life
for them in imitation of Christ.[238]

Jesus so totally identified with Saint Catherine that he gave her his heart
and took hers to himself. This same union and identification, though not in
the same form, can be realized by any Christian. One only needs to be willing
to surrender oneself to the living God and receive in return the Lord's gift of
self, symbolized by his heart. Saint Catherine was set ablaze by the all-
consuming fire and heat of Christ's love for her, and she burned with love for
others with his very heart. The bride similarly exclaims of her bridegroom's
burning, consuming love: "Its flashes are flashes of fire, a raging flame" (v. 6).
Maloney posits that the bride has reached mystical union with her lover: "No
longer does she experience Jesus as an object, loving her from the outside.
Now day and night she is aware that she has become fire, as he is fire. She

---

238. Ibid., 165–166.

cannot determine where her fire ends and his begins. He so completely penetrates every atom of her being that she is fire and he is fire."[239]

Fire sets an object ablaze; it penetrates and consumes an object until it becomes one with itself, such that one cannot distinguish the object from the fire. Christ's love given as the fire of the Holy Spirit consumes our being so that we are transformed to become one and indistinguishable from him.

While it's unlikely we will have the same kind of extraordinary mystical experience as Saint Catherine of Siena, her encounter describes the new level of union we are called to in our lives of Christian prayer and action. Christ really has given us his heart, through his death and resurrection, his sending forth his Holy Spirit, and his gift of his very self: his Body and Blood in the Holy Eucharist. Jesus gives us his life, which no gift could exceed. We give Jesus our hearts, the totality of our lives, our very selves, and no gift could be greater. Together with Saint Ignatius we can make our self-offering to Christ: "Take, Lord, and receive all my liberty, my memory, my understanding, and my entire will. . . . Give me Thy love and Thy grace, for this is sufficient for me" (SpEx 234). We desire that the Lord would take our poor hearts and fashion them after his own—meek, humble, and ablaze with love.

Nothing can extinguish the fire of the Lord's love for us. The Song of Songs closes with the bride's words, "Many waters cannot quench love, neither can floods drown it" (8:7).[240] For the ancient Jews, water was the symbol of terror and distress, as in the flood. Water evoked the idea of evil, for people thought that evil spirits dwelt near the water, waiting to drown unfortunate passersby. Despite water's sinister connotations, the fearless bride is deeply convinced that deep waters cannot drown the love of her bridegroom. Saint Paul likely had this passage in mind when he wrote: "For I am convinced that neither death, nor life, nor angels, nor rulers, nor things present, nor things to come, nor powers, nor height, nor depth, nor anything else in all creation, will

---

239. Maloney, *Singers of the New Song*, 164.

240. Verses 8–14 cannot be seen as part of the original text. They are different in form and content, and contain no poetic style. The characters and subject matter are different. There is no intelligible connection with the previous context. They are likely comments added by a scribe or an elder of Israel. Many scholars agree, as the *New Jerusalem Bible* notes, that these two passages (8–12 and 13–14) were attached only secondarily to the Song. *The New Jerusalem Bible*, gen. ed. Alexander Jones (Garden City: Doubleday, 1985), 1041.

be able to separate us from the love of God in Christ Jesus our Lord" (Rom 8:38–39). Saint Paul's heart continued to burn with the love of Christ in the midst of the floodwaters of persecution and sufferings, evil attacks, and even in the face of death itself.

Now that the bride has matured in her love and totally depends on her bridegroom, she no longer fears the floodwaters of trials and tribulation but endures them in the all-consuming fire of love. Even death cannot quench love, "for love is strong as death" (8:6). Love can be so intense that it can lead to death in the pouring out of one's life for another. Death cannot kill love, but it may be a consequence of the love that lays down its life for one's beloved. Jesus' love resulted in his dying for us, but his love could not die. Instead it expanded beyond the bounds of death into eternal life. We, too, pass through those waters of death to the land where love is transformed and given the infinite capacity of God himself.

The bride has emerged leaning on her beloved as the image of her spouse, as his seal and character mark, conveying his presence by her presence. In his Rules for Thinking with the Church, Saint Ignatius has us cling with heartfelt fidelity to Christ in his Church, the true spouse of Christ. Having been transformed into union by the Lord's consuming fire, we love with his heart and manifest his presence to others.

Questions for Reflection and Discussion

1. To what degree do you depend or "lean" on the Lord in union?

2. Does the image of marital union speak to you of your own union with Christ?

3. How do you see the Church as bearing the character of Christ and being the image, likeness, and representative of Christ?

4. How do you see yourself as a "letter from Christ," manifesting him to the world?

5. What strikes you about Saint Catherine of Siena's experience of exchanging hearts with the Lord?

6. Are you convinced that "many waters cannot quench the fire of love," that none of your trials and distress can separate you from the love of Christ? How have you seen this at work in your life to this point?

Prayer Exercises

1. Consider the bride coming up from the desert, the place of espousal and mystical marriage, leaning upon her bridegroom. Pray with Song of Songs 8:5–7a, and ask for the grace to depend totally on the Lord.

2. Ponder Origen's translation of the bride resting on the bridegroom's "heart" (p. 346). Pray with John 13:21–35, and ask for the grace of deep love for Christ in the midst of painful situations and trials.

3. Reflect on the image of Christ as the Tree of Life (p. 346). Pray with Song of Songs 8:5–7a and Revelation 22:1–6, and ask for the grace to be fully transformed by divine life.

4. Consider Arminjon's words (p. 347) and the image of the seal. Pray with Song of Songs 8:5–7a and Second Corinthians 3:1–6, and ask for the grace of identification with Christ so as to radiate his presence.

5. Ponder some of the parallels between Christ in Luke and the Church in Acts (p. 348). Pray with John 14:11–14, and ask the grace to be an effective witness to Christ.

6. Reflect on the story of Saint Catherine of Siena and her exchange of hearts with Jesus (p. 350). Pray with John 15:1–11, and ask for the grace of mutual indwelling with Christ.

7. Make a repetition on any of the above contemplations, returning to the places of greater movement of spirit (consolation or desolation).

Conclusion

Through the experience of the Spiritual Exercises, we, like the bride, are taken through stages of purification, illumination, and union with Christ our Bridegroom. In the first week of the Exercises, we are purified of sin and receive God's mercy, just as the bride was darkened by sin and made beautiful by grace. We are illuminated by the mysteries of the life of Christ and experience his call in the second week of the Exercises. Similarly, the bride beholds her beloved and is seized by his call to "arise and come away" with him. We journey with compassion in union with Christ suffering, dying, and risen in the third and fourth weeks of the Exercises, transformed into his likeness. Likewise, the bride suffers the loss of her bridegroom and rejoices in his glorious resurgence. She has been transformed to resemble him and radiate his glory. We emerge from the Exercises in the Contemplation to Attain Love imbued with the gifts and charisms of the Holy Spirit "from above," to labor for Christ as his representatives in the Church. In the same way, the bride grows to full stature, symbolizing the Christian built with the gifts and charisms of the Spirit, becoming the seal and symbol of Christ the Bridegroom. In both the Spiritual Exercises and the Song of Songs, the fire of love purifies, enlightens, and consumes the beloved, leading to complete self-abandonment in union with the Bridegroom.

Now that you have completed this book and hopefully many of the prayer exercises, you are a transformed person. You have opened yourself to the experience of God in prayer with the Holy Scriptures, allowing God's word to penetrate your heart. You have removed obstacles and opened dark recesses of your heart to the Lord's grace. Life is no longer the same now that you are more closely united with God. New pathways of seeking God and being receptive to his power at work in you are opened. You will want to persevere in God's grace in both contemplation and action, moving forward with divine momentum. At this point, it will be important to commit more fully to daily prayer with Scripture, perhaps at least a half hour each day. Participate in the Holy Eucharist as often as possible, even daily. Reflect on your experience of God in daily life using the examen prayer. Seek God's presence in all that you do, realizing that he wishes to communicate with you in the midst of every moment of your life. Pursue the support of others in the Church, perhaps in a prayer group or in ongoing adult formation—not just intellectual but spiritual. Seek out a spiritual guide who can continue to help you discern God's presence and action in your life. With your newfound zeal, engage in ministerial outreach according to your own unique gifts and call. Consider making a plan of life with resolutions toward putting your inspirations into practice. Keeping a prayer journal will help you to recall and be faithful to the graces you receive.

Having finished this retreat, look back over your experience of prayer during your time with this book. What are the most important graces you have received? You have learned to pay attention to your many desires and realize that some are deeper aspirations from God to be pursued. Even as you move forward with desires, do so with detachment and freedom. That will allow them to be fulfilled according to God's will. You have come to realize your weaknesses, limitations, and areas in which you are most tempted to go astray, while also knowing the power of God's mercy toward you in your weakness. You have come to greater self-acceptance in Christ and his unconditional love. The Lord gazes on you in a way that bestows his beauty, and you marvel at his beauty in the mutual admiration of contemplative prayer. Jesus calls you first to friendship and then by name to labor at his side in his mission to win over hearts to his love. He makes you aware of his experience of temptations to riches, honor, and pride, and he helps you to win in the battle over these. You have journeyed with Christ in the sorrow of his passion and death, and experienced ecstatic joy with him risen. You have experienced the abundant outpouring of his Holy Spirit empowering you to act in his name. The gifts of the Holy Spirit conform your heart to Christ's, and the charisms of the Spirit enable you to build up the Church in holiness. You move forward with a sense of being a vibrant and cooperative member of the Lord's Body in the Church.

As you reflect on your own personal experiences of God's grace, which ones have been the most striking and profound? Reduce these to one or two key understandings of how God calls you by name, personally and uniquely, and continue to pray over these graces. You will want to keep these in mind in order to allow God to continue to manifest himself in your life as you move forward. Recall your foundational graces at the beginning of each day as you begin contemplative prayer. Keep them alive in communication with the Lord as you receive him in the Holy Eucharist and as you recollect yourself in God throughout the day. Use the examen prayer to consider how you have remained faithful to God's grace in your daily life. As you often return to the Lord in prayer and daily life, these springs of living water will flow forth in your being and become a source of spiritual life for others. Continually give thanks and glory to God for all he has done in you, rejoicing in your new life in Christ!

Appendix

Table of Themes

This appendix correlates themes of the Song of Songs with the Spiritual Exercises.

Song of Songs	Spiritual Exercises	Themes
1:1–4 "Let him kiss me with the kisses of his mouth." 1:4 King takes bride to his inner chamber.	*Introductory Annotations* **SpEx 3** Let the Creator deal directly with the creature. **SpEx 2** For it is not much knowledge that fills and satisfies the soul, but the intimate understanding and relish of the truth. **SpEx 316, 323–4** Spiritual consolation.	Nature of experience of God. Knowing *about* God and knowing God. Hearing about God from others vs. personal experience. Unconscious/conscious experience of God. Spiritual consolation.
1:1–4 "Let him kiss me.... Draw me after you."	*Introductory Annotations* **SpEx 5** Generosity and great desires. Asking for what I want and desire.	Human beings' desire for God. The importance of desires. Discerning desires. Obstacles to desire.
1:2–3 "Your love is better than wine." He alone matters.	*Principle and Foundation* **SpEx 23** Purpose of man.	God and salvation, our supreme end. Other things secondary, use of creatures. All things can lead to God.
1:5 Dark but beautiful. 1:6 "My own vineyard I have not kept."	*First Week* **SpEx 45–90** Meditation on triple sin. Review of personal sin.	Sin objectively, sin in the world. Personal sin—bride is darkened by sin. Exile from self, neighbor, God.

Song of Songs	Spiritual Exercises	Themes
1:9–11 Fast and powerful mare adorned with jewels and ornaments.	Ask for shame and confusion. Experience of mercy and forgiveness. New desire to serve.	Sin deeply wounds but does not ruin. Repentant, she now runs in his ways. Former shackles now ornaments.
1:6 "My mother's sons were angry with me, made me keeper of the vineyard." Bride has suffered wounds from others.	*First Week* **SpEx 45–90** Sin often emerges from wounds suffered at hands of others. **SpEx 63** Consider the causes and roots of our faults to arrive at a "deep knowledge of our sins." Healing of memories. Forgiveness of those who have hurt us.	Consideration of wounds by considering areas of hurt and painful feelings. Healing of wounds and forgiveness. Wounds have made us better persons. Becoming "wounded healers."
1:5–6 Dark and beautiful. Bride's self-acceptance, awareness of love.	*First Week* **SpEx 45–90** Experience of repentance, forgiveness, and mercy. Realizing one is a loved sinner. **SpEx 317–327** Spiritual desolation—especially vulnerable in first week.	Repentance in "turning" and becoming childlike in trust and dependence on God. Self-acceptance in being forgiven. God loves me as I am, even as a sinner. Self-acceptance leads to growth in virtue. Danger of discouragement, desolation.
1:15 "Ah, you are beautiful, my love . . . your eyes are doves."	*Second Week* **SpEx 100–117** Contemplation of the mysteries of the life of Christ. **SpEx 3** Consider how God our Lord is looking at me.	God is first looking at me. Bride aware of lover's gaze. Lord saw us even as living out mysteries, continues to behold us from heaven. She now sees with "dove-eyes"— Spirit enlightened faith.
1:16—2:7 "Ah, you are beautiful, my beloved. . . ." "Sustain me with raisins, refresh me with apples." His left hand under her head, his right hand embracing her.	*Second Week* **SpEx 114–6** Contemplative technique using the imagination. **SpEx 121–6** Application of the senses.	Three modes of the imagination: visual, auditory, kinesthetic. Transforming effects of contemplation. Christ lives out his mysteries in and through us. Raisins, a symbol of fertility— contemplation issues forth in fruitfulness. Rapt in contemplation she is held by lover.

Song of Songs	Spiritual Exercises	Themes
2:8–9 "Look, my beloved, leaping upon the mountains, bounding over the hills."	*Second Week* SpEx 100–117 incarnation and birth of the Savior. Core mystery of our Christian faith and emphasized by Saint Ignatius.	Lover bridges vast distance from heaven to earth, as Christ does in incarnation. Importance of real humanity of Christ, guaranteed by human mother—Mary's role. We imitate Mary in conceiving and bearing Christ—ongoing incarnation.
2:8 "My beloved.... Look, there he stands behind our wall, gazing in at the windows, looking through the lattice."	*Second Week* SpEx 161–3, 275–287 Mysteries of the public life of Jesus. SpEx 104 More intimate knowledge of God made man for me that I may love him more....	"Beloved" in Hebrew means "friend." Jesus calls us friends, not servants. Friendship basis of call, precedes ministry of service. Developing intimacy of friendship with Christ in contemplating mysteries. Characteristics of friendship.
2:10–13 "Arise, my beloved, and come away." Bridegroom's call. Fig trees put forth fruit, vines blossom.	*Second Week* SpEx 91–98 Call of the King (ordinarily this begins the second week, but placed here for continuity with the call of Christ considered over three chapters).	Grace not to be deaf to God's call. Be with Christ, share his lifestyle, his sufferings and glory. Bride awakened from complacency to go with him. Generous offer of self. Bride's emergence and bearing fruit.
2:10–13 "Arise, my beloved, and come away." Bride's choice to follow.	*Second Week* SpEx 169–188 Election: Rules and times for making a choice of a way of life or decisions. SpEx 189 Reform of one's way of life.	Three times of making a decision. Immediate, obvious, and certain call. Through dynamics and pull of spiritual consolations and desolations. Objective analysis—criterion: best glorify God using my unique gifts, also fulfill my personal needs and desires.
2:10–13 "Arise, my beloved, and come away." Personal and unique call.	*Second Week* SpEx 169–188 Sensitivity to Lord's call. SpEx 275–287 Personal call emerging from more intimate knowledge of Christ in contemplating his mysteries.	Personal vocation: The unique and personal way God calls me. At the core of who I am in Christ and the basis for what I do. Examples of Jesus, Mary, and saints who had personal vocations.

Song of Songs	Spiritual Exercises	Themes
2:14 "My dove in the clefts of the rock." "Let me hear *your* voice, let me see *your* face." "Your voice is lovely, your face is beautiful."	*Second Week* SpEx 136–147 Meditation on the two standards. Satan: riches, honor, pride. Christ: poverty, contempt, true humility.	Wants the bride as she truly is, not hiding out of false humility or putting on masks out of pride. Christ's temptations in desert attempt to lead him away from his true identity. Satan tries to lead us to the false self. Ask grace of highest poverty of spirit.
2:15 "Catch us the foxes that destroy the vineyard."	*Second Week* SpEx 32–43 Examination of conscience (ordinarily in first week but placed here to fit the message of the Song of Songs). Five steps: gratitude, petition for light, review of day, forgiveness, amendment. Also a tool of discernment of spirits and help to discovering God in all things.	Foxes represent our evil tendencies toward sin—harm vineyard of our souls. Vigilance in catching these foxes before they ruin vineyard. Review our life, discover and uproot sins and sinful tendencies. Greater praise and thanksgiving for gifts received.
2:15–17 "Catch us the foxes that destroy the vineyard." Mutual belonging of lover and beloved. Lover arriving like a gazelle on mountains.	*Second Week* SpEx 328–336 Rules for Discernment of Spirits.	Foxes represent deception, falsehood. Enemy deceives through spiritual consolation to lead to his wicked ends. Satan's attempt to destroy vineyard of Lord in personal life and apostolate. Wisdom in discerning true path, remaining united to Christ.
3:1–5 "Upon my bed at night, I sought him, but I found him not." Searching the streets for beloved.	*Third Week* SpEx 190–217 Passion and death of Jesus. Grace of sorrow and compassion for Christ sorrowful.	Passion corresponds to loss of beloved. Jesus: "when Bridegroom is taken away" refers to his passion and death. Loss of easy, familiar ways of praying. Darkness in spiritual journey, seeming loss of the Lord. Third week challenge of remaining with Jesus through passion. Last Supper—sacrifice of Jesus, our own. Agony in garden—battle of prayer.

Song of Songs	Spiritual Exercises	Themes
3:1–5 Searching for lost beloved. 5:6–8 Reprise of search, bride now beaten by watchmen.	*Third Week* SpEx 190–217 Passion and death of Jesus.	Confirmation of our call in suffering. Uniting our own sufferings to those of Jesus in passion. We, like bride being beaten, are willing to suffer for Jesus, kingdom.
Song 3:1–5 Searching for lost beloved. "Do not awake love until it is ready."	*Third Week* SpEx 190–217 Passion and death of Jesus. Esp. 208, Sixth and Seventh Day, and 298 Burial of Jesus, vigil in tomb, awaiting resurrection.	Real death of Jesus, his rest in the tomb. Our own deaths— tomb of our heart—death to sin, selfishness, our own will. Awaiting the new life of God generated. Tomb of death becomes a womb of life. Waiting upon God is a fundamental experience in the spiritual life.
3:6–11 King Solomon rising and approaching on throne of glory. 3:11 On the day of the gladness of his heart.	*Fourth Week* SpEx 218–229 Resurrection of Jesus. SpEx 221 Grace "to be glad and rejoice intensely because of the great joy and the glory of Christ our Lord." SpEx 224 Christ's "office of consoler."	Jesus is the "greater than Solomon here." The throne has symbols of incorruptibility and everlasting life. Resurrection and Christ's reign. Compassion for Christ's gladness at resurrection.
4:1–7 "You are altogether beautiful, my love; there is no flaw in you." King extols bride's beauty and many marvelous features.	*Fourth Week* SpEx 218–229 Resurrection of Jesus.	Bride's own transformation and glorification—"rising with Christ." Foreshadowing of future glory that begins even in this life. The effects of the resurrection upon our lives is real and life-changing. Daily experiences of death and resurrection.
4:8–15 "Come with me from Lebanon. . . . Depart from the peak of Amana, from the peak of Senir and Hermon, from the dens of lions, from the mountains of leopards." 4:14–15 "A garden locked is my sister, my bride . . . a fountain sealed. Your channel is an orchard . . . a garden fountain, a well of living water, and flowing streams from Lebanon."	*Fourth Week* SpEx 312 Ascension of Jesus.	The bride is called to depart with her lover from the peaks (4:8–15). Christ not only ascended in glory to the Father's right hand, but takes our nature with him. (*Solemnity of Ascension*) We spiritually ascend with him. Dangers of this world are transcended. Missionary aspect of ascension—bride's garden and trees grow through world.

Song of Songs	Spiritual Exercises	Themes
4:16–5:1 "I come to my garden, my sister, my bride. . . . Eat, friends, drink, and be drunk with love."	*Contemplation to Attain the Love of God* SpEx 230–235 (points 1 and 2). SpEx 231 "Love consists in a mutual sharing of goods." SpEx 234 (point 1) "Recall to mind the blessings of creation and redemption, and the special favors I have received, and finally, how much the same Lord desires to give Himself to me." SpEx 235 (point 2) "Consider how God dwells in all things—creation all around us and within our very selves. . . . We are temples of the Holy Spirit." This indwelling reached its peak in the incarnation of the Word made flesh in Jesus Christ.	The bride invites the bridegroom to come into her garden to taste its rarest fruits. What is hers belongs to him. He does, and calls it my garden, fruits. SpEx 234 corresponds to the themes of creation and redemption in the first week of the Spiritual Exercises. SpEx 235 corresponds to the second week of the Spiritual Exercises and the focus on the incarnation and life of Jesus Christ. The incarnational principle continues in each one of us as God's grace now dwells within us.
5:6–8 The bride has lost her bridegroom, in a reprise of 3:1–5 This loss corresponds to losing him in his act of dying. In her search for the bridegroom, she goes out and suffers in union with him.	*Contemplation to Attain the Love of God* SpEx 236 (point 3) "Consider how God works and labors for me in all creatures upon the face of the earth, that is, He conducts Himself as one who labors."	SpEx 236 corresponds to the third week of the Spiritual Exercises and the labor of the Lord in his passion and death for us, accomplishing the great "work" of our salvation. We consider work as a participation in God's ongoing creative labor. As we, like the bride, go out in all our labors, we suffer with Christ in bringing about his work of salvation.
5:9–6:3 "My beloved has gone down to his garden . . . to pasture his flock in the gardens." Extols features of bridegroom.	*Contemplation to Attain the Love of God* SpEx 237 (point 4) "Consider how all the good things and gifts descend from above, as my poor power from the supreme and infinite power from above; and so justice, goodness, pity, mercy, etc.; as from the sun descend the rays, from the fountain the waters, etc."	SpEx 237 corresponds to the fourth week of the Exercises: divinity of Christ shines forth. All gifts come from above, from Christ and his divinity. All reality can be seen as a participation in God and in Christ. This "going down" from Jerusalem to the garden of the bride and the Church, represents the descent of grace from above. Bridegroom's divinity now shines forth. She extols the features of his Risen Body.

Song of Songs	Spiritual Exercises	Themes
6:4–12 Bride is now as beautiful as the capital cities of Tirzah and Jerusalem, and terrible as an army with banners. Just as the King had arrived surrounded by his warriors, she now resembles him in the intensity of her presence before which he is filled with awe.	*Transition to Daily Life in the Spirit* SpEx 230–237 Contemplation to Attain Love as a recapitulation of the mystery of Pentecost. SpEx 312 Apostles waiting for the Holy Spirit in Jerusalem (first point of mystery of Ascension). The grace of the fourth week is closely related to the grace of Pentecost. The risen Lord exercises his role as Consoler; there the Holy Spirit, the Consoler, does the same work. Many commentators on the Exercises advise to include contemplation of the mystery of Pentecost and the Holy Spirit.	Eph 4:8, 10, 13—The gifts sent by Christ at his Ascension are those of the Spirit in order to bring us to full maturity in Christ. The bride's beauty continues to increase and symbolizes the presence and transforming power of the Holy Spirit who dwells within her, making her more and more like her Bridegroom. The bride represents the Church as the army in battle array (6:4). Saint Paul speaks of the Church as the Bride for which Christ gave himself. She is the place where the Holy Spirit dwells. She is the place wherein we know the Spirit.
6:13 "Return, return, O Shulammite! Return, return, that we may look upon you. Why should you look upon the Shulammite, as upon a dance before two armies?"	*Transition to Daily Life in the Spirit* SpEx 230–237 Contemplation to Attain Love as a recapitulation of the mystery of Pentecost. SpEx 312 Apostles waiting for the Holy Spirit. Proposed additions of contemplations on the Holy Spirit.	The Holy Spirit as the bond of unity between Father and Son and uniter and reconciler of peoples. The Bridegroom's love changes the bride into a person alive with the fullness of God's grace and victorious peace. She demonstrates the dynamic vitality of the Holy Spirit and continues to mediate his presence. She is now seen dancing between two armies or camps, reconciling them.
7:1–6 The bridegroom now beholds his bride in her glory. He extols her body from head to toe in her continued dance.	*Transition to Daily Life in Spirit* SpEx 230–237 Contemplation to Attain Love as a recapitulation of the mystery of Pentecost. SpEx 312 Apostles waiting for the Holy Spirit. Proposed additions of contemplations on the Holy Spirit.	Bride's glory a result of the presence and gifts of the Holy Spirit. These very carnal images are symbolic of her beauty and maturation in the Spirit. The gifts of the Holy Spirit operative in the life of the mature believer, exemplified in the mysteries of the life of the Blessed Virgin Mary.

Song of Songs	Spiritual Exercises	Themes
7:7–13 Bride is described as a palm tree, high and stately, rising to the heavens. The bride's breasts are like clusters of fruit of different kinds—dates, grapes, and apples.	*Transition to Daily Life in the Spirit* SpEx 230–237 Contemplation to Attain Love as a recapitulation of the mystery of Pentecost. SpEx 312 Apostles waiting for the Holy Spirit. Proposed additions of contemplations on the Holy Spirit.	Bride resembles her Bridegroom more and more. Imbued with the Holy Spirit, she becomes another Christ. The towering palm tree symbolizes the mature Christian who has grown and is filled with the Holy Spirit and his gifts. The fruits represent the many and varied charisms of the Holy Spirit that are given to the Church as a whole and to the individual Christian. Because of her fruitfulness, she is able to nourish her children in the Church through her virtuous acts of service.
8:1–2 The bride expresses her desire to lead her beloved into the house of her mother, into the chamber of the one who conceived her. Desires that he would teach her.	*Rules for Thinking with the Church* SpEx 352–370. SpEx 353 The Church as true spouse of Christ, our holy mother, the hierarchical Church. Transition to ordinary life at end of retreat.	The Church is essentially a mother to all the faithful, conceiving and bearing children for God. The Church's role as mother is to give the spiritual life of faith, the supernatural life of grace, of charity, and of the virtues by her teaching and by her sacraments. She educates and nourishes that faith. The bride shows her desire to be taught by her lover (8:2), and the virtue of docility. Retreatant returning to daily life as part of community of faith.
8:3–5 "I would give you spiced wine to drink, the juice of my pomegranates." "O that his left hand were under my head, and that his right hand embraced me!"	*Rules for Thinking with the Church* SpEx 352–370. SpEx 353 We must put aside all judgment of our own, and keep the mind ever ready and prompt to obey in all things the true Spouse of Christ our Lord, our holy Mother, the hierarchical Church. Transition back to life in Church and world.	The virtue of obedience (SpEx 353) helps maintain the bond of unity among the faithful and her leaders. Her surrender of freedom in loving obedience symbolizes her deepest gift of self (wine and juice) to Christ her Bridegroom. Bride's total dependence on her Bridegroom enables her to remain faithful and offer her total surrender to him in love. She knows that his strong right arm encircles her and his left arm is firm and tender beneath her head (8:4). Being a force for unity and ecumenism in Church.

Song of Songs	Spiritual Exercises	Themes
8:5–7 Bride makes an impassioned request that her lover set her as a seal on his heart and on his arm. 8:7 Many waters cannot quench love, neither can floods drown it.	*Rules for Thinking with the Church* SpEx 352–370. SpEx 353 True Spouse of Christ our Lord.	The profound degree of union of bride and her beloved results in her being his very character mark (seal), the expression of his very essence. Image of the Church, the very body of Christ and his representative in this world. The Church as Bride is so one with her beloved that she becomes his presence and instrument as mouthpiece. Now that she has matured in her love and is totally dependent on her Bridegroom, she no longer fears trials and tribulation. Love is an all-consuming fire. She is even willing to die out of love for him.

Pauline
BOOKS & MEDIA

The Daughters of St. Paul operate book and media centers at the following addresses. Visit, call, or write the one nearest you today, or find us at www.paulinestore.org.

CALIFORNIA
3908 Sepulveda Blvd, Culver City, CA 90230	310-397-8676
3250 Middlefield Road, Menlo Park, CA 94025	650-562-7060

FLORIDA
145 S.W. 107th Avenue, Miami, FL 33174	305-559-6715

HAWAII
1143 Bishop Street, Honolulu, HI 96813	808-521-2731

ILLINOIS
172 North Michigan Avenue, Chicago, IL 60601	312-346-4228

LOUISIANA
4403 Veterans Memorial Blvd, Metairie, LA 70006	504-887-7631

MASSACHUSETTS
885 Providence Hwy, Dedham, MA 02026	781-326-5385

MISSOURI
9804 Watson Road, St. Louis, MO 63126	314-965-3512

NEW YORK
115 E. 29th Street, New York City, NY 10016	212-754-1110

SOUTH CAROLINA
243 King Street, Charleston, SC 29401	843-577-0175

TEXAS
No book center; for parish exhibits or outreach evangelization, contact: 210-569-0500, or SanAntonio@paulinemedia.com, or P.O. Box 761416, San Antonio, TX 78245

VIRGINIA
1025 King Street, Alexandria, VA 22314	703-549-3806

CANADA
3022 Dufferin Street, Toronto, ON M6B 3T5	416-781-9131

¡También somos su fuente para libros,
videos y música en español!